Researching Business and Management

Harvey Maylor and Kate Blackmon

palgrave
macmillan

First published 2005 by
PALGRAVE MACMILLAN
Houndmills, Basingstoke, Hampshire RG21 6XS and
175 Fifth Avenue, New York, N.Y. 10010
Companies and representatives throughout the world

PALGRAVE MACMILLAN is the global academic imprint of the Palgrave Macmillan division of St. Martin's Press, LLC and of Palgrave Macmillan Ltd. Macmillan® is a registered trademark in the United States, United Kingdom and other countries. Palgrave is a registered trademark in the European Union and other countries.

ISBN-13: 978–0–333–96407–0
ISBN-10: 978–0–333–96407–1

This book is printed on paper suitable for recycling and made from fully managed and sustained forest sources.

A catalogue record for this book is available from the British Library.

A catalog record for this book is available from the Library of Congress.

10 9 8 7 6 5 4 3 2 1
14 13 12 11 10 09 08 07 06 05

Printed and bound in China

To my mother, Jean Maylor, who died during the writing of this book.
A great lady who always knew the right question to ask (HM)

To my parents (KB)

Short Contents

Long Contents

List of Figures

List of Tables

Preface to Lecturers

This book started life in 2000 as a handout we prepared for our own undergraduate and master's students called 'How to fail your project (without really trying)'. This book was born out of the frustration that both of us experienced in working with many students in their general quest for knowledge, or simply to finish courses and dissertations. Our frustration came from knowing that the students were not making the most of the learning opportunity that their projects presented to them, often for the same reasons, year after year. Not only were they having problems conceptualising and designing their research, they also had problems with providing any critique of the literature that they were using, despite having access to the research methods texts that were available at the time.

Believing we could do better, we set out to write a book that would help our students do good or even excellent research, that would deal with a large percentage of their questions, and that would simultaneously allay our frustrations at the learning opportunity frequently wasted by our students. We are convinced that our book will be welcomed by lecturers and students alike because of:

Our approach

- Our starting point is not that knowledge of research and research methods is useful in itself, but that it needs to be applied for a student to produce excellent work
- We have described research methodologies in an unbiased, easily accessible way, recognising the difficulties many students have in understanding the terminology and often abstract ideas
- We encourage reflection on the business and management literature and have taken a broad and inclusive view of research approaches
- We have used illustrative examples from real-life student research projects, rather than professional research, to illustrate the points being discussed wherever possible and to keep students grounded in reality
- We recognise that good research combines good process with creativity, intuition, self-reflection and just a little serendipity, and these elements can be stifled if the process is made overly complex
- As a result, in this book, we take a student-centred and process-based approach to research projects, following the typical life cycle of a project from concept through to submission of the final report, using a four-stage model

Key chapters

- We have dealt with some of the issues that students find the most challenging – not least finding a topic, managing their projects and communicating the results – and have avoided the intimidating terms and language that many students encounter when academics start to talk about research methods

- We have recognised the prevailing modes of research that students use and provided particular guidance on these – particularly the use of case studies
- We have included chapters on interpreting findings, and reflecting on the project, critical to producing good work and making the most of the learning opportunity, yet not covered in most other research methods textbooks.
- We have clear and detailed sections on ethics and plagiarism

And finally...

- We have put the role of the internet into perspective as a useful but not exclusive medium for research
- We demonstrate how a good project could be made excellent
- And, in all this, we have tried to retain a sense of humour and not lose the excitement (and fear) that comes with doing a research project – particularly when one is trying to do this for the first time.

There is a companion website to accompany the teaching of this book which includes problem-based learning questions with answers, Powerpoint slides and notes, a searchable glossary, weblinks, and tools to help students when designing and writing up their projects. Please tell us if you think there are other resources needed, or you have any comments that you wish to make on this book. We would be delighted to hear from you.

HARVEY MAYLOR AND KATE BLACKMON

Preface to Students

Welcome to our book.

This book originated out of discussions between the two authors concerning student research projects. Both of us were supervising undergraduate, master's and doctoral research students, as well as teaching research methods courses, Harvey to undergraduate and MBA students, and Kate to postgraduate research students.

We found ourselves frustrated by not being able to find the 'perfect' book to recommend to our students. Although many excellent books have been written about business and management research projects, and we mention many of them in this book, few books seemed to combine the **process** of research with the **content** of research. As a student you need to know what to do, how to do it and why you are doing it. This book is our attempt to bring these three aspects of research together.

Furthermore, the nature of student research projects has been changing as courses respond to business needs for student skills. Many business and management programmes now incorporate work placements and/or projects sponsored by businesses as part of undergraduate or pre-experience master's courses. While similar projects have long been common for MBAs, we felt that this new group of students would benefit from a book that understands that they may be new to the business world as well as to formal academic research.

Research projects are also being used to develop skills that are difficult to practise in traditional academic modules, such as team projects. You might feel you could benefit from some help on how to manage the team process as well as your own part of a project.

No research methods book can be comprehensive, especially if it is to be of reasonable size. Therefore, we aim to cover only the issues that are most relevant from an academic or a practical perspective. Students face many of the same issues across all types of projects. So that you can explore issues in more depth, we highlight additional resources in every chapter and at the end of the book.

We aim to predict and answer the queries and concerns students very often voice during research methods tutorials. We have avoided intimidating or over-complicated terms and language to make all the important aspects of research more easily accessible and relevant to you. Additionally:

Our approach

- Our starting point is not that knowledge of research and research methods is useful in itself, but that it needs to be applied for a student to produce excellent work
- We have described research methodologies in an unbiased, easily accessible way, recognising the difficulties many students have in understanding the terminology and often abstract ideas
- We recognise that good research combines good process with creativity, intuition,

self-reflection and just a little serendipity, and these elements can be stifled if the process is made overly complex

- As a result, in this book, we take a student-centred and process-based approach to research projects, following the typical life cycle of a project from concept through to submission of the final report, using a four-stage model

Key chapters

- We have dealt with some of the issues that students find the most challenging – not least finding a topic, managing their projects and communicating the results
- We have included chapters on interpreting findings, and reflecting on the project, critical to producing good work and making the most of the learning opportunity
- We have clear and detailed sections on ethics and plagiarism

And finally…

- We demonstrate how a good project could be made excellent
- And, in all this, we have tried to retain a sense of humour and not lose the excitement (and fear) that comes with doing a research project – particularly when one is trying to do this for the first time.

We wish you every success with your studies.

Introduction

We have written this book for you if you are an undergraduate student in business and management, or a taught postgraduate student taking a research methods module or doing a research project as part of a course. You may also find it useful if you are a postgraduate research student or working in business and management and you are new to research.

This book is for you if you are doing the following type of project:

- An assessed piece of research for a module, such as a coursework project
- An assessed piece of individual or group research for a degree, such as an action project, a portfolio project, a summer project or a dissertation
- An assessed piece of research as part of a placement in a business or other formal organisation
- An assessed piece of research as part of a project sponsored by a business or other formal organisation.

or if you are simply following a research methods course.

You will face many of the same issues whether you are doing a short coursework project or an extended project such as a dissertation, and whether you are working on the project yourself or as part of a research team. If you want to explore issues in more depth, we highlight additional resources in every chapter and at the end of the book.

If you are studying business and management research in a module, this book provides a step-by-step road map for *learning* about research. If you are doing a project for academic assessment or as part of a business placement, it will provide a road map for *doing* research.

Our perspective on the research process

To understand both what to do and how to do it, you need to know why. We have found that books that clearly explain the 'why' of research are usually aimed at experienced researchers or postgraduate research students, and rarely link back to the 'how' of doing research. Most books aimed at the new researcher take what we will describe as the 'cookbook' approach to research, which suggests that doing research is mainly a matter of picking out the right 'recipe' and following the instructions. You can learn a lot from a cookbook, but rarely do you end up with a clear understanding of the overall logic that guides what you are doing, so that you can apply it for yourself. The purpose of this book is to explain both 'why' and 'how' so that you can learn not only to follow a 'recipe', but also to develop your own judgement and style.

By integrating both 'why' and 'how', we hope to get you excited about learning about research, doing a research project and becoming a researcher. Both authors are passionate about research and the research process – doing research, talking about research and teaching research. We have both experienced the frustrations and uncertainties that are part of the intellectual challenge of research, which is more than countered by the satisfaction felt at the discovery of new knowledge, or simply understanding something in a new way that we had never considered before.

On the other hand, each research project is a personal journey. We hope that you can use this book to overcome or at least reduce the obstacles along the way that might keep you from doing good research. This will in no sense reduce the challenge of the topic, but it will remove some of the uncertainty of the process. As shown below, even in the best-planned projects, rarely do we end up exactly where we planned.

Research as a systematic process

This book takes the view that business and management research is a systematic process for finding information about a research problem. Research takes inputs such as previous business and management research and data and transforms them into knowledge that is supported by evidence and theory. Compared with a repetitive process such as manufacturing a television or an automobile, the research process can be disorderly and sometimes even chaotic.

However, we can manage the research process systematically because we can place a structure on it, even if we cannot foresee exactly what will happen at each stage. Even if we cannot plan for intuition or unexpected challenges that arise during the research process, we can expect these to happen and have plans in place to capture these incidents when they do come along.

We recommend that you take a systematic approach to research because you should manage your project, not let the project manage you:

- Ultimately, you – not your supervisor – must manage your research project so that you finish on time and achieve your research objectives. We will demonstrate how to manage your work.
- You are more likely to make the most of your project if you take a structured approach. Taking a structured approach does not mean that there is only 'one true way' of doing research. A structured process is more likely to show you the options you have for doing research in different ways and making an intelligent decision about which way you will do it. This can significantly improve your performance.
- You should make the best use of the time that supervisors and other experts have for you. Throughout this book, we discuss the benefits of taking a proactive approach.
- All research is risky and you need to manage the 'unknown' element of what you are doing. This book will help you to work with this uncertainty.

A systematic approach can enhance your work, rather than constrain it or reduce your own creativity. According to Davis and Parker (1997: 28ff), the advantages of a systematic approach to research include:

- improving your motivation
- improving your task management

- conserving your attention
- reducing errors and omissions
- eliminating redundant processes.

The overall structure of this book

So that you can manage your research project, rather than having it manage you, your first step in understanding and systematically managing your research process is to recognise the major stages that your research will go through. These stages are:

- D1 – Defining your research project
- D2 – Designing your research project
- D3 – Doing your research project
- D4 – Describing your research project

This 4-stage model is shown opposite and illustrates how your activities will progress from defining what you will study to reporting what you found out. Throughout this book, we will use this model of the research process to identify the key activities and ideas that are the most critical during each stage. These activities, and the process itself, are well established. Your challenge is to adopt them for – and if necessary adapt them to – your own research project.

We have structured this book around these four stages. Each stage of the research process is a major part of this book. **Part 1** – defining your research project; **Part 2** – designing your research project; **Part 3** – doing your research, and **Part 4** – describing your research.

Although this model might suggest that you will go through each stage in turn, in reality you may find yourself revisiting previous stages. Research is a cyclical, not a linear process. For example, as you are designing your project you may discover some information that affects how you have defined it, requiring you to briefly return to the project definition stage to revise your definition. Iterating, revisiting previous work to make sure that you are heading in the right direction or to check your course, will help you strengthen your research project.

Part 1 – Defining your research project

The four chapters in **Part 1** focus on defining your research project. You can use these four chapters to get started on your business or management research project. Major questions addressed in these chapters include:

- What is a research project?
- What are the elements of a project brief?
- How do I get started?
- How do I find out more information?

Chapter 2 provides some guidance for managing personal and group projects using project management. **Chapter 3** starts out by helping you to identify and select a topic

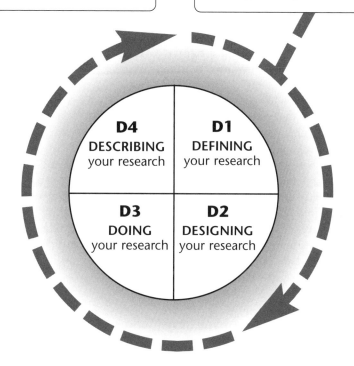

Relevant chapters
4
13 Answering your research questions
14 Describing your research
15 Closing the loop

Key challenges
● Interpreting your findings and making recommendations
● Writing and presenting your project
● Reflecting on and learning from your research

Relevant chapters
1
1 What is research?
2 Managing the research process
3 What should I study?
4 How do I find information?

Key challenges
● Understanding the research process
● Taking a systematic approach
● Generating and clarifying ideas
● Using the library and internet

D4
DESCRIBING
your research

D1
DEFINING
your research

D3
DOING
your research

D2
DESIGNING
your research

Relevant chapters
3
9 Doing field research
10 Analysing quantitative data
11 Advanced quantitative analysis
12 Analysing qualitative data

Key challenges
● Practical considerations in doing research
● Using simple statistics
● Undertanding multivariate statistics
● Interpreting interviews and observations

Relevant chapters
2
5 Scientist or ethnographer?
6 Quantitative research designs
7 Designing qualitative research
8 Case studies/multi-method design

Key challenges
● Choosing a model for doing research
● Using scientific methods
● Using ethnographic methods
● Integrating quantitative and qualitative research

to research. **Chapter 4** will help you to find more information to refine your research project using the library, internet and other resources.

Part 2 – Research design

The four chapters in **Part 2** will explain how to transform your project definition into a research design that describes how you will actually do your research. Because there are so many different ways to carry out business and management research, we will start by identifying the two generic research strategies that underlie particular research designs, and explain what the choice of a particular strategy signifies for your research project. **Chapter 5** identifies the two main research strategies for business and management research, which we will describe as the quantitative and qualitative research design strategies. **Chapter 6** identifies the most popular research designs for quantitative research, while **Chapter 7** identifies the most popular methods for the qualitative research. **Chapter 8** addresses special issues related to case studies and multi-method research.

Part 3 – Doing your research

Once you have developed a research design, you can actually do your research project. The four chapters in **Part 3** focus on using the research design you developed in **Part 2** to collect and analyse your data, and to interpret the results. **Chapter 9** describes some practical and ethical issues that may arise if you are doing an in-company research project, or other research project that involves direct contact with organisations or the public. **Chapters 10** and **11** identify basic and advanced techniques for analysing quantitative data. **Chapter 12** describes structured and unstructured approaches to analysing qualitative data.

Part 4 – Describing what you have found

Your research is only half-complete until you have told other people what you have found out, including any academic and business advisors who you need to report to. The three chapters in **Part 4** help you complete your research project by communicating the results of your research and reflecting and improving on what you have learnt. **Chapter 13** explains what to do with the information you find, that is, how to interpret the results of your data and analysis to see if you have answered your research questions and learnt more about your research problem. **Chapter 14** suggests some ways that you can present your results in a written project report and/or oral presentation. **Chapter 15** looks at how to learn from what you have done.

How to use this book

If you are consulting this book for guidance on specific issues, you can read the chapters in this book out of sequence, but we have tried to structure this book so that we deal with issues in much the same order that you will if you are conducting a major research project, or are taking a course on how to do business and management research. You may want to skim through this book quickly to get an idea of what we will be covering and when, which we summarise briefly below. If you are conducting a project as part of normal work activities, you will find this book helpful in planning and executing your research project, but you might want to skim or skip over some of the sections.

Throughout this book, you will find four different kinds of research examples used to illustrate our discussion. 'Student research in action' boxes present examples from our own undergraduate, master's and postgraduate research students' projects. These examples illustrate both good and bad practice, sometimes both in the same project. We will also occasionally describe some interesting projects that other researchers have published, in the 'Research in action' boxes, to show how more experienced researchers have faced similar issues to those you will face. We also discuss some of our own research, again with examples of both good and bad practice. Finally, we will use some classic research projects, which we describe in more detail in **Chapter 1**, as a continuing theme or motif in the discussion, including classic management studies such as Frederick Taylor's scientific management and the Hawthorne experiments, and classic psychological studies such as Stanley Milgram's laboratory experiment on obedience to authority.

About the authors

Dr Harvey Maylor is Lecturer in Operations and Project Management, and convenor of the Operations and Supply Group at the University of Bath School of Management. For the past five years, he has been full-time MBA projects coordinator. He is the author of the bestselling text, *Project Management* (3rd edn, FT-Prentice Hall, 2003). He has taught post-graduate programmes in project management and research methods at Warwick, Cranfield and Copenhagen Business Schools, at NIMBAS in Holland and Germany, and lately at Kasetsart University, Bangkok, Thailand. He is also a consultant and trainer, and has received funding for his research from the UK goverment, the EU and industry.

Dr Kate Blackmon is Lecturer in Operations Management at the Saïd Business School of the University of Oxford, where she is Deputy Director of Studies for the Undergraduate Programme in Economics and Management, with responsibility for the Engineering, Economics and Management, and the Materials, Economics and Management degrees, and is Fellow and Tutor in Management Studies and currently the Principal of the Postmasters at Merton College. She completed her PhD at the University of North Carolina at Chapel Hill and has previously worked at the University of Bath School of Management, the London Business School, and the International Institute for Management Development (IMD) in Lausanne, Switzerland.

Acknowledgements

The authors and publisher would like to thank the following for permission to use copyright material:

HarperCollins Publishers Ltd for the quotation from *The Phantom Tolbooth* © 2002 Norton Juster.

Kathleen M. Eisenhardt for 'Building Theories from Case Study Research', *Academy of Management Review*, 1989, **14**(4), pp. 532–50.

Every effort has been made to trace all the copyright holders but if any have been inadvertently overlooked the publishers will be pleased to make the necessary arrangements at the first opportunity.

1 Defining your research

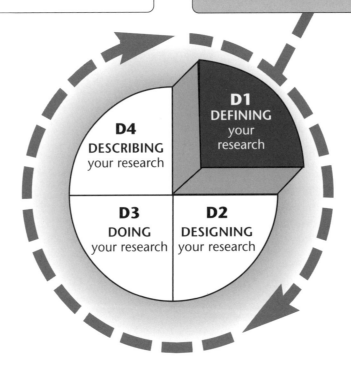

Relevant chapters

13 Answering your research questions
14 Describing your research
15 Closing the loop

Key challenges

- Interpreting your findings and making recommendations
- Writing and presenting your project
- Reflecting on and learning from your research

4

Relevant chapters

1 **What is research?**
2 Managing the research process
3 What should I study?
4 How do I find information?

Key challenges

- **Understanding the research process**
- Taking a systematic approach
- Generating and clarifying ideas
- Using the library and internet

1

D1
DEFINING
your
research

D4
DESCRIBING
your research

D3
DOING
your research

D2
DESIGNING
your research

Relevant chapters

9 Doing field research
10 Analysing quantitative data
11 Advanced quantitative analysis
12 Analysing qualitative data

Key challenges

- Practical considerations in doing research
- Using simple statistics
- Understanding multivariate statistics
- Interpreting interviews and observations

3

Relevant chapters

5 Scientist or ethnographer?
6 Quantitative research designs
7 Designing qualitative research
8 Case studies/multi-method design

Key challenges

- Choosing a model for doing research
- Using scientific methods
- Using ethnographic methods
- Integrating quantitative and qualitative research

2

What is business and management research?
An introduction to the research process

 Key questions

- What is business and management research?
- Why do we do business and management research?
- What are the benefits of taking a systematic approach to a research project?
- What critical issues should you consider as you get started?
- Who are the key project stakeholders?

 Learning outcomes

At the end of this chapter, you should be able to:

- Explain what business and management research is, and why we do it
- Describe a systematic research process for doing research
- Identify the issues you should address before starting your project

Contents

INTRODUCTION

Business and management research plays a familiar part in our everyday lives, even if we don't always recognise it as research. For instance, you often do research without explicitly thinking about it as such, using the library, internet, newspapers and other publications to find out more about organisations and their products and activities. You are doing business and management research when you collect and use information to solve a practical problem, such as visiting a supplier's website to find out more about a new bicycle, using a phone directory to locate a taxi firm or purchasing an air travel ticket over the web.

Businesses and other organisations constantly conduct research. People who work in organisations do research to meet organisational needs, for example to find out about competitors and their products. Sometimes this research is obvious – someone approaches you in the street or contacts you via telephone or email asking you to answer a market survey. Less obviously, organisations unobtrusively collect information on you as a customer using 'cookies' and other software when you visit a website or customer loyalty cards when you visit a shop.

You are also constantly bombarded with new information about business and management. Newspapers report stories about organisations and people, management consultants present their analyses of clients' problems and make recommendations to solve them and organisations themselves churn out a steady flow of information for shareholders, analysts, regulators and the general public.

If you are already doing research, why should you study or learn more about research methods by reading this book? The fact that you are reading this paragraph may mean that you are studying research methods or doing a research project as part of your studies. Or, you may be working in an organisation and need to do some research to solve an organisational problem. Either way, you can benefit from a better understanding of the research process. You can apply the research skills you develop through studying a research problem in depth, as well as the learning and self-reflection that come from the process, in your studies and career. Furthermore, what you learn about research can help you to become a more critical consumer of what you learn in your studies, which are in turn based on business and management research done by professional researchers.

This chapter provides a general introduction to business and management research. **Section 1.1** provides an overview of business and management research. **Section 1.2** explains the wider context of business and management research. **Section 1.3** discusses some critical issues that you should think about as you begin learning about research. Examples of real-life student and scholarly research are a continuing theme in this chapter and throughout this book.

1.1 WHAT IS BUSINESS AND MANAGEMENT RESEARCH?

Our goal in writing this book is not only to present a range of information so that you can pass a research methods course or carry out a particular research project, but also to help you develop skills and understanding that let you manage research through taking a **systematic approach**. You should think of research as a **process** that consists of a specific set and sequence of activities, with tangible and intangible inputs and outputs, such as information, time, resources and knowledge. Something (such as knowledge about the world and actions that are taken based on that knowledge) is transformed as a result of the research process. With this understanding, you can manage research rather than being managed by it or simply hoping that it will all happen for you.

This systematic approach is based on our 4-D model of the **research process** outlined in the **Introduction**. Positioning your research project within this more general framework allows you to identify the choices you will make as a researcher about what to research and how to research it, and the logic that guides these choices. In the research process, even if some aspects of research are always uncertain and unpredictable, a systematic approach will help you manage this uncertainty.

To get you started on thinking about research as a systematic process, this chapter will:

- Describe business and management research
- Introduce our framework for managing the research process
- Show how research fits in the context of business and management.

1.1.1 What is research?

Research is a process of finding out information and investigating the unknown to solve a problem. For many people, 'researcher' conjures up an image of a white-coated scientist beavering away in a laboratory, whilst 'investigator' suggests a hard-boiled private eye snooping around to try to uncover some piece of evidence and thereby solve a crime. However, business and management research generally involves neither 'ivory tower' research in a laboratory nor undercover investigation.

Even before you started reading this book, you probably had some ideas about what business and management research is. You probably know that research involves identifying and gathering information. True, in some small projects, you may only need to find and report information, requiring nothing more than a simple internet search or a quick visit to your library. Although gathering information is an integral research skill, doing business and management research involves much more than searching for information using the library, internet or other resources. Research also requires using this information to solve a problem that is relevant to business and management. This problem can be a practical one faced by a real organisation, or a theoretical one posed by a gap in management knowledge. Research involves identifying a problem, understanding what information is relevant to addressing that problem, getting the information and interpreting that information and its context.

To reflect this larger role of research, we define research as:

A systematic process that includes defining, designing, doing and describing an investigation into a research problem.

What business and management researchers study

Saunders et al. (2003: 3) define business and management research as 'undertaking systematic research to find things out about business and management'. So what exactly does this entail? The scope of business and management research is not as neatly bounded as, for example, inorganic chemistry or nuclear physics. Business and management research covers diverse areas: accounting, finance and economics; human resources and organisational behaviour; strategy and international business; marketing; operations, management science and information systems. Business and management research covers a diverse set of research activities because of its range of topics, links to other areas and study of different social units. Even a single area such as accounting includes a broad range of topics, starting with the distinction between managerial accounting and financial accounting.

This diversity is increased because business and management research draws on other academic areas, including mathematics, statistics, economics, psychology, computing, sociology, anthropology and law. Finance, for example, draws heavily on both economics and mathematics, so if you wanted to study financial markets you would probably need some knowledge of these two areas as well.

Business and management researchers study a diverse set of social units ranging from individuals to nations and even regions. Researchers may study *individuals* such as employees, managers or executives in organisations, and other individuals such as customers and suppliers who interact with them. These shareholders, directors, managers, workers, customers and clients are sometimes described as 'organisational actors'. Researchers also study *groups* of individuals such as work groups, who act together to achieve common goals, or who interact, such as frontline employees and customers. Researchers also study *organisations*, formal or informal groupings of people, including firms and other businesses, and not-for-profit entities such as charities, government agencies or non-government organisations (NGOs). They may also study levels higher than the organisation, such as the supply chain, industry, nation, region of the world or even global organisation. This higher level may be defined around patterns of interaction, such as markets, or location, such as the European Union (EU).

Given these three dimensions of business and management research, you can see the huge range of possible subjects facing the business and management researcher. As we shall see in **Chapter 3**, this can leave you rather spoilt for choice! When you think about what you are interested in studying, you might think about how these individuals and organisations relate to each other. The hierarchy presented in **Figure 1.1** is one way of making sense of the interrelationships and where business and management disciplines fit with these levels.

If business and management research spans nearly every type of human activity, is there anything that makes business and management research unique? How does it differ from other areas such as economics, psychology or sociology that study many of the same issues?

Because business and management is a professional, rather than an academic discipline, research needs to be relevant as well as academically rigorous. Academic researchers are often primarily concerned with increasing knowledge, which may be applied in the future, not just to aid understanding, but also to improve individual and organisational performance. On the other hand, many people, academics and managers alike, believe that the ultimate goal of research should be to help organisations to improve their performance. A major focus of business and management research is on the link between practices and organisational performance. Practices that affect individual and organisational performance may be external – for example the role of national regulation – or internal – for example specific accounting, operations or human resources (HR) practices.

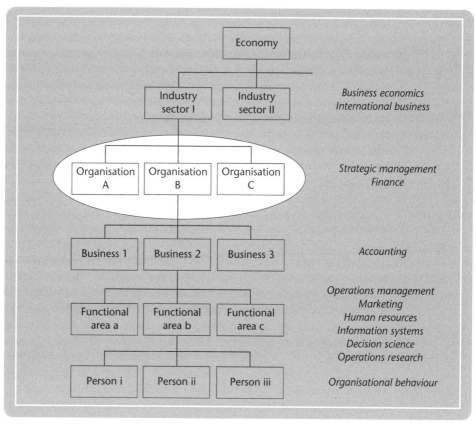

Figure 1.1 A hierarchy of business and management research objects

1.1.2 What research is not!

Even if business and management research is diverse, it is not so broad that any problem you could investigate qualifies as research. There are significant differences between a systematic research process – the journey you are embarking on – and activities such as journalism or consulting.

It can sometimes be hard to tell research, journalism and consulting apart – all three share many characteristics. However, business and management research isn't just a process of collecting and reporting information; it involves creating new knowledge by analysing, interpreting and reporting that information, and by integrating this new knowledge with what we already know. A major goal of business and management research is to create better and more widely applicable theories (we will discuss more precisely what we mean by 'theory' in **Chapter 3**) that will help other people to solve a similar practical problem or understand a research problem better. Further, professional business and management research (what gets published in management journals) must be rigorously checked by other academic researchers (peer review, which we discuss in **Chapter 4**), and is constantly revised or even replaced over time.

Research is not journalism

Many students find it difficult to distinguish between journalism and research. In **journalism**, journalists report information about business and management organisations, people and trends in newspapers such as the *Financial Times* and the *Wall Street Journal* and magazines such as *The Economist* and *Fortune*. A common purpose of both journalism and research is to gather information and present it in an appropriate format. However, a journalist's job is to report the news – what is new or novel – to sell newspapers or magazines or attract television or radio viewers. 'Man bites dog' makes the news headlines because it is new or unusual, not because it adds to our knowledge, or helps us to understand deeper truths about the world or solve particular problems.

An important difference between journalism and research is that other researchers must verify the research findings before they are published. Checking and challenging is an essential, not optional, element of the systematic research process discussed in this book. Newspapers and magazines, however, seldom do much factual checking of the information they report, apart from spell-checking and so fall well short of the standards of peer review. This means that information provided by journalists is not always reliable, even if it is eye-catching and timely.

Of course, journalism and academic research are not always mutually exclusive. Journalists report on noteworthy research findings and the presentations and ideas of leading academic researchers. Some journalists contribute to knowledge as well as just providing information. Some investigative journalism even comes close to or surpasses academic research; however, it is unlikely to have been peer reviewed.

In addition, many academic researchers cross over into journalism, appearing on news programmes and chat shows; providing 'sound bites' on the topic of the day; writing books, magazine articles and newspaper columns for popular audiences; and even presenting television and radio programmes. However, even if someone has immense credibility as a researcher, if what they are saying has not been arrived at through a systematic research process and been checked and challenged by other academics, it is still opinion and/or journalism and not research.

Research is not consulting

The difference between journalism and research is obvious when they are done by different people and reported in different places. (We will discuss the credibility of different sources in **Chapter 4**.) It can be more difficult to tell the difference between **consulting** and research, because they are often done by the same people and reported in the same places (for example *Harvard Business Review*). Professional consultants report their work in books and in-house journals that resemble academic publications, in order to publicise their ideas and promote their services. Some academics wear both hats, carrying out consulting projects and reporting their work as research findings. Famous business 'gurus' such as Michael Porter and Gary Hamel run consulting companies, teach business and management, and publish in academic and non-academic forums.

To understand the difference between consulting and research, let's take a closer look at what consultants do. A consultant is typically engaged by an organisation to solve an organisational problem. The consultant must gather, analyse and interpret information to solve that problem. The output of the consulting engagement will be a set of recommendations, developed by the consultant based on this information, describing how the company should solve the problem. For example, a consultant might be hired by an organisation to provide advice on how to restructure the organisation, and so will need to gather information about the organisation, including finding out the organisation's current structure and defining its objectives. The consultant's report would describe how to restructure the company and address any potential problems in how it might be implemented.

In deciding whether a project is more consulting or research, you should consider both the means and the ends. Whether a project is research or consulting depends on what the consultant then does with that information. Most consulting engagements begin with and end with the specific organisational problem, although a consultant will build up a stock of expertise over time and consulting companies often specialise in particular areas of expertise.

Consultants value the information they gain in a consultancy engagement primarily as an input to future consulting engagements. In fact, consulting firms typically want to keep that knowledge proprietary. When consultants do report their work, it is typically to advertise this expertise in order to attract clients rather than increase the sum of business and management knowledge. As a result, consultants rarely have to justify how and what they investigate except to their client and employer, because the quality of their work is judged by how well it lets the organisation solve a particular problem, not whether it would help other organisations solve similar problems.

Researchers, on the other hand, have a primary responsibility to create and share original knowledge. This means that they must link their research to previous research on the subject, and show that they are adding something new to that knowledge as a result of their investigation. Research by its nature is meant to be shared, not hidden. Finally, as we noted for journalism, it isn't 'research' until it has been validated by other researchers, or peer reviewed.

1.2 BUSINESS AND MANAGEMENT RESEARCH IN WIDER CONTEXT

If we can define business and management research by what it is not, neither journalism nor consulting, we can also define it by what it is, a form of social research and of research in general. This makes it possible for us to identify some characteristics of research projects that both make them unique and create challenges in trying to manage them.

1.2.1 Originality in research

First of all, as we noted above, a business and management research project makes a unique contribution to knowledge. This doesn't necessarily have to be a 'great discovery' or 'grand new theory'. Your project will typically aim to apply existing business and management knowledge in a new context or add a small bit of new knowledge to what we already know. Your unique contribution to existing knowledge may come through:

- new or improved evidence
- new or improved methodology
- new or improved analysis
- new or improved concepts or theories.

Second, business and management research focuses on asking questions and solving problems, rather than just finding out information, as we note above. As we will see in

Chapter 3, the first step in the research process is to identify a research problem that you want to find out more about. A **research problem** can come from either a practical problem (real-life situation) or a theoretical problem (general principles or observations). You might identify a practical problem based on an issue that you have observed in a real-life setting, for example receiving poor service in a store might lead you to study how stores handle customer complaints. A practical problem could also come from issues that have been identified in your courses, or problems that face your organisation or other setting you are interested in investigating.

You could also start with a theoretical problem posed by a business or management topic about which you would like to know more but for which there is incomplete information, for example the best way to motivate workers. Such problems often emerge as you think about how to apply the theories and models learnt in your coursework to real-life settings, or try to understand which of several competing theories best explains how people or organisations actually behave. For example which is better for understanding corporate strategy, Porter's five forces or the resource-based view? It is not always possible to answer either type of problem completely by what you find out in a single research project.

You need to ask one or more **research questions** about your research problem in order to understand more about it. **Chapter 3** will identify a systematic process for identifying research problems and questions that you can transform into research projects, and how these problems and questions can be used to structure your research project.

For example, if you were interested in researching whether agricultural subsidies affect farmers in developing countries, you might investigate the practical problem presented by agricultural subsidies to farmers in developed regions such as the EU, which could potentially put farmers in developing countries out of business. Another way you might approach this problem is from an international business perspective, focusing on the implications of trade barriers. You could start with the theoretical problem of trade barriers, then narrow it down to agricultural subsidies and even further to developing countries.

Either way, you might come up with some questions that you want to answer, such as:

● Do agricultural subsidies to farmers in developed countries make imported products less competitive?
● Should governments in developed countries change their policies to aid farmers in developing countries?

Your research problem and questions *define* your research project and become key inputs to the next stage of the process, *designing* your research, which we cover in **Part 2**. The research design, in turn, drives the *doing* stage of the research process, which is detailed in **Part 3**. Finally, the inputs from these first three stages allow you to *describe* your research, which is the subject of **Part 4**. We described these stages in detail in the **Introduction**.

1.2.2 Types of research activities

We might classify research projects depending on how much they are targeted towards a specific practical problem versus how much they are targeted towards a general theo-

Table 1.1	Three types of research activity

Stage in research	Role of this type of research
Basic research	Research that is conducted to increase knowledge, with little consideration of future applications. Many social science researchers consider their work to be of this type. For instance, research on the behaviour of people under certain conditions may be undertaken (as in Milgram's experiment at the end of this chapter).
Development	This involves taking an original idea, possibly a basic research project, and looking for applications. This may include combining it with other ideas, or changing the original intention. For instance, knowing that people behave in a certain way, considering how this might be applied in practice, for example as part of a training package for in-company use.
Commercial	This involves taking an idea from the possibility of application through to commercial usage. This is a particular skill set of consultants. For instance, they may take the behavioural work developed above and sell it into a firm as part of a training package. There could be further research to evaluate its usefulness in practice.

retical problem. This leads to three general types of project, which are basic research, development and commercial projects and are described in more detail in **Table 1.1**.

Some research projects may fit into more than one classification. You might start by investigating a practical problem and then use your findings to add to the knowledge about a theoretical problem, or you might investigate a theoretical problem in a specific practical context and then identify how to solve similar problems in other practical contexts. A series of research projects that starts with basic research and carries the same kind of investigation through to development, or vice versa, is known as a 'stream' of research.

1.2.3 General issues for research projects

Because many researchers are interested in how ideas are developed and how they are turned into new products or other concrete outcomes, they have conducted much academic study on research projects. **Table 1.2** summarises some other key dimensions or characteristics of research.

1.3 BEFORE YOU GET STARTED

> I keep six honest serving-men, they taught me all I knew. Their names are what and why and when, and how and where and who.
>
> (**Kipling** [1902]1987: 69)

You can use Kipling's six question words to start thinking about your research project:

1. Why am I doing this research project, and what do I want to get out of it?

2. What do I want to find out?
3. Where is the information that I want to find out?
4. Who will want to know what I find out?
5. How will I be assessed?
6. When can I start, and when must I finish, my work?

Table 1.2 Key dimensions of business and management research

Type	Comments
Scholarly versus commercial research	The main motivation for conducting scholarly research is usually to increase our knowledge about business and management. The knowledge that is created may not be immediately – if ever – applicable to a practical problem faced by businesses or managers.
	Commercial research is research that is sponsored (and paid for) by the organisation or individual that intends to apply the knowledge, usually to a practical problem facing the organisation. Commercial research usually has a purpose connected with the central objective of the organisation, be it making money or carrying out a governmental or charitable mission.
	The customers of the output of the project are different in nature. In the first, the acquisition of knowledge is the driver. Commercial research is usually intended for immediate use by the business sponsor, whilst academic research has no clear customer in mind. In the second, the application of the knowledge is the driver.
Scholarly versus student research	Scholarly research is expected to contribute to our knowledge about business and management, whilst student research may only need to apply such knowledge to a practical or theoretical problem.
	To ensure that scholarly research is both original and correct, it usually undergoes peer review – other academics who are knowledgeable about the research topic and/or methods review it to ensure it meets an acceptable level of quality before it is published or presented.
	Student research is usually assessed by a small set of examiners, who must assess it against the project requirements and standards of the institution.
Assigned versus interest-driven topics	The more choice you are given by your project guidelines, the more time you will need to spend defining and designing your research, but you will have a greater opportunity to reflect your own interests and skills.
	The challenges for each are different. Choosing a project is the subject of **Chapter 3** and can be an extensive activity. The assigned project would appear to have an easier start, but defining precisely what the project is about (scoping) can be as extensive an activity as choosing your own project.
Indirect versus direct contact with organisations to gather data	Research projects can involve considerable contact with external organisations or other parties or none at all. Some research, generally known as 'desk' or 'library' research, involves only indirect contact with the organisations or individuals you are studying. In desk research, you will have no direct contact with the source of the data you are analysing, but instead may use the library, internet, archives, computer databases or other sources of data. This is often used when you are studying organisations that are distant in time and/or space.

Table 1.2 cont'd

Type	Comments
	Alternately, you may have direct contact with the organisation and/or individuals you are studying, either face to face, as in interviews or case study research, or by other means, such as postal surveys.
Individual versus group research	Research projects may be conducted alone or as part of a group. Group projects require managing group processes (interactions between group members) as well as the content and the process of the research project. This group process creates the potential for group conflict, although a group can often create synergies.
Single discipline versus interdisciplinary research	Business and management research draws on many base disciplines, including economics, psychology, sociology and mathematics. Your research can be based in one of these disciplines or consider inputs from a number of areas. This will be discussed below and in **Chapters 2** and **3.**

We suggest that, before you start your project, you consider what you are trying to do and why, so that you *begin with the end in mind* (see Stephen Covey's book *The Seven Habits of Highly Effective People* (2005) for a discussion of why this is important). Some of the most successful research projects we have supervised began with students visualising the final project report and then deciding how they would make it happen. Think of your research project not as an arrow that you shoot into the air, which may hit a target only by luck, but as a target pulling the arrow towards it. You might also think about the different people who will be involved in your project and the impact your work might actually make on the world.

1.3.1 Why are you doing a research project?

As you reach the end of this first chapter, you should also consider why you are reading this book, and/or why you are doing a research project. If you are doing research as part of a coursework assignment or degree requirement, one immediate benefit will be to pass the course or get your degree. If you are doing research as part of a work assignment, the immediate benefit will be to satisfy your manager and help your organisation. In both cases, you will be assessed, either formally or informally, on the quality and the outcomes of your research project. Therefore, you may answer the question 'why are you doing research?' with 'to complete an assigned task!'.

However, we argue that learning to do research and becoming a competent researcher are themselves worthwhile. You may find that doing research has long-term benefits, such as improving:

- Your understanding of the research problem you study
- Your competence in doing a research project
- Your ability to manage research as a systematic process
- Your ability to build on other people's research, increasing the credibility of your own work.

Additionally, you can apply your research skills beyond business and management, to:

- Test accepted or new ideas to see if they are true
- Discover new things about the world
- Make sense of the world around you.

To manage research as a systematic process you will need to develop not only practical and analytic skills, but also critical skills. This point is key – if you are not an informed consumer of research, you can't tell what is true and what is merely opinion. Doing research helps you to understand and critically assess research carried out by other researchers, including the research presented in textbooks, academic journals and the popular press. Without this ability to critically assess other people's arguments, as Carl Sagan (1997: 42) commented: 'We become a nation of suckers, up for grabs by every charlatan that comes along' (more of this in **Chapter 5**).

Our experience supports the need for everyone – students, journalists, consultants and managers – to develop a questioning approach to journalists' reports, consultants' recommendations and researchers' findings, as shown in **Research in action 1.1**.

> ### *Research in action 1.1*
> ### CHECK THE ASSUMPTIONS
>
> One company continually worked hard to reduce new product lead times, that is, how long from start to finish it took them to develop new products. Reducing lead times became a real obsession in the firm, but whenever anyone was asked why it was so important, they usually answered: 'Oh, you know that study …'. However, not one person could identify the original source of 'that study'.
>
> From detailed questioning of the managers, it became clear to the researcher that this study was actually a one-line statement quoted in *Fortune* magazine based on some simplistic calculations carried out by a consultancy. Perhaps not coincidentally, the consultancy trained companies to reduce new product lead times. If the managers had approached the study from a more critical perspective, they might have raised questions such as: How reliable is this study? Do these recommendations apply to us?
>
> The point is that we must be able to evaluate the foundations on which we are basing our work or decisions.

1.3.2 Key players in the project

Whether you undertake a research project alone or as part of a team, you need to know what you should be doing at any point in the research process. In the following chapters, we will consider the activities that should be undertaken in each of the project stages. If you are part of a research team, you will also need to know what role each person will be playing. **Chapter 2** will consider the role of the project team in more detail.

Some questions that you might want to ask are:

- Who will be carrying out this research project?
- What will I be doing or be responsible for?
- How should I work with my supervisor?
- How should I work with any external stakeholders for my work?
- What are the requirements of any assessment body?

Your supervisor's role

An important **project stakeholder** will be your main advisor, typically your academic supervisor, but potentially your project sponsor if you have one. The role your main supervisor plays may vary according to the kind of project, for example supervisor implies much more 'hands-on' involvement than coordinator. In coursework projects or job-related research projects, your supervisor will set the project assignment, and may even be the person who marks or assesses it.

If you have a chance to choose your own supervisor or project coordinator, you should try to find out:

- What do other students that he or she has supervised think about him or her for this specific type of project?
- Is he or she interested in the research you will be doing?
- Does his or her personality complement or conflict with your personality?
- How quickly can he or she provide feedback on your work?
- What are his or her plans for the period of research?

Finding out what other students think about a potential supervisor can help you to decide whether he or she might be a good match for your project. Project supervisors who can provide quick, accurate feedback on your research are worth their weight in gold. A good sign is whether your proposed supervisor takes an interest in this kind of project, especially if he or she is interested in the topic and/or research approach you will be taking. However, interest alone is no guarantee of success: every student–supervisor relationship is unique. Personal habits, administrative and other teaching duties, and the number of students he or she supervises can detract from your academic supervisor's time and attention. Furthermore, whether your supervisor is available to provide feedback and other guidance can be affected by sabbaticals, leave of absence, taking a job at another university, retirement or plans to spend the summer in a house in France.

Whether or not you are able to choose your supervisor, you should think carefully about the relationship you are about to embark on. Students sometimes make unrealistic assumptions about their advisors, which can only lead to disappointment. You can use the issues listed in **Figure 1.2** to manage your expectations of what your supervisor will and will not do.

Because this relationship can have such a large impact on a research project's process and outcomes, many institutions now explicitly state what each party is responsible for. The guidelines given in **Student research in action 1.1** are just an example, but you can see how they set out the ground rules right from the start of the project.

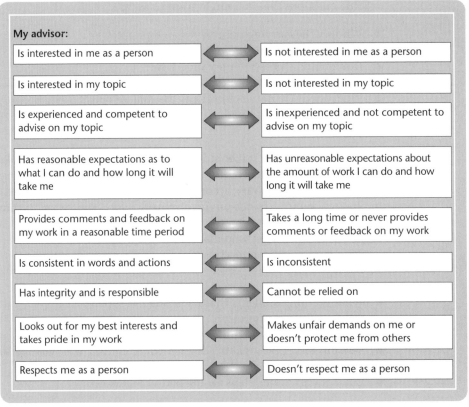

Figure 1.2 Issues to consider in working with a project supervisor
Source: Based on Davis and Parker (1997: 44)

Other people who play a role

You will also need to manage other project stakeholders besides yourself and your supervisor. Try to identify those people who have the information you need. Also try to identify those to whom you will report your findings or make your recommendations. They may or may not be the same people. You should identify these people and start to work proactively with them from the start of your project, since they can help but can also hinder your work. How well you manage them can affect how smoothly the process goes and how successful your project is. This is discussed in more detail in **Chapter 2**.

Always have two plans; leave something to chance. (**Napoleon**)

A key research skill is managing everyone involved in the research project. This includes not only you and any other project team members, but all the project's **stakeholders**. These stakeholders will provide information and/or other inputs that you need. They are also the people who will be the customers for your project's output.

Student research in action 1.1
EXAMPLE GUIDELINES

The student's responsibilities

The student will be expected to:

- Submit a research proposal to the format and timetable as set down in the guidelines
- Draw up a timetable of activities
- Submit an outline of the project report showing what each chapter will cover
- Submit an agreed chapter to generate supervisor feedback
- Keep his/her supervisor informed of any holidays or trips that may affect his/her performance
- Keep the project coordinator and supervisor informed of any circumstances that may affect the submission of his/her project
- Work with an allocated supervisor who may not be his/her first choice
- Be aware of the supervisor's availability during the period of the project, particularly in July, August and September.

The supervisor's responsibilities

The supervisor will provide general guidance in the conduct of a research programme and will act as a 'sounding board' to test various ideas and help in deciding appropriate courses of action (this can include referral to appropriate specialists within the school). This is to help to ensure that the progress made throughout the project and the writing-up of these activities will fulfil the academic requirements of the school.

It is expected that a supervisor will:

- Discuss and assist in the development of the submitted proposal
- Agree a timetable of activities
- Discuss the structure of the written project, that is, chapter coverage and purposes
- Comment on one chapter to advise on how well it matches the set purpose for that chapter and the style of writing
- Advise on issues relating to the theory and/or methodology used in the project
- Examine and mark the completed project.

A supervisor will not:

- Keep track of a student's progress and chase him/her when deadlines are not adhered to
- Read an entire draft copy of the finished project
- Arrange access to organisations used as part of any field work
- Visit any organisations as part of any field work
- Necessarily be an expert in the theoretical or methodological area of a project he/she is supervising.

SUMMARY

In this chapter, we have addressed three main issues about business and management research. First, we have given you an overview of business and management research, and tried to draw a boundary between what research is and is not. Second, we have explained the benefits of understanding business and management research, doing a business and management research project and why you should approach it as a systematic and structured process. Finally, we have explained some issues that you need to consider as you are getting started on your research project, including why you are doing it, what you want to get out of it and who else will be involved in it.

 ANSWERS TO KEY QUESTIONS

What is business and management research?

- It is a process that starts with the determination of a research problem or question, based on an issue of interest
- Research is not journalism or consulting, although there are parallels in the processes with both these activities
- Business and management research considers the roles of organisations, organisational actors and their actions and interactions

Why do we do business and management research?

- Research is conducted for a wide range of intrinsic and extrinsic reasons, including the possibility of discovering new things about something of interest, testing ideas and making sense of complex situations
- Basic research is carried out to establish ideas or principles
- Developmental research is carried out to take these ideas or principles on and bring them one step closer to commercialisation

What are the benefits of taking a systematic approach to a research project?

- A systematic approach allows you to identify the choices you will make as a researcher and the logic that guides these choices
- A systematic approach will remove some of the uncertainty from the process, and allow you to manage the remainder
- The research life cycle is defined by the 4-Ds, from definition, to designing to doing the research and then describing your work
- The process is not linear, but iterative

What critical issues should you consider as you get started?

- Begin with the end in mind
- Look for previous work in this or similar areas, key themes and hot topics, consider methods and look at your timescales and available resources

Who are the key project stakeholders?

- Yourself
- Other members of the project team (if applicable)

- Supervisors
- Examiners
- Project sponsors (if applicable)

REFERENCES

Covey, Stephen R. 2005. *The Seven Habits of Highly Effective People*, rev. edn. London: Simon & Schuster.
Davis, Gordon B. and Parker, Clyde A. 1997. *Writing the Doctoral Dissertation: A Systematic Approach*. Hauppage, NY: Barron's Educational Series.
Kipling, Rudyard. [1902]1998. 'The Elephant's Child' in *Just So Stories*. London: Puffin.
Milgram, S. 1974. *Obedience to Authority*. New York: Harper Perennial.
Roethlisberger, F.J. and Dickson, W.J. 1939. *Management and the Worker*. Cambridge, MA: Harvard University Press.
Sagan, Carl. 1997. *The Demon-Haunted World: Science as a Candle in the Dark*. New York: Ballantine Books.
Saunders, Mark N.K., Lewis, Philip and Thornhill, Adrian. 2003. *Research Methods for Business Students*, 3rd edn. Harlow: Financial Times/Prentice Hall.
Taylor, F.W. [1911]1998. *The Principles of Scientific Management*. London: Dover Publications.
Whyte, William F. 1955. *Street Corner Society*. Chicago: University of Chicago Press.

ADDITIONAL RESOURCES

Collis, Jill and Hussey, Roger. 2003. *Business Research*, 2nd edn. Basingstoke: Palgrave Macmillan.
Easterby-Smith, Mark, Thorpe, Richard and Lowe, Andy. 2002. *Management Research: An Introduction*, 2nd edn. London: Sage.
Gill, John and Johnson, Phil. 2002. *Research Methods for Managers*, 3rd edn. London: Sage.
Jankowicz, A.D. 2000. *Business Research Projects*, 3rd edn. London: Business Press/Thomson Learning.
Partington, David. 2002. *Essential Skills for Management Research*. London: Sage.
Robson, Colin. 2002. *Real World Research*, 2nd edn. Oxford: Blackwell.
Saunders, Mark, Lewis, Phillip and Thornhill, Adrian. 2003. *Research Methods for Business Students*, 3rd edn. Harlow: Financial Times/Prentice Hall.
Sekaran, U. 2000. *Research Methods for Business*, 3rd edn. Chichester: Wiley.
Zikmund, W.G. 2000. *Business Research Methods*, 6th edn. Orlando, FL: Dryden Press/Harcourt College.

Key terms

consulting, 8
journalism, 8
project stakeholder, 15
research, 6
research problem, 10
research process, 5
research questions, 10
stakeholders, 18
systematic approach, 5

1. Identify five ways in which organisations gather information about you for business and management purposes.

2. Can a single research project satisfy the needs of both academic research and consulting? Academic research and journalism?

3. Why do we argue that research reports published in newspapers or business magazines are less credible than those published in journals where they must be reviewed by other researchers before they are published?

4. Review **Table 1.2**. Can you identify a category of research that has been missed out of this table?

5. What do business and management researchers study? Identify at least one study from your classes or textbooks for each level of the hierarchy presented in **Figure 1.1**.

6. What research projects have you carried out so far in your course of study? Why did you do them? What did you find out?

7. Which of the projects would we classify as academic research projects, and which as practical research projects, and what are the differences between the two?

8. Which is more important in business and management research – solving practical problems or increasing knowledge?

9. What are the four stages of business and management research?

10. How can project stakeholders influence the definition, design, doing and description of a research project?

11. Identify the stakeholders in a recent research project or other project you have carried out. What were the needs of each stakeholder and how were they expressed, if at all? If you have carried out projects previously, what have you learnt about the management of stakeholders from this experience?

Read the seven mini-cases below, each describing a particular research project carried out by either students or professional researchers, and then answer the questions at the end.

1: The good student project

A student was asked by a regional development agency (RDA) to investigate how effective the RDA was in promoting good business practice in the region. Early on, the student identified two key customers for this report, the university and the RDA, so she worked with both to make sure that she understood their requirements. The university's requirements were laid out in the project guidelines, which she clarified with her academic supervisor. Her main contact at the RDA put his requirements in writing at an early stage, giving her a definable end objective.

Based on these two sets of requirements, the student decided that the best way to approach the project was from an economic perspective, in which she identified and narrowed down the relevant research done by other people in similar areas, and organised these findings into a framework for evaluating the RDA's practices based on work done elsewhere. The findings reported by other researchers also provided a point of comparison when she evaluated what the agency was doing. Her further investigation of the roles that other agencies were reported to be playing allowed some small-scale benchmarking of the RDA's activities against other agencies.

The project was a phenomenal success. The university awarded it a prize and the agency came away with a much better understanding of how it was supporting businesses in order to innovate. This success reflected an understanding of the needs of both the university and the sponsoring organisation – not always an easy task – and the fact that these needs could be converted into products.

2: The bad student project

The project started with the student demonstrating to the supervisor a piece of software he had been involved in writing. 'This is what managers today need to help them to manage', he confidently stated. 'I want to use my project to validate that this is the case.' Despite objections from his supervisor, he proceeded with his work and tried to construct tests to prove this. As he saw this as 'a practical project', he dismissed any prior academic research as irrelevant to his work. He also rejected using established methods for collecting and analysing data in his testing, preferring to invent these methods himself.

The project failed. It lacked key facets that must be present in all academic projects. These include a basis in prior research – this shows that you have covered what is known already before you start reinventing anything. Furthermore, the use of any method is not self-validating. Justifying your methods is vital to demonstrate that you are able to conceptualise, design, carry out, analyse and report research. This is valued in most academic qualifications.

3: A professional laboratory study: Milgram's experiment

Stanley Milgram (1974) conducted one of the most well-known experiments in the study of human behaviour. His objective was to study obedience to authority. He constructed a laboratory-style experiment using human subjects – in this case male adults residing in New Haven aged 20–50, and selected from a wide variety of occupations. He carried out the experiment twice, using 40 new participants for each experiment.

Each test was carried out on a pair of test subjects. The initial briefing given to the subjects told them that the test was designed to test memory and learning. Unknown to one of the pair was the fact that the other was actually a paid confederate of the researcher. Each was paid and told that their performance in no way affected their pay.

Following a short introduction to memory and learning, a rigged draw took place in which the (naive) subject was assigned the role of teacher, and the confederate the role of learner. A white-coated experimenter stayed in the room with the 'teacher'. The 'learner' was taken to an adjacent room and strapped into an electric chair. The experimenter told the subject that he had to teach the learner a list of paired words. Subsequently he was to test the learner on his recall of the list and to administer an increasing level of electric shocks to punish him for each mistake in the test. The 'teacher' was instructed to increase the intensity of shock by one level for each mistake. The dial was marked with 30 shock levels (15–450 volts), labelled from 'slight shock' to 'danger: severe shock'. The learner, according to the plan, provided many wrong answers, so that before long the subject would have to administer the strongest level of shock. Increases in shock level were met by increasingly insistent demands from the learner that the experiment be stopped. However, the experimenter kept instructing the teacher to continue. (The confederate was not really being shocked, but behaved as though he was increasingly being shocked, up to the level of no response, implying that he was unconscious or even dead.)

Milgram recorded that only 14 out of 40 people withdrew from the test before they thought they had administered the maximum shock. All participants administered at least slight shocks. The remaining majority, despite stating that they would rather not hurt the presumed victim, felt obligated to follow the orders of the experimenter. Although admitting that they had ultimate control over the switch, the experimenter exerted sufficient pressure by simply urging that the experiment must continue to create behaviour antithetical to personal and social ideals. (All the subjects were carefully debriefed following the experiment and reconciled with their 'victim'.)

4: In-house study of text message banking

A high-street bank wanted to know whether it should invest time and significant resources into developing text message banking. With such a service, customers would be able to have balance and transaction information sent directly to their mobile phones, as well as access to other services, including making payments. The overall question was relatively straightforward – should the company invest in this service?

A student research team was assembled to consider this further. They broke the main question down into a number of sub-questions, including:

● What is the main market for text message banking?

● Do people in this group want such a service?

● Would they like it enough to pay for the service?

● How many people would want to sign up for the service if it were free and how many would sign up for it if it were a pay-as-you-go service?

The initial study involved the students finding out who were the greatest users of mobile phones and text messaging services in particular. Their findings were that by far most users of these services were aged 18–30, especially students. Given that the bank was trying to compete in the student market, this presented an intriguing opportunity, which might ultimately be useful outside the single issue of text message services.

The students used various databases such as Mintel to find out more about the usage of mobile phones in this age group. Having established the potential market size, they designed and carried out two further studies. The first was a survey to determine whether this service would be of interest to the market. They chose their respondents carefully and carried out a pilot study of their questionnaire. In addition, they used focus groups to get more information about what kind of service people would be willing to pay for. They obtained many insights from the focus groups, and gained agreement from the bank to launch a small-scale trial of a text message service. From the trial, they were able to answer the third and fourth of their key questions, including estimating the potential market for the service. By rigorously applying well-established marketing research methods, they were able to obtain highly credible results, and produce a report of significance for both their sponsors and their academic institution.

5: The professional ethnographic study – *Street Corner Society*

Whyte (1955) studied groups of young men who socialised together in a thinly disguised Boston in the 1940s. Whyte lived and socialised with these 'disadvantaged' youths, even going bowling and generally living as they did for the period of the study. This gave him a unique insight into the complex social dynamics of the groups – he was able to get 'inside their heads' to understand their thinking processes, in a way that an external observer would never be able to. In this study he 'went native' – completely immersing himself in the environment for the purposes of the research.

6: The professional in-company study: F.W. Taylor's studies of work

F.W. Taylor has been credited with inventing the whole science of 'time-and-motion studies'. In these, a work task is analysed in scientific terms to determine the optimal way for it to be carried out. The time that it takes and the way that it is carried out are the subject of analysis. Taylor developed his techniques in the early years of the last century in a foundry. He studied many manual tasks that were carried out, including the shovelling of ore and ashes into and from furnaces. He would analyse the elements of each task – in the case of ore shovelling, push shovel into ore stack, turn and throw ore in a particular direction at a particular height. By carrying out extensive experimentation and measurement (watching and recording the times and movements on hundreds of occasions), he was able to conclude that the optimum load for a shovel was 21 pounds for the people that he was studying. This meant that they would need different sized shovels – for instance one for ore (small) and a different one for ash (much larger). Redesigning the shovels also increased the productivity of the people doing the shovelling. Other aspects of the job, including the placement of piles of work were likewise optimised. He also paid the workers a bonus for this increased productivity in return for using his scientifically derived methods (see Taylor [1911]1998).

7: The professional in-company study: Roethlisberger and Dickson's Hawthorne studies

The study started as an experiment with a small group of workers in 1927 to determine the conditions that led to fatigue in workers. By doing so, the researchers hoped to be able to determine the optimum conditions under which people could work to increase their productivity. The researchers were very confident about their method and that they would be able to isolate the key variables that would enhance productivity. As is so often the case in research, what they found was not what they expected.

One small part of the study concerned the impact of lighting levels on the productivity of a group of workers. By isolating the group from the rest of the factory, other factors could be eliminated, providing near-laboratory conditions.

Initially the lighting level was raised and it was noted that the productivity increased. At the end of the experiment, the levels were lowered again, and the productivity increased again. This was not expected. The researchers changed their approach to try to uncover why this was happening. They discovered that what was underlying these changes in output were not any of the influences of management (for example through incentives). They found that it was the social processes in the group and their accepted norms (particularly relating to output) that determined their productivity (see Roethlisberger and Dickson 1939).

1. What question or problem do you think the researcher was addressing in each case?
2. How did each researcher go about his/her task? Briefly summarise the method for his/her research.
3. What were the resource requirements in each case in terms of time, level of expertise, and so on for the researchers and how applicable would each approach be for a student project?
4. What were the key findings of each project?
5. How generalisable are the findings in each case, that is, could the finding apply to environments other than the one in which they were carried out?

Relevant chapters

13 Answering your research questions
14 Describing your research
15 Closing the loop

Key challenges

- Interpreting your findings and making recommendations
- Writing and presenting your project
- Reflecting on and learning from your research

4

Relevant chapters

1 What is research?
2 **Managing the research process**
3 What should I study?
4 How do I find information?

Key challenges

- Understanding the research process
- **Taking a systematic approach**
- Generating and clarifying ideas
- Using the library and internet

1

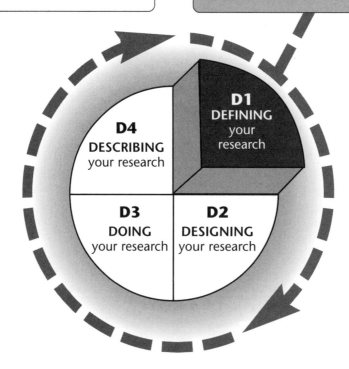

Relevant chapters

9 Doing field research
10 Analysing quantitative data
11 Advanced quantitative analysis
12 Analysing qualitative data

Key challenges

- Practical considerations in doing research
- Using simple statistics
- Undertanding multivariate statistics
- Interpreting interviews and observations

3

Relevant chapters

5 Scientist or ethnographer?
6 Quantitative research designs
7 Designing qualitative research ·
8 Case studies/multi-method design

Key challenges

- Choosing a model for doing research
- Using scientific methods
- Using ethnographic methods
- Integrating quantitative and qualitative research

2

chapter

2

How do I manage the research process?

A systematic approach to project management

 Key questions

- How can project management help me to manage my research project successfully?
- How do I develop and use a project plan?
- How can I monitor my project's progress?
- How can I work effectively with other students?

 Learning outcomes

At the end of this chapter, you should be able to:
- Apply project management ideas to your research project
- Compile SMART objectives, basic plans and activity lists for your project
- Draw a Gantt chart or network diagram and analyse your project schedule
- Keep your project on track
- Identify good practices for managing a group project and dealing with conflict

Contents

INTRODUCTION

From the many student research projects we have supervised, we have identified the two student types described below in **Student research in action 2.1**. Which profile honestly fits you best?

> *Student research in action 2.1*
> **ARE YOU A TYPE 1 OR TYPE 2?**
>
> *Type 1 students.* As soon as the topics for the assignment are issued, these students sprint to the library to start work. They plan out the tasks and, working steadily through them, finish with several weeks to spare. This time can be spent polishing their work, and occasionally gloating over type 2 students ...
>
> *Type 2 students.* As soon as the topics are issued, these students are on the way to the bar. No use rushing the project, of course. It is only in the last few weeks before the deadline that they can ignore it no longer. Massive panic ensues; caffeine keeps them going during the long nights. As all the type 2 students are queuing for the laser printer and photocopier, the project report is submitted late.

More importantly, will a type 1 or a type 2 student manage the research process better and produce better research outcomes? In the past, taking a type 2 approach to your research may have worked for you, but you are leaving your project's success to chance. We don't expect you to magically transform into a full-on type 1, but you can gain many benefits if you adopt at least some type 1 practices in managing your research process. If you define your research project, develop a sensible research design and follow through in executing your project, the systematic approach should maximise your chances of project success. (If you are a full-on type 1 student, you may want to lighten up and enjoy your research project a little more, especially if you are working in a group.)

We cannot say too strongly that *time is key* – particularly when you are working on a research project that is complex or involves many different people. Time is *the* one non-renewable resource in your project – once you have let time slip away, you can never get it back. On the other hand, we have observed that people who carry out projects successfully have consistently made good use of their time. To make the best use of time, you must *plan* your project carefully, but project planning is not the only issue that you must deal with. Over and over, students ignore all the good advice to manage the research process systematically. They hope that 'it'll work out in the end'. However, many research project failures illustrate the old saying 'if you fail to plan, you plan to fail'.

Despite all the evidence that systematically managing your research process will significantly improve your chances of project success, many students object that 'planning and control will interfere with my creativity and academic freedom'. Focusing too much on managing the project, and not enough on actually doing it, could indeed have this result. Intelligently applying the principles set out in the chapter to manage your project, however, should have the opposite effect. You should find the time not only to manage your research process and its outcomes, but also to explore relevant and interesting areas creatively.

You will also need time to learn from the research process. Systematically managing your research project can help you not only improve the quality of the process and outcomes, but also understand your own strengths and weaknesses and how to manage yourself more effectively. How you manage your time (both as an individual and as part of a group) reveals who you are and what you value. If you manage your time well, you will create many opportunities to reflect during your research project, for instance to consider your own preferences for interacting with people and organisations directly or indirectly, or question your assumptions about the business and management world, and the world in general. You can only reflect if you plan and manage your research process from the start.

WHAT IS PROJECT MANAGEMENT?

During the research process, you are embarking upon a 'voyage of discovery'. You need to manage the process of your research project as well as its content. To give you some ideas and tools for managing the research process, this chapter will explain some basic principles of **project management**, which provides you with both a systematic approach to managing projects – which we have consistently advocated in this book for research project – and a large set of tools.

By the end of this chapter, you should understand *what* project management techniques you can apply to managing your research project and *how* to apply them. **Section 2.1** will explain how to define your research process. (**Chapters 3** and **4** will focus on how to define its content.) **Section 2.2** will illustrate how to develop a preliminary plan and how to analyse and improve it. **Section 2.3** will explain how to manage it as you go along.

The ideas presented in this chapter are neither complicated nor difficult, but you will have to use some self-discipline to apply them. This discipline isn't always easy to find, particularly if you have been able to manage past projects such as coursework in your head. We will show that if you take just a few minutes at the start of your research project to develop a detailed project plan, and then review your progress every so often, you can manage your research project more effectively. This is especially important when you need to deal with the uncertainty that inevitably makes the research process challenging and unpredictable. What's more, if the worst happens and your project runs into problems, if you have been actively managing your research project you can demonstrate that you have taken every possible step to make sure that your project succeeded.

2.1 DEFINING YOUR RESEARCH PROJECT

A **project** is a one-off activity carried out with limited resources (particularly time and cost) to meet a given objective. Other definitions can be found in Maylor (2003). Even though most projects follow a common process, a project is a 'one-off' because its content is unique. All projects therefore have some common characteristics, including uncertainty, which need to be managed. When you start a research project, you may not know exactly what you will find out. This is certainly one of the most exciting aspects of research. At the beginning it is often unclear what you will be investigating, how you will investigate it and what you will find out as a result.

Because a research project is a type of project, you can use project management to manage your research project. There are significant differences between the large-scale research projects that typically employ project managers and the relatively small-scale research projects that we are concerned with in this book, but all projects will benefit from a systematic approach to their management. Because project management was originally developed for managing large and complex industrial projects, we will recommend a 'slimmed-down' version for scheduling and managing your research project. Project management should help you to manage your project – a balance between planning and doing – rather than being an end in itself.

The well-developed body of knowledge associated with project management can help you to manage your project systematically. If you plan your project from the start, you can decide on an overall strategy for the project, develop a detailed plan for how you will execute it and monitor your performance along the way. Moreover, you can use the planning process itself to anticipate problems and opportunities along the way, and deal with them proactively rather than simply reacting to them as they occur.

Managing your research project using project management means that you will need to:

● Define your objectives ('begin with the end in mind')
● Plan your work (identify its structure and objectives)
● Control how you spend your resources (particularly time and energy) in the project to achieve your objectives.

In a single chapter, we can only cover the basics of project management. However, because every research project is a project, you may want to follow up with a more detailed investigation of what project management can offer you as a researcher. We provide references in the **additional resources** at the end of this chapter.

2.1.1 Understanding the project life cycle

A **project structure** breaks down a project into stages and identifies the tasks that need to be undertaken during each stage. The **project life cycle** is a generic project structure that can be applied at a high level to the main stages of a research project. By taking a top-down approach, you can use a project structure approach to identify the detailed activities that need to take place in each project stage.

You can use the 4-D model presented in the **Introduction** and repeated at the beginning of each chapter as the guide to your project's life cycle, the major stages that a research project typically goes through during the research process, as shown in **Table 2.1**.

The first step in project planning is to use this project life cycle to identify and reflect on the activities you will undertake in each stage. In the *project definition stage* you will come up with ideas for your research project, expand those ideas into a range of possible projects and select a single main project and a backup (**Chapter 3**). This gives you the basis for identifying your research problem and research questions. The project definition stage may include some activities that take place even before the 'official' project start date.

Table 2.1 The four stages of the research process

Stage	Major outputs	Form
1. Project definition	Research topic, research problem, research questions	Project proposal
2. Project design	Methods for gathering and analysing evidence and testing knowledge claims	Research design
3. Project execution	Knowledge claims, evidence, analysis and interpretation	Findings
4. Project description	New knowledge	Project report

In the *project design stage*, you will develop your research problem and questions into a research design that describes how you will collect, analyse and interpret information to find out more about your research problem. In the *project execution stage*, you will actually collect and analyse data, and interpret your findings. This stage involves the most direct contact with external project stakeholders and the businesses or managers in your research setting.

Lastly, in the *project description stage*, you will report what you did, why you did it, what you found out and what it means. This report will document the quality of both your research process and your research findings. It is never too early to start thinking about what you will need to do in each of these four stages.

The emotional project life cycle

You can also apply the life cycle idea to manage yourself, and possibly your project group, supervisor, sponsor and other stakeholders. Like most researchers, you may encounter these emotions at one time or another (although not always in this order):

- *Enthusiasm* – You have just started the project and you are excited about it.
- *Despondency* – You realise how much you have to do and how much time it will take.
- *Running down blind alleys* – You are wasting time on interesting information or activities that will not contribute to your finished research project.
- *Panic* – You realise that you have too much work to get it all finished in the remaining time.
- *Elation* – You have completed a significant activity or the entire project.
- *Deflation* – You cannot figure out what to do next.

After the original rush of enthusiasm wears off, even experienced researchers often become *despondent* and lose their momentum, because the task can appear to be overwhelming in size or scope. As a result, they often avoid getting stuck in. You can prevent despondency by planning the project like any other business enterprise. The techniques for doing this are discussed in **Section 2.2**.

Most researchers can tell you how much time they have wasted investigating **blind alleys**. These are project directions that initially masquerade as interesting and relevant but ultimately will not help you to solve your research problem or answer your research questions and so represent wasted effort. If you aren't sure whether a certain area is relevant to your research project, you might check with your project advisor and go back to your project proposal and scope (**Chapter 3**). When you are faced with a new line of inquiry, you should ask yourself the 'so what' question – how will pursuing this help you to answer one or more of your research questions? Blind alleys do not answer the 'so what' question, and in short projects they can significantly set back your progress because you do not have enough time to recover if you waste a significant amount of time and effort pursuing them.

As a 'reality check' for a potential blind alley, you should ask:

- What aspects of my research problem (practical or theoretical) does this tell me more about?
- What new information does this add to what I already know about this research problem?
- How would I explain to my academic supervisor or project sponsor what this adds to my research project?
- If it is interesting, but outside the scope of this research project, can I come back to it later as an 'area for further investigation'?

Panic ensues when you realise that the work you have left to do will take longer – sometimes far longer – than the time you have available for doing it. There is no cure for panic, especially when deadlines are approaching, but the best preventive is project planning and control, which we discuss in the next few sections.

Even though project management cannot create the positive emotions or totally prevent you from experiencing the negative emotions listed above, recognising that you will experience different emotions during different phases of the research process can help you to plan for them and take action to prevent them from affecting the quality of your research process and outcomes. For example, whilst you are in the 'enthusiasm phase', you can take action to help to prevent the effects of despondency, blind alleys and panic from being disastrous.

2.1.2 Defining SMART project objectives

Once you have used the project life cycle to identify 'what needs to be done' in each project life cycle stage, you should set **project objectives** for yourself and your research project. These objectives should include both the research objectives that you want to achieve from your research project and any personal objectives. Your **research objectives** describe what you want to achieve from the research project, such as satisfying your project requirements (coursework, degree, work assignment). Your **personal objectives** include any other objectives that you want to achieve, such as supporting your career development, personal interests or job prospects.

Each of your research objectives should be **SMART**, which stands for:

- *Specific* – Where is this research journey taking you? What do you hope to achieve from it? Write it down and use this as a basis for future decision-making

- *Measurable* – How will you determine whether your objective has been achieved (particularly more intangible objectives such as quality)? What steps are on the way to this?
- *Achievable* – Is the target you have set yourself physically possible?
- *Realistic* – Given all that you will be doing at the same time as this, will you really have the time and energy to give this project what it needs?
- *Time-framed* – How long do you have to accomplish each objective?

Once you have identified these SMART objectives, you should identify how you could measure each objective in terms of time, cost and quality:

- *Time* – When each objective needs to be completed. Often, you will be working to a **project end date** (for example submission deadline, agreed dates with supervisors) and you should work backwards from this. Otherwise, determine a realistic time (see below) for the work and set start and end dates accordingly.
- *Cost* – The time, work effort and other resources associated with each objective. Cost is not always a *major* issue, although if you need to travel to interview sites or make long-distance phone calls, photocopy and mail questionnaires, or purchase computer software or databases, costs may be significant. You also should consider the opportunity costs of your project – other things that you could do with your time, such as revising for exams.
- *Quality* – The level of accomplishment you need to reach and the standard you are setting yourself for the outcome (your report/dissertation and any related documents). This will be discussed in later chapters, but it is vital that you set a goal for this.

Goals are high-level objectives that help to guide your decisions before and during the project. Setting these goals sets the course for your journey. **Student research in action 2.2** shows how simple the goal-setting process can be.

Student research in action 2.2
KATYA IN THE WRY

Katya was undertaking an MBA and wanted to do a project in the logistics industry. She identified the following goals and objectives:

- To complete the MBA by submitting a project by the submission deadline – the project to score in excess of 65%
- To gain a working knowledge of leading-edge practices in the logistics industry
- To determine, by the end of the in-company research period, whether this was likely to be an area where she would work in the future
- To make 30 contacts during the period of the project that would be useful in her future career.

Each of these met the requirements of the SMART objectives and she prioritised her life so that she could give the project the time necessary to put in work consistent with achieving in excess of 65%.

2.1.3 Developing a project breakdown

Once you have identified and recorded your goals and SMART objectives for your research project, you can identify the detailed actions you need to take. We suggest that you break down your project life cycle phases into smaller units or **mini-projects** to make them more visible. You can identify goals and objectives for each mini-project, making sure that each goal and objective is linked back to the project's overall goals and objectives.

You should also identify three or four significant events or time points during your project which will define your research project's **milestones**. Each milestone marks the completion of a mini-project. A milestone may occur naturally at the end of each project life cycle phase, or you may want to create some at significant points in the project, such as important deadlines or completing a substantial project output such as a project proposal.

You may also want to break down significant phases, such as the project execution phase, into further mini-projects with their own milestones. For instance, you may decide to spend two weeks on the project definition phase, with a milestone being the submission of a research proposal to your academic supervisor or project sponsor, and a month on investigating the supporting literature, with another milestone being the completion of a literature review (**Chapter 4**). When you have identified all the mini-projects and milestones, you have identified your **project breakdown structure** (**Figure 2.1**). You may find that you need to revisit your goals and objectives once you have identified your detailed actions, but you should be able to see an immediate benefit from breaking down your objectives into **detailed actions**.

Although most of us can manage a simple project in our heads, such as writing an essay or revising for an exam, there are too many activities involved in a typical research project and the structure is too complex for us to visualise all the activities in a research project in the same way. Trying to manage without writing things down can lead you to feeling overwhelmed and despondent, as discussed above. When you write things down, they become visible and therefore more manageable – as the old joke goes, 'How do you eat an elephant? One bite at a time!'

You can also use your project breakdown to identify where problems are most likely to arise. This will allow you to plan alternative courses of action in case they do. For instance, you may need to negotiate access to firms and managers or employees to gather data. This access can take weeks to organise and can delay or even prevent your work from taking place. (In fact, it creates so many problems that we discuss it in detail in **Chapter 9**.) If you know that you might have trouble getting access, then you should identify alternate sources of data – or even alternate research designs – in case you can't get access. For example, one of the authors developed a questionnaire to be administered at an international conference of World Health directors, which would provide the data for an important doctoral paper. Although the questionnaires and her supervisor winged off to Africa as scheduled, the questionnaires mysteriously never reappeared. Fortunately, she was able to analyse an existing data set to pass the assignment.

You might question whether it is worthwhile spending time to prepare a project breakdown if research projects can be disrupted so easily. Because Murphy's Law ('Whatever can go wrong, will go wrong') is especially true for research projects, it is critically important to plan for disruptions, even if you cannot predict what they will be. You should use your project breakdown as a starting point for project planning,

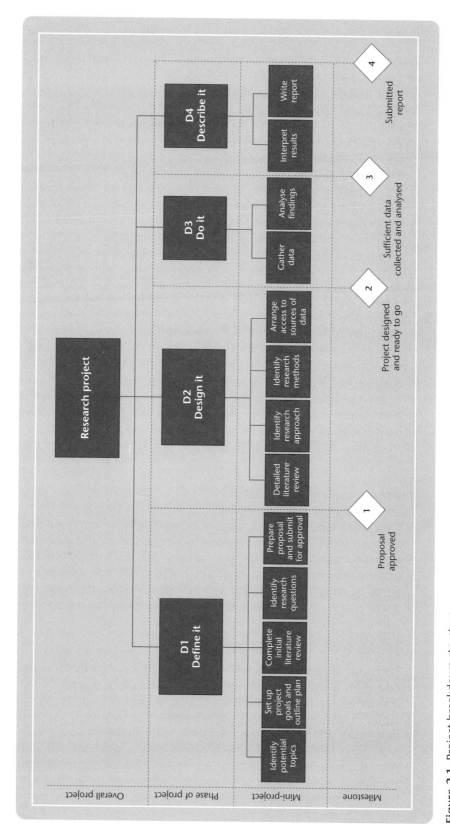

Figure 2.1 Project breakdown structure

which we discuss next in **Section 2.2**, and use this to work through different scenarios, for instance one scenario where everything works perfectly, another where key data doesn't materialise.

We have supervised a few students who failed to plan ahead for such disruptions. They found that academic institutions are notoriously unforgiving and inflexible when asked for deadline extensions when research project delays could have been identified ahead of time and planned for. Normally, you will only be granted an extension if you experience significant medical problems or close family bereavement (and if you have asked for an extension for your mother's funeral, it's not a good idea for her to show up at your graduation – as reported in the *Times Higher Education Supplement*, 10 June 2004). You are unlikely to be shown any mercy if your laptop is stolen or breaks down and you don't have a backup copy of your data and/or project report, or if a project contact fails to deliver promised access or data. (You should check your project guidelines to see what applies to your research project.) If you are being paid to carry out a research project for an organisation, you will probably have even less chance of an extension, since you could be affecting their 'bottom line'.

2.2 PRELIMINARY PROJECT PLANNING

Your project breakdown identified the significant mini-projects that you have to complete as part of your research project, and the goals and objectives for both the mini-projects and complete project. You can now use **project planning** to specify in detail how you will actually execute each mini-project. You can use a project plan not only to manage your project and meet intermediate and final deadlines, but also in case there are problems. To quote Nelson, 'The plan is nothing. Planning is everything'.

2.2.1 Drawing up an activity list

Each mini-project in your project breakdown can be broken down into major activities, and then into smaller activities taking no more than a few days each. This list of major and minor activities becomes your **activity list**. After identifying the complete set of activities, you can identify how long each activity will take, what order you need to carry out these activities in, and what activities you need to complete in order to begin other activities. You will need this information to analyse and improve your project schedule.

Estimating time to complete activities

First, you should estimate how long you expect each activity in your activity list to take. This is simple in theory, but quite difficult in practice. People's estimates of activity times tend to be either hopelessly optimistic ('I will be able to write a 100-page report in two days') or overly generous ('I will allow myself a week to write letters to companies, just in case'). In most cases, estimates are truly guesstimates, since they will always be best guesses. Overoptimism creates problems during the entire project, since you will always be behind schedule, whilst overgenerosity misleads you into thinking you are making good progress when you are making no real progress ('I wrote two sentences today – since the plan was only to write one sentence, I am a whole day ahead!').

Project management can help you avoid both overoptimism and overgenerousness in estimating the time you need to complete a particular activity. You should estimate how much time it will take to complete an activity if you are equally likely to finish it early or late – the finishing time, in other words, where 50 per cent of the time it will take less time to complete and 50 per cent of the time it will take more time.

The resulting estimates are actually much more accurate overall, because your overall objective is to finish the entire research project on time, not each individual activity. It doesn't matter if you finish every individual activity on time, if, in the end, you hand in your project report late. You can use any time saved by completing an individual activity early by immediately starting on another activity. Save up any time saved for the end of the project, when you need it most.

Managing safety/buffer time

Any accumulated time savings or any time that you build into individual activities or the entire project to absorb late finishes is known as a safety margin or buffer. You can use a **safety margin** or **buffer** to make sure that if problems do occur – anything from illness to a computer crashing or losing pieces of research data – your overall project completion will not be delayed.

How much safety margin or buffer you build into your project plan – and where – depends on the uncertainty in your research project and the amount of risk associated with various activities. (We will describe how you can conduct a risk analysis in **Section 2.3.2**.) From project management, we know that you should allow for safety or buffer time at the end of the project, and nowhere else:

> *Planning principle 1.* Every project *must* have a safety margin in the project schedule, and the *only* place to put any safety margin is at the end of the project.

Suppose that you reach your first milestone – a completed draft of your literature review – two days early. You might be tempted to take some time off after spending a few weeks working on your research project, particularly if you are ahead of schedule. If you take time off for a quick city break, a day in the pub or even to polish your draft instead of starting your next activity, you will lose two days' buffer that you could use later to offset a late activity finish, when it really starts to matter. Our second planning principle is therefore:

> *Planning principle 2.* As soon as one activity is completed, regardless of whether it is early or late, the next activity should start straight away.

Identifying sequence and dependencies

In any research project, you will have to complete certain activities before you start other activities. Project managers describe such relationships between activities as **dependencies**. You should identify as many of these dependencies as you can in your project plan because they determine the sequence in which you can carry out your activities, and whether a delay or early completion of any individual activity will affect subsequent activities and the entire project. You may want to write them up in your activity list, as shown in **Table 2.2**.

When there are many dependencies between project activities, a delay in finishing even one project activity almost guarantees that there will be a knock-on effect on

Table 2.2   An activity list for David's project

	Activity	Estimated time (days)	Dependency
	Defining		
A	Define project	10	--
B	Investigate literature and write literature review	20	A
	Designing		
C	Negotiate company access	2	B
D	Develop questionnaire	5	C
E	Pilot test questionnaire	2	D
F	Revise questionnaire	1	E
	Doing		
G	Distribute questionnaires	2	F
H	Collect questionnaires	3	G
I	Enter data from questionnaires into spreadsheet	2	H
J	Analyse questionnaire data	3	I
	Describing		
K	Write up results of data analysis	2	J
L	Produce first draft of project report	10	K
M	Give draft to supervisor for comments	4	L
N	Revise report into final draft	2	M
O	Print out and proofread project report	2	N
P	Copy and bind report	2	P
	Total time required	**72**	

subsequent activities. Leaving things until the last minute means that you will be behind schedule for most of your project, and you will run late in direct proportion to how important finishing an activity is. (We discuss procrastination with respect to writing your project report in **Chapter 14**, so you may want to peek ahead at that chapter.)

If you have followed the steps above, you now have a basic activity list, with activities broken down into chunks or **work packages** that last a few days each, and you've identified the durations and dependencies for each. Now that you have prepared your preliminary project plan, there is one final step you need to take: analyse your project plan and revise it if necessary so that you can achieve your project goals and objectives. The purpose of planning is to allow basic analysis to be carried out. The most basic project analysis will answer questions including:

- How long will the project take?
- Can I complete it on time?
- Do I need to add or remove any activities to make the project fit the time available?
- What happens if one or more elements of the project are delayed?

Although some people can analyse complex projects armed with only an activity list, most people find it easier to analyse project plans where information is presented visually. Two ways to do this are the Gantt chart and the network diagram.

2.2.2 Drawing a Gantt chart

Project managers often use Gantt charts (named after Henry Gantt, who popularised them during the early 20th century for use in production planning) for presenting project plans graphically. A **Gantt chart** is a simple type of chart where time runs from left to right on the horizontal axis. Activities are represented by horizontal bars (see **Figure 2.2**) whose lengths are proportional to the amount of time involved, whilst milestones, which we discussed in **Section 2.1.3**, are indicated by diamonds (lozenges). Gantt charts are easy to read and can be prepared from activity lists by most computerised project management software.

You can use a Gantt chart in project planning to see how long a project will take overall. Once you have marked each of your project activities on a Gantt chart, it is easy to see which activities could overlap if you need to shorten the project. Gantt charts can also be used for **forward scheduling** (seeing how long it will take to complete all subsequent activities starting from a given date) and **backward scheduling** (seeing when you need to start all preceding activities in order to end no later

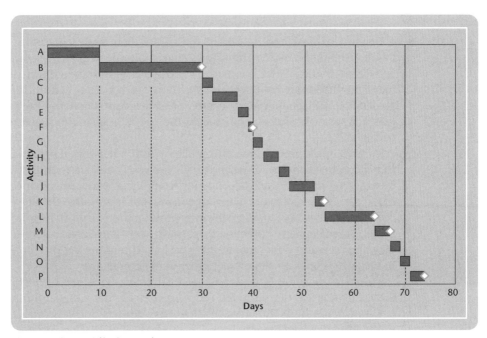

Figure 2.2 David's Gantt chart

than a given finishing date). It is also easier to see dependencies between activities in a Gantt chart than in an activity list.

The Gantt chart for David's project plan is presented in **Figure 2.2** to show you what type of output you can achieve in a Gantt chart. Whilst this chart looks as if it might take a long time to do, once you have learnt to draw Gantt charts, you can draw one in a short time, which will help you to analyse your project plan and make decisions.

The Gantt chart is a model of the system that you hope will achieve your desired results. The process of constructing the model is itself beneficial (you will ask yourself lots of questions in building it), but the main objective is to be able to analyse and optimise your work before you have to do it for real.

You can easily draw Gantt charts using a specialised project management software package such as Microsoft Project or another commercially available package. If you don't have access to project management software, a spreadsheet program such as Microsoft Excel will allow you to construct Gantt charts as a bar chart, but you will need to insert the formulas yourself (these are built in to specialised software). You can even draw a Gantt chart by hand, although it is a bit messy to update without redrawing. However, for simple research projects, this is generally okay.

2.2.3 Drawing a network diagram

Although Gantt charts have been around for a century, many people still find Gantt charts useful for everyday project planning, especially at high levels or for projects where activities have simple dependencies. If you are working on a complex or large project, where many activities are going on simultaneously, or activities depend on more than one preceding activity, you may find it useful to use a network diagram instead. A **network diagram** is like the Gantt chart because it shows what activities you will undertake and their sequence and interdependencies, and is a simple tool that you can master in a few minutes.

One way of drawing a network diagram is to represent each activity as a box, where boxes are linked together by arrows that show the sequence of and dependencies between activities. Since completed network diagrams show flows of activities, you may find them more helpful than an activity list or Gantt chart. In particular, you can use a network diagram to see the effect of early or late starts or finishes on all the activities in a research project, and analyse the effects of changing activity sequences and dependencies.

For a complex project, you will probably find a network diagram useful because it can incorporate multiple dependencies between activities, whilst Gantt charts can usually only show a single dependency relationship between activities. You can easily construct a simple network diagram by hand, but it is more difficult to construct them on a spreadsheet or word-processing programme, so most people use specialised project management software. However, once you have constructed a network diagram, it is easy to incorporate any changes to your project plan or activities and see how it affects your overall project progress or completion.

A network diagram is a useful tool for making decisions or seeing whether your project plan is feasible, although it is no guarantee that you will finish on time. There is always uncertainty inherent in a research project, but you can see the impact of uncertainties as they materialise.

Figure 2.3 shows the network diagram for David's research project. Once David has drawn this first network diagram, he has a complete picture of what activities he needs to complete and in what sequence.

From this network diagram, David should immediately be able to identify some potential problems or conflicts with his project plan. It will take 72 days to complete all these activities in this sequence, but David only has 12 weeks (84 days) before the project is due, and he would rather work five days per week (a maximum of 60 days). Even if David spends six days per week (72 days) to complete the research project, if just one activity is delayed by even a single day, the project will be late: David has not allowed any safety margin or buffer to compensate for anything going wrong or being late. For example, if he has problems with gaining access to a company (always highly risky, as we discuss in **Student research in action 2.4**), there is nowhere in his project plan he can make up this time.

David should reconsider his project plan. He might consider working more than 60 days during the project period, or reducing the amount of time he has allocated to various activities, for example writing his literature review in 15 days instead of 20 days.

His choices will directly affect not only time but also quality:

- the quality of his life, if he decides to work six or seven days per week
- the quality of his project, if he decides to complete some activities in less time.

To minimise how much he has to compromise on either aspect of quality, David reevaluated his plan. Having done so, he recognised that there were some activities he could start before completing the preceding activity, even though the network diagram in **Figure 2.3** shows that in his original plan no activity was started until the preceding activity was completed. In fact, David could and should carry out some activities simultaneously. David could also complete his first activity before the 12 weeks actually start – something we would recommend for most projects.

Figure 2.4 shows David's new network diagram, which shows that, in his revised plan, he will:

- Define his project before the start of the 'official' project period
- Begin negotiating company access before completing his literature review, working on the two in parallel
- Include a buffer at the end of the project to absorb any delays during the project.

Even though with his revised plan David can now complete his project by working 60 days during the 12 weeks, rather than the original 72, this is still risky, as he hasn't allowed a safety margin or buffer in case anything goes wrong. By working every Saturday, he will add 12 days, a reasonable buffer for this project. It will only be useful, however, if David follows the second project planning principle: start the next activity as soon as the previous one is finished.

You can follow a similar process of planning, graphing and analysing your own research project. Once you have developed your own project schedule, you should be able to find ways to improve it. For instance, you can reply to emails, write letters and make telephone calls while you are negotiating access to firms, which would otherwise be wasted time. Similarly, while you are waiting for particular publications to arrive (for example interlibrary loans), you can complete other tasks.

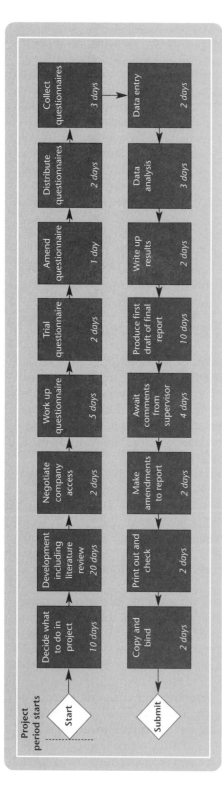

Figure 2.3 Network diagram of David's research project

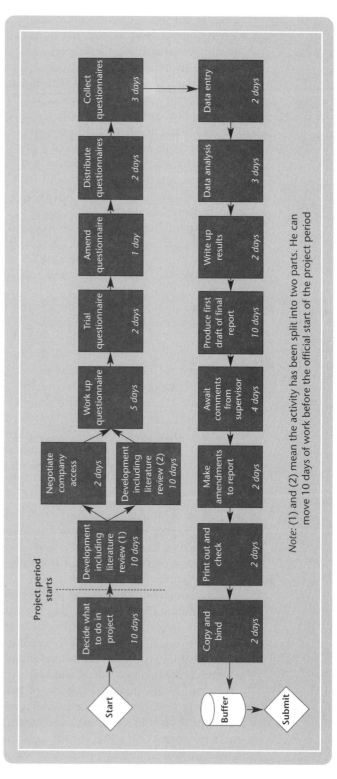

Note: (1) and (2) mean the activity has been split into two parts. He can move 10 days of work before the official start of the project period

Figure 2.4 David's revised network diagram

2.3   MANAGING YOUR RESEARCH PROJECT

If you have been applying the project management ideas and tools presented so far in this chapter to your own research project, you now have:

- a project life cycle, showing the project's main phases
- a project breakdown, showing the mini-projects and milestones
- an activity list, showing detailed activities
- a Gantt chart or network diagram, showing the activities and their dependencies.

This project planning can also help you to deal with project risk – the probability that an activity fails or takes more or less time than you have estimated – and the uncertainties – events that you are unaware of and cannot estimate – that may influence your project.

2.3.1   Monitoring your project's progress

During your research project, you should periodically check your progress by comparing how much work you have completed with your project plan. You can compute how far ahead or behind schedule you are by estimating how long it will take to complete the activities you are working on. You may need to amend your plan periodically as the project progresses. Make sure to update your project plan, and check to see the effects of any changes (they always happen!).

Most importantly, you should count an activity as complete only when it is 100 per cent complete, finished and delivered. Not before! Professional project managers say that a project spends 90 per cent of its time 90 per cent complete.

As well as monitoring your own progress, you should use regular meetings with your supervisor and/or project sponsor to report honestly what you have (and have not) managed to get done since your last meeting. Other people can only give you good advice if you are completely honest about your progress. Remember, too, it's their job to give you advice, not to make sure you turn in your project on time.

Honesty is key. Experienced supervisors often develop an uncanny ability to interpret what students actually mean when they are asked about their progress. For example, 'I'm almost finished' probably means 'I'm just getting started', and, as in **Student research in action 2.3**, 'Everything's going fine' can mean 'It's all gone pear-shaped'. See how not to do it below.

> *Student research in action 2.3*
> **IT'S GOING WELL – HONESTLY**
>
> Martha's project proposal sounded good – investigate how the US retailer Wal-Mart was gaining competitive advantage through the use of its IT and operations capabilities, and whether this posed a threat to European retailers following Wal-Mart's European acquisitions of the British Asda supermarket chain and two German retailers. The project was

undoubtedly current, topical and researchable. Many books and articles had been written on Wal-Mart. Martha even had contacts with one of Wal-Mart's competitors to enable her to collect data.

In her first meeting with the supervisor, research questions and the relevant literature were agreed. Martha enthusiastically spent the next few months reading everything she could find about Wal-Mart, including popular business books, plus lots of newspaper and magazine stories about the company downloaded from the web. She had lots of information about Wal-Mart, little of which could be used to answer the research questions, and not much of it reliable enough to be used in a master's dissertation. Overwhelmed by the sheer amount of material on Wal-Mart, she decided to concentrate on finding out what computer hardware systems Wal-Mart was using, although this was only weakly connected to competitive advantage.

As the summer went on, Martha's supervisor kept asking for information about the progress of the research project, and when he would be able to see a draft – or even a detailed outline – of the project report. She kept reporting that everything was 'fine, honestly', although no written work was forthcoming. On the day that dissertations were due, Martha turned in a project report that rehashed the Wal-Mart story with information everyone knew, but didn't shed any light on competitive advantage or Wal-Mart's effect on European retail competition. The project was a resounding failure.

Avoiding time traps

Because you, not your project supervisor or sponsor, are ultimately responsible for managing your progress, you should be wary of other **time traps** than the blind alleys we discussed in **Section 2.1.1**. These traps often disguise themselves as worthwhile project-related activities, such as tracking down interesting articles you discovered whilst searching for information on the internet. Other time traps include distractions or plain procrastination. Many students find displacement activities such as tidying their rooms or alphabetising their music collection more attractive than getting down to work. None of this helps you to answer your research questions or fulfil other project goals and objectives.

To manage your time more effectively:

- *Set your priorities and keep them.* If this project needs to be your highest priority, make sure it stays that way. If something comes up that might take time away from your project, question how it fits with your priorities, particularly if it seems to offer instant gratification!
- *Use your support network* to help you to stay on track. Tell your tutors, friends and family what you are trying to do and solicit their support. This may help to prevent them from turning into time traps and convert them into cheerleaders.
- *Work when and where you will be most effective.* Are you at your best in the morning, later in the day or at night? Try to schedule your activities so that this is when you are working on your project. Remember that you will be assessed on your project's outcomes, not how long you spent doing it, so work smart!

Table 2.3   Tick sheet for mini-project: complete initial literature review

Activity no.	Activity	Complete? ✓ or ✗
1	Revisit core textbook from taught course to check definitions and sources of further information	✓
2	Library catalogue search for books on specifics of topic	✓
3	Check newspapers (*Financial Times*, *New York Times*, *Le Monde*) for recent general articles	✓
4	Check *Fortune* magazine for relevant stories	✓
5	Do basic search of academic literature on initial keyworks – only pick papers with high numbers of citations (see **Chapter 4**), and identify key authors and themes	✓
6	Read identified material	✗
7	Prepare short statement of findings from the first trawl of the literature	✗

● *Don't leave anything until the last minute.* This is so vital that it deserves emphasising. You may need a lot of time to understand and present complex concepts, and you will certainly need time to polish your written work from a first draft into a final draft.

Another positive measure you can take to manage your time more effectively is to monitor the progress of your project plan. Even a simple tick sheet, as shown in **Table 2.3**, can help you to see whether you are keeping to your original schedule. You can tick off the activities on your project plan once they are completed. If you pin it to a notice board, or somewhere where you look at it frequently, it will show how well you are progressing and help to boost your morale.

2.3.2   Identifying risk and opportunity

Even if you have established a project plan and done your best to stick to it, you can still get derailed. Every research project has a certain degree of **uncertainty** because every project has different inputs, outputs and processes, and generally you cannot determine what these will be in advance. Uncertainty creates both risk and opportunity for you as a researcher.

Risk

Risk is the downside of uncertainty. Put simply, it is what could go wrong in your project or what could intervene that would stop you from achieving your objectives.

Since you can't ignore risk, thinking about risk as you begin your project will help you to manage your project more proactively. **Student research in action 2.4** illustrates how risk can affect project outcomes.

> *Student research in action 2.4*
> **FLAT-PACKED AND BITS MISSING**
>
> Alex proposed to study furniture retailer IKEA for a coursework project that would count for 100% of his mark. IKEA was opening a new store locally, and he wanted to find out more about its operations. After he had corresponded with the store's manager for a period of weeks, the manager regretfully informed him that he could not schedule any meetings with managers for Alex.
>
> Alex's supervisor had warned him not to count on access to IKEA's management, but he had not identified any alternative sources of the information he needed, or an alternative study in case the IKEA interviews didn't work out. As a result, he turned in a poor project, since he had been counting on using those interviews to get the essential data to answer his research questions.

For each mini-project or significant activity in your project plan, you should carry out a risk analysis by asking yourself what could go wrong and what effect it would have on achieving your objectives. A risk is significant if it is likely to occur or even if unlikley would have a major effect on your project's outcomes if it did occur. Where an activity involves significant risk – you do not have control over some elements of the activity – especially when you have to rely on other people for something essential to your project, you should focus on each **risk element** specifically. Ask yourself: 'What will I do if this risk element materialises?' As in the example above, you should identify a contingency plan if the risk level is significant. This is much likelier to leave you prepared, even for risks you do not foresee, rather than ignoring what might go wrong and how it would affect your research process and outcomes if it did.

You can use a simple table such as **Table 2.4** to list the risk elements and the actions associated with them. In preparing the table, you should:

1. *Identify each risk element.* Be creative, but try to avoid being too optimistic or pessimistic when you identify potential risks to your project's completion or success.
2. *Estimate the risk associated with each risk element.* Try to decide how likely it is to occur and what effect it might have on the outcome of your project. Based on the likelihood and effect, rank each risk element.
3. *Identify a plan for managing each risk element.* Try to decide what action you might take if the risk element actually materialises. What are you going to do about it? Ignore it and hope it doesn't happen or spend a few moments thinking about the eventualities?

Avoiding or reducing the effects of risks is called **mitigation**. Some mitigations are included for the highest ranked risks in **Table 2.4**.

Table 2.4 Some risk elements associated with student research projects

Risk	Effect	Rank	Mitigation
Leaving project until it is too late	Project not completed on time or poorly done	3	Start and get ahead of the game; regular meetings with supervisor; arrange to work regularly with other motivated people
Cannot find sufficient literature to build effective literature review	Literature review does not provide good support to the rest of the study	6	
Computer crashes and data lost	Data have to be re-entered and files rewritten	2	Ensure that regular backups are taken; email copies of files to secure storage
Project scope turns out to be too wide or too narrowly focused	Too much work to do or too little depth achieved	4	Regularly review your scope as the project develops, say once a month
People who have promised data don't provide them	Reduced amount of data to analyse	1	Provide means of controlling the data coming in to allow you to remind people about the need to provide data; offer an incentive for their early provision
Someone else picks a very similar project	Risks of being accused of plagiarism	5	

We could, of course, have listed many more risk elements, and you may want to spend a few minutes listing any that are relevant to your research project. Once you have thought through a risk element table, you are better prepared to deal with even those risk elements you haven't foreseen.

Opportunities

Opportunity is the positive side of uncertainty. You may discover something new in your research project that you did not expect, or be offered the opportunity to develop your work into another area. How you deal with such opportunities can influence your project's outcome significantly, as shown in **Student research in action 2.5**.

Student research in action 2.5
THE DEUX JOHNS

John and Jon were investigating the motivation levels of key managers and how this was or could be monitored by human resource (HR) managers over time for an MBA project. During the project, they established what they believed to be a managerial ability of managers, which they called 'dynamic criticality'. This was the ability to discern well within a situation; to identify, from a mass of data, the elements of importance; to act on these elements, ignoring more spurious elements or noise; and to change this focus as the reality changed. They believed that this ability was underutilised in the selection criteria most firms used when choosing managers. Indeed, in their interviews with general managers, this ability appeared to be one of the most needed, but in interviews with a group of HR managers, this factor was not recognised.

John and Jon focused their work on developing a profile of dynamic criticality and were contemplating putting together a series of exercises to test the strength of this factor in an individual. This would have taken a considerable amount of time leaving them with little time to complete their main work. Further, dynamic criticality did not actually address the research questions in their project. They needed to decide whether to continue developing a model and testing for dynamic criticality, which might not even be possible, and which their supervisor believed had been tried already, or refocus on their original project, and pursue the new idea at a later date.

Imagine that, like John and Jon, you have a 'blinding insight' into what you believe is some vitally important area, related to your study but not directly connected to your research questions, halfway through your project. This is a great opportunity. Should you:

- *Pursue it* – ditch everything else and go with the new idea? After all, research is about being creative, isn't it?
- *File it for later* – it sounds good now, but will it sound so good in a few months time? Park it somewhere safe (for example write a one-page summary of your idea), and if you have time, explore it when the main work is complete.
- *Ignore it completely* – you'll soon forget it anyway, and concentrate all your efforts on the main work. There'll be another great idea coming along anytime now.

If you decide to pursue an opportunity that arises after you have defined your research project, you risk having to discard all the work you have done up to that point, for example any data you have already collected. This is highly risky in a short project, because you may not have enough time to change direction and complete your study, as illustrated by **Student research in action 2.6**. Furthermore, you risk taking a chance on an insight that may not be big enough to support your project, particularly if you are attracted to it because no one else has yet researched it. Even if you believe that you have a cutting-edge insight, in reality there are very few new ideas in business and management studies.

Student research in action 2.6
SLEEPERS AWAKE

Whilst investigating a large bed manufacturer's distribution and marketing system in order to identify opportunities for cost savings, Juanita became interested in how the company introduced new products. It was an interesting process, with what appeared to be huge opportunities for improvement. Indeed, as the investigation progressed, she spent more and more time looking at new products and less looking at the distribution and marketing systems. This deviation from her research questions was not noticed until she submitted her project report to her university supervisor. Neither the company nor her supervisor was impressed with the change, which had not been sanctioned by either side, despite the opportunity for the organisation that the new project presented.

On the other hand, if you have a well-defined project plan and have made good progress, you might be able to risk a limited exploration of the new insight rather than discarding what you have done so far. Quickly check out what is known about the area or ask the opinions of some knowledgeable experts such as your project advisor. You should be able to decide fairly quickly whether the insight adds value to your project, and whether you can build on your original research plan.

Finally, even though pursuing or postponing your insight may create extra work for your project, you may lose out if you ignore it completely. Insights are gems. You should keep track of them even if their time has not come, and even if you have to adapt, combine or otherwise modify them to use them – whatever you do, don't lose them.

2.3.3 Working as part of a project team

If you are doing a project as part of a group, you will also need to include how you will manage the group process as part of your project planning and ongoing management. Students increasingly work together on research projects in pairs or groups for both educational and practical reasons. Employers value graduates who can work effectively with other people, whilst the expansion of the higher education system in the UK creates pressures for fewer individual assessments. Either way, working as part of a project team or group means that you will need to manage the *interpersonal* as well as the personal and research process.

Working on your research project with other people increases both risk and opportunities. Our experiences in supervising students working together raises some intriguing questions. Why do some research project teams work really well together, whilst others end up not speaking to, hating or even wanting to physically harm each other? Why do some project teams produce highly creative results, whilst others, despite the inclusion of some very creative people, produce mediocre work?

Team dynamics can significantly affect the research process and outcome: just as uncertainty created both risks and opportunities, teamwork can create either **synergy** – better results than the individuals could create working alone – or disruption – worse results than working alone. Synergy is more rare than people assume and it will only occur under certain circumstances. It isn't automatically created when people work together.

Since group dynamics is taught in most business and management courses, we recommend that you review your course materials and/or discuss this with course tutors if you do have significant problems. Organisational researchers have studied group and team performance for a long time, and knowledge of group processes can be useful in managing this 'third dimension' of business and management research.

Because group work is so common in degree programmes and businesses, most people start with some experience of working together towards common goals. In order to manage group processes as systematically as you are managing the rest of the research process, you might want to review **group process models**, for example 'storming, norming, performing' (Hackman 2002), or 'collection, entrenchment, resolution, synergy and decline' (Maylor 2003: 229–31). Many students have found it useful to look at **group role descriptions**, such as Belbin (1993), to see how to make the best use of each person in the group. Larson and Lafasto (1989) have identified the following characteristics of highly effective groups:

- They have a clear, elevating goal – a sense of mission must be created through the development of an objective which is understood, important, worthwhile and personally or collectively challenging
- The responsibilities of each group member are worked out and communicated, and each person is held accountable to the group for the discharge of these responsibilities
- They have an active communications strategy, based around face-to-face meetings but also encompassing the use of emails, text messaging and so on
- They have competent team members, with a balance between personal and technical competence
- They foster a collaborative climate – encouraging reliance on others within the team, and where good work is performed, it is recognised
- They set high standards – through individual standards, team pressure and knowledge of the consequences of failure
- They deal with conflict as and when it arises.

You may want to devote some time during your first team meeting establishing how you will handle the group process, and these points help to establish some goals for managing it. This is another aspect of 'beginning with the end in mind', one of the themes of this book and this chapter in particular. These points help to establish the principles that groups are going to work with.

We will focus below on some ways to reduce group conflict created by task-related conflict in a group project. In particular, we have found it effective to manage the initial project start-up, group meetings and communication, and allocation of group responsibilities, which are particular leverage points for establishing good group practices.

Managing group meetings

Although there is no way you can escape group meetings completely, if not carefully managed they often take up a good deal of time relative to what they actually accomplish. You are more likely to get things accomplished if you try to manage meetings as systematically as the rest of your research process. In this section, we provide a few suggestions about good practice, so you can make the most of the time you and your group spend on your research project:

1. *Always meet with a specific purpose.* Your project group needs a specific reason to get together. A meeting should not be held just for social interaction, because you have a regular meeting scheduled or to give everyone a warm fuzzy feeling of progress. Each meeting should have a clear purpose, for example to update weekly progress, compile data or plan the project report.

2. *Prepare before the meeting.* Circulate in advance the location and timing, agenda and any background on the items to be discussed. The agenda should tell team members what information they will be expected to update during the meeting and what critical issues they may need to discuss. You should also take into account that most people's attention declines to zero after 20 minutes, and after two hours you are unlikely to make any constructive progress: people will agree to anything at this point simply to get out of the meeting.

3. *Manage the meeting.* Nominate someone to chair the meeting, whose role it is to facilitate constructive debate while limiting the scope of discussion to the matter in hand. Unless the group agrees otherwise, the role of chair should rotate between meetings. The chair should make sure that the discussion moves forward, rather than getting stuck debating the same points, prevent any one member from dominating the discussions and regularly summarise progress and ask for conclusions to be drawn based on the discussions. A skilful chair will be able to steer the group towards consensus and away from majority rule. This makes sure that everyone has bought in to a decision, and makes carrying it out far easier than if there is dissent.

4. *Follow up the meeting.* Nominate someone to record the minutes of the meeting, and then send copies of the minutes with action points and responsibilities listed against each (see the example in **Table 2.5**). A meeting's conclusions and action points should fit on one side of A4 paper so that they are read rather than filed or thrown away. These minutes and action points then form the basis of the next meeting's agenda, so that the person who said they would carry out a task has a natural responsibility to the group to do it. They also know that should they fail to carry out an action, this will be identified at the next meeting.

Table 2.5	Sample of minutes of group project meeting

Date and time: 21 February, 10.30p.m., All Bar One

Present: Chloe, Andre, Felia, Yee Ping

Apologies: Bill (emailed 20 February to say in hospital after hang-gliding accident)

Agreed and signed the minutes of the last meeting prepared by Felia.

During this meeting we discussed our creative strategy and the budget. Everyone was happy with progress but Yee Ping had had difficulties getting the information she needed about billboard costs.

Main outstanding issues	Action
Chloe to help Yee Ping with budget information (to be ready for next meeting on 28th)	C & YP
Felia to complete mock up of life-size orange kangaroo (bring to meeting on 28th)	F
Andre to liaise with Chloe and Yee Ping to finalise budget spreadsheet (during the week)	A
Bill to get himself out of hospital as quickly as possible to edit the report (28th)	B
Next meeting 28 February, 5p.m., Saracen's Head. Minutes prepared by Andre	All

Source: Adapted from Nairn (2003)

Managing group communication

You may be able to use email (or texting) to substitute for face-to-face meetings and other forms of contact. However, when things start to go wrong, relying on email can quickly make them much worse. Because email lacks the cues such as body language that we use in interpreting what other people mean, as compared with what they say, we can easily misinterpret what an email says. This can lead to unnecessary friction in a group. Regular emailers and texters have developed their own shorthand of symbols such as ☺ that can add some of the human element to a message (for a list of emoticons see emoticon.com).

Managing responsibilities

In an individual project, it is clear that you are responsible for each and every activity. In a team project, you must clarify the responsibilities of each member and the entire

Table 2.6   Activity table

Activity	When	Who	Notes
Write outline of Chapter 4	Mon a.m.	All	
Write section 4.1	Mon p.m.	HT & MR	
Complete graphics for Chapter 3	Mon p.m.	WF	
Complete telephone interviews	Mon p.m.	KR	
Write section 4.2	Tues a.m.	HT & WF	Relies on 4.1 being complete
Outline presentation	Tues a.m.	MR	
Write section 4.3	Tues p.m.	HT & WF	Relies on 4.2 being complete
Transcribe telephone interview data	Tues p.m.	KR & MR	Relies on interviews being complete
Analyse interview data	Wed a.m.	KR & WF	Relies on transcription being complete
Write section 4.4	Wed a.m.	HT & MR	Relies on section 4.3 being complete
Write conclusion to Chapter 4	Wed p.m.	HT & MR	Needs all 4 sections complete
Outline Chapter 5 – data analysis	Thurs a.m.	All	Relies on chapter 4 and the data analysis being complete
Write up data analysis	Thurs p.m.	KR & MR	
Extract key findings into presentation	Thurs p.m.	HT & WF	
Prepare graphics for Chapter 5 and presentation	Fri a.m.	WF	
Compile report and check flow	Fri a.m.	HT, KR & MR	Needs all sections complete, graphics to be inserted for Chapter 5 later
Integrate Chapter 5 graphics and print report	Fri p.m.	All	
Practise presentation	Fri p.m.	All	

group. This is much simpler if you have already prepared a well-defined project break-down and activity list, as discussed in **Section 2.1. Table 2.6** shows how each activity has been allocated to one or more team members. This table does more than allocate responsibilities, however, it also shows when activities need to be completed and the dependencies between them (in the notes column). You should prepare an updated activity table for each team meeting so the team can monitor and control progress against the project plan.

You can also use an activity table to reduce conflict by making the group process more visible. Although some people might be reluctant to commit themselves to a project schedule and thus uncomfortable with such an activity table, when you cannot see who is responsible for which activities, you cannot see the consequences of activities not being completed.

An activity table will work better when the way you assign responsibilities takes account of each team member's skills and preferences. Some people may prefer to work only on activities that make use of their existing competences (for example volunteering to analyse data after doing well in statistics), whilst others may want to try out new activities to develop new skills (for example volunteering as an editor to learn how to edit). Not everyone needs to be a technical specialist but not everyone has to learn how to do everything. Support and tolerance are more important.

Dealing with conflict

Working with other people can be stressful – naming one of the group process phases 'storming' or 'entrenchment' in the group dynamics literature attests to that. It's almost inevitable that differences in personalities or opinions about the research process will create conflict within a project team. Whilst managing the teamwork process to minimise potential sources of conflict is a pre-emptive strategy, you should also think about how you will handle conflict when it does arise. This is especially useful when conflicts occur due to differences in people's expectations and perceptions of what is happening.

Three principles for managing conflict, especially between two team members, are:

- Deal directly with the person concerned, wherever possible
- Seek first to understand, then be understood (discussed in Covey 2005)
- Assume that people are acting from good intentions until proven otherwise.

 ## SUMMARY

If you do not define, plan and monitor the research process, you are leaving the success of your work to chance. You can use project management to manage your research project systematically. Systematic management also creates an opportunity for you to reflect on the research process and your own learning.

Project management provides a way to identify the structure of your project (project life cycle), the activities you need to conduct (activity list) and your goals and objectives (SMART). You can turn these into a detailed project plan, which you can analyse to see whether your project plan is feasible and sensible. You can make this plan visible by using a Gantt chart or network diagram, which will also make it easier to monitor your project and take action if necessary to get back on track.

As well as using project management in defining, planning and monitoring your research process, project management also provides some insights into two topics that might affect your research process and outcome: risks and opportunities that you cannot foresee but which might materialise due to project uncertainty; and managing the group process if you are working with other people.

ANSWERS TO KEY QUESTIONS

How can project management help me to manage my research project more systematically?
- Identifying actions and establishing goals and objectives
- Developing a project plan
- Monitoring progress and taking action when necessary

How do I develop and use a project plan?
- Take a top-down approach to breaking down the project, for example the project life cycle. Start with considering the project as a series of activities
- Use SMART objectives to 'begin with the end in mind'
- Break the project down into manageable work packages, estimate the times for each work package and the dependencies between the activities
- Analyse your project plan using your activity list, Gantt chart or network diagram. Use visual tools including a network analysis or Gantt chart to analyse and then communicate your plans
- Carry out a basic risk and opportunities analysis

How can I monitor my project's progress?
- Recognise that you will go through many different stages in your feelings towards your work
- Do not rely on your own assessment of your progress or hide information from your supervisor
- Use your plans as a basic benchmark for your progress
- Always start each activity as soon as possible, and include a safety margin or buffer at the end of your project

How can I work effectively with other students?
- Managing the group is as important as managing the project
- Use group meetings effectively
- Communicate with care – particularly emails
- Deal with conflict rather than avoiding it

REFERENCES

Belbin, R.M. 1993. *Team Roles at Work.* Oxford: Butterworth Heinemann.
Covey, Stephen. 2005. *The Seven Habits of Highly Effective People,* rev. edn. London: Simon & Schuster.

Hackman, J. Richard. 2002. *Leading Teams: Setting the Stage for Great Performances.* Harvard, MA: HBS Press.

Larson, C.E. and Lafasto, F.M.J. 1989. *Teamwork.* London: Sage.

Maylor, Harvey. 2003. *Project Management,* 3rd edn. London: Financial Times Management.

Nairn, A. 2003. Guidelines for Group Projects. University of Bath internal publication.

ADDITIONAL RESOURCES

Belbin, M. 1993. *Team Roles at Work.* Oxford: Butterworth Heinemann.

Brown, M. 1998. *Successful Project Management in a Week,* 2nd edn. Abingdon: Institute of Management/Hodder & Stoughton.

PMI 1996, 2000, 2004. *A Guide to the Project Management Body of Knowledge.* PMI, PA (parts are downloadable free from www.pmi.org).

Web resources

www.lboro.ac.uk/service/std/myrp/myrp.html.

www.unigis.org/powerpoints/managingresearch.

www.shef.ac.uk/stdu/solar/research.

Key terms

activity list, 36	mini-projects, 34	project structure, 30
backward scheduling, 39	mitigation, 46	research objectives, 32
blind alleys, 31	network diagram, 40	risk, 45
buffer, 37	opportunity, 47	risk element, 46
dependencies, 37	personal objectives, 32	safety margin, 37
detailed actions, 34	project, 29	SMART, 32
forward scheduling, 39	project breakdown structure, 34	synergy, 49
Gantt chart, 39	project end date, 33	team dynamics, 49
goals, 33	project life cycle, 30	time traps, 44
group process models, 50	project management, 29	uncertainty, 45
group role descriptions, 50	project objectives, 32	work packages, 38
milestone, 34	project planning, 36	

Discussion questions

1. Is project management applicable to student research projects?
2. What is the difference between a mini-project and an activity?
3. How many goals should you try to achieve in a single project?
4. Why should objectives be 'SMART'?
5. Are there any other ways of expressing objectives rather than time, cost and quality?
6. Why should you manage the research process systematically, as well as the research outcomes?
7. Why don't groups always perform up to the potential of their most capable members?
8. Who is responsible if the group process falls apart? Who could you ask for advice if you start having group problems?

Workshop

It is noticed that people often have to make significant changes in their lives when they go into higher education, either from school, travelling or a work environment. In order to be able to assist people in making this transition, it is necessary to understand the nature of these changes better. You are to plan a three-month research project that will investigate an aspect of this change.

Task

1 For a limited time, discuss the above scenario. What would you be interested in investigating as part of this project (for example could be social adaptation or financial adaptation to the new environment).

2 In order to accomplish this, we recommend that you put together an outline plan, which can be improved later as you develop the detail. For now, complete the main elements of the pro forma plan given below.

Project description (include aspects and planned output from the project, for example report, presentation guide for new students)

Objectives (SMART)

Overview plan

Phase	Main activities	Who responsible	Time required	Milestones	Gantt chart (shade in: one box = one week)
D1: Definition					
D2: Design					
D3: Execution					
D4: Description					
Buffer (very important – don't forget it)					

Risks

Risk	Effect	Ranking (likelihood + effect)	Mitigation (what will you do to prevent or deal with this risk occurring

Communications (briefly describe the nature of regular communications, meetings, checkpoints with supervisors, interim reports (if any) and means of dealing with conflicts)

Workshop pro forma

Relevant chapters

13 Answering your research questions
14 Describing your research
15 Closing the loop

Key challenges

- Interpreting your findings and making recommendations
- Writing and presenting your project
- Reflecting on and learning from your research

4

Relevant chapters

1 What is research?
2 Managing the research process
3 **What should I study?**
4 How do I find information?

Key challenges

- Understanding the research process
- Taking a systematic approach
- **Generating and clarifying ideas**
- Using the library and internet

1

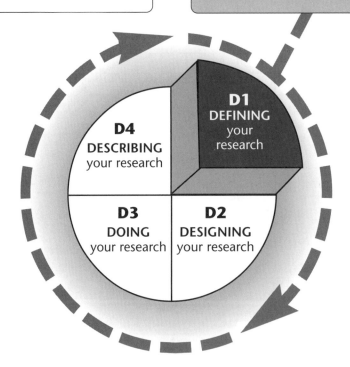

D4 DESCRIBING your research

D1 DEFINING your research

D3 DOING your research

D2 DESIGNING your research

Relevant chapters

9 Doing field research
10 Analysing quantitative data
11 Advanced quantitative analysis
12 Analysing qualitative data

Key challenges

- Practical considerations in doing research
- Using simple statistics
- Understanding multivariate statistics
- Interpreting interviews and observations

3

Relevant chapters

5 Scientist or ethnographer?
6 Quantitative research designs
7 Designing qualitative research
8 Case studies/multi-method design

Key challenges

- Choosing a model for doing research
- Using scientific methods
- Using ethnographic methods
- Integrating quantitative and qualitative research

2

chapter 3

What should I study?

Generating and clarifying ideas for your research project

 Key questions

- Where do ideas for research topics come from?
- How can I choose between several potential research topics?
- What characterises a good research topic?
- Why should I use research questions to focus my research?
- How can I use a project proposal to define my project scope?

 Learning outcomes

At the end of this chapter, you should be able to:

- Generate ideas and select an idea for your research project
- Identify your research topic
- Distinguish between satisfactory and unsatisfactory research topics
- Develop researchable research questions
- Develop a research proposal

Contents

 **INTRODUCTION**

The starting point for your research project is deciding what you will study (Lundberg 1999). 'What am I going to research?' is one of the most important questions you will ask. Your research topic will be developed into your research design, which describes how you are going to research it, covered in **Part 2**. Needless to say, you should choose your research topic carefully, because you will have to live with it, often for a long time.

This chapter presents a systematic process for generating, selecting and refining ideas for research topics. If you have been assigned a research problem by your academic supervisor or business sponsor, you may think that you don't need to generate ideas. This may limit your freedom somewhat, but you still can bring some creativity to generating and selecting ideas and defining your project and developing a research design.

In coming up with good ideas, you may have to deal with many creative and personal issues. Not surprisingly, many students find choosing a topic the most challenging stage of their research project. Sometimes this is because they have no idea of what they want to do or how to come up with ideas; other times, it is because they have too many ideas and no notion of how to choose between them. We will suggest how you might manage either problem. This is an example of where understanding the boundaries between chaos and order can help you to manage your research.

Section 3.1 will explain how to generate ideas from real-world organisations, business and management research, and your own personal and career interests. Combined with brainstorming and other methods such as mind mapping – it is vital for you to generate several ideas here – you can identify ideas that are potentially worth researching.

Although you can easily find good advice about *how* to come up with ideas that you can turn into a feasible and worthwhile research topic, you may find surprisingly little specific guidance about *what* a research topic is. This chapter focuses not only on how to generate and select ideas for research topics and turn them into research problems, but also what a research topic actually is.

At this stage, to make sure that your research topic will satisfy your project guidelines and assessment criteria, read them carefully when you are defining your project – another example of 'beginning with the end in mind'. **Section 3.2** describes how you can select the best idea based on the project requirements and your interests. You can filter your ideas against the characteristics of a good research project. We also describe how to refine your idea from a research topic to research problems and research questions.

When you select an idea to develop, you should make sure not only that you will find your project interesting and worth doing, but also that it is manageable – you can actually get it done in the time and with the skills and other resources you have. In **Section 3.3** we describe how you should define the scope of your project once you have selected a promising research topic and a backup – what you are going to do and, just as importantly, what you are not going to do. A good way to do this is to prepare a project proposal, which will answer the questions that your supervisor or sponsor will typically ask about your project. You can also use a well-developed project proposal to tell other project stakeholders what you will do in your project, which makes it easier for them to provide support and feedback.

After you have finished this chapter, you should be much clearer about what you are going to research, even if you have to revise your research topic once you have done some library research on it, as covered in **Chapter 4**. Otherwise, you may be trying to solve a problem that has already been solved, or one that no one can solve. Such revisiting is not unusual in research projects – they are seldom linear. However, if you approach this systematically, you should waste much less time and effort defining your research project.

3.1 GENERATING IDEAS FOR YOUR RESEARCH PROJECT

Deciding what the project will be about and where and with whom it will be conducted is an important part of your research project (Blaikie 2000: 14). Good ideas for research topics come from all kinds of places: the business and management world, the subjects you have studied in your course and your own personal interests. A systematic approach to generating, selecting and refining these ideas is key to project success (Gill and Johnson 2002).

You may already know what you want or must do, but it's important not to close down the idea-generating process too early. While some projects may not allow you any leeway in defining your topic, nearly every project has enough flexibility that you can – or even be required to – be creative about what you are going to study and how you are going to study it. We suggest that in this stage you identify as many ideas as you can, rather than just one perfect idea. You will learn how to rank and select the best one in **Section 3.2**.

We strongly recommend that you don't decide *what* you will research based on *how* you will research it. That is, don't choose a research topic just because you want to try out a particular way of gathering data – such as a survey – or a particular way of analysing data – such as conjoint analysis (unless your project requirements make this unavoidable). While you should definitely take research methods into account, you should cast your net more widely when you select your topic, otherwise, as the old saying among project supervisors goes, 'if the only tool you have is a hammer, everything starts to look like a nail'.

You should balance order and chaos in generating ideas. Creativity lies on the border between them, where you have generated enough ideas so you can choose the best one, but not so many that you feel overwhelmed and unable to get started, or too few so that you ignore the chance to learn. You should try to identify enough ideas so that you can choose the one that suits you and satisfies your project stakeholders, including your sponsors. You can often incorporate features of the ideas you reject into your research project.

As you can see in **Figure 3.1**, people start from different places in generating ideas. Some people start with many ideas, others with no ideas and a few with one main idea that they will end up researching. Most people start somewhere between the two extremes. If you start with many ideas, you should aim to converge on a few possibilities, and then select one main idea. If you start with no ideas, you should aim to generate several ideas that you can choose among. Even if you start with one main idea, you should revisit that idea to see whether it will actually lead to the best project that you can do.

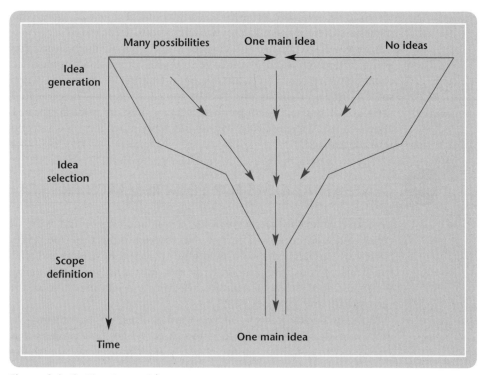

Figure 3.1 Getting to one idea

Although this figure may make the process seem simple – generate some ideas and pick the best one – many students find this stressful. Some students have absolutely no idea of what they would like to research for their project, and no clue about how to come up with some ideas. You cannot truly own your project unless you want to find out more about some practical or theoretical problem. You will be just 'going through the motions' (Whedon 2001). We describe how to overcome this in **Section 3.1.1**.

Other students come unstuck the first time they have an unconstrained brief – they can do anything within the entire subject area of business and management – resulting in an overload of possibilities and uncertainty about where to get started. This uncertainty conflicts with the pressing need to get on with the project, which leads to **project paralysis**. If this describes you, don't worry, there are many ways out of it and we will be describing them in **Section 3.2**.

Students who start off with a single fixed idea, an unshakeable view of what they are going to do and how they are going to do it often run into significant problems later on in their research project. This is more risky than not being able to come up with ideas. If you choose your topic without exploring other possibilities, you are unlikely to be successful. You have probably not considered the possibilities adequately and have rushed into making a choice too early. You will miss what you might learn from the early exploration of a subject area, and might have to change your topic significantly anyway. Indeed, absolute certainty at this stage is usually a cover-up for massive ignorance – 'not knowing what you don't know' – as illustrated in **Student research in action 3.10**. The antidote for too much early certainty is to explore your research topic and come up with possibilities to investigate further. Once you start to explore potential ideas, you will find that your certainties are replaced by questions, rather than vice versa.

For instance, suppose you are looking at how to motivate employees in your organisation and have decided that you will take Maslow's 'hierarchy of needs' as the main theoretical basis for your research. Without doing some background research on this model of human behaviour, you may not realise that many studies question the basis of Maslow's model, its applicability and usefulness. If you don't find these articles early on, you risk 'building on sand'. If you only find these studies when you are writing up your research, you may have to go back and make major changes to your project, which you may not have the time for. Even worse, if you don't find them and you turn in recommendations or findings based on at least partially discredited research, you will be embarrassed, at best, when this is pointed out to you. Don't assume that your work will be so compelling that your project examiners will overlook this flaw.

3.1.1 Generating ideas

According to Weick (1992), good research often starts with an issue that catches your attention – something that presents a puzzle or is interesting. Although you may find ideas to explore anywhere, student projects usually come from either real-world business and management settings (practical problems) or from business and management research (theoretical problems). However, you may also find ideas in your own personal interests and experiences, the subjects you have already studied and projects that other students have already carried out, or even from brainstorming.

You can think of an idea as an interest or a general area of inquiry that you want to pursue (Booth et al. 2003: 36). Lundberg (1999) suggests that a **research idea** is general enough to describe anything that you might research:

- a phenomenon
- an issue
- a problem
- a question to study
- a general theme
- an area of behaviour
- a body of theory.

Early on, your ideas may be as broad as 'service management', 'research and development', 'the film industry', or 'humour'. As we noted above, don't worry so much about the quality of your ideas at this point but on quantity: generating enough good ideas so that you can choose the best idea (and possibly a backup if the first idea is risky). *Don't lose your ideas: write them down.* Maintaining a file of your ideas will help you to keep track of potential research topics. You will need to nurture your most promising ideas into research topics, and your best topics into research problems and research questions through further reading and some library research.

These ideas are too general to research, but we describe how you can focus them into research topics and then into research problems and research questions. Your **research topic** is a general area of business and management that you can investigate and describes what your project is about. A good research topic will lead to either a practical or a theoretical problem that you can address in your research. As well as a research topic and research problem, you will need to identify a **research setting** where you will conduct your project, and a **sample** of organisations, people or other social units where you will collect your data.

3.1.2 Sources of ideas

Ideas from real-world managers and organisations

Many interesting ideas come from problems that face business and management organisations in the real world, **practical problems** that the organisation needs to solve. If you are sponsored by an organisation or are working in an organisation while you are doing your research, you will probably be expected to focus on a practical problem identified by either you or the organisation. For instance, your organisation or sponsor may want to know how to answer questions such as:

- How can we reduce our purchasing costs through developing a supply strategy (implementing a particular practice)?
- How can we retain customers who are defecting because of bad service (solving a particular organisational problem)?
- How can we get more undergraduate students to apply for our credit card (improving the organisation's performance)?

Your ideas may also be the result of personal experience, as was the case in **Student research in action 3.1**.

Student research in action 3.1
A RESEARCH TOPIC THAT 'STUCK'

Elmar had been an IT consultant before he started as a postgraduate research student. He was shocked and appalled by the number of large IT projects that failed, despite the millions of pounds spent on them. Such failures were often reported in newspapers. When he started his studies, he found that many academic articles also investigated the problem of why IT projects failed. But no one had any definite answers – indeed the literature was littered with prescriptions that did not appear to provide any benefit to managers in managing their projects successfully. Clearly, there was an opportunity for him to do some interesting research. The research project has clear practical implications for managers.

Even if your research is not sponsored by a particular organisation, you may be interested in practical problems faced by organisations or other social units. You might try looking at journals such as the *Harvard Business Review* or *European Management Journal*, magazines such as *Fortune* or *Management Today* or newspapers such as the *Financial Times* or *Wall Street Journal* for those practical problems that are currently 'hot'. Some of the topics recently suggested by such sources include:

- Should charities try to brand themselves (a type of organisation)?
- How do traditional music retailers plan to compete with music downloaded over the web (an industry)?
- How is Nike responding to ethical concerns about the labour practices of its overseas subcontractors (an organisation)?

- Under what conditions should companies buy back their own stock (an organisational problem)?
- Do women managers still face a 'glass ceiling' in investment banks (a group of employees)?
- How do children exercise 'pester power' to get their parents to buy them products advertised on television (a group of consumers)?

If you are required to apply or test a management theory or model as part of your research, you should be aware that not every interesting real-world problem is relevant to academic knowledge. This is important. We have seen research projects fail because the student has not identified a problem for which the research project is a solution. This often happens when a student falls in love with a computer model or other abstract solution and tries to find a business or management problem to apply it to. Remember the hammer analogy. Or, the solution is already well known, and there is nothing new about applying it, but the student hasn't done enough reading to see that this has been discussed already. We will give some tips later on how you can investigate business and management research to find out which ideas you can turn into researchable topics.

Notice that each question above involves a problem that an organisation, its members or society must solve. For example, if downloaded music didn't affect either current or future sales of recorded music, there wouldn't be much to go on. If no problem is involved – you just want to gather information – you might ask yourself whether it is really research.

One useful way to generate a research topic is to take an idea from one context and examine its application in another. **Student research in action 3.2** is an example of this.

> ### Student research in action 3.2
> #### THE CATHERINE WHEEL
>
> As a committed vegetarian and ethical consumer, Catherine was interested in farmers' markets, farm shops, and other places that people could buy organic fruit and vegetables besides the major supermarket chains. In her MSc dissertation, Catherine had surveyed customer attitudes towards online grocery shopping. For her PhD, she decided to combine her ethical interests with her interest in e-business and find out more about what kinds of customers bought organic fruit and vegetables online, and how small organic producers tried to market their products to customers. As she worked on her idea, she realised that it would be interesting to find out whether the models of service quality that she had applied in studying online supermarkets could actually be applied to studying small producers.

Starting with a practical problem will help you to identify the research setting where you will do your research. This will often be centred on the organisation you are sponsored by, are working in or are interested in. You might study a part of the organisation, the entire organisation, its supply network or its industry. On the other hand, you may want to study another research setting to find out information that will be useful to your **focal organisation**. If you want to investigate a practical problem faced by a legal firm, you may want to research how the problem is handled in the medical profession. Research on charities may involve investigating for-profit firms. Part of the solution will be to describe how to implement what you learn in this new context.

Ideas from business and management research

Your other main source of ideas is the research that has been done on business and management. Many interesting ideas for research projects come from **theoretical problems** faced by business and management researchers rather than the practical problems faced by business and management in the real world. If you aren't working for or with an organisation, you might decide to start by identifying theories, models or concepts that other researchers have developed to see whether you can confirm, disprove or extend them. Even though you may be able to apply what you learn in your research to practical problems faced by business and management, your main goal is to increase knowledge by filling in any 'gaps' in what we know about that theory or model.

Theoretical problems are problems of incomplete knowledge that researchers need to solve to understand the world better than when they started. A theoretical problem exists when researchers lack complete knowledge about a theory or model that applies to some aspect of business or management, when they cannot use the existing theory or models to explain what goes on in the real world, or when they do not know which theory or model to apply in a particular situation. They may need more knowledge of the contexts in which to apply this theory or model, or of the concepts to include or exclude from the model. It might also mean that they do not know what concepts belong to that theory or model.

You might look for theoretical problems in various places. You might decide to investigate a particular theory, model or concept mentioned in your studies, such as 'lean production' or 'virtual teams'. You can look for theoretical problems in textbooks (for example Kotler et al.'s *Principles of Marketing* (2004) or Grant's *Contemporary Strategy Analysis* (2004)), academic books (for example *The Machine that Changed the World* (Womack et al., 1995) *Laboratory Life* (Latour and Woolgar, 1986)), or academic journals (for example *Academy of Management Journal* or *European Management Journal*). You might have read about some interesting research findings in a newspaper or a journal. Even looking through the tables of contents of some management journals may give you some ideas about what concepts, models and theories are currently on the research agenda. Your academic supervisor might have some suggestions for you to investigate.

You may have read about a particular theory, model or concept and want to know more about it, or disagree with it and want to challenge it. You might identify an interesting research topic by asking 'what if' you try to apply a theory or model in a new context. For example, you might investigate whether you can apply a model of employee motivation developed for manufacturing employees to lawyers. If you find out that the model does apply, this makes the model more universal or more 'robust'; on the other hand, if it does not apply, this makes the model less universal and more limited.

You can also identify theoretical problems by thinking about generic questions such as the 'practice–performance link' discussed in **Chapter 1**. Is there a theoretical problem that interests you and is relevant to business? Are practices developed in the context of large, multinational companies, for example ISO 9000, applicable in other contexts, for example small and medium-sized enterprises (SMEs) or public services?

You could also start with a concept instead of a problem. Based on what you have learnt about organisational citizenship behaviour (OCB) in your organisational behaviour classes, you could think up questions such as:

- What behaviours should we include in OCB? (concepts)
- Are there differences in OCB between full-time and part-time workers? (context)
- Do Western models of OCB apply in China? (context)
- Does OCB affect customer loyalty? (outcomes)
- Does deviant workplace behaviour affect business unit performance? (outcomes)

If you start with a theoretical problem, as with a practical problem, you will need to identify a research setting where you can investigate your theory, model or concept, and a sample of organisations, people or other units from which you will gather your data. Since you don't have a ready-made research setting, you may need to do some library or internet research to see what research setting might be appropriate.

Projects often benefit from a degree of serendipity. Hence the statement we made in the **Preface** that you will not necessarily end up where you intended with your research. **Student research in action 3.3** illustrates just one of the times that this has happened in the work of the authors of this book.

Student research in action 3.3
AN ABSORBING PROJECT

Intrigued by an article on technology cycles by Tushman and Anderson (1986), Kate decided to investigate how major changes in technology affected company survival in high-tech industries. Her supervisor brought an article on a new theoretical concept, absorptive capacity (Cohen and Levinthal 1989, 1990), to her attention as a factor that might affect company survival in turbulent environments. To study whether absorptive capacity affected company survival, Kate needed to find at least one industry or sector where she could gather data. She investigated a number of industries, and narrowed them down to reduced-instruction-set-computing microprocessors, high-definition television, and supercomputers. Even though all three industries were interesting, a chance conversation during a transatlantic air flight with a venture capitalist convinced her to study supercomputers for her thesis.

So which is a better place to start, a practical problem or a theoretical problem? Research that starts with a practical problem often focuses on developing recommendations for solving the particular practical problem in that particular context. Remember the discussion in **Chapter 1**, though, so that you can keep your project from being strictly a consulting project (unless that is your remit). You will need to link your research back to larger issues of business and management knowledge. If you are working on a sponsored project, you need to keep in mind that the organisation's main focus is on resolving the practical problem it faces. On the other hand, you need to be clear on how your project will contribute to business and management knowledge.

If you start with a theoretical problem, you will usually emphasise your contribution to knowledge, the findings about the particular theory, model or concept that you have investigated in your particular research setting. Your findings should contribute

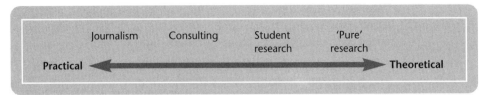

Figure 3.2 The range of approaches to solving interesting problems

to knowledge about that theory or model. As we noted, this does not always mean that you have to come up with a new theory or a new model. Your project might simply add to our understanding of which theories and models do or do not apply in this type of organisation (or other context), find out something new that can be used to improve the model or theory, or even, in some cases, discredit it. The organisation will expect you to deliver some useful output, usually in the form of an analysis, recommendations and an implementation plan.

People have strong opinions on whether the main emphasis of business and management research should be to solve practical problems **(mode II research)** or theoretical problems **(mode I research)**. This is part of a longstanding debate over whether research should be immediately relevant to solving industry's problems or to increase knowledge without any immediate application. This is illustrated by the differences between basic research, development and commercial research, described in **Chapter 1**.

As shown in **Figure 3.2**, all business and management research has both a practical and a theoretical side, but the balance between the two may vary. Business and management research is more than information-gathering (journalism) or applied problem-solving (consulting) as we argued in **Chapter 1**: research adds to our knowledge about business and management. Your research project will contribute to this knowledge, no matter how small your contribution.

Other sources of ideas

What if you have considered these sources and still don't have any ideas? If you are stuck for ideas and haven't been able to identify any practical or theoretical problems that really 'grab you', you might want to be a bit more creative. Why not brainstorm? **Brainstorming** is a technique for generating and selecting ideas. You should try to come up with as many ideas as you can, without censoring them or subjecting them to critical review. Brainstorming is probably more practical for a group than an individual, but try sitting down somewhere quiet with a blank sheet of paper and free-associating. Include a variety of potential sources of ideas for brainstorming such as your personal interests, your studies or other students' projects. If your idea doesn't interest you, you probably won't be committed enough to do a good project.

Your personal interests

Many students overlook an obvious source of ideas, their own interests. Whilst this is not always necessary or even possible, it is worth considering your interests as you define your project. You may be able to develop one or more of your hobbies, sports and other interests into a topic that reflects your own personality and character. After all, you have to live with the project – sometimes for up to a year – so it may as well be something that inspires you!

Finding something about your project that interests you is especially important if you are working on a project that extends over several months, even if you are working on an assigned project or as part of a research team. You need to 'own' some part of the project, even if it is just part of the process, such as finding out how to design a questionnaire, use a particular statistical technique that you are interested in, or taking responsibility for editing or doing the graphic design of the finished report.

Some examples of projects that students have developed from their own interests are given in **Student research in action 3.4**. Each student developed a research project that allowed him or her to explore a personal interest, and also led to a research problem with both practical and theoretical aspects.

Student research in action 3.4
PROJECTS BASED ON STUDENT INTERESTS

- A football fan combined his love of Manchester United with his interest in marketing to develop a study of the impact of sports sponsorship on the sponsoring organisation.
- A student with a serious interest in 'retail therapy' carried out a study of the e-marketing potential of luxury goods.
- A highly entrepreneurial student studied the practices and associated success (or otherwise) of local entrepreneurs.
- A student who did a lot of work with local charities conducted a human resources study of the work performance differences between the voluntary and the private sectors.
- A student who had served in the military conducted research into commercial project management, and used the project to establish an interest, which subsequently led to a job.

Your studies

You should also consider ideas that come from your studies more generally, such as classes that you have enjoyed or where you have performed your best, since these usually reflect your natural interests and abilities. Your academic performance may also indicate what you are interested in or good at: it is difficult to do a good project if you don't have the knowledge or skills to carry it through. One of Harvey's students, whose best marks were in finance, initially refused to consider a finance project because he didn't intend to pursue a career in that area. When he thought about his personal and research goals for the project, however, he relented and decided to do a project in financial management, which he carried off with distinction. You should also look at your past coursework assignments to see whether you have already completed a short assignment that you could expand or follow up, given more time, to investigate a topic more deeply.

If you start with a project based on a taught course or coursework assignment, you may find it easier to identify the main topics and relevant research. This will be important when you get started on your literature search and literature review, as we will see in **Chapter 4**. This may also make it easier to identify an academic supervisor who can support your research project.

Other students' projects

A look at projects that other students have completed might spark off some ideas. Many schools keep lists of previous student research projects in the projects office or library or even let you look at previous projects. They may also be listed on your library's web catalogue. If you can look over a list of previous projects, or even at some projects themselves, it may be worth spending some time to see if you can generate some ideas of your own. The following are some examples of recent projects:

- An investigation into knowledge management in the use of rehearsal for natural disaster planning
- Cross-cultural management – the role of individual managers
- Environmental policies – are they worth the recycled paper they are written on?
- A Delphi study on the future of B2B e-commerce platforms
- Virtual teams or virtual chaos? A study of a dispersed workplace
- Information systems strategy and cost justification: visible and invisible benefits
- The impact of ISO 9002 on company performance
- The role of information intermediaries in the distribution of corporate financial reports
- An investigation of the role of regional development agencies in improving business performance
- How much does it cost to gain a customer? A study of the economics of marketing in a law firm
- Will the new requirements for financial reporting prevent another Parmalat or Enron?
- The use of humour in management
- A review of the construction of the facilities for the Athens Olympics

If you still haven't come up with any ideas that seem appealing, you might consider:

1. *Reflecting on your own personal experiences* related to business and management. Frustration is often a great seed for management research ideas. If you have had a bad experience of service quality in a shop, you may want to find out just how widespread bad service is or the causes of such encounters.
2. *Thinking back to lecturers and other speakers you have heard.* Has anyone presented you with an idea that you thought was particularly well thought-out or you could relate to and wanted to find out more about?
3. *Talking to other people to see what they are interested in.* What are the pertinent issues at the moment? For example, you might find out that someone you know has bought or sold something interesting on eBay. This might lead to a question such as 'Can we start to make all our purchases through eBay or other auction sites?'
4. *Reading general articles, journals, books and newspapers.* Good sources for current topics include the *Financial Times*, *Fortune* magazine, *Harvard Business Review*, and trade publications such as *Computer Weekly* and *The Grocer*. These can help you to identify 'hot topics' that may present good opportunities for both interest and career, and add some relatively unique element to the work.

5. *Surfing the internet using a search engine such as Google.* Do a random search just to see where it leads you.

3.1.3 Which research ideas are worth pursuing?

Once you have developed some potential ideas, before you select one to develop into your research topic you should make sure that none is a 'dead end' in practical or theoretical terms. Just being interesting does not mean that something is worth studying. An idea is only worth exploring if you can develop it into a research topic, a statement of the general area that you plan to research. A research topic 'sets the researcher on a specific path and defines the territory to be explored' (Blaikie 2000: 45). We suggest that you spend a few minutes now to make sure that you could transform any of these ideas into a good research topic. If you can state your research topic as a problem, you are doing well.

In **Section 3.2**, we will describe how to actually narrow down the contenders into one or two ideas that you can take forward. We suggest that you ask the following questions about each of your ideas:

1. Does it meet the project requirements?
2. Is it relevant to at least one practical problem faced by business and management?
3. Is it relevant to at least one theoretical problem faced by business and management researchers?
4. Can I identify a research setting and research sample in which I could gather data?
5. Can I do it with the time and resources available to me?
6. Am I interested in doing it?
7. Is it worth studying?

We suggest that you score each of your ideas using the following system: 0 = No, 1 = Yes, 2 = Outstanding. You should drop any projects that score one or more 0s from further consideration. We will explain in **Section 3.2** how to choose the best idea out of those that are feasible. Use your project requirements to think about what your project needs to do and the criteria it needs to meet.

If you forget to apply the second and third criteria above to potential research topics, this can create significant difficulties later in your research process. Whether you start with a practical or a theoretical problem, your research must apply both to what goes on in the real world – the practical problems faced by businesses and managers – and to business and management theory – our accumulated academic knowledge about organisations and the people in them. Every business and management research project should therefore be relevant for practice – what business and management actually do – and theory – what we know about business and management. We describe how to use the library, internet and other knowledge resources to do this in **Chapter 4**. You may also want to get advice from your supervisor. Don't forget about your coursework.

You may need to do some research to link potential research topics to theoretical problems before you go any further. Even if you start with a practical problem, you will need to identify the business and management knowledge you can apply to define your research topic, design how you will investigate it and describe what you find out. Managers often lack this knowledge and/or the time or skills to find it. This business and management knowledge that you apply may be a theory or model that you have learnt about in your coursework. For example, if you have studied purchasing and supply management, you can identify appropriate models for analysing the organisation's purchasing and supply practices, and other models for improving it. If you can't identify any relevant theories or models from your studies, you will need to search for a theory or model that applies to this specific situation, which we explore in more detail in **Chapter 4**.

There must be something about your research topic that we do not know, but we ought to know, either to solve a practical problem or to add to incomplete information. A potential topic is only worth pursuing if it leads to one or more research problems you can investigate. As we will discuss later in this section, this means you need to be able to link your research topic to one or more areas of business and management studies and to a practical problem faced by business and management. This investigation can focus on solving a real problem or applying, extending or clarifying a theory or model.

Suppose that you don't have any particular practical or theoretical problem in mind when you are getting started on your research project. How can you bring together a practical problem and a theoretical problem? As we have said previously in this book, you may have to go through several rounds of identifying a practical problem and seeing if you can possibly link it to some area of business and management knowledge, or identifying a theoretical problem and seeing if you can possibly link it to a research setting. No matter whether you start with a practical or a theoretical problem, you must bring both of them together when you define your research problem. So, if you start with a practical problem, you can use theoretical knowledge from your business and management studies to solve that practical problem. If you start with a theoretical problem, you can add to our understanding of that problem by investigating a practical situation. You can see this in **Figure 3.3**.

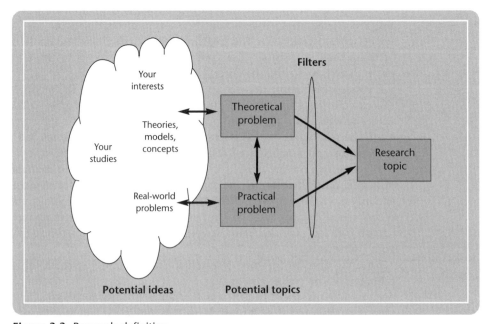

Figure 3.3 Research definition

3.2 SELECTING THE BEST IDEA

Once you have developed a list of potential research topics that meet the basic criteria we described above, your next step is to decide which idea you will actually go forward with. If you are doing an individual project, you may want to pick the idea that interests you the most. If you are not sure which one you should pick, or if you are working in a project team, here is a structured approach from project management you might find useful.

3.2.1 Characteristics of a good research topic

You can use the characteristics of a good research topic that we list below as the baseline for identifying suitable topics and ideas. The most important things to consider are your project requirements, but there are other characteristics of a good research topic that you should consider. They are fairly general, but you can use them to filter research topics as they emerge and revise others. They will also help you decide among different projects you might pursue.

Topic satisfies project guidelines

Any project you take on must satisfy your project requirements and any other expectations of your project supervisor and your examiners. A sponsored or placement project must also satisfy your manager and the organisation's expectations as agreed in the project brief or sponsorship agreement. Balancing the needs and expectations of your academic and business sponsor can be tricky, as we discuss in **Chapter 10**, because they can often come into conflict.

Your project requirements may list specific skills and knowledge you need to demonstrate in your project, such as:

1. Demonstrating your knowledge of the work covered during the course.
2. Identifying and constructively critiquing the work already carried out in the area.
3. Relating theory/best practice to actual practice in organisations.
4. Designing appropriate research questions and selecting appropriate methods to carry them out.
5. Analysing and reporting your findings.
6. Drawing conclusions from the work.

To see how to meet these criteria, you may find it helpful to look at some project reports submitted by former students, as we suggested in **Section 3.1.1**, to see how much work you will need to do and what standard of work you need to achieve. You might also want to talk to your supervisor and/or sponsor to see what effort they expect. For some academic projects, such as a dissertation, you may well be expected to put in as much effort as you would for a full-time job. This would obviously affect your ability to take paid work during this period. For other projects, you might be expected to put in the equivalent of one day per week during the project period.

Topic is feasible

A research problem is not feasible unless you can investigate it with the time and other resources that you have available. This sounds obvious, but students often propose research topics or problems that require more time than they have to spend or access to resources beyond their means. **Chapter 2** explained how to use project management to plan your project, including your project plan, milestones and work breakdown. You should rule out any project that will take more than 80% of the time you have available to work on it.

You should also think about what other resources you will need to investigate this topic. For instance, if you plan to investigate the marketing strategies of blue-chip companies by interviewing top managers, needless to say, you should reconsider your idea unless you already have personal contacts in those firms who already have agreed to take part in such a study. It is unlikely that you will be able to interview even one manager based on 'cold calling', so you will have to rely on publicly available information, which rarely gives any particular insight into the actual strategies being pursued or why and results in unsatisfactory projects. We showed this in **Student research in action 2.4**.

Topic has a manageable scope

A project should have an identifiable beginning, end and boundaries. A good research problem has a well-defined and realistic purpose. It doesn't try to change the world. Many students start out with an overambitious project, for example they aim to 'change the world', or at least significantly 'fix it'. Whilst we applaud this sentiment, you will rarely be able to achieve this – nor is it really appropriate – in a student project. A project with realistic goals, for example understanding a particular area better or applying something you have learnt in your course to solve a particular problem, is much likelier to succeed. Finding out something revolutionary is a bonus, not an objective.

Like other project supervisors, we have given this piece of advice to students more times than we can count. Your idea must be focused enough for you to do a thorough job, but not so small that it is trivial. This chapter will discuss how you can narrow down a research topic. Project scope will come up formally in **Section 3.3.2**.

Topic has symmetrical outcomes

Even if you will not be formally assessed on your research project's outcomes, you will put a lot of time and effort into it. You should therefore make sure that whatever the outcome of your early work, you will still have a project to work on and your outcome will not be irrelevant or trivial. Make sure that your research topic leads to **symmetrical outcomes**, so that no matter what you find out, your findings are both interesting and relevant, or your recommendations are valid and relevant. Not having symmetrical outcomes will be fatal to your research if you are investigating a 'yes or no' question, and the answer is only interesting if you find one. This is especially important if your research is done in sequential stages: one part of your project depends on what you find out in an earlier part. This is often true of exploratory or qualitative projects. The need for symmetry is illustrated in **Student research in action 3.5**.

> *Student research in action 3.5*
> **BRUCE'S FRUIT MARKET**
>
> Bruce was asked to investigate a major supermarket's supply chain for fresh fruit. The project brief stated that he should investigate the supply chain and identify where suppliers were consolidating their products. If, as the supermarket expected, this was in northern France, how might the supermarket influence the supply chain by providing additional facilities, warehousing, and so on?
>
> In the first phase of his study, Bruce found that suppliers mainly consolidated and stored fruit in the UK. This meant that the second part of Bruce's project, which had originally been intended to be the main part of the investigation, was now irrelevant because the supermarket already had enough warehouse facilities in the UK. Thus, he could only complete half of the project, which left him without enough material to flesh out a full research project.

Guess what? Bruce hadn't designed his research so that the first part of the project investigations had symmetrical outcomes. If only he had known about the concept of symmetric outcomes, he could have framed his research questions so that the second half of his project would be worth doing no matter what he found out.

You should think carefully about the questions you are asking in your research in order to spot any asymmetric outcomes. For example, 'Why do lower income households tend to die younger?' assumes a positive answer to the implied question – 'Do people from lower income households (however you decide to define this) actually die younger?' If you can show that people from lower income households do die younger, for example using national statistical records, you can investigate the question, 'Why might this be true?' On the other hand, if you initially found out that people from lower income households didn't actually die younger, the answer to your question is, 'Well, they don't', and your project would not be wildly successful. It might be better to ask 'How does household income affect health and mortality rates?'

Topic is relevant to business and management practice

Your findings and/or recommendations should have more general usefulness, that is, someone else could take your findings and apply them to a similar set of companies or people, or use your project as a starting point for further research or application. A good research project will add to our knowledge about a practical problem and/or theoretical problem, if not both. This continues the theme of building on previous research.

Topic is linked to business and management knowledge

You should have selected a research topic that you can link to at least one area of business and management research (or research in supporting disciplines such as economics or psychology) so that you can develop the theoretical problem. As we will see in **Chapter 4**, you will need to use previous studies when you define your research problem and questions, and when you select your research methods. You will need to develop a literature review (**Chapter 4**) and discuss key findings (**Chapter 12**).

This can be a problem if you are looking at leading-edge technologies or other new areas. For example, when the web was first becoming popular in the 1990s, students researching e-commerce found it difficult to find enough articles to do a good literature review, because the area was so new.

What you find out in your research should contribute to our knowledge of a practical or theoretical problem, that is, it has at least one original aspect. You do not have to provide a new grand theory or make a substantial addition to our existing knowledge, but you should enable us to understand one small aspect of what you have covered a little better than when you started.

Findings/recommendations will satisfy all your project's stakeholders

Students often find that academic and business sponsors have different ideas about what they should do in their project. If you have different project stakeholders who each have conflicting needs and expectations, you may find it difficult to satisfy all of them. You need to think about these competing project stakeholders from the start and make sure that you build in the necessary work to meet the needs of each into your project plan. We cover more of the issues of managing in-company research projects in **Chapter 9**.

Your examiners will probably focus on how your research can help them to understand a theoretical problem – aspects of your topic that they want to know more about. Your academic institution requires an academically sound piece of work that demonstrates knowledge of the subject area and an ability to design and carry out research, present, analyse and draw conclusions from the results.

On the other hand, your business sponsor or collaborator will probably focus on how your research can help them to understand a practical problem – aspects of business and management practice that they need help with. They will worry less about how this was arrived at rather than whether your recommendations can be implemented and whether they will help to solve that particular problem. Sometimes, and this can be very difficult for students to resolve, you may be expected to produce recommendations that support what the manager has already decided, not what the best solution is for the organisation, as illustrated by **Student research in action 3.6**.

> *Student research in action 3.6*
> **THAT'S NOT WHAT WE WANTED TO HEAR!**
>
> A team of students spent a year studying the excellent community outreach work being done by a faith-based organisation. Towards the end of their research, the students found out that very few of the underprivileged young people being serviced by the organisation were actually aware of its strong religious beliefs, and those who did know, did not want to be associated with that particular religion. Although this was an interesting finding, with significant implications for their sponsor, the students were told, in no uncertain terms, that they should not mention this finding in their project report.

You may even need to write a different report for each important stakeholder. Few managers will wade through a 20,000-word report to reach your recommendations in your last chapter, even if your report is beautifully bound and laid out! One managing director commented, 'if the blurb on the front doesn't grab me, I don't bother reading it'. This is not what you want to hear if you have worked hard on every page of your project report. We will return to this in **Chapter 14**.

Finally, don't leave yourself out of this equation. You should identify what you want to get out of the project in terms of your research and personal objectives, as discussed in **Chapter 2**. As you start to define what you will do in your research project, you should give some serious thought as to why you are doing the project and what you want to get out of it. A good research project should satisfy your own needs, as well as those of project stakeholders. Even if you have been assigned a research topic or sponsored project that you are not really interested in, you may need to complete your degree requirements or fulfil your project placement requirements. On the other hand, you may be passionate about what you plan to study or see it as a stepping stone to a good job or a promotion. You may be interested in part of the research project, such as learning how to do an action project or analyse questionnaire data.

3.2.2 Selecting the best idea

So, how do you identify the best project? We suggest that you follow the process described in **Student research in action 3.7**. You can construct a similar table by listing your ideas and rating them against the assessment criteria and any other criteria you decide are important. You can make the ranking process more complex by using numerical ratings and/or weighting the factors by their importance. Whether you use a simple or more complex table to rank potential projects, this structured approach allows you or your project team to make a reasonable choice based on your own criteria, and can greatly assist the group in uniting behind a particular decision.

Student research in action 3.7
OOPS! WE DID IT AGAIN

As part of a course at the University of Bath, a group of students must run an event or carry out a particular task to demonstrate their ability to plan, execute and review a group project. They are assessed on the originality of their idea, the quality of the planning process and the content of the report reflecting their experiences during the project.

One group had a meeting and came up with a number of ideas. The group wanted to choose the best project out of the following:

- Producing a yearbook for their class group
- Developing a short video to promote the course they are studying
- Organising a formal ball for the entire department
- Organising a treasure hunt one Sunday
- Organising an 'accident awareness' day for schoolchildren.

The group's next activity was to decide what criteria to judge the proposal against. They first identified three criteria based on how the project would be assessed:

- whether the idea was original
- whether the idea would demonstrate project management skills
- whether it would enable them to produce a good report.

The group then added four more characteristics of their own that they wanted their project to have. These were:

- it should sufficiently stretch the group
- it should not depend too heavily on other people for its success
- it must not require them to undertake any large financial risk
- it must be fun for the group to do.

They then put the projects into a table, and agreed a set of ratings, as shown in **Table 3.1**.

Table 3.1 An example rating table

	Originality	Demonstrates skills	Produces a good report	Stretching	Independent of others	Avoids financial risk	Fun
Yearbook	✗	✓	✓	–	–	✗	✗
Video	✓	✓	✓	✓	✓	✗	✓
Ball	–	✓	✓	✓	✗	✗✗✗	✓
Treasure hunt	✗	–	✗	–	–	✓	–
Accident awareness day	✓	✓	–	✗	✗	✓	–

Given these ratings, they saw that there was one clear choice for them – the video – as it had the most ticks. They also saw that they needed to manage the project's financial risk (cost of hiring editing facilities and production of the finished product) carefully.

Even if one idea is clearly ranked higher than others when you have gone through the ranking process, we recommend that you identify a second project as a backup in case the first one doesn't work out. Having an alternate or 'safety' project available is especially important when your first project is risky, for example if you need to arrange access to an organisation or data set, as such access often falls through.

3.2.3 Refining your research topic

So, now you are down to a single research topic that you have identified or been assigned. What next? For most students, this is narrowing down the research topic to a manageable scope. (Most students start out with a topic so broad it would take a thousand students working for a thousand years to finish their research project.) We suggest that you do this by developing research questions.

Research questions

If your research topic describes the general area you will investigate, your **research questions** define those areas of the topic you will investigate. They will be the main focus of your project, because they will guide what you do in your project. For example, you might develop a research topic of 'service quality' from service management, or 'dual-career ladders' from 'research and development'. These topics could then generate research questions.

Well-constructed research questions will identify the scope of your research project and guide the plan for your project, because they will determine the business and management research that you use to support your project, the data you collect and how you report your research. According to O'Leary (2004: 29), your research questions should:

- Define your research topic – the business or management phenomenon that you will focus on
- Define the nature of your research – whether your main goal is to describe, explore or explain this phenomenon
- Define the issues you will explore – what aspects of the phenomenon you will find out about
- Indicate whether you foresee a relationship between the concepts you are exploring – develop any propositions or hypotheses.

You should try to express any good research problem as a question that is interesting to both managers and academic researchers. **Student research in action 3.8** describes how one student developed some potential research questions.

Student research in action 3.8
UP THE ARSENAL

Alex needed to come up with an idea for her summer research project. She was a passionate fan of the Arsenal football team, which she had followed since she was a child. Putting together the idea of doing research on one or more football teams with the topics she had studied in service management, Alex came up with some potential research questions, including:

- Were football stadiums trying to become friendlier to female fans?
- Were football clubs focusing more on retailing merchandise or entertaining fans?
- What physical aspects of football stadiums encouraged or discouraged female fans from attending?

Alex also made sure that there was enough support in the academic literature to support her project at a level appropriate for an MSc dissertation. She identified previous studies of female sports fans by Coddington (1997) and Crawford and Gosling (2004) that she could use for her academic framework.

Other research questions that our students have asked include:

- Why do people buy organic produce from small farmers over the internet?
- Do project management techniques reduce IT project failures?
- How can we calculate all the environmental impacts associated with projects such as building a road or bridge?
- Do multinational top management teams work together differently from single nationality ones?

Most students find that they need to cycle between their research topic and research questions several times to end up with a feasible set of research questions and a suitably focused research topic. It is not unusual for students doing a PhD to spend a year clarifying their research questions, even if they have started with a well-defined research topic. Most undergraduate or master's students don't have the luxury of spending so much time! We highlight some of the most common problems below.

No significant contribution. You should avoid, where possible, asking research questions that have already been answered, since you run the risk of doing trivial research. On the other hand, if we only *think* we know the answer, usually because we think the answer is 'common sense', the question might well be worth asking. **Research in action 3.1** demonstrates where a researcher believed that the existing answers to a particular question were inadequate, and went on to make a major contribution to business and management research as a result.

Research in action 3.1
I CAN'T BELIEVE IT'S NOT FAYOL!

Like Henry Mintzberg, you have probably encountered a number of models of 'what managers do' during your studies. At the time Mintzberg started his doctoral thesis, researchers and managers accepted Henri Fayol's description of what managers do, which is to 'plan, organise, control and coordinate'. For his doctoral research, Henry Mintzberg watched five managers for a week each, and recorded what each one did during that week, analysing their incoming and outgoing post, and their conversations. Mintzberg concluded that Fayol and other formal models of managerial decision-making did not describe adequately what managers actually did, which he identified as comprising ten different roles (Mintzberg 1971). As well as being a significant triumph of 'fact over folklore', Mintzberg's research led to significant research in managerial decision-making.

Biased or self-answering questions. You should try to avoid choosing or stating research questions so that you have already determined what the answer will be before you start by how you frame the question. Even if you expect to find a certain answer, based on your experience, the theory or model you are using or what your academic supervisor or project sponsor expects, you should frame your research questions so that you remain open to contradictory evidence or unexpected findings. If you don't, you may miss out on the opportunity to discuss what you have found. In **Student research in action 3.9**, the student was open to findings that were not expected and as a result produced a most interesting piece of work.

Student research in action 3.9
ONE-POTATO, TWO-POTATO … YOU'RE HIRED!

Anjali was studying how small and medium-sized companies recruited and selected their employees. She expected to find that they used selected structured methods, as these were widely discussed by both academics and practitioners. However, in the firms who had agreed to give her access to their recruitment methods, it became clear that they selected employees based on interviews only, and that supposedly 'objective' methods (for example personality profiling) were not used. This presented great opportunities for discussion, and then gave rise to further questions, including 'Why didn't these firms use structured techniques for recruitment?'

On the other hand, unexpected findings can become gifts to your research project. In the Hawthorne experiments, researchers failed to find any link between lighting and worker output, but this led them to question what factors actually influenced output in the relay assembly group. Was it the style of supervision? Was it the chance to make more money? Was it the attention from the supervisor? Elton Mayo's explanation that strong social ties created higher performance, even if his interpretation of the data has been challenged by later researchers (see Gillespie 1993), was significantly more interesting for management research than the original question about electric lighting, since it opened up many possibilities for research into the human and social side of managing employees.

Unanswerable questions. Beware of research questions that you cannot answer by gathering and analysing data. Some research questions are simply unanswerable, for example metaphysical questions about good and evil, or right or wrong. This is not the same as the study of business ethics or topics such as corporate social responsibility, though!

Using the literature to support your research topic and questions

Students who have been exposed to natural sciences research often wonder whether they should develop propositions or hypotheses from their research questions. The answer is, 'it depends'. In some research projects, as we will see in **Chapter 5**, you may be expected to further refine your research questions into more specific statements about what you expect to find in your research project at this point. Depending on how specific these statements or predictions are, they may be called research propositions or research hypotheses. You may need to read **Chapter 5** and then come back to this section to see whether this is the case for your own research project.

The work that you do now exploring the area is vital, and will initially expand the possibilities for your work – in line with the model presented in **Figure 3.1**. You may find this easier to do if you use a mind map, a hierarchy of concepts or a Venn diagram, which we describe below.

If you can't find at least one business and management area that your topic fits into, then you may find it difficult to develop and support the theoretical side of your research project. Although this sounds obvious, students often take such a narrow view of a research topic that they conclude that no one else has ever identified it, as shown in **Student research in action 3.10**.

Student research in action 3.10
I AM THE GREATEST

Roy walked into his potential supervisor's office and claimed that the issue of staff pay and rewards in lean manufacturing systems had not been properly studied, but 'the rest of the management world had been too dull to notice'. When the potential supervisor asked him to support this claim, Roy said that he could find little of any relevance on this topic in the operations management literature, and his research project would therefore break new ground.

Roy's proposed research topic was clearly important, relevant and of interest to business. It was also probably true that there was little research in operations management on pay and rewards. So what might be wrong with this picture? Management has been formally studied for over 100 years, and the chances that everyone had ignored such a major research problem are small – not zero, but small, as most topics have been covered in some way, in some form. Relatively little is completely new in management.

Roy's potential project supervisor, therefore, found it hard to believe that no research had been done on the topic and, in fact, he knew that a major study of pay and rewards in lean manufacturing had been published by Delbridge and Lowe (1997). Roy had ignored the fact that pay and reward is a major concern of human resource management (HRM), not of operations management. Not surprisingly, a brief review of the HRM literature revealed that his proposed topic had been extensively studied. Even so, there was scope for him to investigate this topic by building on the existing research on pay and rewards in HRM and lean manufacturing in OM.

If Roy had identified the two different concepts he wanted to study as 'pay and reward' and 'lean production' and realised that they belonged to two different areas, he would have realised that he should be looking at his topic not only as 'how pay and reward affect lean production' but also 'lean production affects pay and reward', which would have led him to both the HRM and the OM literature. Then, rather than trying to invent a new area of study, with the risk that his project findings would merely replicate previous research such as Delbridge and Lowe's study, he could have used this research to focus or frame his study more clearly. For instance, he could have tested the findings of Delbridge and Lowe's study in his own sample of manufacturing firms that had adopted lean production. This would have added to both the HRM and OM literature, since his findings could be used to validate Delbridge and Lowe. Furthermore, he could potentially have used Delbridge and Lowe's research methods to help to design his own research study, which would have saved a lot of time and effort.

As this example suggests someone, somewhere has covered almost any business and management topic you could think of. Don't try to reinvent the wheel unnecessarily. Most research projects that are worth doing build on one or more existing areas of knowledge, and in **Chapter 4** we will discuss some ways you can identify those areas. This also presents a challenge if you can draw on more than one area: you will need not only to select your topic carefully, but also to consider what subject or perspective you will approach that topic from. This will make a big difference in how you define and execute your research topic, and help you to avoid some problems that commonly plague students.

At this stage you should look for two main types of material:

- *General overviews* of your topic, for example textbooks or review articles
- *Model studies* – the type of study you would like to carry out, which yours can add to, provide points of discussion or generally be based around in some way.

Student research in action 3.11
IS ANYBODY LISTENING?

One student found an article by Barclay and Benson (1990), who reported that fewer than 8% of the managers they studied were aware of any recent published studies on the areas in which they were working. He decided to investigate whether the management literature actually affected managers' behaviour. The student decided to see whether his study would find similar low levels of awareness and try to find reasons for the low level of awareness. This would both replicate Barclay and Benson's findings and try to extend them.

Using a mind map to refine your research topic

Figure 3.4 shows a mind map (aka a spider diagram) that Omozo, an MBA student, used to help structure his thoughts on his project on graduate recruitment practices in UK retail banking. He put the main topic in the centre of the map and the main issues related to this around it. The sub-issues are then clustered around each of the main issues.

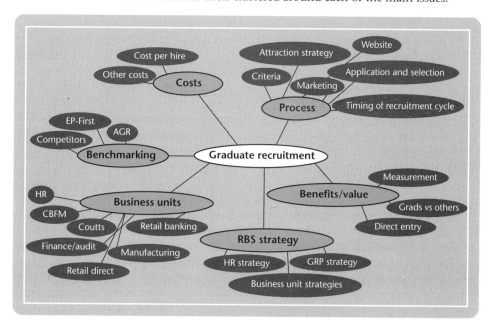

Figure 3.4 Mind map of graduate recruitment project
Source: Courtesy of Omozo Ehigie

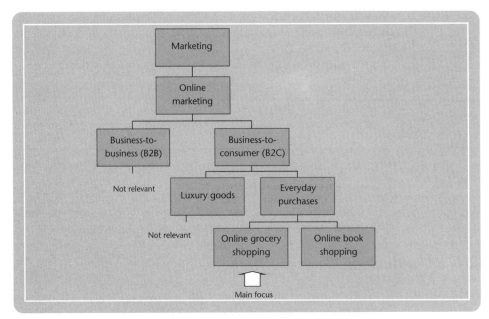

Figure 3.5 A hierarchy of concepts

Using a hierarchy of concepts to refine your research topic

One way to narrow down what you want to research is to draw a **hierarchy of concepts**, which will help you get specific with your practical and/or theoretical problem. Some students start off with a really broad focus, such as 'Why do organisations fail?' This is a perfectly good starting point, but it would be impossible to investigate in a single research project. Often, students need to go through several iterations on each concept in their research questions to narrow them down into a manageable topic and questions. For example, if your particular interest is marketing, this can be broken down into business-to-business marketing (B2B) and business-to-consumer marketing (B2C). You decide that your interest is in the B2C area. How might this area be broken down? The potential hierarchy of concepts for this project is shown in **Figure 3.5**.

Many concepts easily fall into hierarchies. Thinking about how your research might fit into a conceptual hierarchy can be useful at many points in your project, as you will see in **Chapter 4**. If you go up a level in the hierarchy, you have a more abstract, and therefore broader, concept to deal with; if you go down a level, you have a less abstract, and therefore narrower, concept to deal with.

Using a Venn diagram to refine your research topic

An important aspect of refining your research topic is to see where it fits into the business and management research. If your proposed research project fits into two or more areas of study, you may want to use a mapping technique such as Venn diagrams to show where your topic fits with the subjects that you have studied, because this makes it much easier to see what research people have already done in the area.

Drawing a **Venn diagram** can help you focus your search for previous research (see **Chapter 4**). Some research topics are studied only within one field, for example the ethics of marketing to children is mainly of interest in marketing. Many research topics, however, fit into several areas. For example, total quality management (TQM) is a substantial topic in both operations management and human resource management. Some research topics are also studied within business and management's base disciplines, such as economics, sociology or psychology.

As shown in **Figure 3.6**, by looking at the overlap between more than one topic, or more than one field, you can narrow down the scope of your topic considerably. Although each of the areas in **Student research in action 3.12** was well known, the project's originality came from integrating the three. Original work often takes place at the intersection between different areas of study, because you can then draw on relevant aspects of each, but also combine multiple views of your topic.

Student research in action 3.12
TALK TO ME

Amit decided that he would investigate call centres. He started by trying to identify previous research on the specific topic of 'call centre management', but not much had been published under that specific topic heading. After talking to his supervisor, he realised that call centre management was studied in three areas: human resource management (well understood), operations management (well understood) and service management (also well understood). The project therefore existed at the intersection of the three areas, as shown in **Figure 3.6**. His challenge was to bring these three areas together.

Amit could not possibly investigate HRM, OM and services in a single project. His next step was therefore to choose one as his main perspective on the topic. For instance, Amit could choose to take an operations-based approach, if he were mainly interested in the process (what people do), a service-based approach, the way in which the employees interact with the customers, or an HRM-based approach, the human interactions with the system.

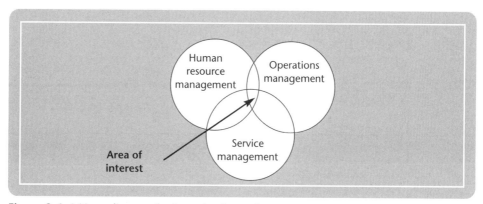

Figure 3.6 A Venn diagram for investigating call centres

3.3 DEVELOPING A RESEARCH PROPOSAL

Once you have identified your research problem and research questions, you are ready to start on your research. First, however, you need to communicate it to both yourself and other people. You might try writing down what you want to do as:

- A 'working title' – doesn't have to be snappy, just a few words that say what it is you are doing.
- A picture – some people find it most helpful at this stage to draw a mind map, or represent their project with a picture, photograph, collage or drawing.
- A 'sound bite' or 'elevator pitch' – imagine a friend asking you what you are doing for your project. You have precisely 15 seconds to tell them, before his or her eyes glaze over and he or she rushes off. What will you tell him or her about your work?
- An **abstract** – 100–150 words that summarise what you are thinking of doing.
- A research proposal – a formal document that describes what you plan to do in your project.

3.3.1 Writing a research proposal

Once you've narrowed down your topic area and identified your research problem and research questions, you can now formally state them in a **research proposal** to your academic advisor and/or business sponsor as part of your project. Whether or not you are required to present a formal project proposal, we recommend this as part of your research process. There are many reasons that you should do this, including to:

- Clarify your own ideas
- Document your ideas so that you can discuss your project with other people, including potential supervisors, partners and collaborators
- Provide a formal starting point for the project and a point of reference that you can come back to during the study should things not progress as you plan.

If you have been given a proposal format to follow by your organisation, you should follow it. If you haven't, many students have successfully used the format in **Table 3.2** for a variety of projects. It is worth putting some effort into completing the proposal at this point. If you can fill in all the boxes, you have at least considered the major issues.

Table 3.2 An example of a research proposal

Working title	Don't worry too much about the title at this point, it is generally accepted that it will change during the project – but insert a few words that summarise your ideas.
Main discipline (for example strategy, finance, operations and so on)	What approach will you be taking? Use a Venn diagram to help with this one.

Table 3.2 cont'd

Project discussed with	This should include anyone relevant to your project, and anyone else who could usefully ask pertinent questions on the subject, maybe an academic or tutor, or someone related to the application of the issue you are planning to investigate. We always suggest that you gather as many opinions as possible at the start of the project.
Background to the study	Fill in how the project came about – was it your idea? If not, how did it emerge?
Management issues	What are the people who are working with this problem facing? How is the problem evident? What has been done already about the issue, and how is it manifesting itself today? For instance, it may be the issue of interest is an ongoing problem with industrial relations that results in regular stoppages or industrial disputes. It may recently have come to a head because of new commercial pressures.
Research questions/ propositions/ hypotheses	Insert the main and the subsidiary questions/propositions/hypotheses here.
Project objectives	What do you hope to achieve by carrying out this piece of research? What are your personal goals? What do you hope the project will find?
Project scope	What is going to be covered by this project and is there anything you want to specifically exclude? (See further note below.)
Sources of academic information	What are the main review articles, books and your 'hook article', if relevant?
Sources of data	This will be covered later, but for now, have an idea of what you might do to answer your research questions, within the constraints of the available time and resources. In particular, you should consider whether you will be able to answer your research questions by using: ● existing information, desk or library research ● indirect contact with organisations, for example questionnaires ● direct contact with organisations, interviews or in-company research.

3.3.2 Identifying your project scope

Your **project scope** states 'what's in and what's out'. Identifying your project scope will help you focus your work. It is a good touchstone later on when you are in danger of being distracted or face a choice about what direction your project should take. If you are working as part of a project group, it can help to keep the whole group focused.

The project scope will describe your research topic, research questions and the main perspective you will take on your topic. This does not stop you from considering other perspectives but, pragmatically, you will have to limit the input from other areas. You will also need to put some boundaries around the subject material you will be considering. For instance, will you consider a single firm, a sector, a type of organisation (for example not for profit, governmental, small to medium-sized enterprise) or a generic view of your topic?

SUMMARY

In this chapter, we have described how to generate ideas for your research project. Some research will start with a practical problem. You may be interested in this practical problem, or you may be assigned a project brief by a business sponsor. Other research starts with a theoretical problem, a problem of incomplete knowledge that you may discover or are assigned by an academic supervisor or lecturer. Either way, business and management research usually involves finding both a practical and a theoretical aspect to your research topic.

This chapter has also provided some guidance on generating research ideas and filtering them to find the best idea. If you start with too few ideas, you may not have enough to select a high-quality idea. On the other hand, if you start with too many ideas, you may not be able to narrow them down. We have discussed a ranking mechanism for selecting the best idea for your research project.

Once you have selected a topic, you should be able to develop a project proposal – a document for communicating to others what you plan to do. You can use a project proposal to gain academic approval and practical support for your project.

 ANSWERS TO KEY QUESTIONS

Where do ideas for research topics come from?

- By creating some initial chaos, reading, discussing a wide range of potential issues, creating a number of possible topics, then focusing your work onto one issue that you will develop
- The process of developing ideas includes reflection on experience, teaching and looking at previous projects, as well as considering why you are doing the project, then choosing the subject perspective you will use to approach the topic

How can I choose between several potential research topics?

- You should choose between topics by defining the criteria your project will be evaluated on and selecting the one that most closely matches the criteria. If there are areas that do not match the criteria, the project should be specified to make sure that key criteria are met

What characterises a good research topic?

- These can be summarised in seven general points – a well-defined purpose, wider implications than the project context, it is feasible, there is a basis in the literature but there is something novel about the study, it is practical, the outcomes are symmetrical and the project satisfies the stakeholders
- It must interest you
- It must fit with the requirements of your institution

Why should I use research questions to focus my research?

- A main overall question will provide a focus for your work

● Breaking the main question down into smaller research questions should provide a comprehensible breakdown of the activities you will need to carry out

● Research questions are a readily understandable means for you to explain 'what is my research project about?'

How can I use a project proposal to define my project scope?

● The proposal will allow you to demonstrate the background and importance of your work, the research questions, hypotheses and propositions, state the intended methods for carrying it out and the basis for it in the literature

● The proposal requires you to start being specific about your ideas – to define what you are going to investigate and, just as importantly, what you are not going to investigate

REFERENCES

Barclay, I. and Benson, M.H. 1990. The Effective Management of New Product Development, *Leadership and Organisation Development Journal* Special Issue, **11**(6): 1–37.

Blaikie, Norman. 2000. *Designing Social Research.* Cambridge: Polity Press.

Coddington, A. 1997. *One of the Lads: Women who Follow Football.* London: HarperCollins.

Cohen, Wesley M. and Levinthal, Daniel A. 1989. Innovation and learning: The two faces of R&D, *Economic Journal*, **99**(397): 569–96.

Cohen, Wesley M. 1990. Absorptive capacity: A new perspective on learning and innovation, *Administrative Science Quarterly*, **35**(1): 128–52.

Crawford, Garry and Gosling, Victoria K. 2004. The myth of the 'Puck Bunny': Female fans and men's ice hockey, *Sociology*, **38**(3): 477–93.

Delbride, R. and Lowe, J. (1997). Manufacturing control: supervisory systems on the 'new' shopfloor, *Sociology*, **31**(3).

Gill, John and Johnson, Phil. 2002. *Research Methods for Managers*, 3rd edn. London: Sage.

Gillespie, Richard. 1993. *Manufacturing Knowledge: A History of the Hawthorne Experiments.* Cambridge: Cambridge University Press.

Grant, R.M. 2004. *Contemporary Strategy Analysis.* Oxford: Blackwell Publishing.

Kotler, P., Saunders, J. and Armstrong, G. 2004. *Principles of Marketing: European Edition.* Harlow: FT/Prentice Hall.

Lundberg, Craig C. 1999. Finding research agendas: Getting started Weick-like, *The Society for Industrial and Organizational Psychology*, American Psychological Society available on http://www.apa.org.

Mintzberg, Henry. 1971. Managerial work: analysis from observation, *Management Science*, **18**(2): 97–110.

O'Leary, Zina. 2004. *The Essential Guide to Doing Research.* London: Sage.

Tushman, Michael L. and Anderson, Philip. 1986. Technological discontinuities and organisational environments, *Administrative Science Quarterly*, **31**(3): 439–65.

Weick, Karl E. 1992. Agenda setting in organizational behaviour: A theory-focused approach, *Journal of Management Inquiry*, **1**(3): 171–82.

Whedon, Joss. 2002. *Once More with Feeling.* New York: Simon & Schuster.

Womack, J.P., Jones, D.T. and Roos, D. 1995. *The Machine That Changed the World: The Massachusetts Institute of Technology 5-million-dollar, 5-year Report on the Future of the Automobile Industry*, New York: Rawson Associates.

ADDITIONAL RESOURCES

Campbell, John P., Daft, Richard L. and Hulin, Charles L. 1982. *What to Study: Generating and Developing Research Questions.* Beverly Hills, CA: Sage.

Collis, Jill and Hussey, Roger. 2003. *Business Research,* 2nd edn. Basingstoke: Palgrave Macmillan.

Daft, Richard L. 1984. Antecedents of significant and not-so-significant organizational research. In T.S. Bateman and G.R. Ferris (eds). *Method and Analysis in Organizational Research.* Reston, VA: Reston Publishing.

Davis, Murray S. 1971. That's interesting: Toward a phenomenology of sociology and a sociology of phenomenology, *Philosophy of Social Science,* 1: 309–44.

Easterby-Smith, Mark, Thorpe, Richard and Lowe, Andy. 2002. *Management Research: An Introduction,* 2nd edn. London: Sage.

Jankowicz, A.D. 2000. *Business Research Projects,* 3rd edn. London: Business Press/Thomson Learning.

Kaplan, Abraham. 1964. *The Conduct of Inquiry.* San Francisco: Chandler Press.

Lawrence, Paul R. 1992. The challenge of problem-oriented research, *Journal of Management Inquiry,* 1(2): 139–42.

Lundberg, Craig C. 1976. Hypothesis generation in organizational behavior research, *Academy of Management Review,* 3(1/2): 5–12.

Maslow, A. H. 1970. *Motivation and Personality,* 2nd edn. New York: Harper & Row.

Partington, David. 2002. *Essential Skills for Management Research.* London: Sage.

Robson, Colin. 2002. *Real World Research,* 2nd edn. Oxford: Blackwell.

Saunders, Mark, Lewis, Phillip and Thornhill, Adrian. 2003. *Research Methods for Business Students,* 3rd edn. Harlow: Financial Times/Prentice Hall

Sekaran, U. 2000. *Research Methods for Business,* 3rd edn. Chichester: Wiley.

Taylor, Frederick W. 1947. *Scientific Management.* New York: Harper & Row.

Weick, Karl E. 1983. Management thought in the context of action. In S. Srivastva (ed.) *The Executive Mind.* San Francisco: Jossey-Bass.

Weick, Karl E. 1989. Theory construction as disciplined imagination, *Academy of Management Review,* 14(4): 516–31.

Wren, Daniel A. and Greenwood, Ronald G. 1998. *Management Innovators: The People and Ideas that Have Shaped Modern Business.* Oxford: Oxford University Press.

Zikmund, W.G. 2000. *Business Research Methods,* 6th edn. Orlando, FL: Dryden Press/Harcourt College Publishers.

FREQUENTLY ASKED QUESTIONS

- **Does the project have to be leading edge in management terms: does it have to address a hot topic from the current management literature?**

No – the project does not have to be fashionable to be good. Many topics have disappeared from the management agenda for no reason other than the field appears to have moved on to the next big idea. For instance, during the 1990s, many firms adopted particular approaches to quality management and then abandoned them when other ideas came along. Quality management is still a good topic for investigation – as there is plenty written on it and practitioners are still interested in to how to gain benefit from good quality management.

- **How do I know the precise objectives of the project and the balance that is required between theoretical and practical issues?**

The precise objectives of the project should be set out in course documentation and are always worth referring to – not least because they can clarify the requirements of the project and the balance point between theoretical and practical issues. The discussion of the role of theory/best practice and other practices is in **Chapter 4**.

- **Why do I need to include this theory when what I am looking at is profoundly practical?**

This is easy to understand, but where does this theory generally come from? It comes from people studying the practical, and theorising from it. As Hebb (1963) famously commented, 'There's nothing so useful as a good theory'. In addition, you will usually need to show that you have covered the existing knowledge on a topic – it is usually a central purpose of the project work. Moreover, the existing knowledge base should help you to make sense of, or at least structure the issues in the area that you are considering.

- **Do I really have to prepare a written scope and proposal?**

Whilst some institutions require you to present a written proposal, others will accept a discussion of your proposals. We suggest that the few minutes that it takes to prepare the proposal are worthwhile, as it provides a point of reference for the project as it progresses and will help to keep you on track, if you refer back to it regularly.

1. If you have access to a set of project requirements for your academic work or business project, use them to answer this question. What are the requirements of projects that you will be carrying out? Investigate the documentation provided by your institution and compare them with the characteristics of a 'good project' included in this chapter.

2. 'Previous work is so yesterday. Why not just start it again? After all, it was about time there was some fresh thinking in management.' What do you think of this statement?

3. Where do you position yourself in **Figure 3.2**?

4. What are the sources of ideas that you could usefully use for your project either to start you off or expand on the ideas that you have?

5. Does every research project have to be linked to a particular business and management area of study? Why or why not?

6. What are the ethical implications of using previous student projects as a source for your own project ideas?

7. How would you express your ideas at different stages in the development of those ideas? How would a mind map be used here?

8. How can filling out a research proposal improve the quality of the research process?

9. How can defining your project scope at this stage of the research process improve the quality of the research project?

This workshop comprises two short group exercises, intended to illustrate the different processes that people go through in trying to reach a decision when there are a large number of possibilities for that decision.

10-minute exercise (1)

Your group has been awarded a (fictitious) potential business start-up grant of £100,000. What are you going to do with this? You have 10 minutes to agree on an idea and present it in order to 'win' this money.

Debrief discussion questions (1)

1. What are your ideas (summarise to one idea per group)?

2. How did you choose which of your ideas to run with?

3. What happened in the 10-minute session – was there any structure to the activity? Did all people contribute or was it dominated by one person? How was the information collected?

4. How effective was this process at getting to 'the best idea'?

5. Plot the process that the group went through onto **Figure 3.1**. How did each of you respond to such a wide brief?

10-minute exercise (2)

We now introduce some 'rules' for the process:

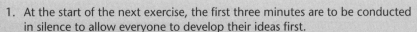

Workshop cont'd

1. At the start of the next exercise, the first three minutes are to be conducted in silence to allow everyone to develop their ideas first.

2. Appoint someone as facilitator (not the most dominant person from the first exercise). The role of the facilitator is to clarify ideas and help to ensure that everyone is assisted in making their contribution.

3. No ideas are rejected and nobody is criticised for ideas (some of the wackiest ideas when combined with others can produce superb concepts).

4. Combine but don't eliminate ideas.

5. Use Post-its (or index cards) to write your ideas down (one idea per Post-it or index card) and then compile a mind map of the issues as in **Figure 3.4**.

Task

You have been assigned to a project team to carry out a research project. The general area that you have come up with is the evaluation of critical success factors for small businesses. Your initial evaluation of the area shows it to be large and you will need to focus the topic onto a more limited question that you want to ask.

1. For three minutes, working individually, write down your ideas.

2. For two minutes review each other's ideas, without discussion.

3. For five minutes, arrange the topics into a mind map (as **Figure 3.4**).

Which is the most interesting of these that the group would pursue?

Debrief discussion questions (2)

1. What were your main ideas?

2. How did the group work this time round (better or worse)?

3. How did you make decisions?

4. What would you do differently in group situations in future – both to avoid the potential for failure from the issues you have identified, and in terms of the process for making decisions in project groups?

Task

Use the basic idea you have identified to complete a project proposal similar to the one provided in **Table 3.2**.

Relevant chapters

13 Answering your research questions
14 Describing your research
15 Closing the loop

Key challenges

- Interpreting your findings and making recommendations
- Writing and presenting your project
- Reflecting on and learning from your research

Relevant chapters

1 What is research?
2 Managing the research process
3 What should I study?
4 How do I find information?

Key challenges

- Understanding the research process
- Taking a systematic approach
- Generating and clarifying ideas
- **Using the library and internet**

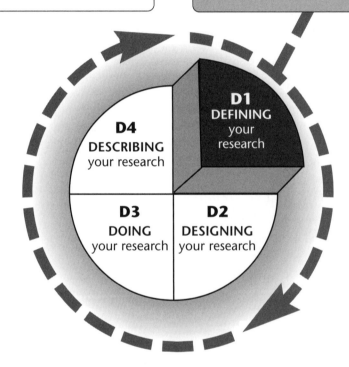

Relevant chapters

9 Doing field research
10 Analysing quantitative data
11 Advanced quantitative analysis
12 Analysing qualitative data

Key challenges

- Practical considerations in doing research
- Using simple statistics
- Understanding multivariate statistics
- Interpreting interviews and observations

Relevant chapters

5 Scientist or ethnographer?
6 Quantitative research designs
7 Designing qualitative research
8 Case studies/multi-method design

Key challenges

- Choosing a model for doing research
- Using scientific methods
- Using ethnographic methods
- Integrating quantitative and qualitative research

How do I find information?
Using the library and internet as knowledge resources

 Key questions

- Where and how do I find information for my research project?
- What business and management research is relevant to my research project?
- What theories, models and concepts are relevant to my research topic?
- How do I find more information about my research setting and sample?
- What methods for collecting and analysing data have other researchers used?
- How do I use this information?

 Learning outcomes

At the end of this chapter, you should be able to:

- Use the library and internet to find information
- Plan your literature search
- Critically analyse business and management research on your research topic in a literature review
- Make appropriate use of business and management research by avoiding plagiarism and copyright violations, and by giving appropriate credit to the source of other people's words and ideas in citations and reference list

Contents

INTRODUCTION

Figuring out 'What should I study?' is the first step in defining your research project. After reading **Chapter 3**, you should have a better idea of your research topic and questions. But you still need to ask more questions in defining your research. This chapter will help you decide 'What do I want to find out about it?'

Whether you started your project with a practical or theoretical problem, an assigned brief or free choice, you need to know what information you might use in your research project, where and how to find it, and how to use it. Working with the business and management literature is essential (O'Leary 2004: 66): you must draw on other people's research to define and support your own project. Even though each research project creates some new knowledge, it must first build on other people's research. In Isaac Newton's words: 'If I have been able to see farther than others, it was because I stood on the shoulders of giants' In turn, your own research findings will contribute to other people's research projects in the future.

This chapter describes a systematic process for finding and using information about your research problem and research setting. This will help you to answer the following three questions about your research project:

1. What theory, models or concepts can I apply to my research topic?
2. What can I find out about my research setting?
3. How can I collect and analyse data to answer my research questions?

You may hear people refer to the process of searching for this information as 'searching the literature', but many people are unsure of exactly what we mean by the 'literature'. Does it include business magazines, such as *Fortune, Harvard Business Review* and *McKinsey Quarterly*? What about web pages, textbooks? You will also need this information to support a critical analysis (Gill and Johnson 2002: 24) called a 'literature review'. You should also understand the difference between the knowledge that professional researchers have (**academic information**) and information about people and organisations that is created as a byproduct of their activities (**empirical information**). (Empirical means 'relating to the real world'.)

The best place to start your search for both academic and empirical information is your library. Libraries not only hold books, they provide a gateway to all kinds of printed and electronic information. Your librarian can be helpful, especially if you don't have the knowledge, skills or time to develop a good search strategy (but don't expect your librarian actually to do your work for you). Another useful source of information is the internet, particularly the World Wide Web. Even though the web holds much more information than any library, as well as powerful search engines that will help you find it, you should rely on it mainly as a source of data rather than a definitive academic reference.

Section 4.1 describes the different sources of information that you might consult during your literature search, including books, periodicals and electronic publications. It considers the credibility of different sources for answering your research questions. It also describes the role of the library and internet in your literature search.

You should know how to use the library, internet, and other sources of knowledge *effectively* if you are to do good research. Using an organised search process, as explained in **Section 4.2**, is essential to finding and using information and managing the information you find (or overcoming not finding it).

Section 4.3 presents some technical skills you will need. We will also explain how to write up a literature review and outline some different approaches to structuring it. We will also explain how to give appropriate credit for other people's words and ideas to avoid plagiarism – intellectual property theft – and briefly introduce ideas about copyright and taking notes. You can use these skills not only in your research project but also in your coursework and your work.

After you have finished this chapter, you should have all the information you need to decide what you will do in your research project. You can follow the systematic process described in **Part II** of this book to turn your project definition into a research design that explains 'How will I study it?' In addition, you can use these skills for both research and study beyond a particular research project.

4.1 WHAT INFORMATION DO YOU NEED?

Most students wonder why they should spend time in the library or on the internet searching for information rather than getting started now with what they regard as research, that is, writing a questionnaire or starting to collect data. Many project disasters start in this stage when students plan inadequately or not at all, rather than when they are actually doing the project.

You will make much better use of your time and other resources if you develop a systematic plan for how you will do your research before you actually do it. If you manage your search for information systematically, you are more likely to find the right information and, more importantly, the right *amount* of information. You need to find not so much that you are overwhelmed but not so little that you have nothing to build on.

In our experience as supervisors, students who don't search systematically end up looking in the wrong place, or in the right place for the wrong information. To search systematically, you need to know:

- What am I looking for?
- Where should I look?
- How should l look?
- What should I do with what I find?

Activity

Briefly record the answers to each of the questions above.

What am I looking for?

Where should I look?

How should I look?

What will I do with the information that I find?

Once you have read the chapter, you should come back and revisit these answers.

 4.1.1 ### What kind of information is relevant for your project?

As noted above, you need to search for information about:

1. Your research topic – what other researchers have found out
2. Your research setting and sample – where to get your data and from whom
3. Your research methods – how to collect and analyse these data to answer your research questions.

Whether you have started with a practical or a theoretical problem, you will need to search the literature systematically to find previous business and management research on your research topic and research questions, key terms we defined in **Chapter 3**. In some research projects, you will gather all this information and develop a detailed and complete research plan before you start collecting data. In others, you may only sketch out the broad detail of what you want to study and then collect more information in parallel with doing your research.

Reading about your research topic will show you what other people have found out about it. You will need to know what **conceptual frameworks** – theories, models, concepts and relationships between concepts – are associated with your topic. You also need to decide what data you will gather to find out more about your research topic and to answer your research questions. But how do you know what data you need to collect – or even what questions to ask – unless you have investigated the knowledge that already exists about your topic? Read on.

Information about your research topic

When people speak of doing a **literature search**, they usually mean the process of finding out more about a research topic, in particular a theoretical problem. The **literature** is the record of other people's research. It contains information about research topics, questions and data that accumulates as researchers conduct research projects and report their findings. These conceptual frameworks are essential for developing your research topic and questions.

To make it clear what your are looking for, this book uses the term 'the literature' to describe the sources of academic information, usually academic books and journals published by professional researchers. Academic information is vital to narrowing down your research topic and developing your research questions, which we will further refine into the idea of 'knowledge claims' later in this chapter.

From reading other people's research, you can understand and explain:

1. Exactly what research questions you want to answer
2. Why your research problem is important
3. What other researchers have found out about it.

Information about your real-world setting and sample

The other important information you want to search for is information about your research setting and sample. You will need to identify a real-world setting and find out more about the organisations, people or other entities you want to investigate. A thorough search will help you find or justify your research setting – the context in which you will investigate your research problem – and sample – the sites in which you will gather your evidence or the entities you will gather it from. You will also need to think about what methods you can use to gather this information and test your knowledge claims. To make sure that you can answer your research questions in your research setting and with your sample, you may need to cycle back and forth between academic information, which is often abstract or at least not related to the specific people or organisations you are studying, and empirical information about the people and organisations you are investigating.

If you are starting from a practical problem, such as a sponsored project with a business sponsor, you may have little leeway in choosing your research setting, but you will still need to decide what evidence to collect and how to collect and analyse it. If you are starting from a theoretical problem, you may have more freedom in choosing your evidence and research setting.

Since business and management is not purely theoretical but engages with the real world, conceptual frameworks are only useful if they help us understand the real world a bit better than when we started. Your literature search will help you identify and collect the empirical information or 'evidence' about what organisations and people actually do in the real world that you need to answer your research questions.

Empirical information is often useful for describing the context – or setting – for your research project. If you don't have any choice about your research setting or have already chosen one, you can do some research to find out what research has been conducted in that setting. If you haven't already chosen a research setting, you can identify potential settings for the research you want to do. For example, if you are investigating airport management, you can find out who the major firms are, such as BAA, and what airports they manage. If you have already identified a likely setting, you can identify its size, geographic distribution, history and trajectory, key players, financials and so on. In some cases, empirical information may even become the main source of data for your research project, as we will describe in **Chapters 6** and **7**.

The difference between 'the literature' as a specific body of knowledge and the literature as information in general is often confusing. Remember that in this context the literature refers to the *academic* literature. It is important to understand the difference between academic information from research and the empirical information about organisations, people and practices that accumulates as journalists, consultants, market researchers and people and organisations themselves report on business and management activities. You may need support from the academic literature to justify your research setting and sample, but information about your setting and sample usually comes from outside the academic literature and from sources of empirical information instead. The academic literature is almost exclusively published in journals, monographs and scholarly books. Empirical information is typically published in completely different sources, such as company publications, newspapers, business magazines, trade publications, popular books and so on.

If you are having trouble finding research that seems relevant to your project, this difference may be your problem. You may find it helpful to separate what you want to study into your **knowledge claim** – the theoretical problem that you want to find out more about – and your **evidence** – the information that you want to collect in the real world to find out more about it. Otherwise, you may be searching too narrowly for previous research projects that have investigated your research problem and your research setting simultaneously, leading you to conclude that no one has done any work on your research topic. As shown in **Student research in action 4.1**, not seeing the difference between a research problem and a research context causes needless confusion for students as they define their research.

Student research in action 4.1
SOME STUDENTS NEVER GET IT, DO THEY?

Yuraporn was completely clear when she started her research project that she wanted to investigate 'how to implement human resource information systems in Thai subsidiaries of multinational corporations'. She kept insisting to her supervisor that there was no research on this, which was probably true. However, if she had separated this into the research problem 'how to implement human resource information systems' – and the research setting – 'Thai subsidiaries of multinational corporations' – she could have identified a clear (and substantial) topic area in human resource information systems. By defining the research problem and research setting separately, she would also have seen links to other related topics, such as information systems and cultural aspects of human resources.

A knowledge claim generally centres on a topic that is interesting to researchers and managers. One knowledge claim currently being investigated from many different aspects is whether family-friendly policies such as flexible working can benefit the organisation as well as individual workers. You could investigate a knowledge claim such as this in many different research settings: two that have been investigated include law firms and high-tech companies.

The reality is that your research problem and research setting will seldom converge in a single piece of work. Multiply the number of research topics by the number of research settings, and you will see why this is so. Remember that your research setting is *not* your research topic. You can study the same research topic in many different settings (not to mention many research topics in a particular setting). The topic remains the same no matter what setting you are investigating.

Information about research methods

The third type of information you should look for is information about the methods you can use to collect and analyse data to answer your research questions. Research reported in the academic literature will describe the research methods that researchers have used to investigate a particular research problem and what kind of data they have collected and analysed. You can decide whether these research methods are appropriate for your own research project or whether you want to use different ones. **Parts 2 and 3** will explain research methods in detail.

You should look for information about suitable research methods in books and articles about how researchers studied your research topic, and in books or articles about research methods in general. General research methods books provide an overview of the research process. They may be aimed at undergraduates (for example Collis and Hussey 2003), taught postgraduates (for example Gill and Johnson 2002), research postgraduates (for example Easterby-Smith et al. 2002) or practicing managers (for example Saunders et al. 2003).

Other books focus on smaller aspects of research in more detail. Sage Publications (http://www.sagepub.co.uk) is the main specialist in the research methods area. It publishes everything from short, focused guides to a specific research method to specialised books and journals. These sources of information about research methods will come in useful once you have narrowed down your choice about collecting and analysing data, as they provide detailed, step-by-step guides. Some even aim to provide complete packages for doing a particular kind of research, for example for conducting a focus group or a survey.

Putting it all together

In **Chapter 2**, we described the emotional project life cycle. As you start grappling with the academic and empirical literatures, you may find your enthusiasm slipping into despondency or even despair. Do not fear! If you use a systematic process to search for information about your research problem and setting, your literature search will help you to develop a research project that is both interesting and original. As you search the literature, you will see opportunities to position your research and how your research can contribute to practical and theoretical knowledge.

Since there are few opportunities to identify a 'new-to-the-world' research problem, the research topic and research setting you choose may be your strongest claim to originality. If you are mainly interested in finding out about a theoretical problem, applying or testing your theory or model in a real-world setting will make your research more than just speculation. You can use your empirical evidence to support or disconfirm what you propose. Even if you are mainly interested in answering a practical problem, linking your research to a theoretical problem will help to keep your research from being just journalism or consulting. The **Student research in action 4.2** is an example of how a practical issue can be approached by linking it to a theoretical problem.

> *Student research in action 4.2*
> **IDENTIFYING AN OPPORTUNITY AND CONTRIBUTION**
>
> As we saw in **Student research in action 3.2**, Catherine began her research project with an interest in food retailing over the internet, with a project on customers' perceptions of service quality of online supermarkets in hand. For her doctoral research, she decided to investigate online small organic food retailers, a very different segment. As she read the literature on web service quality, she realised that rather than simply substituting online purchasing for physical shopping, as with grocery shopping, customers might have different motives for buying organic food over the internet.
>
> This led her to investigate the consumer marketing literature, a very different area of research. The consumer marketing literature directed her to theories of consumption, including Thorstein Veblen's theory of trickle-down consumption. By reading research written from this different perspective, she realised that she needed to take into account the fact that people purchase goods not only for their utility, but also for satisfying emotional needs, displaying an affiliation with certain groups, marking a significant life passage or expressing personal and social aspirations. Since nearly all the research on website quality was written from a technical perspective focusing on the design and efficiency of transactions, she identified the potential to do research that would fill in an existing 'blank spot'.

You may need to explore different combinations of research topic and questions, research settings and research methods before you make your final decision. As **Figure 4.1** suggests, you don't have to choose your research topic first and then decide on a setting. You might need to consider potential topics and potential settings.

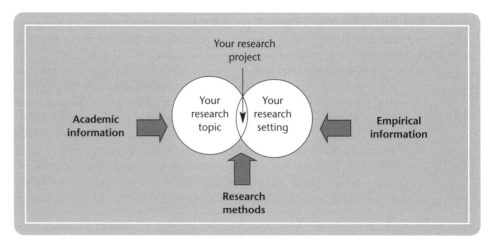

Figure 4.1 The relationship between research problem and research setting

What to look for: types of information and search domains

Now that you have some idea of what to look for, where should you start looking for this academic and empirical information about your research problem, setting and methods? In this section, we will describe what to look for and where to look for it. We will briefly describe the main kinds of sources that business and management researchers use in their search for information, including books, periodicals, databases and electronic publications. In **Section 4.2**, we will help you to identify search processes to find them and use your time and other resources effectively.

Peer review and credibility

When you are deciding what information you should be collecting, you should think not only about what you are going to use the information for, but also whether the information is appropriate for the purpose, especially the credibility of different sources. Different sources of information attract different amounts of scrutiny. A book published by an academic press has been reviewed carefully; no such scrutiny applies to web pages.

The process used to make sure that published research meets quality standards is **peer review**. Any peer reviewed book, article or conference proceeding has been carefully reviewed by other academics working in the same academic area. The highest standard of review is **double-blind** review, where the reviewers do not know who the author is, and authors do not know who is reviewing their work. This reduces the bias that might otherwise creep into the reviewing process.

Books

Books can be a good source of both academic and empirical information. In the UK alone, over 100,000 books appear every year (although this number includes fiction and other types of books that may not be useful to research). If you go onto a website such as Amazon.com or one of its country subsidiaries, you will be able to get an idea of how many books are in print on your research topic.

The internet is becoming a useful resource for finding books, especially ones that are rare or out of print and out of copyright. Depending on your research problem, you may be able to identify specialist collections of online books. The Gutenberg Foundation (http://www.gutenberg.org) has been especially active in publishing books online as they go out of copyright, and has put thousands of books in electronic form (e-texts) on the web, where you can access them free of charge. You can also purchase electronic books on both specialist sites and mainstream sites such as Amazon.com.

Compared with the explosion of online materials, books may seem old-fashioned, but they can be authoritative sources of information. They may also be the best sources of historical (noncurrent) information. On the minus side, because it takes a fairly long time to research, write and publish a book, the information in books may not be up to date in rapidly changing fields.

We can further divide the most relevant books for research into:

- **Textbooks** – books written specifically to support teaching, a good source of standard information, but unlikely to be comprehensive or up to date. Typically focused on a subject (marketing) or discipline (management). Examples include: Kotler (2004) *Marketing*, Slack et al. (2004) *Operations Management*, Brearley and Myers (2003) *Principles of Corporate Finance*.

- **Monograph** – a specialist book written on a single subject by a single author or a set of authors.
- An **edited volume** – a book compiled by one or more editors from a series of papers or chapters written by different authors. These may be specially commissioned or report the proceedings of a conference.
- Undergraduate and master's **dissertations** and doctoral **theses** – formal reports on research projects submitted by students to fulfil a degree requirement.
- **Reference books** – dictionaries, encyclopaedias, yearbooks, writing guides, thesauruses and statistical abstracts.

There are also many *popular business-related books* – books written for a general audience, typically by non-academic authors, for example, *In Search of Excellence* (Peters and Waterman 2004), *The One Minute Manager* (Blanchard and Johnson 1982), *Who Moved My Cheese?* (Johnson 2003).

Undergraduate and master's teaching relies heavily on textbooks and articles that interpret business and management research for nonacademic readers. Although textbooks are a good place to start, you should not stop there, especially if you are doing an extended or narrowly focused research project.

Not all books are equally credible, however, as sources of academic information. When you spot a book that looks likely to be useful for your research, you should ask yourself: 'Who wrote it? Why did they write it? Who published it?' If the book's authors or editors belong to a major research university, in most instances, they are more likely to be aware of and concerned about the standards for good research than a freelance author who is writing to make money.

Similarly, you should think about the book's main audience – is it scholars, students, managers or the general public? In a book written primarily for other researchers rather than a general audience, the authors are more likely to try to meet the standards for good research. On the other hand, authors writing for popular audiences such as managers often base these books on other people's research findings and not their own original research. (These books for popular audiences are sometimes called 'airport books' because they are designed and written to attract the attention of a traveller passing through a busy airport and looking for something to read on the journey.)

Finally, you should think about the organisation behind the book. If a book is published by an academic publishing house or a mainstream publishing house, the authors or editors are more likely to meet the standards for good research. If you can't find information about the book's authors or intended audience, you might use the publisher's reputation as a guide to the book's credibility. Academic publishing houses include university publishers such as the Oxford University Press and the University of Chicago Press, professional associations and commercial publishers such as Palgrave Macmillan, McGraw-Hill, Routledge and Sage. Books from these publishers are more likely to have been carefully reviewed by other academics and professional editors to make sure that the information in them is valid and reliable. For this reason, if you want to rely on evidence from books, you should try to rely on books from reputable presses.

Commercial publishing houses include Harvard Business School Press and the Free Press. Many have high standards but a few may not enforce the same kinds of peer review and professional editing – a case of 'let the buyer beware'. Similarly, some conference proceedings, such as the Academy of Management Proceedings are peer reviewed but some publish any paper that is accepted to be presented.

Given this range of books, and their different levels of credibility, how do you know which type of book you should emphasise in your literature search? This will depend on the goal of your research (solving a practical or theoretical problem), the size of your project and what degree you are studying for. A theoretically focused project should emphasise the more academic sources, whilst a practically focused project should emphasise the more practical books, all other things being equal. This may be a good question to ask your academic supervisor or project coordinator.

Periodicals

The second major source of academic and empirical information you should investigate is **periodicals**. Periodicals may appear regularly – daily, weekly, monthly or yearly – or irregularly. They include familiar sources, such as newspapers and magazines, and those that may be less familiar, such as academic journals.

Your library may have the most recent or current issue of a periodical on display. Libraries typically shelve older issues together, sometimes in bound volumes. They may also store older periodicals, especially newspapers, as **microfilm** or **microform** copies to save space and prevent physical damage to the originals by handling or the passage of time. You usually need a special reader to view microfilm or microforms. Electronic copies, which readers can view over a library's intranet or the web, are increasingly replacing microfilm and microforms.

The main periodical types that are relevant to your research are:

- **Academic journals** – peer reviewed periodicals, either general management (for example *Academy of Management Journal, British Journal of Management*) or subject-specific (for example *Journal of Marketing, Journal of Finance, European Journal of Operations Research*), which are mainly targeted to scholars.
- **Managerial journals** – periodicals, typically *not* peer reviewed, either general management or subject-specific, which are written for managers rather than scholars.
- **Newspapers** – daily or weekly publications of general interest, such as *The Times*, or special interest, such as the *Financial Times*.
- **Magazines** – weekly, monthly or quarterly publications of general interest, such as *Fortune* or *Management Today*, or special interest, such as *The Grocer*.

The quality of academic and empirical information varies across different types of periodicals, as for books. When you are looking at an article in a periodical, you should ask yourself, just as for a book, 'Who wrote this? Why did they write it? For whom is it written? Who published it?' Again, how much you should rely on each type of periodical depends on whether you are trying to solve a practical or a theoretical problem (although remember every research problem will have both an empirical and a theoretical component). Your academic supervisor will expect you to demonstrate more knowledge of the academic information than your business sponsor will. Your use of various types of periodical will also depend on other factors such as the type of project and the degree you are studying.

Most of your conceptual framework should come from academic journals. They may appear a bit formidable at first, especially if you are used to reading textbooks and articles from the *Harvard Business Review*, which may contain exactly the same information but be written to communicate to a popular audience. Academic journals are written for an academic audience with a detailed knowledge of the subject area and any specialist terms. They report the research methods in detail, together with mathematical equations or statistics if used. If you find them tough going, you may want to consult the **Additional resources** to help make sense of what has been written.

Because articles in academic journals are peer reviewed, they are more likely to be credible than general interest publications such as newspapers and magazines. However, they often have long lead times between when an article is first submitted and when it is published, sometimes two to four years, so that the information may not be current. **Table 4.1** gives examples of some academic journals and their intended audiences.

Many students find the articles in managerial journals, such as those shown in **Table 4.1**, easier to follow, because, although many of the authors are academics, they write mainly for managers and the public. Their main purpose is often to interpret serious academic research or trends for managers, so you should find them much easier to read than academic journals. The credibility of articles in managerial journals can be variable: journals such as *Harvard Business Review* and *California Management Review,* are as strict in reviewing articles as the good academic journals, but some managerial journals do not peer review submissions. Managerial journals may still be worth looking at even if you are doing a mainly academic project, because they tend to have shorter lead times than academic journals (typically six months to a year) so you may be able to find information that is more current than in academic journals. This may be important when you are researching new or emerging topics, where the articles published in academic journals have not yet begun appearing.

Business and trade magazines and newspapers such as *The Economist, Business Week,* and *Fortune* can be good sources of information about people, organisations, industries, countries and economies. Because they are published frequently, there is a much shorter lead time between the event being reported and the report being published. This also means that they can identify new and emerging trends more quickly than

Table 4.1 Examples of journals by audience

Type	Examples	Remit
General management	● *Academy of Management Journal* ● *British Journal of Management* ● *European Management Journal*	Covers a wide range of management topics written by academics for an academic audience
Discipline-specific	● *Journal of Operations Management* ● *Journal of Finance*	Covers a range of management topics within a specific subject area
Managerial	● *Harvard Business Review* ● *MIT Sloan Management Review* ● *California Management Review* ● *Business Horizons*	Covers a wider range of management topics written by academics for a managerial audience

academics can identify, study and write about them. On the other hand, you should keep in mind there is no peer review for the articles in these magazines – their main goal is to sell articles, not report on academic research.

Other sources of information

Company publications include news releases, brochures, financial reports, product specifications and so on. The internet contains millions of personal, organisational and corporate web pages, and the number of pages is growing exponentially. Many students have capitalised on the web's potential as an almost unlimited source of images, sounds and other knowledge resources. You should not rely on web pages for academic information, but they may be useful sources of empirical information. Anyone can put up a website, without any restrictions on the content, so they are less credible than peer reviewed research, or even unreviewed research. Additionally, pages can disappear as quickly as they appeared, so you may not be able to count on continued access to a web page.

More and more information is published electronically, whether in the form of electronic versions of printed books, articles or other publications, or publications that only ever existed in electronic form. Any information presented in this book on electronic publications will quickly go out of date, but some you might find useful are databases, electronic books and web pages.

A **database** is a compact way to present economic and other statistical data. It contains information structured in a unique way, which can be presented in a printed format such as OECD publications, electronically on magnetic media or on CD-ROM. Many business and management databases are now available to multiple users on networked CD-ROMs, including:

- *AMADEUS* (Analyse MAjor Databases from European Sources) – A database of annual accounts and graphed data for public and private European companies that can be searched by name, country or industry.
- *FAME* (Financial Analysis Made Easy) – A database of annual accounts and graphed data for public and private UK companies that can be searched by name, country or industry.
- *Forrester* – Reports on trends in technology and their impact on business.
- *Mintel* – a UK database of market reports in key areas of retail, leisure and finance.

We will describe these in more detail in **Chapter 6** when we discuss the analysis of secondary data.

Making sense of the types of information

Figure 4.2 presents a preliminary overview of sources of information, roughly classified by whether they are typically sources of academic or empirical information. When academics talk about searching the literature or doing a literature review, they usually mean the left-hand side of the figure. However, you can apply the search process to finding empirical information about organisations, people and practices on the right-hand side.

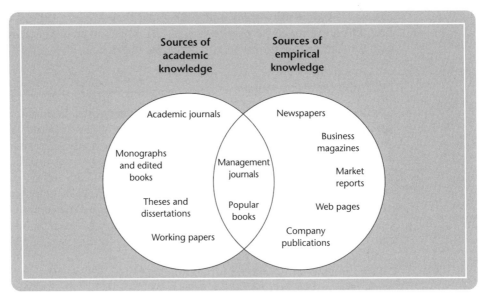

Figure 4.2 What do we mean by 'the literature'?

4.1.3 The library and internet as sources of information

As noted above, you will need to find both academic and empirical information to finish defining your research project (what you will study), and to begin designing it (how you will study it). The library and the internet are your most important gateways to both academic and real-world knowledge, and the two main knowledge resources you will be using in this stage of your research.

The library as a source of information

Your main library will generally be a 'one-stop shop' for your research projects. Most university libraries provide general support for mainstream study and therefore focus on general resources. You may need to consult other libraries, especially if your research problem is especially narrow or unusual.

Different libraries vary in the range and volume of resources. (If you are on a placement in or sponsored by an organisation, you may also have access to a corporate or organisational library.) Smaller universities often provide a single university library for all their students and faculty, whilst large universities may have dozens of libraries. If your institution has more than one library, some libraries may specialise in providing mainly teaching-related resources for undergraduates, such as multiple copies of core textbooks, and others in research-related resources for faculty and other scholars. You may have access to a departmental or faculty library specifically devoted to business and management studies.

A **copyright depository library** gets a copy of every book published in the country. Such libraries include the British Library in St Pancras, London, the Bodleian Library of the University of Oxford and the Library of Congress in the United States.

Specialist libraries are library-sized specialist collections. A large university may contain several or many specialist libraries (Oxford has over 100 libraries!) to serve faculties, departments, schools or other groupings. Specialist libraries may also be associated with museums, hospitals, charities or other stand-alone specialist institutions. You will usually need a reader's card or special permission to consult a specialist collection or visit a specialist library, as they are only rarely open to the public.

Some libraries also hold specialist collections relating to a particular topic or person. If you wanted to study scientific management, for example, you might want to visit the Stevens Institute of Technology, which maintains a specialist collection of materials on Frederick W. Taylor, many of which are unique. These are usually of more interest to postgraduate research students or professional researchers.

You may have already used your library to find assigned readings for classes and look up information for essays and projects. The library has traditionally been and is still your most important knowledge resource for finding academic knowledge, and can be a useful source of real-world knowledge. However, few people know how to take full advantage of the library's resources. Your library may hold periodic library inductions that provide basic training in using library resources, and there may be an electronic induction session on your library's intranet. Your library may provide handouts or training – if you haven't done so already, take advantage of this free help.

Find out whether your library employs a **subject librarian** who specialises in business and management studies, or a more general specialist in social sciences who takes responsibility for business and management studies. This librarian may be able to point you to brochures or information sheets that answer common questions about research in business and management studies. Beyond that, your subject librarian can provide expert knowledge on what resources are available to you and where and how to look for them.

To locate materials held by your library, you will need to use your library's catalogue, which may be a card catalogue, or available electronically over the web or on the library's intranet. The **catalogue** lists information about each book, serial or other entry. You can search the catalogue using the index, an alphabetical list by the first word (excluding a, an or the) of the title, or a keyword search of the author, title, date or subject.

Your physical access to these resources may vary according to the type of library and the library's regulations. In an **open-stack library**, you can roam through the shelves, or stacks, by yourself. This can be useful, since you may spot interesting-looking books or other resources in the neighbourhood of whatever you are looking for. In a **closed-stack library**, you will have to place a request for the resource, which will be fetched by someone else, and may take minutes, hours or even days to appear. Some libraries operate under both systems, with older or rarer resources kept in the closed stacks and newer ones kept in open stacks.

Your library can provide access not only to the physical resources housed in a physical building, but also to electronic resources that literally span the world. University libraries were originally founded to hold books, which at the time were too scarce, expensive and valuable for any person to own more than a few. Today's libraries contain not only books but also other useful types of information such as reference books, periodicals, theses and multimedia resources. You can access resources beyond the physical capability of even the largest bricks-and-mortar library through a **virtual library**. In particular, virtual libraries provide electronic access to journals and other serials, sometimes in addition to and sometimes instead of hard copies – some periodicals appear only in electronic form now.

If you identify a resource that looks interesting but isn't held in your library, it might be worth checking with your library and/or subject librarian whether it is possible to borrow the resource or have a copy made through the interlibrary lending system. In the UK, it is possible to borrow many books from the British Library through such loans.

The internet as a source of information

Published information – whether in printed or electronic form – is expanding so fast that any library can only hold a small sample of it. You can search the web for text, images, sounds and videos using various search engines. The web has billions of pages: to search through them efficiently, knowing how to use search engines such as Yahoo!, Google and AltaVista is important.

Even the most comprehensive search engine does not cover all the pages on the web. **Metasearch engines** submit searches to multiple search engines simultaneously so you cover more of the information available on the web. They may also do useful things with the results, such as removing duplicate results, providing keywords or clustering the results. Metasearch engines include Ixquick, which claims to be the world's 'most powerful metasearch engine', and KillerInfo.

You should probably search for academic resources through your physical or virtual library first, and then use the web to follow up any intriguing references you find. The internet, particularly the web, is now often the first place to look up information, but the library has the edge on reliable information since it has 'gatekeepers'. Since anyone can publish anything on the web, knowing whether what you have found is accurate and useful may be difficult, so you should begin your search using your university library and then follow it up using the internet.

Moreover, the web, like other new technologies, has been exploited by people with unfriendly motives as well as altruistic ones. Although it is more difficult inadvertently to enter a porn site than most people claim when caught downloading pornography, it is not unknown for pornographers to hijack respectable-sounding sites or even 'legitimately' set up domains with names close to respectable sites. Furthermore, websites can download spyware or malware onto your computer without your knowledge which can report on your activities, or even perform nefarious activities such as logging every keystroke and transmitting credit card numbers. At the very least, they can considerably slow down your computer's performance. These days, it's a good idea to install your own software to guard against such unwanted programs, just as other programs help to guard against viruses and spam. These programs, which may scan your computer for unwanted 'visitors' so that you can remove them, or prevent them from being downloaded in the first place, may be available as shareware or by subscription. If you use the internet a lot, you should check your computer frequently for unwanted programs.

Whatever search engine you use may also let you use a 'family filter', which will cut down on 'adult content' results in your search. If you are looking for information on the business entrepreneur Richard Branson and his various Virgin enterprises, you probably won't be interested in naked pictures of Branson or worse! If you do need to look up something that might be linked to such sites, for example if you are looking at the drug Viagra, you should design your search carefully to restrict your results to legitimate sites.

4.2 HOW SHOULD YOU SEARCH?

An ideal search starts broadly and quickly narrows down to a focused search for just the right amount of information. As we noted above, you will be looking for information about your research topic, research setting and sample. You may find it easier to search for these separately rather than together. You will probably be looking in different places and for different kinds of information.

Even if you have started with what you think is a focused research problem, you will probably be able to find quite a lot of leads that you could investigate, especially when you are searching for information about both your research problem and research question. It's easy to waste hours or even days in the library or on the internet and come up with a lot of interesting information that doesn't help you to make progress in your research.

If you spend a little time developing a search strategy, you will spend less time searching and be more likely to find what you are looking for. We will describe two search strategies that you can use to search the library and web. As usual, you may need to consult more specialised resources – see the **Additional resources** at the end of this chapter.

4.2.1 Defining what you are searching for

The logical place to start is with your literature search for information about your research topic. In **Chapter 3**, we noted that some research topics fit neatly within a single field, while others cut across fields or even into other disciplines.

You may want to search:

1. Within a particular field of study in business and management, such as finance, marketing or organisational behaviour, where your topic is studied
2. In related fields of management, when a topic is studied across more than one field of business and management
3. In related disciplines, such as economics, psychology or statistics, when a topic is studied in less applied areas.

If you are investigating a research topic that fits within a single business or management field, you are likely to find all of the information that you need in the books and journals related to the area. For example, net present value calculations are typical of finance, whilst manufacturing planning and control systems are typical of operations management. Additionally, if you are studying a research topic that spans more than one discipline, for example research on e-commerce and e-business cuts across many management areas, you may need to search in several different management fields, even if you end up deciding to stick with just one perspective on your topic. Since business and management studies draw from outside areas such as economics, sociology and psychology, you may need to decide whether you should extend your search to other disciplines.

A good way of keeping track of this is to use a mind map, the hierarchy of concepts or the Venn diagram presented in **Chapter 3** to help you to identify all the relevant perspectives on your research topic. **Figure 4.3** shows a further example of the use of mind maps, where a student used this technique to demonstrate the complexity of the area she was studying.

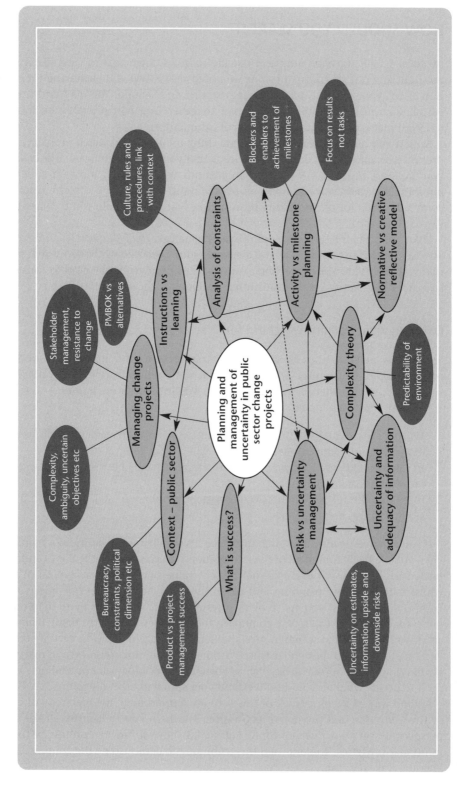

Figure 4.3 Mind map of literature search relevant to public sector change projects

Source: Courtesy of Liz Heywood

What to look for

Your top priority is to find a focused set of academic books or journal articles that will let you identify:

- What are the main arguments related to my research problem?
- What key concepts have other researchers identified as important?
- What key frameworks, if any, have other researchers developed, including propositions and hypotheses?
- What key theoretical perspectives have other researchers applied, and are there different ones?
- What methods have other researchers used to collect and analyse data?
- What are the most important findings in these articles?
- What key themes link these articles? Are there any gaps?

We suggest that you start with your textbooks to identify at least one or two key articles or authors who work on your research topic. This can be tricky, especially when different fields call the same topic by different names, for example purchasing versus procurement. We will discuss potential problems with searching by keywords below.

If you get stuck, you should ask your project supervisor for some leads – he or she may know a surprising amount about the topic. Even if you don't end up keeping these articles or authors in your set of core articles, this is probably easier than starting with a random search of books, academic journals and the web.

4.2.2 Deciding how to search

Even if you know what you are looking for, one of the biggest problems in searching for information is getting started. If you are starting without a good idea of what you are looking for, we suggest two strategies, shown in **Figure 4.4**, the snowball search and the keyword search. You can use the results of your first search to adjust your strategy – to make your search broader or narrower.

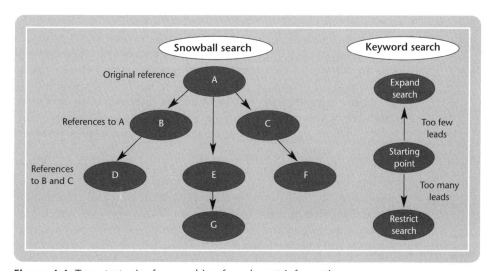

Figure 4.4 Two strategies for searching for relevant information

If you can find the name of a key author in your topic area in a textbook or assigned reading, you might want to use a **snowball** or **egocentric search**. Your first step is to identify one or more key works – usually books or articles -- by that author on the topic. You can then see what previous research that author has used by looking at the references or bibliography – a sort of intellectual 'family tree' where these works represent the generation before this key work. You can apply the same procedure to the key references to see what sources they refer to – the 'grandparents' of this work. You can keep this search strategy going until you have run out of likely-looking authors to pursue. One problem with this strategy, though, is knowing when to stop. Another is that if there is more than one important stream of research, you may not be able to identify the other(s) using this strategy.

If you have started with a key work published more than two or three years ago, you can also see who has been influenced by it – its 'children' and 'grandchildren' so to speak. You can see who else has referred to this author by using a specialised database such as the International Social Science Citation Index that keeps track of references and citations.

So when should you stop looking? Students frequently ask their academic supervisors: 'How many sources do I need for this project?' Some students mistakenly think that their project examiners measure the quality of a literature search based on the number of different sources in the bibliography. The right answer is: 'Enough to get the job done.' It is more important at this stage to strive for quality rather than quantity. You should try to identify a few high-quality academic articles closely related to your research topic, rather than everything that someone has written about your research topic. You will not have the time to read more than a few articles or books thoroughly, anyway, or skim read more than a few dozen.

Another way to search is to identify a conceptual framework or other key idea that gives you focused **keywords** which you can use to search, such as 'organisational citizenship', 'behavioural finance theory' or 'ISO 14000'. You can use a **keyword search** of your library's catalogue and/or databases such as Business Source Premiere to identify a starting set of authors and articles. We discuss keywords below in the context of searching more efficiently.

Searching more efficiently

The number of books in a good library, the number of articles on a particular subject and the number of web pages may be beyond human comprehension. If you don't know what you're looking for, or you don't use the right search terms, you will only get mediocre results. Your results when you search your library's catalogue, electronic databases or the web will only be good as your search strategy. This includes the sources you are searching, the means you use to search them and the terms you use to define your search.

You should start by making sure that you are searching the right source for the information you want. As we have noted, information related to your theoretical problem is more likely to come from the academic literature, whilst information related to your practical problem is more likely to come from empirical sources. Make sure that you are not searching in the wrong place, and check that you have not combined your academic and empirical searches.

You should also put some effort into identifying the best keywords to describe the key concepts you are investigating. A keyword search will be most effective if your keywords are neither too broad (will lead to too many results) nor too narrow (will lead to too few results). This means that you need to understand the key concepts you are looking for so you can define your search parameters. If your keywords are too broad, you will get too many 'hits' to be able to investigate the, for example, 'marketing' or 'operations'. This may require some experimentation, or you may need help from your supervisor, subject librarian or information specialist.

Many concepts can be expressed as synonyms or close alternatives. For example, if you wanted to find out more about total quality management, relevant results might be listed under 'total quality management', 'total quality', or 'TQM'. Business Source Premier, an electronic publications database, includes a thesaurus that lets you see what terms you can use to search effectively. Similarly, AltaVista has a built-in 'intelligent agent' that gives you alternative or related terms.

Each search engine also uses a particular **syntax** that describes how you should enter your search terms and how you can combine these search terms to increase the relevance of your results. Library catalogues and electronic publications databases often predefine specific fields to increase the power of your search. For example, if you wanted to search your library for books by Frederick W. Taylor, you could specify him in the author field; if you wanted to search for books about him, you could specify him in the subject field; and if you wanted to search for books either by or about him, you could do both.

SU (Taylor, Frederick W)
TI Taylor, F W

Most search engines also give you the power to search by either one criterion at a time or two or more criteria. These often draw on a mathematical function known as Boolean logic, in which the basic operators are *true, false, not, and* and *or*. Using *and* and *not*, you can restrict your search, using *or*, you can widen it. Boolean logic is a powerful tool for researchers. Suppose that you wanted to look for information on cross-cultural research on the psychological contract. If you simply typed in 'cross-cultural psychological contract' your search results would identify any research that covered any of these three terms – a very large number indeed. If you typed in 'cross-cultural and (psychological contract)' you would narrow down the search to only those works that included both 'cross-cultural' and 'psychological contract' – a much smaller number. If you wanted to start with articles that focused on this topic particularly, rather than just mentioning it, you could further specify the search using TI to indicate that the search engine should look for that word(s) in the title; SU to tell the search engine to look for that word(s) in the subject; AU to find a particular author. The syntax is as follows: 'ti (cross-cultural) and (ti (psychological contract))' which would only identify those works with both terms in the title. You could also use *or* to expand the search or look for alternative terms, for example if you thought 'cross-cultural' and 'international' might be used as synonyms: '(ti (cross-cultural) or ti (international)) and (ti (psychological contract))'.

Don't forget that American and British spellings often differ, so that you may want to search for both 'organisational' and 'organizational' to identify works from both sides of the Atlantic.

4.2.3 Reading and recording what you find

If you are used to getting your information mainly from textbooks and other sources where academic research has been 'translated' for you, you may find reading academic articles, especially in some of the more heavy-duty journals, hard going. You may find the books by Girden (2001) and Locke et al. (2004) useful in understanding how to read this kind of article.

Locke and his colleagues (2004: 77) suggest that you are less likely to be overwhelmed by your reading if you take a systematic approach to recording the details of your reading and organising your records. They suggest that for each article you read, you should record the following information on a single sheet of paper:

1. *Citation* – the complete details of the study
2. *The purpose of the study* – why did the authors do it and why did they think it was important?
3. *Theoretical background* – how does the study fit with the literature?
4. *Sample* – who did the authors study?
5. *Research setting* – where did the study take place?
6. *Method* – how were the data gathered?
7. *Data* – what data were gathered?
8. *Analysis* – how were the data analysed?
9. *Results* – what were the primary results of the analysis?
10. *Conclusions* – what did the authors say about the results?
11. *Limitations* – how should we interpret the study?
12. *Significance* – what did you learn from this study?

Activity

Use the above format to record the information from one of the articles you have identified. Have you recorded any information that you would normally have missed? Has anything been left out that you would normally include?

 4.3   ## HOW SHOULD YOU USE THE INFORMATION YOU FIND?

Once you have searched the literature, what should you do with the information you have found? One thing you can do is write a literature review that provides either the foundations or the jumping-off point for your research. Whether you write this as part of defining your project or as part of describing your research will depend on your approach to your research, which we will describe in **Chapter 5**.

Some researchers will collect all their academic and empirical information before they start collecting and analysing data. They will identify and develop any theories, models or concepts during the project definition stage. Any propositions or hypotheses that they investigate will need to be based in the literature. They will also need to gather all the information that they need to design their research. If you take this approach, you should be able to draft much of your project report before you start collecting and analysing your data.

On the other hand, other researchers may do a broad search of the literature during the project definition stage, and postpone any major engagement with the literature until they have started their data collection and analysis. This is because they may not know what major themes will emerge from their data, so they cannot predict what theory, models or concepts they will need to explain their data.

If you are expected to write a formal literature review as part of your project report, you may find it worth consulting more detailed guides to searching the literature and writing a literature review. For the social sciences, Chris Hart has written two excellent full-length books, *Doing a Literature Review* (1998) and *Doing a Literature Search* (2001). Other books are listed at the end of this chapter in **Additional resources**.

No matter when you write your literature review, you need to know how to use the material you have found correctly. Giving appropriate credit when you use someone else's words or ideas is a crucial research skill. You need to learn the principles of citation and referencing, so that you can refer to other people's research when you are writing. This will help you to avoid plagiarism, which is intellectual property theft and taken seriously in academic institutions. You should also avoid violating copyright law by understanding the limits to the fair use of other people's published and unpublished information, including web resources.

4.3.1 Writing a literature review

Unlike journalism and consulting, the business and management research on your research topic forms a key part of your research project. A formal literature review, as we noted above, is a part of the project definition or project description phases of any research project. A **literature review** is a critical analysis of the business and management research on your topic that positions your research in its theoretical context, shows that you understand the current state of the research topic and supports any conceptual framework (theories, models, concepts, hypotheses) that you plan to investigate.

You therefore make a major contribution to your research project with your literature review by finding and interpreting other people's research. Writing a literature review shows that you understand the research that has been done on your topic, and can even be an output from your research project. Being able to critically analyse the literature and use it to support your arguments is a key research skill.

In a literature review, you must do more than show that you have read what has been published about your research topics, including the arguments and evidence that other authors have presented. You must do more than summarise other people's research, the 'laundry list' approach, which is more likely to put your reader to sleep than get them excited about your research. A critical review evaluates not only individual research reports, but also the entire topic area, identifying the strengths and weaknesses of existing research and any gaps that your research might fill.

This review creates the 'opening' in the literature that you are going to address in your research project. You can use this discussion to show that your research topic is worth studying and your project will contribute to business and management knowledge. You might want to show that your research will contradict what everyone has always thought or explore an area that is new to the world.

Davis (1971) suggests some ways you can argue this in your literature review:

- 'It has long been thought ...' – this is what researchers have always taken for granted

- 'But this is false ...' – but some or all of this may not be true
- 'We have seen instead that ...' – the new assumptions are true
- 'Further investigation is necessary ...' – new research is made possible by this logic.

One way to organise your literature review is around the themes that emerge (or fail to emerge) as you read the literature. What categories might emerge? Golhar and Stamm (1991), for example, identify three key themes in the just-in-time literature as JIT's role in global productivity, differences between JIT and other systems such as MRP and OPT, and the practices associated with JIT, and classify the articles they read into one of these three key themes.

Hart (1998) identifies three evaluation structures for writing up the literature review:

- *Summative* – describes what is known about the research problem
- *Analytical* – describes the basis for investigating the research problem
- *Formative* – compares and contrasts the various points of view on the research problem.

Another way of organising your literature review, suggested by Creswell (1994), is to structure one section around each of your key concepts. For example, if you are examining the relationship between customer satisfaction and the steps that organisations take to recover from service failures, you might write a section on customer satisfaction, one on service failure and another on service recovery. You would then need a final section that explains the relationship between failure/recovery and customer satisfaction, which acts as a 'hook' to set up your own research project.

If possible, you should look at some literature reviews that have been published in your topic area, or even your research problem. Blackwell's *International Journal of Management Reviews* specialises in management reviews and the well-established *Journal of Economic Literature* does the same for economics. You might also search your electronic publications database for literature reviews that have been published as stand-alone articles. Some recent examples include:

- Heneman, Robert L. 2003. Job and work evaluation: A literature review, *Public Personnel Management*, **32**(1): 47–71.
- Kitchen, Philip J. and Spickett-Jones, Graham. 2003. Information processing: A critical literature review and future research directions, *International Journal of Market Research*, **45**(1): 73–98.
- Luo, Wenping, Van Hoek, Remko I. and Roos, Hugo H. 2001. Cross-cultural logistics research: A literature review and propositions, *International Journal of Logistics: Research and Applications*, **4**(1): 57–78.
- Bartell, Sherrie Myers. 1998. Information systems outsourcing: A literature review and agenda for research, *International Journal of Organization Theory and Behavior*, **1**(1): 17–44.
- Mitchell, Vincent-Wayne. 1995. Organizational risk perception and reduction: A literature review, *British Journal of Management*, **6**(2): 115–33.

No matter which approach you choose, the end result should be, as Hart (1998: 198) argues, a literature review that:

1. Demonstrates that you clearly understand the research topic

2. Identifies all the major studies related to your research topic
3. Identifies the different points of view on the research topic
4. Draws clear and appropriate conclusions from prior research
5. Clearly states a research problem
6. Proposes a way to investigate the research problem
7. Demonstrates the relevance and importance of the research problem.

As we mentioned at the beginning of this chapter, you may write your literature review early in your research as the basis for your research plan or later on to integrate it with your data collection and analysis. We will describe which one you might choose in **Chapter 5**. We will also return to the literature review in **Chapter 13** and **Chapter 14**.

4.3.2 Giving credit to other people's words and ideas

When you use the academic or empirical information you have found, you should always give appropriate credit to others for their words and ideas by identifying the original source. The correct way to do this in your project report is to cite the source of the words or ideas in the body of your project report. You should also list the source at the end of your project in the **references**, a list of sources or a bibliography.

Citing other people's words and ideas in your text

As you write your project report, you should give credit each time you refer – directly or indirectly – to someone else's words and/or ideas in the form of a **citation**. The three common systems for citations in academic writing are author–date (Harvard), numbered (Vancouver) and notes (footnotes or endnotes).

Your project requirements should give you specific instructions how to format citations and set up your reference list. If not, consult your project supervisor, project coordinator or librarian to see what local practice is. If your project coordinator or sponsor has asked you to use a particular system, he or she will be annoyed if you don't use it.

Citations are so important that national standards and international standards have been developed for citing published and unpublished sources:

● The International Standards Organisation (ISO) has published ISO 690:1987 *'Information and documentation – Bibliographic references – Content, form and structure'* and ISO 690-2:1997, *'Information and documentation — Bibliographic references – Part 2: Electronic documents or parts thereof'*
● The British Standards Institute (BSI) in the UK has published three standards for citations, BSI 1629, *'Recommendations'*; BSI 5605, *'Recommendations for citing and referencing published materials'*; and BSI 6371, *'Citations to unpublished documents'*

These are not the only sources of citation standards. Professional editors and authors in the UK use the *Oxford Style Manual* (Ritter 2002), while those in the USA often rely on *The Chicago Manual of Style* (2003), the most authoritative source of information for American writers and editors. A version of *The Chicago Manual of Style* condensed for students is Turabian (1996). Publishing houses, such as Harvard Business School Press and journals, such as the *Academy of Management Journal* generally set and publish their own standards for citations.

Citing in style

We recommend that you use the **Harvard author–date system** for citations and references, unless you have specific instructions otherwise. It is the most common system in business and management, along with many other social sciences. (Occasionally, business and management researchers use the **Vancouver system** of numbered references or Chicago system of footnotes.)

In the Harvard system, 'you know immediately whose work has been referred to and when it appeared' (Baker 2000: 227). 'It saves space and delivers a cleaner and simpler text than do notes of any kind' (Dunleavy 2003: 126).

Table 4.2   Examples of Harvard author–date citations and references

	Single author	Two authors	Three to six authors
Entry in reference list	Pentland, B.T. 1992. Organizing moves in software support hot lines, *Administrative Science Quarterly*, **37**(4): 527–48.	Sutton, R.I. and Hargadon, A. 1996. Brainstorming groups in context: Effectiveness in a product design firm, *Administrative Science Quarterly*, **41**(4): 685–718.	Voss, C.A., Roth, A.V., Rosenzweig, E.D., Blackmon, K. and Chase, R.B. 2004. A tale of two countries' conservatism, service quality, and feedback on customer satisfaction, *Journal of Service Research*, **6**(3): 212–40.
Making reference to ideas but not quoting or paraphrasing			
Direct reference	Pentland (1992)	Sutton and Hargadon (1996)	First reference:* Voss, Roth, Rosenzweig, Blackmon and Chase (2004) Second and subsequent references: Voss et al. (2004)
Indirect reference	(Pentland 1992)	(Sutton and Hargadon 1996)	First reference:* (Voss, Roth, Rosenzweig, Blackmon and Chase 2004) Second and subsequent references: (Voss et al. 2004)
Quoting or paraphrasing the author's words			
Direct reference	Pentland (1992: 529)	Sutton and Hargadon (1996: 690)	First reference:* Voss, Roth, Rosenzweig, Blackmon and Chase (2004: 221) Second and subsequent references: Voss et al. (2004: 221)
Indirect reference	(Pentland 1992: 529)	(Sutton and Hargadon 1996: 690)	First reference:* (Voss, Roth, Rosenzweig, Blackmon and Chase 2004: 221) Second and subsequent references: (Voss et al. 2004: 221)

* Many publishers use et al. even for the first reference

Whatever system you are using, you must give credit to other people's words and ideas whenever you quote someone's words directly or indirectly by paraphrasing them and whenever you quote someone's ideas, directly or indirectly. We give some common examples in **Table 4.2** below, but you should consult a technical guide such as the *Oxford Style Manual* or whatever source your project guidelines direct you to for comprehensive and precise directions for citations.

In the Harvard system, you cite the source of anyone else's words or ideas that you are generally referring to in your project report by giving their name and the date of the published (or unpublished) material. As you refer to a source in your text, you should refer to a single author by his or her last name alone (Bloggs 1990), more than one author by their last names (Bloggs and Golightly 1992) and an organisation by its name (OECD, *Wall Street Journal*). After the first reference to three or more authors (Bloggs, Golightly and Sprog 1994 – but see also note to Table 4.2), you will refer to the source using 'et al.' to refer to the second and subsequent authors (Bloggs et al. 1994), but you will always refer to two authors by both their names (Bloggs and Golightly 1992). Students often find it difficult to work out how to use 'et al.', the Latin phrase that stands for 'and others', not 'and another'. Always cite both authors when there are only two, but use et al. for three to six authors for all references after your first reference. When there are seven or more authors, use et al. for even the first reference.

The author–date combination is usually enough to make sure that each reference has a unique citation, but some authors are prolific enough to publish more than one article in a year. In this case, you should add a letter of the alphabet to the year (Bloggs, 1997a, Bloggs 1997b), to make sure that each source has a unique citation.

When you are *directly quoting* or *paraphrasing* someone else's words or a specific idea, to avoid plagiarism, you should refer to the page you found the words or idea on, and set those words so that it is clear they are not yours. You can set quoted material in one of two ways:

1. for short quotations or paraphrases, enclose the words in quotation marks
2. for longer quotations or paraphrases, block indent the entire set of words.

Making sure that you give other people appropriate credit is a key research skill. You need to understand the principles involved, take careful notes and refer back to these notes when you are writing. We will return to this in **Section 4.3** below.

Constructing a reference list

When you write your project report you will need to provide a **reference list** of the sources you have cited. (We will discuss where in your project report your reference list will go in **Chapter 13**.) Your project guidelines will usually give you more specific information about how to do this, and many business schools and universities have a standard set of guidelines for students. You can find technical guidance on preparing a reference list in your project guidelines and the books listed in the **Additional resources** at the end of the chapter. Your supervisor may also have strong preferences for or against a certain format.

The main things to remember are:

● The list should be in alphabetical order by the first author's last name, for example Smith, John or Smith, J.C. depending on the format you are using.

- If there is more than one work by the same author:
  - Single-authored works come first; if there is more than one they are listed in ascending order by date; for example Smith, J.C. (1992) followed by Smith, J.C. (1993).
  - Multiple-authored works come next, in order of the second (and so on) author's last name.
- All references are combined in a single list unless your project requirements tell you to separate them, that is, do not include separate reference lists for books, articles, newspaper, web references and so on.

When you are writing up your research, citing your sources and preparing your reference list will be much easier if you have kept a comprehensive list of the sources you have consulted. Even if you think you will end up using only some of the sources, try to record everything you have consulted systematically. Otherwise, no matter how hard you look, you will never be able to find one or two key references again! If you later want to find some information that you half-remember reading but haven't recorded where you found it, it will take you a lot of time in the library or on the computer trying to track it down, or you will have to leave it out of your report. The number of references you are missing will be directly related to the closeness of your project end date!

If you record details of each source in the format required for your reference list or bibliography, you will spend less time formatting your references during the critical writing up period. This record might be in a Word document, a spreadsheet or a specialised referencing software program such as EndNote or Reference Manager.

You may find slight differences between different formats, such as whether to use quotation marks around journal article titles, how to capitalise titles, whether to enclose date references in parentheses and so on. If you make sure that you have all the information you need to hand, you will save yourself a lot of work. A standard example is shown in **Table 4.3**.

Many students skimp on their reference lists because they run out of time, have not recorded their sources or do not think that the reference list is important. Your references may be the first place that experienced examiners look (Rugg and Petre 2004). If you have an incomplete, poorly formatted, thoroughly inadequate reference list, your

Table 4.3	Standard formatting for references
Books	**Name. Date published. *Title*. Where published: Publisher.**
Monograph	Aldrich, H.E. 1999. *Organizations Evolving*. London: Sage.
Chapter in an edited volume	Ventresca, M.J., Szyliowicz, D. and Dacin, M.T., 'Institutional innovations in governance in the global field of financial markets', in Djelic, M.L. and Quack, S. (eds), *Globalization and Institutions: Changing the Rules of the Economic Game,* Edward Elgar, 2003.
Article in an academic journal	Meyer, A.D. 1991. Visual data in organizational research, *Organization Science*, **2**(2): 218–36.
Article in a business/ trade publication	Roth, D. 1999. Putting fluff over function, *Fortune*, 03/15/99, pp. 163–5.

reader is likely to start reading your project report with the impression that you have carried out the rest of your research in an equally shoddy manner. If you misspell, miscite, or otherwise mangle something that your reader, your reader's supervisor or your reader's best mate has written, you can be sure that this will jump right out at them! And be assured that it will be the one citation for which you have failed to provide a reference (usually because it is obscure and you can't find it again) that your reader will flip to your reference list to find.

Taking notes

Your conscientiousness in taking notes will affect not only how useful the information you get out of your sources will be to your research project, but also whether you can give credit to these sources and avoid plagiarism. Before laptops, photocopiers and laser printers, researchers used to write notes by hand on index cards, to which they would refer when writing up their research project. One set of index cards recorded the precise details of each reference source consulted, often in more detail than required for the reference list. For example, you might want to include the call number of any library book, so that you could find it again quickly if you need to. The other set of index cards recorded both paraphrased information and exact quotes from these sources. Because of the amount of hard graft involved in making notes on index cards, researchers tended to learn best practice quickly.

Today, most of us make notes directly on laptops or desktop computers. Furthermore, instead of having to consult resources physically in the library, most of us can either photocopy or download materials, so that we have our own copy of it. This means that it is easier to collect the information physically. It also means that if you file your printed copies in an organised way as you go along, it will be much easier to lay your hands on that critical paper when you need it, instead of having to search frantically through a three-foot high stack of paper at the last minute. You should carefully record information about web pages and other internet sources that you consult, especially those you find using a search engine, metasearch engine or portal, since there is no guarantee that a page you consult today will still be around tomorrow, even if you have bookmarked it.

However you choose to deal with your source material, the key principles of taking notes are the same:

- record your sources, not only for your reference list but also so that you can easily find them again
- record your information, and make sure that you distinguish clearly between quoted (or narrowly paraphrased) material and summarised material.

4.3.3 Ethical problems to avoid

Because you are using other people's ideas and words, of which they have intellectual if not legal ownership, this stage of your research can raise technical and ethical issues that may be new to you. You absolutely must avoid plagiarism. You do this by citing your sources. You should also be wary of copyright violations, which you may commit even if you do give credit to other people.

Plagiarism

Plagiarism, not giving appropriate credit to other people for their ideas, is an increasingly serious concern for researchers – who should avoid committing it – and examiners – who hope to avoid seeing it. Booth et al. (2003: 167) put it bluntly:

> You plagiarise when, intentionally or not, you use someone else's words or ideas but fail to credit that person. You plagiarise even when you do credit the author but use his exact words without so indicating with quotation marks or block indentation. You also plagiarise when you use words so close to those in your source, that if you placed your work next to the source, you would see that you could not have written what you did without the source at your elbow.

Most universities now have strict policies against plagiarising. Whether you plagiarise deliberately or accidentally, because it is stealing, if you are caught, you will be punished. You could face penalties ranging from failing the piece of work in which plagiarism was committed, failing the unit for which the work was submitted and even expulsion from the degree course. Since there is no statute of limitations on plagiarism, you could be risking your degree even if you think you have got away with it: if plagiarism is detected some years later, your degree could still be rescinded.

Whether you think that plagiarism is acceptable or not, given the risk of getting caught and the severity of the punishment, the amount of effort that it would take you to plagiarise successfully is probably more than the effort it would take to give credit appropriately. You might also consider whether plagiarism is compatible with learning.

Despite the enormous rise in the cases of plagiarism reported today, students are probably no more predisposed to plagiarise than past generations: new computer and communications technologies have vastly facilitated plagiarism. It is easy to use the web to search for information and copy or download it in text form, tempting students to copy large amounts of material and *deliberately* plagiarise by incorporating this material without changing or acknowledging it, or only thinly rephrasing it. Because many students take notes and compose their drafts directly on the computer, careless note-taking and drafting can aid and abet *inadvertent* plagiarism by confusing other people's words with your own. Even professional writers who should know better have been found plagiarising: recently several popular historians were severely embarrassed when plagiarism was detected in their books.

It has been argued that international students are at a disadvantage because the ground rules about plagiarism are different in different cultures, especially at undergraduate level. There is no cultural relativism in plagiarism. Despite the standards applied in your own culture, you will be judged by the rules that apply where you are taking your degree. 'Ignorance of the law is no excuse.' You should review your student handbook and/or code of ethics to make sure that you are complying with them.

Universities, especially those that teach large class sections, have started using software programs that can detect probable plagiarism. However, most experienced markers don't need software to tell whether a student is plagiarising, although it is very efficient at finding the plagiarised source by comparing it with printed texts. Most plagiarism is so obvious that it can be spotted right away: plagiarised text seldom sounds the same as text the student has written. (Of course, if the student has plagiarised the entire document and the examiner has never read anything else by this student, this won't apply.) Examples of practices we have experienced are in **Student research in action 4.2.**

> ### *Student research in action 4.2*
> ### STUPID PET TRICKS
>
> A lecturer gave a student a copy of a paper he had written. Later, he was surprised to find large sections of the paper repeated word for word in the student's thesis.
>
> Another student plagiarised three entire pages, word for word, from Geert Hofstede – probably the best-known author on international management culture – in his transfer paper. This did not impress his examiner with his academic integrity.

Avoiding copyright infringement

Beyond plagiarism, the use of other people's research has ethical implications in the area of what you are actually allowed to photocopy, download, copy or quote. Before the web and virtual library resources, our ability to record information was limited to taking notes on index cards, or the cost and availability of photocopying. Today, we can print out or photocopy printed material, such as articles and books, free or cheaply. This makes it easy, in most cases, to photocopy or download enough published material for a specific project or even more. We can also download images, sounds and other media from the internet with the click of a mouse. **Student research in action 4.3** shows how what can appear relatively straightforward procedurally, may not be acceptable practice.

> ### *Student research in action 4.3*
> ### THE WAY FORWARD – OR WAY OUT OF BOUNDS?
>
> Corey wanted to study how humour was used in office settings to defuse tense situations. He decided that he would analyse the British television series *The Office* as part of his summer research project. Since he had videotaped the three series of the programme, he planned to use these tapes as the basis for his research. He also planned to illustrate his research using images from the show's website and some fan websites, and quote some of the dialogue in his report. As long as he acknowledged the source of the material, he figured it would be OK. A casual conversation with one of this book's authors, who was writing this chapter at the time, alerted him to potential problems. When he brought this up with his supervisor, they both agreed that he needed to investigate this much more carefully.

In contrast to how easy it is to print out or photocopy material, or download files, our permission to use materials created by other people is becoming more limited. Other people's work is generally protected by **copyright**, whether it is published or unpublished (for example a thesis), for a long period of time (often up to 70 years after the author's death). Materials that are covered by copyright include:

● Literary, dramatic, musical and artistic works (for example books, plays, musical scores and paintings)

- Computer-generated works, databases, sound recordings, films, broadcasts and cable programmes.

Even if something you want to quote, photocopy or reproduce electronically does not have the © symbol and a copyright statement, it is still copyrighted as long as it is an original work in material form. (It is, however, good practice to include a statement such as '© 2005 University of Swindon. All rights reserved' on anything you publish in written or electronic form to remind other people.)

In the UK, the Copyright Licensing Authority (CLA) licenses universities, libraries, museums and other educational institutions to photocopy extracts from magazines, journals and books. A notice from the CLA should be next to any photocopying machine you use, which tells you what you are and aren't allowed to copy.

Understanding copyright is important because copyright law restricts:

- what you can photocopy from magazines, journals, books, music scores and other publications
- what you can quote from unpublished materials
- what you can download from websites and other internet sources
- what you can quote or otherwise reproduce in your project report (written or oral presentation) or on web pages and other electronic publication of your research.

Copyright is covered by national, EU and international law. (The most recent UK law is the Copyright, Patents and Design Act 1988, although the EU Directive on Copyright has now been adopted. The international standard is the Berne convention for the protection of literary and artistic works.) Reproducing or downloading materials for educational purposes, such as a coursework assignment, has traditionally been governed by the principle of **fair dealing**, which means that you are allowed (within limits, of course) to reproduce and use various materials if your purpose is study, criticism or review. Under the principle of fair dealing, you can copy:

- 5% or one chapter, whichever is greater, of a book
- 10% of a small book or report of 200 or fewer pages
- one article from any one issue of a journal.

However, use of these materials for commercial purposes (which technically includes sponsored research or any other research for which you will be paid) does not fall under fair dealing.

If you plan to use material from the internet in your research or project report, you should make sure that you understand the copyright restrictions that apply to electronic works, such as web pages, including the text, images, data and other materials you may find. The principle of fair dealing does not apply here. You may be allowed to print out a copy of a web page for personal use, but unless the web page gives permission or you have explicit permission from the author or copyright holder, that is all. If you want to quote text from a website, you need copyright permission from the author (or copyright holder, if not the same), rather than just acknowledging the source of the material as for traditional publications. The Joint Information Systems Committee (JISC) and the Publishers Association have published a code of conduct that you may want to consult.

Another area where copyright law may prevent you from using material without explicit permission from the author is unpublished material. This includes (in the UK and many other countries) student theses and dissertations, student projects and unpublished company reports, such as memoranda or minutes of meetings.

Traditionally, materials used in essays and research reports that have only been produced for examination, such as doctoral theses, have been considered as 'fair dealing'. However, you should note that copyright restrictions do apply to downloaded cartoons (for example Dilbert) and images from web pages, which frequently show up in student reports and presentations. These would probably not be considered 'fair dealing' because electronic resources are excluded. If you find a nifty picture of Barbie on the internet to illustrate your report on advertising to children, it is definitely not fair dealing to download that picture and use it to illustrate your report or presentation without the permission of the copyright owner. Given that it may take up to a year to get copyright permission, and most student projects are considerably shorter than a year, you should be careful about keeping to 'best practice' when doing your research and writing up your findings and/or recommendations.

You should also note that, even if you are accessing material in other countries using the internet, you are restricted by:

- the copyright law of the country where the website is hosted
- the country in which you are downloading or using material
- international law.

One last word. As well as being careful about other people's rights, you should make sure that you understand how copyright applies to your own research project, including your written report and any electronic publications, such as web pages. In some cases, your university may own the copyright to your work. If you have been sponsored by a business or organisation, they may own the copyright to your work, even if they have only provided access or sponsorship. You should check this explicitly rather than assuming anything.

 ## SUMMARY

Being able to identify, find and make use of information from the library, internet and other knowledge resources in your research is a key skill and one that will affect the quality of your research project. Understanding how to define and set up searches is a useful skill.

Your physical library contains books, periodicals and multimedia resources that will help you investigate the academic research on your research problem and the empirical knowledge about your research setting. Virtual library resources provide electronic access to even more resources, including financial and economic databases and periodicals. Your librarian can also be a valuable resource in helping you to refine your search and telling you about extended library services such as interlibrary loans and access to other academic and specialist libraries.

The internet, especially the web, gives you global access to information, but managing the quality and the quantity of information can be a problem. Global search engines and metasearch engines, along with subject-specific portals, can help you to deal with the size and complexity of the web.

Once you have found relevant information, you need to manage and use it. The academic information about your research problem can be used in a literature review, which covers the theories, frameworks, concepts and research methods employed by other researchers on the same or relevant research problems. You can use the information about your research setting to develop your research methods further.

An important aspect of this process is learning how to give other researchers appropriate credit for their words and ideas. Deliberately or inadvertently omitting this credit is plagiarism, a form of intellectual property theft that can lead to severe penalties. You can avoid plagiarism by good practice in taking notes, giving credit in your writing by citing the authors who have contributed ideas and words and constructing a reference list or bibliography that gives a complete list of these sources. Learning the correct format for citations and references is another useful skill.

 ## ANSWERS TO KEY QUESTIONS

Where and how do I find information for my research project?

- Your physical and virtual library should give you access to books and periodicals that tell you what previous research has been done on your research problem
- Textbooks, monographs, edited books, conference proceedings, reference books and periodicals (especially academic journals and annuals) which report previous research are your main sources
- You can use the internet, especially the web, to search for additional information, such as working papers and reports

What business and management research is relevant to my research project?

- Primary research – information you collect yourself from people and/or organisations
- Secondary research – information you collect from already published sources
- The internet can be used to identity and acquire information about your research project and research setting

What theories, models and concepts are relevant to my research topic?

- Looking at previous academic research will give you information about the theories, models and concepts that are relevant to your research topic

How do I find more information about my research setting and sample?

- Business and trade publications, including newspapers and magazines
- Books and reports on specific areas, including marketing reports from organisations such as Mintel, and financial databases such as AMADEUS and FAME
- The web may be especially useful in searching for information about your research setting, since many businesses, organisations and so on have web pages

What methods for collecting and analysing data have other researchers used?

- Analyse how researchers have collected and analysed data in previous research on your research problem
- See if there are any different methods being applied in related research problems
- You can consult the research methods literature itself – specialist books, journals, and articles on research methods, including general research guides and specific technical guides

How do I use this information?

- Good notes will help you to make sense of the information
- Writing a literature review will help you make sense of what previous researchers have done and found, help you to develop a research design and give you a head start on writing your project report
- Giving other researchers appropriate credit for their words and ideas is a key skill here

REFERENCES

Baker, Michael J. 2000. Writing a literature review, *Marketing Review,* **1**(2): 219–47.

Blanchard, K. and Johnson, S. 1982. *The One Minute Manager.* New York: Morrow Books.

Booth, Wayne C., Columb, Gregory G. and William, Joseph M. 2003. *The Craft of Research,* 2nd edn. Chicago: University of Chicago Press.

Brearley, R.A. and Myers, S.C. 2003. *Fundamentals of Corporate Finance.* London: McGraw-Hill.

The Chicago Manual of Style: For Authors, Editors and Copywriters, 2003. 15th edn. Chicago: University of Chicago Press.

Collis, Jill and Hussey, Roger. 2003. *Business Research,* 2nd edn. Basingstoke: Palgrave Macmillan.

Creswell, John W. 1994. *Research Design: Qualitative and Quantitative Approaches.* Thousand Oaks CA: Sage.

Davis, Murray S. 1971. That's interesting! Towards a phenomenology of sociology and a sociology of phenomenology, *Philosophy of Social Science,* **1**: 309–44.

Dunleavy, Patrick. 2003. *Authoring a PhD: How to Plan, Draft, Write and Finish a Doctoral Thesis or Dissertation.* Basingstoke: Palgrave Macmillan.

Easterby-Smith, Mark, Thorpe, Richard and Lowe, Andy. 2002. *Management Research: An Introduction,* 2nd edn. London: Sage.

Gill, John and Johnson, Phil. 2002. *Research Methods for Managers,* 3rd edn. London: Sage.

Girden, Ellen R. 2001. *Evaluating Research Articles from Start to Finish,* 2nd edn. Thousand Oaks, CA: Sage.

Golhar, Damodar Y. and Stamm, Carol Lee. 1991. The just-in-time philosophy: A literature review, *International Journal of Production Research,* **29**(4): 657–76.

Hart, Chris. 1998. *Doing a Literature Review: Releasing the Social Science Research Imagination.* London: Sage.

Hart, Chris. 2001. *Doing a Literature Search: A Comprehensive Guide for the Social Sciences.* London: Sage.

Johnson, S. 2003. *Who Moved My Cheese?* New York: Andrews McMeel.

Kotler, P., Saunders, J. and Armstrong, G. 2004. *Principles of Marketing: European Edition.* Harlow: FT Prentice Hall.

Locke, Lawrence F., Silverman, Stephen J. and Spirduso, Waneen W. 2004. *Reading and Understanding Research,* 2nd edn. Thousand Oaks CA: Sage.

O'Leary, Z. 2004. *The Essential Guide to Doing Research.* London: Sage.

Peters, T. and Waterman, R.H. 2004. *In Search of Excellence: Lessons From America's Best-run Companies.* New York: Profile Business.

Ritter, Robert M. 2002. *The Oxford Style Manual.* Oxford: Oxford University Press.

Rugg, Gordon and Petre, Marian. 2004. *The Unwritten Rules of PhD Research.* Maidenhead: Open University Press.

Saunders, Mark, Lewis, Phillip and Thornhill, Adrian. 2003. *Research Methods for Business Students,* 3rd edn. Harlow: Financial Times/Prentice Hall.

Slack, N.D.C., Chambers, S. and Johnston, R. 2004. *Operations Management.* Harlow: FT Prentice Hall.

Turabian, Kate L. 1996. *A Manual for Writers of Term Papers, Theses and Dissertations,* 6th edn. Chicago: University of Chicago Press.

 ## ADDITIONAL RESOURCES

Delamont, Sara, Atkinson, Paul and Parry, Odette. 1997. *Supervising the PhD: A Guide to Success.* Buckingham: Open University.

Delamont, Sara, Atkinson, Paul and Parry, Odette. 2004. *Supervising the Doctorate.* Maidenhead: Open University Press.

Fisher, D. and Hanstock, T. 1998, *Citing References,* Oxford: Blackwell.

O'Dochartaigh, N. 2001, *The Internet Research Handbook,* London: Sage.

Resources on copyright and plagiarism

Lyons, P. (ed.). *JISC/TLTP Copyright Guidelines.* JISC and TLTP 1998. (ISBN 1 900508 41 9)

Oppenheim, C., Phillips, C. and Wall, R.A. *The Aslib Guide to Copyright.*

Web documents

http://ahds.ac.uk/copyrightfaq.htm

http://www.leeds.ac.uk/library/rights/faq.htm
Answers some frequently asked questions about copyright, especially electronic works

http://www.ariadne.ac.uk/issue5/copyright/

http://www.ukoln.ac.uk/services/elib/papers/other/
The JISC/TLTP Copyright Guidelines

eLib – The Electronic Libraries Program
JISC and Publishers Association guidelines on copying electronic materials

British Association of Picture Libraries and Agencies

The Copyright Licensing Agency
Information on the CLA, copyright, CLA licences, and an excellent directory of copyright organisations

Design and Artists Copyright Society
For information on copyright in artistic works, collection society for licensing of slide libraries and so on

Her Majesty's Stationery Office
Information on crown and parliamentary copyright, the copyright unit, electronic texts of statutory instruments (SI), and publishing/copyright guidance notes

Ordnance Survey
Information on OS products, crown copyright and licensing for OS mapping

Performing Rights Society Ltd

World Intellectual Property Organisation (WIPO)
For information on international copyright treaties

Key terms

academic information, 96
academic journals, 105
catalogue, 109
citation, 119
closed-stack library, 109
conceptual frameworks, 98
copyright, 125
copyright depository library, 108
database, 107
dissertations, 104
double-blind, 103
edited volume, 104
empirical information, 96
evidence, 100
fair dealing, 126

Harvard author–date system, 120
keywords, 114
keyword search, 114
knowledge claim, 100
literature, 98
literature review, 117
literature search, 98
magazines, 105
managerial journals, 105
metasearch engines, 110
microfilm/microform, 105
monograph, 104
newspapers, 105
open-stack library, 109
peer review, 103

periodicals, 105
plagiarism, 124
reference books, 104
reference list, 121
references, 119
snowball (egocentric) search, 114
specialist libraries, 109
subject librarian, 109
syntax, 115
textbooks, 103
theses, 104
Vancouver system, 120
virtual library, 109

Discussion questions

1. Should you consult the internet or the library first to find out more about the theoretical aspects of your research topic?

2. Can you believe everything you read on the internet?

3. Why is the process of peer review considered so important in scholarly publishing?

4. 'If I am trying to solve a practical problem, reviewing the literature is irrelevant.' Discuss.

5. In quantitative research, is it OK to do your literature review after you've collected and analysed your data?

6. 'A good literature review is one that describes everything ever written on my topic.' Yes or no?

7. Why is knowing how to use citations and references an essential skill for researchers?

8. Is ignorance of your university's rules about plagiarism an adequate defence if you are caught?

9. Is plagiarism a 'victimless crime'?

10. Is anything on the internet 'fair game' as far as research materials go?

Workshop

Task

Using the topic area that you identified in **Chapter 2** or **3** workshop, carry out a basic literature search. You should:

1. Identify the subject area(s) relevant to your topic, and note the main texts for these subject areas.

2. Check in your library and at online bookstores for specialist books on the area.

3. Carry out a search of newspapers and business periodicals.

4. Identify keywords and do an internet search.

5. Use your library online journal article service to identify potentially relevant articles.

6. Browse through relevant journals in hard copy in your library to identify current views of this general area.

7. Classify the type of publications that you have found using the classifications of books and periodicals from this chapter.

8. Prepare a mind map of the topic area.

2 Designing your research

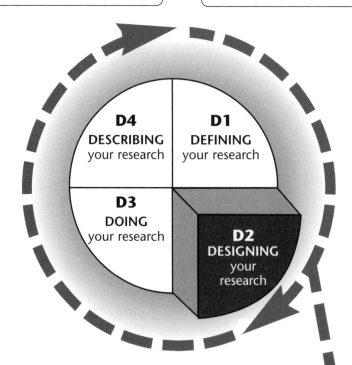

Relevant chapters

13 Answering your research questions
14 Describing your research
15 Closing the loop

Key challenges

● Interpreting your findings and making recommendations
● Writing and presenting your project
● Reflecting on and learning from your research

4

Relevant chapters

1 What is research?
2 Managing the research process
3 What should I study?
4 How do I find information?

Key challenges

● Understanding the research process
● Taking a systematic approach
● Generating and clarifying ideas
● Using the library and internet

1

D4
DESCRIBING
your research

D1
DEFINING
your research

D3
DOING
your research

D2
DESIGNING
your
research

Relevant chapters

 9 Doing field research
10 Analysing quantitative data
11 Advanced quantitative analysis
12 Analysing qualitative data

Key challenges

● Practical considerations in doing research
● Using simple statistics
● Understanding multivariate statistics
● Interpreting interviews and observations

3

Relevant chapters

5 Scientist or ethnographer?
6 Quantitative research designs
7 Designing qualitative research
8 Case studies/multi-method design

Key challenges

● **Choosing a model for doing research**
● Using scientific methods
● Using ethnographic methods
● Integrating quantitative and qualitative research

2

chapter 5

Scientist or ethnographer?
Two models for designing and doing research

Key questions

- How can I answer my research questions?
- What are the scientific and ethnographic approaches to research design?
- What is the 'logic of research' for business and management research?
- What roles do theory and data play in management research?
- What are the assumptions underlying the scientific and ethnographic approaches?

Learning outcomes

At the end of this chapter, you should be able to:

- Decide whether to answer your research questions using a scientific, ethnographic or eclectic approach
- Explain the research process and content associated with each approach
- Explain how research philosophy enables us to understand the principles underlying consistent research design

Contents

INTRODUCTION

Part 1 explained how you can define your research topic and the research questions that you will be working on, and plan and schedule how you will carry out your project. In **Part 2**, we consider the next stage of your research process – that of research design. A research design includes the general approach you will take to answering your research questions, as well as the specific techniques you will use to gather, analyse and interpret data.

This chapter introduces two major research design approaches, whilst the remaining chapters in **Part 2** consider how to gather data and the chapters in **Part 3** consider how to analyse data. The approach you select influences your research plan, your role in the research process and how you assess the quality of your research. We characterise the first approach as the scientific approach, exemplified in this book by Frederick W. Taylor and the Hawthorne researchers, and the second approach as the ethnographic approach, exemplified by William Foote White. The scientific approach is influenced by the logic of research in the natural sciences and is associated with research projects that focus on quantitative data. The ethnographic approach is influenced by the logic of research in the social sciences and is associated with research projects that focus on non-quantitative – or qualitative – data.

Before you can decide which approach may best suit your research project, you need to know more about them. In **Section 5.1**, we describe each research approach, and the essence of each approach. This is vital. You should make sure that you understand this before continuing with your research. In **Section 5.2**, we explain how each approach influences the timing and sequence of your research tasks, especially the use of theory and the relationship between theory and data in the research process. In **Section 5.3**, we explore the broader implications of each research approach, which include not only the process of your research project but also its content: each research approach is linked with a different world-view and 'theory' of research, which influences what research questions you can ask, what methods you can use and what data you can collect.

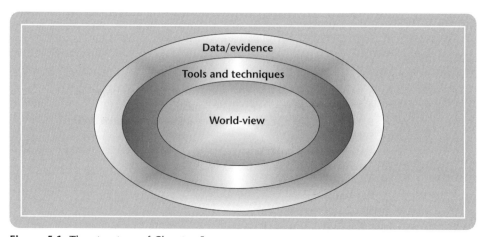

Figure 5.1 The structure of Chapter 5

We provide a summary table at the end of each section. We believe understanding your research approach will improve your project. First, understanding these two approaches will help you to understand why there are so many different ways to do business and management research. It will help you to make good choices about your selection of research methods, make them in a justifiable way and recognise the implications of these choices. If you are using this book to help you to conduct a research project, the approach you choose will affect your research process from this point forward and, as a result, your path through the rest of this book. **Chapters 6, 10 and 11** focus on research methods associated with the scientific approach. **Chapters 7, 8 and 12** each focus on research methods associated with ethnographic research. How you interpret and report your research, discussed in **Chapters 13 and 14**, will depend on which approach you choose. Both approaches have implications for how you work inside an organisation, as we discuss in **Chapter 9**.

Second, understanding your research approach will help you to assess other people's research, particularly the business and management research you find in your literature search. After you have read this chapter, you should understand why research is a better way to answer questions about the world than is journalism or consulting.

5.1 WHAT ARE THE SCIENTIFIC AND ETHNOGRAPHIC APPROACHES?

Once you have identified your research questions, you need to put together a plan that describes how you will collect and analyse data to answer those research questions. Every research project follows roughly the same process outlined in the plan for this book:

1. Define a research topic and research questions
2. Design your research
3. Do your research – collect and analyse your data
4. Describe your research – interpret and report your findings.

However, this only describes the research process in a very generic way. There is still quite a bit of variety in how you might design, do and describe your research. In an ideal world, you could choose the best combination of research methods – how you will collect and analyse your data – to answer your research questions.

However, as we show in **Figure 5.2**, your research design will be subject to various constraints. In the real world, your choices are limited by the time and resources you have available and the amount of effort you are prepared to invest in your research project. These constraints also include the theory and any prior studies you are looking to emulate or repeat, and any subject preferences. If you are working on a sponsored project or placement, you may be limited to investigating the practical problem and setting of this project. Your personal preferences also need to be taken into account – you may prefer certain kinds of research questions and certain research methods, and you may select the best research topic to suit these questions and methods. We will return to these issues later in this chapter.

A major influence on your research design will be the topic you are studying and the 'rules' for doing research on that topic and in general. These rules deal with the **logic of research**, and describe what research questions you can ask and what methods you can use to answer them.

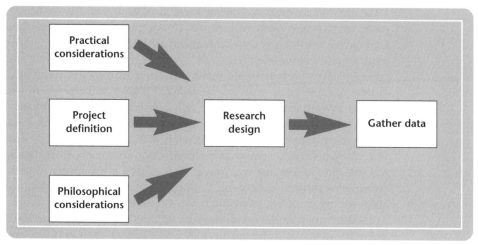

Figure 5.2 Where do you go from here?

As noted above, the two main approaches to research design in business and management can be described as the scientific and the ethnographic. Before we describe these two approaches in detail, **Student research in action 5.1** shows how an awareness of the differences between these two approaches led a student project team to radically redefine their project brief and do an outstanding project. It also demonstrates the choice of research design and the interplay between this and your research questions.

Student research in action 5.1
A LITTLE DAB'LL DO YA

A toiletries manufacturer sponsored an undergraduate student project team to find out why sales of their male grooming products had the highest marketing share among 14 to 16-year-olds but only a miniscule share among 18 to 22-year-olds. The company had already commissioned extensive consumer marketing research that gave them specific details about product usage. The company wanted some more in-depth information before they invested in a revised advertising campaign.

The students started by discussing how to find out more about this problem. The company could provide the students with access to point-of-sales data from supermarkets, pharmacies and other retail outlets. The students first considered using a traditional market research approach to find out more about attitudes towards the brand among university students. Whilst they did not have the resources to send out an army of market researchers armed with clipboards or personal computers to ask male university students a barrage of questions, they could use focus groups and questionnaires to find out what grooming products the men used and why they used those particular products. They were certain to be able to get enough students to complete the questionnaires to carry out statistical analysis of the questionnaire results. The focus groups would help them understand what questions to ask on the questionnaires.

This type of research, gathering data by asking questions that you have decided in advance, is consistent with the scientific approach to business and management research. As you will see in **Chapter 6**, questionnaires are a popular method of gathering data that answer specific, well-defined questions, whose answers can be expressed as numbers for statistical analysis. If they chose this research design, the students would need to make sure that they constructed their surveys carefully, selected a representative sample of students, and collected enough data for statistical analysis to be valid. This is consistent with the scientific approach to research, which focuses on quantification. Many researchers prefer the scientific approach, because they understand what the numbers mean and can take action based on them, for example to advise the company how it could reverse the drop among older consumers by targeting its marketing to likely buyers.

> *Student research in action 5.1 cont'd*
>
> On reflection, however, the students realised that the interesting question for them was not 'who' purchased (or didn't purchase) the company's products, but 'why' the market share changed so emphatically with age group. They decided to study the role that grooming products played in the life of male students – something that market research and POS figures could not reveal. They used video diaries, collages and other creative research techniques to find out more about what was going on. This focused their attention on the question of 'what influences what products male university students purchase', rather than who purchases them and how much they purchase.
>
> The use of video diaries, collages and other creative techniques resulted in data that were mainly impressions, words and pictures, rather than numbers. To make sense of these data, the students needed to find patterns of common meanings and interpret them as themes, rather than analysing them statistically.

This type of research, gathering data to answer questions that are themselves suggested by the data, is consistent with the ethnographic approach to business and management research. As you will see in **Chapter 7**, direct observation is a popular way of gathering data that answer questions that cannot be specified in advance and are better represented as words than numbers.

> *Student research in action 5.1 cont'd*
>
> At the end of the project, the students had made some fascinating and revealing findings about male university students and their relationship to male grooming products, including the significant amount of time most male students spent in front of the mirror getting their look just right, the need to have the 'right labels' in their rooms or bathrooms and the widespread sniffing and even borrowing of products among friends. These findings helped the company to understand that the popularity of their products among 14–16-year-olds actually *created* the sales gap when men got to university, in particular when their mothers were no longer buying their toiletries and they made their own choices.

By choosing between a scientific approach and an ethnographic approach, the students were choosing between measuring behaviours and finding meanings associated with those behaviours. Because measurement and meaning are different aspects of social behaviour, the scientific approach and the ethnographic approach are associated with different research methods, although this is a matter of 'more often' than 'always'. If the students had chosen the scientific approach, they could have used surveys to gather students' impressions and feelings in the form of words, or they could have counted the occurrence of various motifs or behaviours in the video diary and other qualitative data. The students could even have combined different methods in a single study, which we will consider in **Chapter 8** on case study and multi-method research designs.

5.1.1   Scientific and ethnographic approaches to research and the research process

In this chapter, we will use the terms 'scientific' and 'ethnographic' to contrast the two main research approaches. This does not mean that ethnographic research is *unscientific*, or that scientific research excludes the study of cultures. We have chosen these terms because they reflect the main world-views associated with the two approaches, as well as the main sources of methods, techniques and thinking. The key characteristics of the two approaches are summarised in **Table 5.1**.

In the example above, the students chose between collecting data that were best expressed as numbers – quantitative data – and data that were difficult to reduce to numbers – qualitative data. Because different research methods are often used for the collection or analysis of quantitative and qualitative data, the research methods themselves are often described as quantitative or qualitative. Indeed, the terms 'quantitative' and 'qualitative' are often used to describe the overall research approach. According to O'Leary (2004: 99), however: 'For my money, the two most confusing words in the methods world are quantitative and qualitative.'

Whether you choose a scientific or an ethnographic approach will have a major effect on your research process. These two approaches have 'alternative starting and concluding points, [and] different steps between these points' (Blaikie 2000: 25). In the scientific approach, you develop a complete research plan before you start to collect data. If the students had chosen a scientific approach, they would decide exactly what data they wanted to collect to find what was happening with the brand and its

Table 5.1   A comparison of the scientific and ethnographic approaches

Characteristic	Scientific approach	Ethnographic approach
Questions that can be answered	What, how much	Why, how
Associated methods	Survey Experiment Databases	Direct observation Interviews Participant observation
Data type	Predominantly numbers	Predominantly words
Finding	Measure	Meaning

customers. Before they started collecting data, they would specify in precise detail what questions they needed to ask to collect those data, so that they could develop a standardised questionnaire to give to a large number of male students. This approach often requires a fairly extensive literature review, in order to make sure that you ask the right questions. By deciding on the questions in advance, you can limit the responses to a simple set of responses or even just numbers (for example 'What hair products do you currently buy?', 'How frequently do you buy them?'). These answers can be quickly transcribed onto a spreadsheet and analysed using statistics to identify patterns of behaviour. This is a highly *structured* approach to doing research: the students could identify each stage in advance and each stage could be carried out relatively independently.

In contrast, by choosing the ethnographic approach, the students let the precise nature of the observations of male student behaviour and even some of the questions to emerge as they were doing their research. In this case, the students decided they needed to closely observe how male students actually used grooming products 'in the wild', so that they could build up a picture of these behaviours rather than trying to identify all the questions and data they would need in advance. They needed some starting point to help them to decide where to look and what to look for, but they didn't do a detailed literature review until they started making sense of the materials they had collected. The data themselves – video images, collages and verbal impressions – are different from survey responses. As you can see, this represents a more *unstructured* approach to doing research. Each stage of the study depended on what emerged from the data they had collected – in particular by analysing the themes they saw.

5.1.2 The scientific approach – a brief overview

A brief look at the management literature will show the influence that the scientific approach has had on the development of the body of knowledge. The workshop in **Chapter 1** discussed Frederick W. Taylor and the Hawthorne experiment researchers as examples of the scientific approach to business and management research, along with Stanley Milgram.

A fundamental principle of the scientific approach is: 'If you can measure it, you can understand it' (Michael Faraday). For example, F.W. Taylor was concerned with applying the 'scientific principles' he had used in experimenting with tool steel to managing workers. Here, he analysed what the workers did by measuring their movements – the loads, the distances moved and the time that each movement took. By understanding what they did, he was able to redesign the work they undertook and propose better methods for doing tasks. He also proposed extending this logic to how workers should be supervised and managed. This shows an early emphasis on the scientific approach and on measurement in business and management research.

We will now discuss some other characteristics of the scientific approach, the worldview of scientists and the subjects associated with the approach.

How do scientists view the world?

The scientific approach originated in the natural sciences, including biology, chemistry and physics, which are mainly concerned with natural objects and phenomena. Research from a scientific approach is based on making observations using our senses or through the use of scientific instruments or other measuring devices. Scientific research focuses on measurement as the way of understanding something of interest. The scientific researcher looks for general patterns, which can be interpreted as theories or 'laws'. Consider Newton's laws of physics, for instance, which predict general properties of matter and motion and are predominantly derived from experimentation and observation. Scientists view the natural world as real and capable of being studied *objectively*, that is, scientists do research 'as if' they can study the world without being influenced by personal opinions or beliefs about what they will find. Whether scientists support a particular political party, religion, or football team should not influence what they discover or what they choose to study.

This approach to doing research on the natural world has been adopted by many researchers for doing research on the social world, including business and management research. Instead of looking for physical laws, scientific researchers may seek to develop general principles about how people, organisations or social systems behave. They focus on what these social units have in common, rather than individual differences. For example, the market research carried out by the consumer products firm identified a general problem – that sales of their products dropped as their target consumers aged. But this only identified what happened, not the reasons underlying the drop. Scientific research by the students might have clarified this, but might not have revealed the deeper meaning of the drop in market share.

Who are the 'scientists' in business and management research?

Business and management researchers who use the scientific approach in their research often come from subjects that look at physical systems or the general behaviour of people, organisations or other social units. For example, finance research often investigates the behaviour of investors in financial markets, with personal information about these investors being irrelevant. Subjects associated with the scientific approach include economics, finance, consumer marketing, operations management, information systems and decision sciences such as operations research and management science. This does not mean that researchers in these areas only take a scientific approach, but it is the 'prevailing approach' in each of these areas.

The role of theory in developing a research design

In the scientific approach, an extensive literature review often takes place as part of developing the research design. The concepts and relationships identified in previous research often form the foundation for the present research project. In some cases, the research project itself focuses on collecting data to test a theory or set of propositions put forward by another researcher. Motivations for doing this kind of research include:

- *Replication* – can we duplicate what the original researchers found out?
- *Extension* – can we find similar results in different contexts?
- *Comparison* – which theory (among competing theories) is the most useful to explain or predict the world?

For instance, one student wanted to test whether the Balanced Scorecard (Kaplan and Norton 1992) could be used to motivate employees. The student formally stated the relationship as the hypothesis: 'The level of employee motivation will be higher where the Balanced Scorecard has been adopted than where it has not been adopted.'

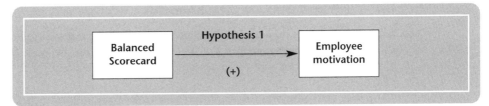

Figure 5.3 A conceptual framework

He then developed a research project to collect data to test this hypothesis. In this case, he found that the staff reported being more motivated in the departments where the Balanced Scorecard was being used. Whilst this particular research did not prove that adopting the Balanced Scorecard *caused* motivation to be higher, only that they occurred simultaneously, the data supported this link between the Balanced Scorecard and motivation.

In the scientific approach, researchers often use a literature review to develop a **conceptual framework** that describes both the key issues and concepts they are interested in and the relationships they expect to find between them (Blaikie 2000: 27). A conceptual framework or model is often included as part of an academic article that takes the scientific approach. For instance, the student who was studying the relationship between the Balanced Scorecard and employee motivation had a simple conceptual model, as shown in **Figure 5.3**.

The scientific method

The scientific approach is derived from a particular way of doing research known as the **scientific method**, a generally accepted set of procedures for developing and testing theories. It is an idealised model to arrive at what scientists consider to be truth. The key ideals of this model are objective observation and measurement and careful and accurate analysis of data. In applying the scientific method, scientists try to set aside their preconceptions about how the world works and gather data using 'objective' methods such as laboratory experiments, where they are able to control conditions and repeat experiments over and over again with only slight variations. Such a *closed system* allows them to rule out alternative explanations for their findings and propose that (at least under certain conditions) one thing is linked to another.

We can only use objective methods if we ourselves are objective. The researcher must be separate from what he or she is studying in order to be objective. This distance may come from physical distance (for example sending out a postal survey), social distance (for example the authority of the researcher as a 'social scientist') or procedure (for example separating the planning and execution of research). This distance, as well as external control by peer review (see **Chapter 4**), makes sure that personal bias is minimised.

When the social sciences started to become recognised areas of study, they were highly influenced by the logic and process of scientific research, so they borrowed the scientific method for the social sciences. The scientific model for research has thus significantly influenced social research, both as 'the way' to do research and as a way not to do research. Although business and management researchers study different topics and use different methods from natural scientists, many researchers believe that the scientific method is the best way to do research, 'as if' we are natural scientists.

The scientific approach – a practical example

As described above, if you take the scientific approach, you may be able to write nearly all your research report before you ever collect any data. Because this approach is highly structured it is often appropriate for a short project since you know how long each stage will take.

Suppose that you were researching customer satisfaction with an online travel retailer and have decided to use an online questionnaire to gather data about customer satisfaction. Before you start collecting data, you could:

- Come up with a series of research questions and hypotheses to test customer satisfaction, for example 'Customers who are highly satisfied with their first online purchase are more likely to repurchase from the same retailer.'
- Specify each aspect of your research plan before you start collecting data (this will be covered in detail in **Chapter 6**).
- Design, pre-test, and pilot your survey before you started collecting your data.
- Set up a spreadsheet for your data, and even run some statistical analysis with dummy data.
- Calculate the number of responses you need to test your hypotheses.
- Design your research report.

As described above and shown in **Figure 5.4**, quantitative research is relatively straightforward once you have decided what research questions you will ask. Although you might have to revisit some issues, once you have decided how you will collect and analyse your data you have made all the major decisions that will affect your research process.

5.1.3 The ethnographic approach – a brief overview

Although the scientific method and the scientific approach unquestionably influenced the early development of business and management studies, the ethnographic approach and the ethnographer as role model are equally important. **Ethnography** is concerned with the study of culture and is an important research approach in areas such as anthropology and sociology. Early ethnographic research focused on exotic, faraway people, such as the American Samoans studied by Margaret Mead in the South Pacific. However, many ethnographers today focus on cultures closer to home, such as high-tech workers, Harley-Davidson owners or even *Star Trek* fans.

An ethnographer is more likely to pick up on differences between cultures if he or she tries to blend in and learn from watching rather than walking around with a clipboard and a list of questions. Ethnographic study is more open-ended – ethnographers start not knowing exactly what they might find or even how they might get there. Much of the learning will emerge along the way and from the journey itself. Ethnography is much better at finding out about meaning rather than measurement, through investigating feelings, attitudes, values, perceptions or motivations, and the state, actions and interactions of people, groups and organisations. In interpreting these, researchers consider their properties – hence the association of ethnography with qualitative research.

The study of 'street corner society' by William F. Whyte described briefly in **Chapter**

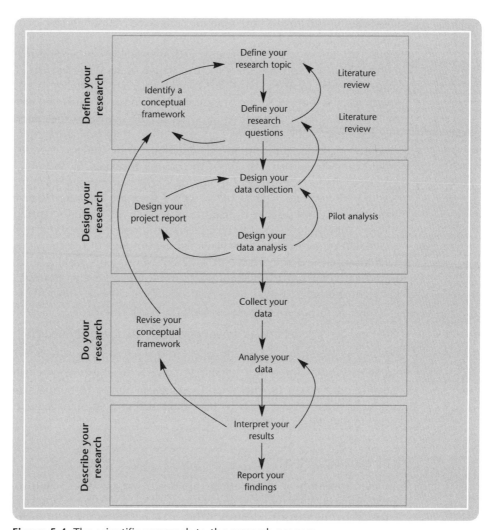

Figure 5.4 The scientific approach to the research process

1 is often citied as a classic professional ethnographic study. In a brief student project, it might be impossible to achieve this deep immersion, but many placement or sponsored projects offer students a chance to experience life from the perspective, albeit a temporary one, of a member of or a participant in the organisation or social unit being studied. Even if this isn't possible, many student projects can benefit from using the unstructured tools and techniques associated with ethnography, including observation and interviews, as an alternative to the structured tools and techniques associated with the scientific approach.

How do ethnographers view the world?

Whilst the scientists claimed objectivity about what they were researching, ethnographers emphasise the extent to which the world, especially the social worlds such as business and management, is subjective and shaped by our perceptions. If we perceive what we are studying (for example the complex dynamics in employer–employee relations) to be a certain way, there is rarely an instrument that will confirm or deny that view. Any view of what is happening is thus *subjective* – it depends on your viewpoint. Ethnographers emphasise the extent to which views differ between individuals, and across cultures, so that the extent to which research is actually based on indisputable social 'facts' is limited. For instance, consider a course of study you have undertaken. It is likely that there will be differing views on the success of the course – some people will have enjoyed it, others may not have done so. In evaluating the course, we could compile quantitative measurements describing how students viewed the course that would provide us with data about the course, focusing, for instance, on the average ratings of the lecturer. Under this approach, the perception of each individual matters less than the average. This would fit with a scientific approach. We could also investigate satisfaction with the course through different students' perceptions. Here, all views would be considered to be relevant, and reveal more about the expectations of individual students, how their views (or perceptions) of the course were formed, and why they viewed the course in different ways. This would be an ethnographic approach. What you learnt about the course would differ significantly between the two different studies.

Who are the 'ethnographers' in business and management research?

Ethnographers often have backgrounds in the subjects mainly concerned with studying people, either individually or collectively, and how they behave. They draw on those disciplines for theory and research methods. In business and management research, these subject areas include human resources management, organisational behaviour and organisational science.

Ethnographic method

In the discussion of the scientific approach, we saw that scientists are concerned predominantly with trying to uncover general laws or patterns, similar to the laws being investigated by natural scientists. Ethnographers try to uncover meaning in a specific situation by studying it intensively. This *depth* is characteristic of ethnographic research.

Wherever possible, ethnographers study issues of interest in their 'natural settings', by involving themselves in the workplace or, in the case of the student project discussed at the start of the chapter, in the lives of the group of people they researched. This emphasises field work – being physically present in the setting being studied. Ethnographic research, thus involves the role of the researcher, the effect of the researcher on what is being studied (you can imagine the impact a loud person may have on the group dynamics of an otherwise quiet group, and the effect this would have on the research if they are concerned with studying group dynamics) and potential sources of bias. Because it takes place in these natural settings, where the researcher cannot control conditions, ethnographic research takes place within an *open system*.

Ethnographers point out that all researchers are human and cannot be completely objective, and therefore will inevitably introduce some sort of bias or subjectivity into the research process. Even experimental research, usually held up as a model of objectivity, can be influenced by researchers, as summarised in **Research in action 5.1**.

> ### *Research in action 5.1*
> ### RESEARCHING THE ROLE OF THE RESEARCHER
>
> Rosenthal and Fode (1963) conducted an experiment to test the effect of experimenter bias, specifically whether experimenters' expectations affected experimental outcomes. Rosenthal and Fode gave student subjects five rats to train to run a maze. Students were told that they had either 'bright' rats, specially bred to run mazes quickly, or 'dull' rats, which were not.
>
> The students found that the 'bright' rats performed significantly better over 50 trials than the 'dull' rats, but the two groups had been actually given rats bred under identical conditions and randomly labelled as either 'bright' or 'dull'.

Just how objective were the experimental results reprinted by the students? Was it not a scientific study carried out in a laboratory environment? Were the conditions not controlled? The students' preconceptions impaired their objectivity in both training and measuring the performance of the rats. This reinforces the ethnographers' belief in subjectivity, and they argue that a challenge in research is recognising your own biases. We will return to this theme later. Natural science researchers argue that objectivity is improved when individual research experiments are designed with controls, such as the 'double-blind' experimental design for conducting medical research, where neither the doctor nor the patient knows whether an active or inactive (placebo) treatment has been administered. They also argue that the scientific community as a whole minimises individual researcher bias through replication. For example, the inability of the scientific community to replicate 'cold fusion' showed that the original study was biased in some way and so disproved its existence.

Practical application of ethnography

Many ethnographers prefer to enter the field (that is, start their data collection in the setting they are investigating) with a completely open mind about what they will find. They will do everything possible to rid themselves of their own biases about the situation into which they are going and prevent other biases developing (for example by reading a critical newspaper article concerning their research setting). They will then let the data (for example what people tell them) dictate the way they proceed with the study and the findings. This is known as 'being led by the data'. They argue that this minimises the likelihood that what they observe and record in the field will be determined by prior beliefs.

In many instances, though, it is not truly possible to do this; all researchers go into the field with some orienting ideas. Thus, many researchers prefer to enter the field with at least some preparation, without developing explicit conceptual frames or instruments such as questionnaires for testing or gathering data, so that the themes (the conceptual framework, as discussed above and in **Chapter 4**) will emerge during the study. This is more typical of student projects and dissertations, where time constraints and other practical considerations (such as people wanting to know what you are going to ask them before they will agree to interviews) are important.

As we have already seen, if you choose an ethnographic approach, you will spend less time planning your research, since you can begin collecting data with a relatively broad topic, and more time actually gathering and analysing data. Ethnography as carried out by Whyte may not be the best approach for a short project – it is fundamentally uncertain and we do not recommend this approach, unless you are being closely supervised by an experienced researcher who has specifically selected the research setting and research method and will work with you on making sense of the data as you go along. However, we do suggest that a form of **bounded ethnography** is entirely appropriate – it combines the practicality of the time-limited project with the ethnographic method. In a bounded situation, you may not reach the level of depth that you would if you were able to explore an issue in unlimited depth. However, you need to finish a project report and provide at least limited answers to your research questions. For this reason, we advocate bounded ethnography as an entirely appropriate approach for student projects.

We can demonstrate this by returning to the earlier example of researching customer satisfaction with an online travel retailer and take an ethnographic approach. Rather than setting up hypotheses, an appropriate research question might be: How do customers judge the quality of travel websites? To answer this question, you could decide to use interviews and observation (for example sitting with customers as they try to make enquiries and bookings online) and, consistent with this, only specify the broad outline of your research process before you start collecting data. Once you have started collecting data, you might:

- Change the data you collect and the methods you use to collect it. For example, if it becomes clear, after the first round of interviews and observations, that speed of response/refresh rates are vital for some people, you could investigate why this is so by conducting further targeted interviews. If you wanted to know if different customers rate speed differently, you could revert to a scientific approach and prepare a questionnaire.
- Decide how to analyse and interpret your data – again emergent, so only planned as far as the analysis of your first set of data.
- Once you have done the first set of data analysis, you will have identified the main themes emerging from your data and can search the literature for conceptual frameworks to support your findings.

As you can see from this example and **Figure 5.5**, if you choose an ethnographic research approach, it will be more recursive than the scientific approach. To put it more formally, it will be an *iterative* (stages looping back to previous stages) rather than a *linear* process (one stage follows another in sequence). Defining, designing, doing and describing overlap significantly. As we have seen, your data collection and data analysis strategies might only emerge once you have started doing research. You may start describing your research, as you will see in **Chapters 7** and **12** before you have finished doing it, and you might identify your conceptual frameworks late in the process.

This messiness is characteristic of ethnographic research. In some ways, it represents the natural way that we solve problems in real life, compared with the linear process of the scientific approach.

A final thought on the practicalities of the ethnographic approach to research concerns your own attitudes and preferences. Some researchers are content to live with this messiness and relative lack of structure; others believe that you should do some

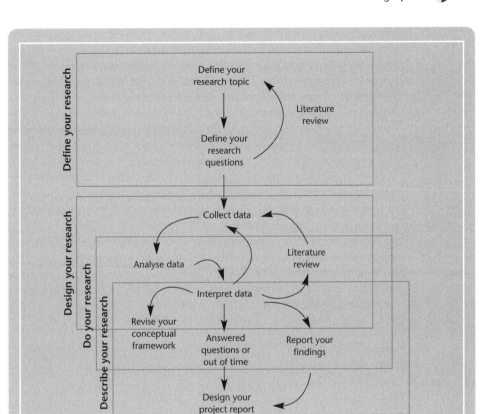

Figure 5.5 A qualitative research process

preliminary research so that you are adequately prepared to observe and record data. If you are the kind of person who might travel alone for the first time by hopping on a plane to the other side of the world, with no hotel reservations, no return ticket and no fixed plans, you might find that a completely 'data-led' approach might suit your personal beliefs and preferences. On the other hand, if you are the kind of person who needs to know what you are doing every day, where you will be staying and when you will be coming home, you might find this an unsettling experience.

As we noted above, most business and management researchers prefer to start collecting data with at least some preparation, although they may not develop an explicit conceptual framework or structured approaches to collecting data (**Chapter 6**). This is more likely to lead to success in a student project, since you do not have the luxury of starting over again if things go wrong and you face many practical constraints such as time.

5.1.4 The logic underlying the two approaches

We have seen that your approach must be consistent with the question you are answering, and your choice will limit the appropriate research methods. If you take the scientific approach, you will need to develop a detailed research plan before you start collecting data. Your first step is to translate your research questions into hypotheses or specific questions, which will determine what data you will collect and how you will collect them. If you take an ethnographic approach, you may only develop a broad research plan before you start collecting data. Your first step is to translate your research questions into a research setting and a preliminary method for collecting data – but not what data you will collect.

But why is this so? Couldn't you collect data and then decide what hypotheses to test, or develop a detailed plan before you start an ethnographic study? Neither of these is impossible, but to do so violates the spirit of each type of study described earlier. The different process for each approach reflects a different logic of research. In scientific research, you will start by developing a specific question based on your research problem, or a hypothesis from a theory or conceptual model that you develop or borrow from the literature.

Your data are then used to answer that specific question or prove or disprove the hypothesis. This is known as **deduction** because the literature will lead to your question or hypothesis. In ethnographic research, your major logical task is to develop concepts and/or a conceptual framework from your data, which is known as **induction** because the data will lead to it.

Deduction – the logic of the scientist

The purpose of deduction is to provide a structured process for testing a general rule or theory using data about a specific instance. Starting with a theory or conceptual framework that may explain a behaviour or a social phenomenon you are interested in studying, you deduce one or more hypotheses from the theory to test, which will guide how and what data you collect. You then analyse your data to see whether they do or do not support the theory. Hypothesis testing in quantitative research usually takes place through the following process:

1. Select a method such as an experiment, survey or secondary data analysis (**Chapter 6**) to collect data
2. Collect data in the form of numbers or transform them into numbers (**Chapter 10**)
3. Use statistical techniques to analyse these quantitative data (**Chapters 10 and 11**)
4. Decide whether to accept or reject the hypothesis based on the statistical analysis
5. Decide whether the results challenge or support the theory or conceptual framework from which the hypotheses were generated (**Chapter 13**)
6. Report the results in numbers, tables and charts (**Chapter 14**).

If you are not testing a specific theory or hypothesis (as in the marketing research project described in **Student research in action 5.1**), omit step 4.

We stated that the methods for scientific research were typically good for collecting quantitative data. However, as we will see in subsequent chapters, you can also test your hypotheses using qualitative data collected using qualitative methods (Blaikie 2000: 10). For now though, we will associate quantitative methods with the scientific approach.

Within the scientific method, going from data back to hypotheses to theory is known as **verification**. You can only show whether your hypothesis is true for the data that you have collected and analysed. If you have done a good job of deducing your hypotheses from your theory, you can make the argument that your theory has been strengthened or weakened by your findings. As you and other researchers test hypotheses in different studies, then theories become stronger or weaker. As theories become weaker, they are replaced by better theories; as theories become stronger, they replace weaker theories. In **Student research in action 5.2**, the student sets out to challenge whether an 'accepted theory' holds in a particular context.

Student research in action 5.2
BIG HAT, SMALL CATTLE

Neil was interested in using his research process to investigate SMEs. He noticed that much of the management literature, in particular the literature on 'best practices', was based on studies conducted on large, often multinational corporations. He wanted to find out how relevant these 'best practices' were to SMEs, and specifically whether his experience that they rarely produced benefits for SMEs – also suggested in the small business literature – was more generally true.

Neil conducted a study to see whether SMEs were adopting 'big business' best practices and whether these practices were associated with performance improvement. His conceptual framework was based on the proposed link between the issues or concepts of 'employing big business best practices' and 'achieving performance improvement'. His hypothesis was 'Employing big business best practices is associated with achieving performance improvement.' This was consistent with the mainstream management literature, but not the small business literature or his own experience, and was what sparked his interest in the project in the first place. He prepared and piloted a questionnaire and then surveyed some small businesses.

Neil discovered that SMEs who had adopted best practices based on big businesses were failing to see any benefits from them. He failed to verify the hypothesis from mainstream management literature and he concluded that these big business ideas were questionable for SMEs. This helped support the small business literature, which argued that a 'one-size-fits-all' approach of using big business ideas in SMEs was inappropriate. Neil's conclusions suggested that researchers should specifically consider the small business context in future research.

The philosopher of science Popper (1959) argued that there is no such thing as objective observation and thus since theories can never be proven to be true, they can only be proven to be false. His classic example concerned swans. If we have never visited the southern hemisphere (or zoo), we might believe that all swans are white. No matter how many white swans we saw, however, we would never be able to prove this unless we could examine every swan in the world. On the other hand, if we set out to disprove the hypothesis that all swans are white, then we could do so by seeing just one nonwhite swan. Popper's argument was that since a single exception such as one single black swan anywhere would disprove a hypothesis, we should only accept a hypothesis as provisionally true (not disproved) rather than proved. As a result, he recommended that a researcher should set up a hypothesis so that it can be disproved (doable) rather than proved (impossible). This approach is known as *falsification*.

Induction – the logic of the ethnographer

As shown above, the logic of induction is that the researcher will generate theory from data. The data can be analysed to identify **patterns,** for instance if there appears to be a pattern that people you meet at the weekend smile more than people you meet during the week, you may conclude that there was something in this. You can generalise these patterns as a conceptual framework or theory, for instance by stating that from your observations, either 'people in general are more happy at the weekend than they are during the week,' or that 'the people you associate with at the weekend are generally more happy than those you associate with during the week'. Such general patterns are what we mean by theory. They are different from the kind of grand theory that you have read about during your literature reviews, but can be classed as a theory, nonetheless.

Researchers often rely on induction when they are researching an area without theory to guide the development of hypotheses (and hence which data to collect). In this case, a researcher will want to collect data about as many aspects as possible of what he or she is studying, and induce the theory from the data, as you will see in **Chapter 12**.

Researchers also use induction when studying an area in which they believe that relying on a conceptual framework or even a high-level theory might bias data collection towards evidence that supports (or in some cases contradicts) that framework. For example, ethologists (researchers who study animal behaviour) may go into the field without having studied primate behaviour intensively, so that they do not try to impose existing research frameworks on what they observe, which might prevent them from observing something important.

5.1.5 The relationship between research approaches and theory

If the scientific approach to research relies on a deductive logic, where you collect data to test theory, and the ethnographic approach relies on an inductive logic, where you collect data to generate theory, clearly the relationship between theory and data differs significantly in the two approaches. Philosophers have debated this relationship between data and theory for many centuries (Easterby-Smith et al. 2002: 27).

The deductive logic is associated with individual projects that emphasise theory *testing*. A stream of quantitative research projects can be used to build theory by testing, revising and then retesting the new theory. However, this does require multiple projects and multiple testing phases, of which a student project could form a small part.

The inductive logic is associated with research projects that emphasise theory *building*. A stream of projects can be used to test theory by comparing the theoretical arguments generated in each, for instance in different contexts.

You will also see researchers alternate between research approaches in a single project. For example, a researcher might use an ethnographic research design for theory-building research, and then follow it up with a scientific design for theory-testing research.

Table 5.2 provides a summary of **Section 5.1**. It builds on the content of **Table 5.1** and is further expanded on in **Tables 5.4** and **5.6**.

Table 5.2 Summary of the scientific and ethnographic approaches (1)

Characteristic	Scientific approach	Ethnographic approach
Archetype	Experimenter operating in a laboratory	Researcher present or participating in the field of interest
Questions that can be answered	What, how much	Why, how
Starting point	Structure for data – you know what you need to collect – theory-led	Unstructured – what you need to do emerges – data-led
World-view	Objective – the researcher is independent	Subjective – the researcher is part of what is being researched
Objective	To find general patterns or laws – generality	To understand meaning in one specific situation – depth
Underlying logic	Deduction	Induction
Who uses?	Predominant in economics, finance, operations research, management science, marketing	Predominant in human resource management, organisational behaviour, organisational science
Role of theory	Testing of theory through development of hypotheses, collection of data, verification	Generation of theory through pattern analysis
Process	Predominantly linear, sequential, ordered	Predominantly iterative, over-lapping, messy
Associated methods	The scientific method, of which surveys are an example. Modelled on closed-system experiments, minimising bias, but limiting the possibilities of discovery	Video diaries. Recognises social systems are most likely to be open systems, and tries to recognise personal biases and keep an open mind
Data type	Predominantly quantitative, predetermined	Predominantly qualitative, for example a series of statements or impressions
Finding	Measure	Meaning

5.2 WHY DOES THE RESEARCH APPROACH REALLY MATTER?

Up to this point, we provided a general overview of the research approaches. This is important, because you need to identify or select your approach before you go any further in your research process. In this section, we show that the approach you choose will significantly affect your research content as well. Although you might select either approach to study a given research topic, you might not be able to ask the same research questions, because the two approaches make different assumptions about

'How do I understand the world?' and 'How can I study the world?' These are actually two sophisticated questions. They go beyond the logic of research and the relationship between theory and data. Research philosophy provides a way to answer these questions because it allows us to identify and understand the logic of inquiry, the 'rules of the game' for a research approach.

If you have the freedom to choose your research design, whether you choose a scientific or an ethnographic research approach will influence:

1. *What research questions can I ask?* – should I focus on 'why', 'how', or 'what'?
2. *What methods or techniques will I use to collect my data* – methods taken from science or social science?
3. *What type of data will I be collecting?* – quantitative or qualitative data?
4. *How will I analyse my data?* – statistical analysis or thematic analysis?

You do not necessarily need to understand research philosophy to answer these questions. Indeed, if you see your research project as a one-off, or if you are working to a narrowly defined project brief, you can plan your research pragmatically. You may not need to address these questions in your research project, but you should understand whether the decisions you make in the rest of the research process are consistent with your research questions. In the bigger picture, the approach you take will affect what you study, how you study it and why you study it. Understanding the two research approaches will also help you to read and understand the business and management literature. This section explores how research philosophy underlies the two approaches.

5.2.1 Research philosophy – where does it fit?

Your choice of research approach reflects deeper issues about research and your own personal beliefs and values. So that we can discuss research philosophy, we will start by defining some terms we need, and later incorporate the elements of **Table 5.2**. Unfortunately, there isn't general agreement in the research literature on where these elements fit into the hierarchy, or even what elements belong in the hierarchy, so the best we can do is try to be consistent in this book. Whilst we can't completely avoid engaging with complex issues, there is an underlying simplicity to research philosophy, which we will describe here as a hierarchy from abstract to concrete, as shown in **Figure 5.6**.

At the highest level of our hierarchy is **research approach**, a strategy or a general logic for answering research questions. We have already identified two main research approaches for business and management as scientific and ethnographic. Knowing or deciding which research approach you will take roughly defines how you will actually do your research and what you will study.

Next comes **research philosophy**, which is the 'rules of the game' or the logic of inquiry governing each approach. You can think of research philosophy as being 'the study of study' – it studies how we study issues. The two branches of research philosophy that concern business and management research are the **philosophy of science**, the high-level rules that set out the ideal way to carry out scientific research on the natural world, and the **philosophy of social science**, the high-level rules that set out the ideal way to carry out research on the social world. We have already examined the

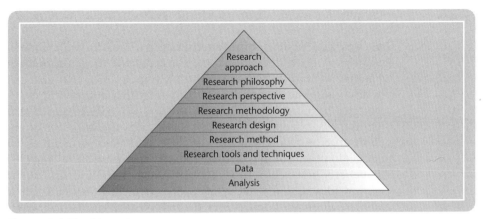

Figure 5.6 The hierarchy

philosophy of science through the scientific approach, and the philosophy of social science through the ethnographic approach.

Because of the fundamental assumptions made by the philosophy of science and philosophy of social science (objectivity and subjectivity, for instance) about the world and the best way to study it differ, we can never combine the two in one part of one study – they are incompatible ways of studying the world. They might be used to great effect at different times and for different purposes, for example in sequential studies.

We can further break down the research approach into the **research perspective**, which describes the set of assumptions about the world and the best way to study it, that underlie your research.

Research methodologies, describe how to translate the research perspective into a way of studying the world. If research philosophy concerns the 'study of study', then research methodology concerns the 'study of how to study'.

A research methodology may be implemented through several different **research designs**, the plan for conducting your study, through translating your research methodology into specific **research methods**, the techniques you use to collect and analyse data. In turn, research methods comprise specific techniques and tools, the physical or electronic artefacts associated with particular methods, for example a web survey, a questionnaire or an interview schedule. At the bottom of the hierarchy we have data and analysis. Methodologies, designs, methods, data and analysis are the subject of **Section 5.3**.

5.2.2 Research philosophy – what is it?

Research philosophy describes a 'theory' of research in a particular field and explains the assumptions that underlie the research approaches. These assumptions mainly concern the nature of reality and how we can know reality. Research philosophy describes our **ontological** assumptions about the nature of reality – what is considered to exist and, just as importantly, what does not exist in the environment we are studying.

Wait a minute, how can we study something that doesn't exist? You might reasonably treat social objects, such as organisations, jobs, work roles and so on, as being just as real as physical objects, such as rocks, cars and buildings. However, rocks and work roles are real in different ways. Rocks can be argued to have an objective reality independent of researchers and their understanding, even if you didn't know what a rock was, you would probably recognise it as real if you stubbed your toe on it. Researchers who study physical objects usually find that an **objectivist** ontology suits what they want to research and how they want to research it – they deal with what is physically real and do not consider anything that does not fit in with this 'reality', such as social objects.

On the other hand, although the person with the work role of 'manager' is a real person, the concept of manager isn't a natural concept, and therefore the idea of a manager has been **socially constructed** – it isn't a physical or tangible idea. The role of the manager has evolved over the past couple of centuries and different people have different ideas about what a manager is/does, depending, for example, on their national culture, the point in time they are considering and their experience of people who have borne the title 'manager'. Many social researchers argue, therefore, that even though we treat social concepts such as 'manager' or 'organisations' as real in everyday life, it is inappropriate to treat them as objective in the same way that a geologist would a rock. A **subjectivist** ontology may therefore be more appropriate for studying many business and management phenomena since human behaviour, whether at the level of the individual or the social system, differs significantly from the behaviour of natural objects.

Ontology therefore helps us identify what we accept to be real and therefore what we can study – the objectivist focuses on physical evidence, while the subjectivist accepts that reality can be constructed, by patterns of behaviour for instance.

Another major idea to take away from research philosophy is that your research approach should be consistent with your **epistemology** or epistemological assumptions. Epistemology concerns what is and isn't considered as knowledge in a field. For instance, to an ethnographer, people's opinions provide useful data about a situation – this is acceptable knowledge in this field. To a scientist, however, objective data are preferable, and the use of people's opinions as data may require rigorous scrutiny, for example only in the form of multi-item scales.

The two extreme epistemological positions in business and management research are **positivism**, which is derived from the philosophy of science, and **subjectivism**, which is derived from the philosophy of social science.

We will build the above into our hierarchy at the end of this section. There are, however, some variations in the epistemological approach that a researcher can take between positivism and subjectivism. **Table 5.3** below describes some of these. They may be relevant to your project, or at least help you to make sense of some of the business and management literature you have come across.

In our experience, few business and management undergraduate or taught master's student projects go much further in exploring research philosophy, especially ontology and epistemology, than we have gone this far in this chapter. Indeed, should you wish to go further, we strongly recommend that this is agreed with your supervisor and be part of the requirements of the project.

Table 5.3 demonstrates the variety and complexity of research in the business and management area. It has been studied for over a hundred years, and draws on methods that have been developed over considerably longer than that. If you need to go down one of the above routes, you should consult a specialist source – many examples are contained in the additional resources at the end of this chapter.

Table 5.3 Research approaches

Epistemology	Ontology	Comments
Positivism	Objectivist	Used extensively in the management literature
Realism	Objectivist	Becoming much more popular
Critical realism	Objectivist	Acknowledges that management researchers cannot directly know reality but they can study the world 'as if' they can – the knowledge of reality can be 'good enough'
Interpretivism	Subjectivist	The goal of research is not to explain human behaviour, but to understand it. A fairly mainstream epistemology for business and management researchers
Constructionism	Subjectivist	Focuses on the collective construction of social phenomena
Subjectivism	Subjectivist	Focuses on the 'multiple realities' that exist when social reality is imposed by social actors rather than being constructed or interpreted

The content is therefore the set of beliefs about what we are researching and the world. **Table 5.4** builds on **Table 5.2** and now includes the research philosophy and perspective.

5.3 HOW DOES RESEARCH APPROACH INFLUENCE RESEARCH DESIGN?

Most students do not usually sit around and debate the nature of reality, existence and knowledge. So, what can a knowledge of research philosophy, in particular ontology and epistemology, do for you as a researcher? Specifically, how does the research approach influence the research process?

As we have noted above, whether you take a scientific or ethnographic approach to research will affect many, if not all, subsequent decisions you make about your research. This section discusses two implications you should think about before you start making your decisions about research methods:

- The criteria by which the quality of research is assessed
- Auditing your intentions of your research using a research profile.

5.3.1 Quality criteria in research

The goals of scientific research

Researchers who follow the scientific approach generally agree on the standards for judging whether research is good or not good. The goal of such research is *statistically*

Table 5.4 Summary of the scientific and ethnographic approaches (2)

Characteristic	Scientific approach	Ethnographic approach
Research philosophy	Philosophy of science	Philosophy of social science
Research perspective	Positivism Realism Empiricism	Interpretivism Constructivism Subjectivism
Archetype	Experimenter operating in a laboratory	Researcher present or participating in the field of interest
Questions that can be answered	What, how much	Why, how
Starting point	Structure for data – you know what you need to collect – theory-led	Unstructured – what you need to do emerges – data-led
World-view	Objective – the researcher is independent	Subjective – the researcher is part of what is being researched
Objective	To find general patterns or laws – generality	To understand meaning in one specific situation – depth
Underlying logic	Deduction	Induction
Who uses?	Predominant in economics, finance, operations research, management science, marketing	Predominant in human resource management, organisational behaviour, organisational science
Role of theory	Testing of theory through development of hypotheses, collection of data, verification	Generation of theory through pattern analysis
Process	Predominantly linear, sequential, ordered	Predominantly iterative, overlapping, messy
Associated methods	The scientific method, of which surveys are an example.Modelled on closed-system experiments, minimising bias, but limiting the possibilities of discovery	Video diaries. Recognises social systems are most likely to be open systems, and tries to recognise personal biases and keep an open mind
Data type	Predominantly quantitative, predetermined	Predominantly qualitative, for example a series of statements or impressions
Finding	Measure	Meaning

significant and *generalisable results*. Statistically significant means that the findings are unlikely to have occurred by chance alone (discussed further in **Chapters 11** and **12**).

The goal of many quantitative studies is generalisability – drawing conclusions about a group from a sample. You can only generalise the findings of quantitative research if you can first show that they are valid and reliable.

Validity refers to how accurately we have conducted our research. For instance, if you were trying to measure customer satisfaction, have the measures you used really measured customer satisfaction or a related concept? Also, did you have enough responses to justify the findings you are claiming? If, as the scientific method proposes, the world is objective and knowable, then the main source of error in our data will be our research method.

Reliability means that you or another researcher would get the same findings if you repeated your study. For example, if you studied the relationship between the location of the till and theft from the till in your high-street bookstore, you should find the same relationship in the bookstore on any high street. Another way of describing reliability is repeatability. Research findings are only reliable if the world itself is uniform.

The goals of ethnographic research

People take one of two positions on the criteria for assessing the quality of ethnographic research, depending on where they start. Some researchers, mainly North American, see the goal of such research to be as rigorous as scientific research. They therefore apply the scientific method to data gathered using ethnographic research designs, or qualitative data gathered using quantitative research designs such as surveys. These researchers usually design their research projects to follow the process that we defined in **Section 5.1** as being closer to the scientific method. This group would be more likely to seek the same qualities in the their findings as scientific researchers – validity and generalisability.

Others do not agree, stating that scientific criteria are incompatible with the ethnographic research approach. Most ethnographers argue that the standards for assessing the quality of qualitative research must differ from those for quantitative research. If the goal of scientific research is statistically significant and generalisable results, then the goal of qualitative research is *valuable*, and idiographic or *transferable* results (O'Leary 2004: 7). Either way, ethnographic researchers need to be as careful as quantitative researchers in reporting how they designed their research and how they collected and interpreted their data.

In understanding the value of the research, the process for analysis of data needs some further discussion. The ethnographic researcher may rely on intuition to guide the analysis and interpretation of findings, rather than rules or procedures. It is in this uniqueness of the situation and the intuitive analysis that the value arrives. It is valuable because it is original.

Most ethnographers disagree that researchers can be objective, and even question whether objectivity is a desirable quality in research. Instead, researchers should recognise that all human beings are subjective, but that subjectivity can be managed in social research. Two ways of managing subjectivity are **neutrality**, developing strategies to avoid unrecognised subjectivity that might bias research findings, and **transparency**, acknowledging subjectivity (O'Leary 2004: 59). Following an agreed procedure for generating theory from data helps to demonstrate neutrality. Explicitly stating your own position helps to demonstrate transparency.

Ethnography requires the researcher to see through other people's eyes and interpret events from their point of view (Bryman 1988). The ethnographer may even need to adopt the viewpoint of the people being researched in order to understand what is going on. This may be illustrated by thinking about how you might research business and management in another culture. If you try to study it from your own (native) perspective, you may not really comprehend what is going on. You might need to think as a person from that culture in order to understand the social reality. This is a major concern in international business research – in part it is about resisting the 'Americanisation' of management, in part about the value of differences between cultures.

If the world is not uniform, dependability may be a more realistic research goal than reliability. **Dependability** refers to the repeatability of the process of inducing theory from data, rather than the repeatability of the findings themselves.

Some researchers question whether uniform criteria can actually be established for ethnography, since every study will differ on essential criteria. They regard the emphasis on universal standards as trying to promote an artificial and unworkable consensus, in the presence of 'multiple realities'.

On the other hand, you will probably need to refer to some standards to assess the quality of your research, if you take an ethnographic approach. You might want to suggest that your work:

● makes a contribution to understanding some aspect of social reality
● is original in some way
● has been conducted in a correct manner, as far as possible, and you have identified any potential source of bias
● is both interesting and true.

 ### 5.3.2 Auditing your research using a research profile

You can profile your research design and decide whether your plan is consistent or incon-

---

Table 5.5 A research profile

Aspect	Scientific			Ethnographic
Focus	Measurement	✓		Meaning
Definition	Collecting and analysing data	✓		Exploring instances and examples
Objective	Testing general principles		✓	Examining individual differences
Ideal model	Natural sciences	✓		Social sciences
Research questions	What, how much		✓	How, why
Theory	Theory-testing	✓		Theory-generating
Reasoning	Deductive	✓		Inductive
Researcher	Objective and independent		✓	Subjective and involved
Data	Quantitative – numbers and categories		✓	Qualitative – words and symbols
Data collection	Remote or brief	✓		Up close and extended
Typical methods	Surveys, experiments		✓	Observation, interviews
Data analysis	Statistics	✓		Thematic
Quality	Validity, reliability, generalisability	✓		Dependability, richness

sistent. We show a research profile in **Table 5.5**. This researcher is obviously confused, mixing elements of scientific and ethnographic research approaches inconsistently.

You might want to build a profile of your research and perhaps the key exemplars you have identified in your literature search. Good research tends to be consistent – by

Table 5.6 Summary of the scientific and ethnographic approaches (3)

Characteristic	Scientific approach	Ethnographic approach
Research philosophy	Philosophy of science	Philosophy of social science
Research perspective	Positivism Realism Empiricism	Interpretivism Constructivism Subjectivism
Archetype	Experimenter operating in a laboratory	Researcher present or participating in the field of interest
Questions that can be answered	What, how much	Why, how
Starting point	Structure for data – you know what you need to collect – theory-led	Unstructured – what you need to do emerges – data-led
World-view	Objective – the researcher is independent	Subjective – the researcher is part of what is being researched
Objective	To find general patterns or laws – generality, statistically significant results	To understand meaning in one specific situation – depth and valuable, transferable results
Underlying logic	Deduction	Induction
Who uses?	Predominant in economics, finance, operations research, management science, marketing	Predominant in human resource management, organisational behaviour, organisational science
Role of theory	Testing of theory through development of hypotheses, collection of data, verification	Generation of theory through pattern analysis
Process	Predominantly linear, sequential, ordered	Predominantly iterative, overlapping, messy
Associated methods	The scientific method, of which surveys are an example. Modelled on closed-system experiments, minimising bias, but limiting the possibilities of discovery	Video diaries. Recognises social systems are most likely to be open systems, and tries to recognise personal biases and keep an open mind
Data type	Predominantly quantitative, pre-determined	Predominantly qualitative, for example a series of statements or impressions
Finding	Measure	Meaning
Data analysis	Statistical, through rules or procedures	Thematic, through intuition
Quality	Validity, reliability, generalisability	Makes a contribution, good use of recognised method, neutrality or transparency

consistent we do not mean that every box must be ticked for one or the other approaches, but that there is a logic for any deviation. For example, you could use statistics and inference on data that were collected in qualitative form, but you might want to consider if this is the best method or the best use of your data.

5.3.3 Scientific versus ethnographic research

Table 5.6 summarises all the elements of each approach, as constructed through this chapter.

 ## SUMMARY

In this chapter, we have presented the two main approaches to business and management research. The scientific approach is based on the logic of scientific inquiry, and uses the scientific method as the model for research endeavour. The ethnographic approach rejects scientific inquiry as inappropriate for studying the social world, and takes the methods of social science, particularly ethnography, as its model.

We began by describing the implications of choosing the scientist or ethnographer as the role model for your research. Quantitative research is relatively linear and predictable once you have decided how you will collect and analyse your data. On the other hand, qualitative research is cyclical and unpredictable – how you will collect and analyse your data emerges as you are actually doing your research.

Besides the process implications, it is important to understand the implications of your research process for what you can study and how you can study it. Some research is associated with research designs that try to replicate the scientific process in social settings. Other research is associated with research designs that try to replicate ethnography. Research philosophy helps us to understand the differences between the two and make sure that a research design is internally consistent.

 ## ANSWERS TO KEY QUESTIONS

How can I answer my research questions?
- You must select an appropriate research design
- You must collect and analyse data
- You must report your findings

What are the scientific and ethnographic approaches to research design?
- The scientific approach is focused on the collection and analysis of numerical data – a process known as social measurement
- The ethnographic approach is focused on the collection and interpretation of a wide array of data – a process for understanding social meaning

What is the 'logic of research' for business and management research?
- Scientific research follows a deductive logic
- Ethnographic research follows an inductive logic

What roles do theory and data play in management research?

- Theory can be used to develop hypotheses for scientific research, and guide the collection of data
- Data can be used to develop theory in ethnographic research and guide the selection of theory

What are the assumptions underlying the scientific and ethnographic approaches?

- Underlying the scientific research approach are the assumptions that the world is real and knowable, we can be objective and all phenomena can be reduced to a set of numbers
- Underlying the ethnographic research approach is the prime assumption that the world is complex and only knowable through interaction with the social systems that it contains

REFERENCES

Blaikie, Norman. 2000. *Designing Social Research*. Cambridge: Polity Press.

Bryman, A. 1988. *Quantity and Quality in Social Research*. London: Routledge.

Cooper, D.R. and Schindler, P.S. 2001. *Business Research Methods*, International edition. Singapore: McGraw-Hill Book Company.

Easterby-Smith, Mark, Thorpe, Richard and Lowe, Andy. 2002. *Management Research: An Introduction,* 2nd edn. London: Sage.

Kaplan, R.S. and Norton, D.P. 1992. 'The Balanced Scorecard – Measures That Drive Performance', *Harvard Business Review*, Jan–Feb, pp. 71–9.

O'Leary, Z. 2004. *The Essential Guide to Doing Research*. London: Sage.

Popper, K. 1959. *The Logic of Scientific Discovery*, London: Hutchinson.

Rosenthal, R. and Fode, K. L. 1963. The effect of experimenter bias on the performance of the albino rat, *Behavioural Science*, **8**: 183–9.

ADDITIONAL RESOURCES

Crotty, Michel. 1998. *The Foundations of Social Research: Meaning and Perspective in the Research Process*. London: Sage.

Hollis, M. 1994. *The Philosophy of Social Science: An Introduction*. Cambridge: Cambridge University Press.

Kaplan, A. 1964. *The Conduct of Inquiry: Methodology for Behavioural Science*. San Francisco: Chandler.

Potter, G. 2000. *The Philosophy of Social Science: New Perspectives*. Harlow: Prentice Hall.

Rosnow, R.L. and Rosenthal, R. 1997. *People Studying People: Artifacts and Ethics in Behavioural Research*. New York: W.H. Freeman.

Schutt, R.K. 1996. *Social World: The Process and Practice of Research*. Thousand Oaks, CA: Pine Forge Press.

Searle, C. 1996. *The Quality of Qualitative Research*. London: Allen Lane.

Shermer, M. 1997. *Why People Believe Weird Things: Pseudoscience, Superstition, and Other Confusions of Our Time*. New York: W.H. Freeman.

Weick, K.E. 1979. *The Social Psychology of Organising*, 2nd edn. Reading, MA: Addison-Wesley.

Key terms

bounded ethnography, 148
conceptual framework, 143
deduction, 150
dependability, 160
epistemology, 156
ethnography, 144
induction, 150
logic of research, 137
neutrality, 159
objectivist, 156

patterns, 152
philosophy of science, 154
philosophy of social science, 154
positivism, 156
reliability, 159
research approach, 154
research designs, 155
research methodologies, 155
research methods, 155

research perspective, 155
research philosophy, 154
scientific method, 143
socially constructed, 156
subjectivism, 156
subjectivist, 156
transparency, 159
validity, 158
verification, 150

Discussion questions

1. Why should you consider research philosophy between the research definition stage and the research design stage?

2. Are there any research methods that can only be used in quantitative research and any that can only be used for qualitative research?

3. If the overall goal of research is to find 'truth', why should we judge qualitative research by the standards of quantitative research, or vice versa?

4. Is it acceptable in quantitative research to develop hypotheses from 'interrogating' a large data set with statistical techniques? What principles might this violate?

5. Why do we need to know about research philosophy?

6. What subject areas within business and management are likely to take a quantitative or qualitative approach?

7. Why should we try to disprove a hypothesis rather than to prove it?

8. What is 'truth' in the context of the research that you have come across? How close to 'the truth' do these research projects come?

Workshop

Task

Review the cases discussed in the Chapter 1 workshop.

1. Classify each of these projects as having used either a scientific or an ethnographic approach.

2. Use the research profile of Table 5.5 and profile two of these projects. How consistent is the research design in each case (as far as is possible to tell from the descriptions)?

3. Identify your own 'natural' research approach (the one that fits best with your own world-view), using Table 5.1, 5.2 or 5.3. Identify the strengths and weaknesses of this approach.

4. Find someone with a different 'natural' approach and compare views.

Relevant chapters

13 Answering your research questions
14 Describing your research
15 Closing the loop

Key challenges

● Interpreting your findings and making recommendations
● Writing and presenting your project
● Reflecting on and learning from your research

4

Relevant chapters

1 What is research?
2 Managing the research process
3 What should I study?
4 How do I find information?

Key challenges

● Understanding the research process
● Taking a systematic approach
● Generating and clarifying ideas
● Using the library and internet

1

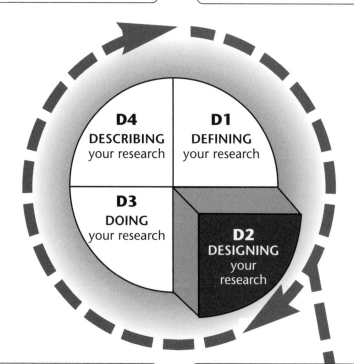

Relevant chapters

9 Doing field research
10 Analysing quantitative data
11 Advanced quantitative analysis
12 Analysing qualitative data

Key challenges

● Practical considerations in doing research
● Using simple statistics
● Undertanding multivariate statistics
● Interpreting interviews and observations

3

Relevant chapters

5 Scientist or ethnographer?
6 **Quantitative research designs**
7 Designing qualitative research
8 Case studies/multi-method design

Key challenges

● Choosing a model for doing research
● **Using scientific methods**
● Using ethnographic methods
● Integrating quantitative and qualitative research

2

chapter

6

Quantitative research designs
Using scientific methods for social measurement

 Key questions

- What methods for collecting data are associated with the scientific approach?
- How can I design a research project to analyse documents or databases, conduct a survey or run an experiment?
- How can I use these methods as part of a qualitative research design strategy?

 Learning outcomes

At the end of this chapter, you should be able to:

- Design a research study using secondary analysis, a survey or an experiment
- Discuss the strengths and weaknesses of each design
- Identify how we judge the quality of research designs for social measurement

Contents

 **INTRODUCTION**

'Don't you know anything about numbers?'

'Well, I don't think they're very important', snapped Milo, too embarrassed to admit the truth.

'Not important!' roared the Dodecahedron, turning red with fury. 'Could you have tea for two without the two – or three blind mice without the three? Would there be four corners of the earth if there weren't a four? And how could you sail the seven seas without a seven?'

'All I meant was –' began Milo, but the Dodecahedron, overcome with emotion and shouting furiously, carried on.

'If you had high hopes, how would you know how high they were? And did you know that narrow escapes come in all different widths? Would you travel the whole wide world without ever knowing how wide it was? And how could you do anything at long last,' he concluded, waving his arms over his head, 'without knowing how long the last was? Why, numbers are the most beautiful and valuable things in the world.'

(Juster, The Phantom Tollbooth, 1954: 174)

After reading **Chapter 5**, you should have an idea whether you will model your research on the scientist or the ethnographer. If your role model is the scientist, you will find this chapter especially useful, because the research methods here are most closely associated with the scientific approach, even though you could also consider using the research methods presented in **Chapter 7**. The methods in this chapter are secondary analysis, surveys and experiments, and are commonly used in business and management research.

This chapter provides a general overview of these research designs, provides some preliminary guidance for designing an informal study and describes their main strengths and weaknesses. They are worth considering if you want your findings to be quantitative, statistically significant and generalisable, and for your research to be as objective, reliable and reproducible as possible.

In **Section 6.1**, we describe how you can collect data to answer your research questions through methods that involve indirect contact only with organisations or people as a data source. This is known as secondary analysis because the sources of data, such as government surveys, proprietary databases, documents or statistical databases, have almost always been created for purposes other than your research project. Secondary analysis can reduce difficulties with gaining access to people or organisations, but it may be difficult to find exactly the data you need to answer your research questions compared with more direct methods. You might select secondary analysis as a main technique if you can answer your research questions using data other people have already collected, or if you can construct your own data set from documents or other materials, but it is often combined with other research methods.

If your research questions can't be answered by analysing existing data, or if you need direct contact with organisations to collect data specifically for your research project, you may want to consider using a survey, described in **Section 6.2**. Survey research is so popular that many people often considered it to be synonymous with business and management research. A survey collects the same information about some or all of a group's members, and includes familiar techniques such as interviews, questionnaires and structured observations. Since you want to draw conclusions about all the group's members without necessarily gathering information from each member of the group, you will need to consider sampling issues carefully. You can use a survey to collect information directly through face-to-face or voice-to-voice interviews, or at a distance through the post, email or web questionnaires. Because surveys are so common, if you choose a survey design you may be able to use an existing survey, build your own survey from existing questions or even develop your own questions.

We also describe experiments as a research design for business and management research in **Section 6.3**. Experiments come closest to the ideal of the scientific model of research because they let researchers test cause-and-effect relationships. However, laboratory experiments are rare in business and management research because little business and management takes place in controlled settings; there is a good deal of use of experiments in natural settings such as field and quasi-experiments like taste tests. No matter what setting, important ethical issues as well as design issues are raised by experiments, because they can affect people's lives, as shown in **Research in action 6.1**.

Research in action 6.1
OUCH!

In June 2004, British newspapers and television news programmes reported on a study presented at the European Society of Human Reproduction and Embryology conference claiming that even just carrying a mobile phone in a pocket reduced men's sperm counts. Based on a survey of 221 men over 13 months concerning their mobile phone usage and their sperm counts, Hungarian researchers proposed that mobile phone usage reduced sperm counts by about one-third.

A report such as this, if accurate, would be alarming in view of the widespread usage of mobile phones in developed countries. Many people were sceptical, however, of the report's conclusions. The survey compared heavy and light/nonusers of mobile phones, but failed to take into account any other factors that might be associated with lower sperm counts among mobile phone users or other studies that found higher sperm counts generally in countries with high mobile phone usage, such as Finland.

After reading this chapter, you should have a better idea why and how you might use one of these designs, choose the most appropriate one for your research, and understand each well enough to get started, although you may need to consult more specialised guides for detailed design. You can read about different statistical techniques in **Chapters 9** and **10**, which cover basic and advanced statistics. Even if you don't plan to use one of these methods in your research project, these designs are commonly used to collect data which can then be cited in journalism and consulting, for example public opinion polls and medical research such as clinical trials. Furthermore, an understanding of these three methods will be helpful if you want to analyse critically how people have collected and analysed data in the articles you have found in your literature search.

6.1 DESIGNS FOR SECONDARY ANALYSIS

In this section, we will describe how you can use **secondary analysis**, analysing previously collected data as your main research design. Secondary analysis is used to describe a research design based around collecting (or acquiring) and analysing secondary data, data that you do not directly collect from organisations or people in their natural settings. In its strictest sense, secondary analysis means analysing data that someone else has already analysed, but it also is used for analysing data that you collect indirectly about people and organisations rather than from them. Your data may have been collected by other people for other purposes, or extracted by you from such sources. This section will describe the main sources of data for secondary analysis and how you can use secondary analysis to analyse data from:

● An existing data set such as a large-scale survey or a commercial database
● A data set that you have created yourself from published or unpublished materials such as company archives, document analysis, or from observing people or organisations without interacting with them (unobtrusive analysis), as shown in **Student research in action 6.1**.

You might choose to use secondary analysis as your research design when:

● Someone else has already collected the data you need, and you can use them to answer your own research questions
● You want to study a social unit that you cannot contact directly because of geographic distance or other access problems
● You want to study the historical activities of social units or social units that no longer exist (historical data), or covering an extended period of time (longitudinal data).

Student research in action 6.1

Frances and Kate were interested in whether high-street banks were responding to pressures for corporate social responsibility (CSR). They decided that one measure of this would be whether the banks had included a statement of their policy regarding diversity on the company website and the content of that policy (if there was one). They collected data from the 25 major banks and building societies in the UK. They also used publicly available information such as reported profits and return on assets to see what influenced these statements. Although this only revealed information about a small part of the banks' CSR activities, it agreed closely with other information about this sector, including market research on customer perceptions and regulatory actions. This secondary analysis gave them some good ideas for doing further research in which they collected information directly from bank customers about their perceptions of their own banks.

Research projects that are based on indirectly collected data are sometimes called **desk/library research** projects, because you do not have direct contact with organisations or people in collecting your data. If you decide to use secondary analysis as your main research method, you should check with your project supervisor and/or business sponsor to see if this meets your project guidelines, because some project guidelines require you to collect primary data. If you are working on a sponsored project, you should check to see if secondary data are acceptable to your project stakeholders, as they may want you to collect primary data to support your findings.

6.1.1   Using existing data sets: surveys, commercial databases, and other sources

Despite the volume of data available in business and management research, few students consider analysing data already collected for other purposes (Saunders et al. 2003: 188). However, it may be worth looking to see if someone has already collected data that may be relevant to your research problem. We have already described library and internet search processes in **Chapter 4** as two ways to find information about your research problem and research setting, an essential part of any research project. You can also use these search processes to identify data to answer your research questions. If you are lucky, someone has already collected the data you need to answer your research questions, and, if you are especially lucky, they have created an electronic database with the kind of information you need in an appropriate format. If you are inordinately lucky, you can gain access to this information and it will be free.

Secondary data are stored in data archives, commercial databases, market reports and company archives. Government departments, trade associations, market research organisations, commercial research organisations, academic research units, newspapers, businesses and other organisations all collect and publish information that may be relevant to answering your research questions. This information may be available in printed form, CD-ROMs, online computer databases or internet sites.

Researchers who use this method usually describe the data differently depending on how it is stored and organised. A **data set** is a set of information collected by academic or professional researchers about one or more social units using a consistent research design or research protocol. A **database** is a structured data set, usually a matrix of data that allocates a row to each social unit (for example organisation, household or person) and a column to each variable or other measure related to that social unit. An **archive** is a collection of documents, images and other data in unprocessed form, which you might process into a data set or a database.

You can use this method to analyse documents and other records you collect from organisations, data that are stored in data repositories such as archives and data collected through unobtrusive measures. You are collecting data specifically for your research project, but your research design still counts as 'secondary analysis' because you are not directly observing, interviewing or surveying the people or organisations you are studying. The documents you are using as sources have already been produced for another purpose rather than being created specifically for your research project, even though your data do not exist until you 'interrogate' the documents (O'Leary 2004: 180).

If you are considering secondary analysis, some questions you might want to explore early on include:

1. *Are the data free, or will you have to pay for them?* In some cases, buying a particular data set will cost hundreds or even thousands of pounds – beyond the reach of most student projects.
2. *Are the data available in computer files, or will you have to enter the data yourself?* Many older data sets are only available in printed tables, or sometimes in obsolete computer formats such as punched cards.
3. *Do the data cover the organisations and the phenomena you are interested in?* It is unlikely that the people who collected the data originally were interested in exactly the same research questions you want to answer in your research, so they may have omitted some data that are relevant to your research and included irrelevant data. Furthermore, data sets tend to focus on large industrial organisations so the sample may be biased.
4. *Are the data accurate?* Research on commercially produced data sets such as Compustat has shown that the data are not always correct, due to either collection or entry errors. You will sometimes need to spend as much time checking your data as if you had originally collected and entered it yourself.

Advantages and disadvantages of secondary analysis

Analysing secondary data may save you time and effort (although not always money). People collect data in many fields of business and management and make those data available. Some companies who conduct market research and publish market reports and consult, such as Mintel and Gartner, specialise in making data available for a fee.

Some areas of management use secondary analysis as a core research design. Secondary data abound in accounting and finance, because companies have to report their financial performance. For example, many financial studies are based on data from financial databases that have been put together by government or for-profit organisations, such as records of stock prices. Studies of technological innovation may use counts of patents derived from patent databases.

Some of the advantages and disadvantages of secondary analysis are listed in **Table 6.1** below. Bryman and Bell (2003: 213) discuss some of these aspects in more depth.

Producers of secondary data

Secondary data can be found everywhere. People and organisations collect information about many aspects of business and management. Governmental and quasi-governmental bodies such as international trade bodies collect and publish statistics about a wide variety of activities, such as trade statistics. Corporations publish annual reports and file information related to stock offerings and other significant activities. Markets such as the New York Stock Exchange are a source of detailed information about transactions such as share prices. Any of these could be used in research. Although it is relatively rare for undergraduate or taught master's research projects compared with postgraduate research projects, sometimes you may be expected to analyse data that have already been collected by your supervisor or your institution.

You may find the terms primary and secondary confusing (just to complicate things even more, you may even see references to tertiary data or sources). **Primary data** are data you have collected yourself specifically for your project and **secondary data** are data other people have collected for their own research projects or commercial purposes. Understanding what terms you should use for your data and sources is not as

Table 6.1 Secondary analysis in perspective

	Advantages	Disadvantages
Effort	Saving money and time in data collection Allowing more time for data analysis	Need to familiarise yourself with the data Need to manage large and complex data sets May be expensive
Analysis	Access to high-quality data Comparing subgroups or subsets within the data sample Comparing subgroups or subsets in other countries Opportunity to analyse data longitudinally	Lack of control over data quality Limited to data already collected May be biased in unobservable ways May not answer your research questions
Contribution	Reinterpret original findings Fully exploit data set	May not be seen as being as rigorous or relevant as purposefully collected data Does not build as many research skills as direct methods

important as understanding why we want to know whether your data are primary, secondary or tertiary.

The main thing to keep in mind is the difference between 'primary' and 'secondary' as the difference between 'new' data and 'reused' data. Your distance from the source of the data will affect the quality of the data and ultimately the quality of your findings or recommendations. The farther away you are from the data source, the more cautious you need to be about its reliability; on the other hand, the closer you are to the data source the more cautious you need to be about the potential bias of the researcher and the researched.

Social surveys as sources of secondary data

A major source of information about organisations, households and people is **survey data**. The internet has revolutionised researchers' ability to identify and access large-scale survey data for secondary analysis. These survey data include data from **censuses**, surveys that collect data from every member of the group being studied, **repeated surveys**, surveys that collect data continuously or at regular intervals, and **ad hoc surveys**, surveys that collect data only once. Since we will discuss survey designs in **Section 6.2**, in this section we will focus on using survey data rather than how to design and administer a survey.

The UK, in particular, is taking a leading role in making survey information available through the web with the Economic and Social Data Service (ESDS), founded jointly in January 2003 by the Economic and Social Research Council (ESRC) and the Joint Information Systems Committee (JISC). The ESDS coordinates storage and access to **data archives**, which are repositories for survey data. Four ESDS research centres currently provide access to key economic and social data for secondary analysis:

● The UK Data Archive (UKDA) at the University of Essex

Table 6.2   Examples of online data sources provided through ESDS

ESDS Government Surveys

Labour Force Surveys/Northern Ireland Labour Force Survey	General Household Survey/Continuous Household Survey (Northern Ireland)
Family Expenditure Survey/Northern Ireland Family Expenditure Survey	National Food Survey/Expenditure and Food Survey (new combined National Food Survey and Family Expenditure Survey)
Family Resources Survey	ONS Omnibus Survey
Survey of English Housing	Health Survey for England/Welsh Health Survey/Scottish Health Survey
British Crime Survey/Scottish Crime Survey	British Social Attitudes/Scottish Social Attitudes/Northern Ireland Life and Times Survey (and the former Northern Ireland Social Attitudes)/Young People's Social Attitudes (periodic offshoot of the BSA)
National Travel Survey	Time Use Survey

ESDS Longitudinal

British Cohort Study (BCS70)	British Household Panel Survey (BHPS)
Millennium Cohort Study (MCS)	National Child Development Survey (NCDS)

ESDS Qualidata

The Peter Townsend collection featuring studies on poverty and the life of older people, *Family Life of Old People* (1955), *The Last Refuge* (1959) and *Poverty in the UK* (1979)	The Paul Thompson collection comprising the major life history interview study of *The Edwardians* (1975)
Stan Cohen's (1967) *Folk Devils and Moral Panics* focusing on the genesis and development of 'moral panic'	Dennis Marsden and Brian Jackson's research papers, including their data for *Education and the Working Class* (1962)
Goldthorpe et al. (1962) *The Affluent Worker* undertaken to test the thesis of working-class embourgeoisement	

ESDS International

OECD Main Economic Indicators	OECD Main Science and Technology Indicators
OECD Quarterly Labour Force Statistics	OECD Social Expenditure Database
OECD Measuring Globalisation	OECD International Development
OECD International Direct Investment Statistics	OECD International Migration Statistics
NS Time Series Data	UNIDO Industrial Statistics
UNIDO Industrial Demand Supply	IMF Direction of Trade Statistics
IMF International Financial Statistics	IMF Balance of Payment Statistics
World Bank World Development Indicators	World Bank Global Development Finance
United Nations Common Database	Eurobarometers
European Social Survey	International Social Survey Programme
World Values Surveys and European Values Surveys	

- The Institute for Social and Economic Research (ISER) at the University of Essex
- The Manchester Information and Associated Services (MIMAS) at the University of Manchester
- The Cathie Marsh Centre for Census and Survey Research (CCSR) at the University of Manchester.

If you are studying in the UK, you may be able to access many different kinds of data through these centres, including large-scale government surveys, qualitative data sets, international data sets and longitudinal data sets, as shown in **Table 6.2**, and illustrated in **Research in action 6.2**.

Research in action 6.2
BRITAIN AT WORK

Many academic researchers have conducted secondary analysis on the Workplace Employee Relations Survey (WERS) data set. The survey is conducted by the Centre for Social Research (formerly SCPR). It started in 1980 as the quadrennial Workplace Industrial Relations Survey (WIRS), surveying British establishments with 25 or more employees, and was renamed WERS in 1998 and extended to workplaces with 10 or more employees. The survey provides 'statistically reliable, nationally representative data on workplace relations and employment practices'.

The research team publishes primary analysis of each survey. Secondary analysis of the data has been conducted by other researchers, who may not have any connection with the project except through the data. These secondary analyses include journal articles, master's dissertations and doctoral dissertations.

See for example:

http://www.data-archive.ac.uk/findingData/werAbstract.asp;

http://www.niesr.ac.uk/niesr/wers98/Bib2004a.pdf

There are many advantages to using archived survey data as a source of data for a research project. The survey data provide you with access to much larger samples than you could hope to ever collect. Surveys such as these are designed and conducted by teams of experts, so that the quality of the research design, instruments, data collection and data processing is very high.

As well as data from a single source such as WERS, you can also combine data from different sources, as shown in **Research in action 6.3**.

Research in action 6.3
COUNTRY MUSIC ... THE MUSIC OF PAIN

To see whether country music and suicide rates were linked, sociologists Steven Stack and Jim Gundlach combined data from the Radio and Records Rating Report, which reported on the size of the country music listening audience in 49 US metropolitan areas, with suicide rates for those areas from the annual Mortality Tapes compiled by the Inter-

University Consortium for Social and Political Research at the University of Michigan in the US (Stack and Gundlach 1995). They proposed that the two would be related, because the themes of country music dealt with the same issues that sociologists associate with suicide. This touched off a debate in the journal *Social Forces* over the link, with other sociologists arguing that divorce, gun ownership, living in the south and poverty accounted for both suicide and listening to 'country radio' (also see Stack and Gundlach 1992, 1994).

To use archived survey data, you first need to find out what surveys exist and then gain access to them, which is not always easy. Projects such as ESDS provide comprehensive listings of the survey data they hold, but you may have to use some of the tools and techniques for searching discussed in **Chapter 4** to find other surveys.

Even if you find a survey or other source whose data may help you answer your research questions, you may not always gain access to that data. Whilst many government and academic research centres make summary results and even raw data from their surveys available to researchers, you may only be able to obtain summary results of surveys conducted by commercial research organisations by paying and they may charge more than most student projects could afford. In some cases, however, they may not want to share this information with anyone else.

Commercial databases as sources of secondary data

Proprietary databases are data sets or databases created to be sold. These are often the best source of access to company financial data. You may have access to some proprietary data sets through your department or library, if they subscribe. **Company-specific databases** give company names, sales, profits, geographic profiles, industry profiles and other useful data. Because these databases are compiled and published by commercial organisations, they typically sell the results or charge for access to them. **Chapter 4** discussed some of these databases, but a few of the most popular ones include market research archives such as Mintel, and financial databases such as AMADEUS and FAME.

AMADEUS and **FAME** are two popular company financial databases. These are based on the financial reports and other data provided by companies to governments, securities overseers and investors. You can use these databases to find company accounts data for public and private companies, and can download selected data to create your own custom database.

Marketing information can be essential for projects involving either consumer or industrial products, especially if you are studying a marketing problem or your research setting is consumer-oriented. **Market research reports** are another type of proprietary information that students find useful for research projects. These reports may be published by commercial market or consumer research organisations, or trade associations.

Many business schools subscribe to Mintel market reports. **Mintel** is a consultancy company that:

publishes over 45 reports each month, covering a wide range of sectors and focusing on topical marketing issues. Divided between UK-specific, European and

USA reports, Mintel reports analyse market sizes and trends, market segmentation, and consumer attitudes and purchasing habits, as well as assessing the future of the market. By providing a comprehensive picture of the consumer, Mintel's reports provide thorough analyses of specialist sectors, breaking down often complex issues into easy-to-understand sections.

(http://www.mintel.com/docs/pubs.htm)

For example, if you were studying food consumption, you might want to consult Mintel's June 2004 report extensively exploring the yoghurt market in the US. Other reports listed on the site examine the beer market, book retailing, analgesics and household cleaning products.

Trade associations are another good but often overlooked source of information about the commodity or organisations they represent. For example, the National Hot Dog and Sausage Council's website (http://www.hot-dog.org/) provides extensive information about the sales of 'tube steak' in the US. Information on this site includes:

- General market information (reports on *The Size and Scope of the US Market for Hot Dogs 2003* and *The Size and Scope of the US Market for Sausages 2003*)
- Consumption by geographic area (reports on the *Top Ten Hot Dog Eating Cities* and *Top Ten Sausage Eating Cities*)
- Special reports, such as how many hot dogs are eaten at baseball games in the US (a report on *2004 Major League Ballpark Consumption*).

6.1.2 Creating your own data sets: archival research and unobtrusive observation

In the previous section, we described surveys and databases as sources of data for secondary analysis where the data had already been collected and processed for you. If you are interested in secondary research but you can't identify a data set or database that contains the information you want to analyse to answer your research questions, you may want to create your own data set from materials that you collect or that have been collected by organisations or other researchers but not processed and analysed. As we noted above, although you might be the first person to collect and analyse this data, it is still generally considered as secondary analysis because you are relying on data you are not collecting directly from organisations or people. Below, we will describe some features of archival research.

Data from documents and archives

In some research projects, you may want or need to gather data without any direct contact with organisations or people. You might choose to analyse documents, whether they are company records, publications or other sources.

Research that takes a historical perspective can often only rely on documents and other records for evidence, since the organisations and people being studied no longer exist to be interviewed or studied. These materials may be held in library or company **archives**, collections of documents or other artefacts that organisations or people create as part of their ongoing activities. Research that uses only secondary data, especially if it focuses on documents, is sometimes called **archival research**, whether the information is actually held in an archive or not, because the same techniques are used for recording and analysing information. Many placement projects involve investigating archival data, as shown in **Research in action 6.4**.

Research in action 6.4
KATE'S ABC

As part of a summer job between completing her MBA and starting her PhD, Kate worked on a project for a telecoms manufacturer looking for ways to reduce the costs of materials management. As part of this project, the author and her colleague analysed the purchase orders that had been made over the past year, to identify the items that fell into A*, A, B and C purchase categories. This meant organising and sorting through tens of thousands of purchase orders (historical data), using data downloaded from the division's mainframe into a format viewable in a spreadsheet program. This allowed the organisation to identify the costs associated with purchase orders and thereby assess whether electronic purchasing would be cost-effective.

Secondary data can provide otherwise lost insights into management decisions outside any respondent's living memory, so business history and management history tends to focus largely on archival research. A company's archives can be a rich source of data, since it may contain detailed information that has never been made public and hence never analysed. Company archives may contain catalogues, reports, records of transactions and minutes of meetings, all of which tell us what happened in the past. Researchers may also use other archival materials such as images (photographs, film, video), sounds and other nonwritten materials in doing their research. Archival records can show what people actually (recorded as) thought or did at the time, since organisational members have not reinterpreted archival records through hindsight – as the saying goes, 'Success has many fathers but failure is an orphan.' On the other hand, archives typically only capture a small part of what goes on in an organisation, because they cannot capture informal and verbal interactions.

Some organisational researchers have used archival research to look at how change unfolds over decades, rather than the few months or years that a particular research project would normally take. They may even span centuries, as illustrated in **Research in action 6.5**.

Research in action 6.5
I'LL DRINK TO THAT!

Glenn Carroll and Anand Swaminathan (2000) were interested in how the emergence of microbreweries contradicted a long trend towards greater concentration in the beer brewing industry. Carroll and Swaminathan used archival sources to identify the companies that entered and exited the brewing industry in the US over a long period. They used archival sources to construct life histories of 2251 breweries in the country, including microbreweries, brewpubs, contract brewers and mass producers. To identify all the brewers, they relied on industry histories, trade publications and web pages, rather than collecting information

> directly from existing firms. This is something that would have been, practically, almost impossible to achieve by direct measurement – not just in terms of the logistics of visiting all the firms, but the relative availability of data on firms that no longer existed.

You can also analyse 'texts' that are not words, such as films, television commercials and programmes, magazines advertisements, advertising coupons or bumper stickers. This kind of research can be extremely creative. Even though it is unlikely that you could find a database or a data set of, let's say, how commercials portray people drinking coffee, you could gather these materials and create your own data set to analyse. Consumer researchers, for example, have reported studies in the *Journal of Consumer Research* based on materials as diverse as comic books, romance novels, television commercials and popular television programmes. These are all artefacts created by organisations and used by people.

You might only want to use archival materials as a source of descriptive information, such as names, to create a record of key events in a company's history or as a source of illustrations, but you can also use them in a much more structured way to generate information you can analyse statistically. Various techniques are available for **structured content analysis** to find and count how often concepts, ideas or other 'meaning units' occur within documents or other texts. There are various computer programs you can use to make this task easier.

Major issues in archival research are similar to issues in large-scale survey data archives:

1. *How do you find out what archives exist?* As we noted in **Section 6.1.1**, public organisations such as the government, charities, trade associations and universities may make information available about their archives and even provide public access to those archives, but company archives are usually private, closely controlled, and difficult to find out about and access. Additionally, corporate and other business records may disappear when those businesses disappear through merger, acquisition, bankruptcy or dissolution.

2. *How do you gain access to these archives?* Access to most archives, especially those in private hands, is usually tightly controlled. You may need to use some of the tips for gaining access to people to gain access to archives. We discuss this issue in more detail in **Chapters 8** and **12**.

3. *What data do I need and how should I structure them?* Since you are not working with data in a predefined data set or database as for survey or proprietary databases, you will need to make these decisions yourself. It may take two or more passes through the data to collect all the information you need.

4. *How much time will it take?* Archival research is often time-consuming and open-ended. Archival research is usually slow compared with the other kinds of data gathering described in this chapter and the next, since you will have to go through many documents, and you may not be able to make photocopies or even take notes by hand if there are restrictions because of confidentiality or the condition of the materials. Therefore, extensive archival research may not be appropriate for short- or medium-length research projects, since the time needed to identify, access and collect data may be longer than the time you have available.

5. *Is there another way to get these data?* Can you interrogate any company sources or

databases to get the same information? Archival data may be the only records relating to long-ago events or defunct organisations.

Data from unobtrusive measures

You can also use secondary analysis with **unobtrusive measures**, data gathered indirectly from research subjects (Webb et al. 1966) by observing the traces they leave in the physical environment or other natural settings. These data are collected in the natural setting of organisations and people, unlike archival data. There can also be traces such as the forwarding of emails, posts on message boards, and so on.

Such **found data** result from the identification of physical traces, physical changes in the environment due to erosion or accretion. Whilst a variety of unobtrusive data are available to the researcher, researchers need the skills of a forensic scientist, detective or archaeologist to find and interpret these clues. Creative sources of unobtrusive data include:

> wear on the floor tiles surrounding a museum exhibit showing hatching chicks to measure visitor flows; the size of suits of armour as an indicator of changes in human stature over time; and (tongue in cheek) the relationship between psychologists' hair length and their methodological predilections. (Lee 2000: 2)

An unusual but interesting source is described in **Research in action 6.6**.

Research in action 6.6
IT'S NOT RUBBISH, IT'S RESEARCH … HONESTLY!

In studies of household consumption, people often consciously or unconsciously misreport what and how much they consume of various products. To find out what people actually buy, consume and throw away, many researchers have turned to analysing household waste – finding out what's in people's rubbish bins. This can be used to complement survey data ('what people said they did' versus 'what they actually did') or as a stand-alone research design.

In 1973, the Garbage Project at the University of Arizona started to analyse people's household rubbish using the same techniques that archaeologists use for studying ancient populations. A number of studies have used 'household archaeology' or garbage-ology to study business and management problems. For example, Wallendorf and Nelson (1986) studied the contents of nearly 1600 waste bins to determine whether Americans of European and Mexican backgrounds differed in the use of body care products, including 'personal cleansers, household cleansers, oral hygiene products, odour fighters, hair care products, skin care products, cosmetics, feminine protection products, over-the-counter drugs, and aspirin'. In another project, Reilly and Wallendorf (1987) studied differences between the foods consumed by these two groups based on the contents of their rubbish bins.

Unobtrusive measures can complement other data especially if you want to collect data about sensitive issues or do not have direct access to respondents, they are unwilling to answer questions or the act of asking questions might affect the answers (Lee 2000: 1). For example, when people are asked questions directly, they tend to overreport behaviours or attitudes they perceive as positive or **socially desirable**. If recycling household rubbish and giving to charity are considered as positive social behaviours, people will report doing more of these than they actually do. Not surprisingly, people also tend to underreport undesirable behaviours, such as drinking too much or wasting food.

Activity 1

List three behaviours of interest to business and management researchers that might not be accurately reported.

How could you get accurate information about these behaviours?

Would it be easier or harder than studying attitudes or beliefs?

Is secondary analysis right for you?

Whether you are taking a scientific or ethnographic approach to research, you will probably find yourself doing some secondary analysis, even if it is not the only method you use for collecting data to answer your research questions. If someone else has collected the right data and you can gain access to it, you should make use of it if you can. People and organisations create large amounts of secondary data as part of their everyday activities, and, as we have seen, some proprietary secondary data sources are even deliberately created and maintained as a source of revenues.

Some researchers find the challenge of archival research or unobtrusive measures exciting because it requires 'thinking outside the box'. If you are a fan of Sherlock Holmes, for example, you may recognise some of the detective's methods in unobtrusive research. If you are interested in historical or longitudinal research, this may be the only way to find out about people and companies.

Other business and management researchers, particularly in areas such as finance, accounting and business history, consider secondary analysis to be the only proper way to do research. (This makes writing chapters on methods for data collection in research methods books in these areas fairly simple.) This is often the only way they can accumulate the large number of observations they need to do statistical testing.

You may want to look ahead to **Figure 6.8** if you think you might be interested in secondary analysis, but are not sure. You should also read through **Sections 6.2** and **6.3** before you decide.

6.2 DESIGNS FOR SURVEYS

Many people think first of survey designs such as questionnaires when they think about business and management research. Interviews and questionnaires are popular ways to gather data about organisations and people (Gray 2004) and find out what people and organisations think, believe or do. They are a fairly natural way of getting information, because we usually ask someone else when we want to find something out. You may want to conduct your own survey to gain information directly from people or organisations, especially when secondary data aren't available.

Surveys can be the quickest and cheapest way of finding out information when you don't have time for intensive research designs such as observation or you are especially interested in studying groups rather than individuals. On the other hand, most people underestimate how difficult and time-consuming it is to design an effective survey that will actually answer their research questions. Questionnaire design and administration can be surprisingly difficult to get right, and the effort involved in getting enough people to agree to be interviewed or return your questionnaire is often underestimated. Unless you do a good job of designing your questions and sample, you may not get the information you need or be able to draw any conclusions. You might even end up discarding all the data you have gathered because the answers are irrelevant, wasting your time and resources and your respondents' time. The worst-case scenario is getting few – or even no – completed questionnaires back.

This section will describe the basics of survey design and administration, including the three main techniques of structured interviews, questionnaires and structured observations. You may want to follow up this information with a specialist book on interviewing or questionnaires from the **Additional resources** at the end of this chapter. Neither, however, will substitute for hands-on experience:

> Questionnaire design cannot be taught from books; every investigation presents new and different problems. A textbook can only hope to prevent some of the worst pitfalls and to give practical, do-it-yourself kind of information that will point the way out of difficulties. (Oppenheimer 1992: 1)

Activity 2

Unsurprisingly, 95 per cent of adults say they wash their hands after using the toilet. However, the American Society of Microbiology reports that only 78 per cent of people actually wash their hands after using the toilet. Of those who wash their hands, only half use soap and only half wash for 15–20 seconds.

What do you think accounts for the difference in the figures above?

How could you collect data to see which figure was more accurate?

Are there any legal or ethical questions that this might raise?

6.2.1 What is a survey?

A **survey** is a way to collect data from a range of respondents by asking them questions. Surveys are especially useful for capturing facts, opinions, behaviours or attitudes. Some familiar tools and techniques are associated with survey designs, including questionnaires, structured interviews and structured observations.

Although survey design can be identified by general principles, a particular survey can take many different forms. **Structured interviews** are conducted face to face, over the telephone or electronically, but they are still based on a standard set of questions (which may be called an instrument or a schedule). **Structured observations** record your observations of people's behaviours over a period of time, for example in work study. **Questionnaires** ask people to record their answers to a series of questions on paper or electronic forms; and are sometimes sent by post. However, you can also hand out questionnaires to respondents in person, and collect them in person, or leave them somewhere for people to collect themselves and return (for example store comment cards). Most surveys are conducted at only a single point in time, but surveys can also be used to collect longitudinal information if conducted continuously or at regular intervals of time.

Is a survey the right design for you?

A survey is not always the best way to answer your research questions. You might want to look ahead to **Figure 6.8** if you are considering a survey.

You should consider a survey if you want to collect data from a large number of respondents and have a limited time for collecting data from each of them or cannot visit them in person, or if you need to collect a large number of responses to analyse statistically. If you want to use a structured interview or questionnaire, your respondents must be able to understand and answer your questions with minimal explanation or without your being physically present. If you want to use structured observation, you may need to do this unobtrusively. You should also consider whether you are asking questions that your respondents might find sensitive or data they might only provide anonymously.

On the other hand, you should rule out a structured survey technique if it is not clear who might have the answers to your questions, you do not know in advance what you want to ask, you need to explain your questions in detail or you need to capture this kind of unstructured information by observation or other means. You should also rule out this approach if your questions or data will change as you do your research. If any of these are true, you might consider the unstructured interview and other techniques presented in **Chapter 7**.

Structured interviews

One of the most common techniques used in all types of business and management research is the **interview** – asking someone questions directly. The structured interview – where you ask the same questions in the same order to every interviewee – is the type of interview mostly closely associated with the scientific approach. (We will discuss other types of interviews in **Chapter 9**.) Taking a structured approach makes sure that the data you collect are consistent across interviews, by minimising the differences between the people you have interviewed and differences between different researchers or different interviews. This fits with the scientific model described in **Chapter 5**.

Ways of conducting structured interviews include:

- *Face-to-face interviews* – typically a one-to-one interview where you and your interviewee are present in the same location. Face-to-face interviews capture the most detail, both verbal and nonverbal, but are the most expensive to conduct because of time, distance and travel. Occasionally, you might conduct the interview as part of a team. You might also interview more than one person at a time, for example all adult members of a household in a consumer marketing study of how the decision to buy a new refrigerator is made.

- *Telephone interviews* – typically a one-to-one interview over the telephone between you and your interviewee. Since neither of you needs to travel, telephone interviewing is less expensive than face-to-face interviewing, and you may be able to conduct more telephone interviews in a given amount of time. However, the large number of unsolicited telephone interviews for marketing and political research may make people reluctant to participate in them and, if you are trying to interview people in organisations, you may find it difficult to get past the reception switchboard. The growth in web cameras and mobile phones equipped with video capabilities may increase the popularity of telephone interviews for business and management research, and overcome the loss of nonverbal information. You might also interview someone by email or fax, rather than over the phone, but this is more similar to questionnaires, which we explore below.
- *Structured observations* – although in structured observation you are not directly asking any questions, you are interrogating the behaviour of the person being observed and recording the information on a schedule. Mystery shoppers may use such a schedule when they unobtrusively follow people around and record details of what merchandise people look at, touch, try on and purchase, as described by Underhill (2000). Another use of structured observation is the time and motion study, associated with F.W. Taylor.

Issues in interview administration

Although we will go into sampling in more detail in **Section 6.2.3**, you should consider which respondents you are likely to include in or exclude from your survey if you choose one of the three structured interviewing techniques we list above. For example, telephone surveys have been found to undersample people with low or high incomes. In the UK, while most households have a landline, a high percentage of numbers are ex-directory (unlisted), so that you may have trouble developing an accurate sample frame. Furthermore, many people, mostly younger ones, are giving up land lines in favour of mobile phones, which are also ex-directory. Similarly, many people do not have email accounts, so you may be limiting your sample if you send them out this way.

Your 'script', or list of questions, is known as an **interview schedule**. You may standardise not only your questions, but also the range of answers that your respondent can choose from, as we discuss below. Using an interview schedule is convenient because it usually provides space for you to record the answers directly on the form. Standardising your questions, however, doesn't completely limit what you can ask. You may want to probe, ask for further information or explore unexpected answers.

Most professional survey researchers now use **computer-assisted protocols for interviews** (CAPI). Besides making it easier to standardise questions and responses, CAPI allows you to record responses directly on the computer and transfer them to the program you will use to analyse them. You are less likely to create errors than if you are entering them from a paper-based form.

You should try not to influence the answers you get by how you conduct your interviews. **Chapter 7** will discuss how you should behave as an interviewer in more depth. Some issues that apply specifically to structured interviews include:

1. *Consistency*. Make sure that you ask questions in exactly the same way and the same order during each interview. If you need to explain a question to your interviewee, make sure that you are consistent with the instrument and building standard **prompts** into your interview schedule may help to maintain this consistency. If you interpret or embellish the question with an example or additional information based on what you think, such as 'Well, I think that this means ...', you may influence the answer you get.
2. *Completeness*. Make sure that you have asked every question and not left any out. You may sometimes be tempted ask questions out of order if your interviewee starts talking about a subject you know comes up later in the interview schedule, but besides making it more likely that you will omit questions, this can contribute to a lack of consistency between interviews.
3. *Accuracy*. Make sure that you are recording the replies exactly. If you are only recording answers to closed-ended questions, make sure that you are ticking the right boxes. If you are recording answers to open-ended questions, make sure that you are capturing them exactly.

Even using an interviewing schedule, you may have a hard time maintaining consistency across interviews if several people in your project group are conducting interviews. You should hold a practice session before you start interviewing, so that everyone asks the same questions in the same way. You might try round-robin interviewing until you are satisfied with the consistency across interviewers. You may need to hold a refresher session after a certain number of interviews to make sure that variation hasn't crept in. This is especially important if there are major differences between interviewers. In the *International Service Study*, for example, researcher Chris Voss flew over from the UK to the US to train the American interviewers (Voss et al. 2004). By doing this, he made sure that no significant differences in the way the research was being conducted could creep in.

Because interviewing is so often used for commercial research, including consumer marketing and public opinion research, codes of ethics have been developed that address most of the issues you might encounter if you use a structured interview. Obviously, you need to consider ethical issues and informed consent if you plan to record a telephone interview. We will discuss this issue further in **Chapter 9**.

Self-administered questionnaires

Probably the most familiar survey design is the questionnaire, in which a respondent answers your questions directly, without you present. This difference in who does the asking and recording is significant. Your respondents interact with you only through the structured and standardised list of questions (and often answers), in a **self-administered questionnaire**.

Like interviews, questionnaires vary in how they are delivered to and collected from the respondent. The main methods are:

● *By post* – you send your questionnaire to your respondent by post and the respondent returns the completed questionnaire the same way. This postal questionnaire is popular because of its geographic reach – you can send a questionnaire to anywhere in the world that post is delivered.

- *Deliver and collect* – the questionnaire is handed out or left in a convenient location, and the respondent returns the completed questionnaire to the surveyor or a convenient location such as a clearly labelled box. Comment cards on restaurant tables and in hotel rooms are simple examples.
- *Email surveys* – the questionnaire is sent as an email or attachment to an email for your respondent to complete and return. You will obviously need a list of email addresses to send surveys. It is ethically unacceptable for you to send unsolicited mass emails (**spam**), no matter how well intentioned.
- *Web surveys* – you direct respondents to a web address – or they arrive at it from other links – to fill out a computer-assisted set of questions. This is becoming increasingly popular, not least because the software can record answers for you in a file or database and you do not have to re-enter them manually. You can also post intermediate or final feedback on the results on your website, which may be interesting to your participants. Although, increasingly facilitated by proprietary and general purpose software, there is less control over who answers and how many times they answer.

Issues in questionnaire administration

Your questionnaire design will have to be very clear because you are not interacting with your respondent. If you are considering using a self-administered questionnaire, there is a well-established literature on best practice for questionnaire design and administration (for example Foddy 1993; Oppenheimer 1992). We will present some of the main topics in questionnaire design and administration in this section, but we can cover only a few here. If you decide to use a questionnaire, you should consult some of the sources listed at the end of this chapter in **Additional resources**.

The main advantage of questionnaires over interviews for collecting data from a large number of people becomes obvious when you consider the cost per response. Once you have developed a questionnaire, the cost of administering one additional questionnaire is very low – the cost of photocopying and postage or hosting the website. The costs of scaling up from 100 to 200 questionnaires, or 1000 to 2000 questionnaires, are relatively small. By comparison, each additional interview is as expensive as every other interview. On the other hand, if you are scheduling interviews rather than cold-calling, you are only out the cost of a phone call or letter if your contact decides not to participate; given the low response rate to unsolicited questionnaires, you may be sending out 5–20 questionnaires for each one you get back – this can add up if you want to get a large set of responses to analyse.

The trade-off is the quality of the information you collect in an interview or questionnaire. You can only get the answers to the questions you have asked on your questionnaire, but a structured interview does allow some potential for capturing additional information and insights. Furthermore, you are less likely to have missing data problems with interview data, since you are interacting directly with your respondent. People often skip questions on questionnaires if they do not understand them or are bored. We have seen many questionnaires returned only half-complete. You also can capture more spontaneous feedback from your respondents, especially nonverbal feedback, in an interview, although in a questionnaire you can include a section at the end such as 'Any other comments?'

Since you are not asking the questions in person, your respondent cannot ask for directions, clarifications or prompts, so good questionnaire design becomes essential. If you want people to fill out a questionnaire, it needs to be short and clear, which usually means simple questions with predefined responses (we discuss this below). If you make a major design error, you cannot easily correct or recall a questionnaire once it has been delivered. If you do change your questionnaire or web questionnaire, you may not be able to use the early data. Since you usually interview people one at a time rather than simultaneously, you have more of a chance to mend your interview schedule if you find out that it is flawed.

6.2.2 Survey design and administration

Although many students think that survey design is simple and quick, for example you can design a survey in an afternoon session, survey design and administration is actually an intensive process and you must go through quite a few rounds drafting and redrafting your questions before your first participant is interviewed or fills out a questionnaire.

Developing or adopting a survey instrument

Although we discuss instrument design in detail below, you should consider using an existing survey and/or questions before you design your own. We recommend that you look at some examples of surveys from your literature search. Many articles and books include a copy of key questions – or even the entire survey instrument – or offer to provide them on request. For example, Zeithaml et al.'s *Delivering Quality Service* (1990) includes a copy of their *Service Quality Questionnaire*. Remember to ask permission to use a survey or a questionnaire unless the author has explicitly given permission in the source. (If you can't find any examples of how someone has investigated your research topic using structured interviews or questionnaires, you might question whether survey design is appropriate before trying to develop your own.)

We also recommend that you look at some examples of large-scale social surveys. In the UK, the Economic and Social Research Council (ESRC) supports the Social Survey Question Bank in the Centre for Applied Social Surveys at the University of Surrey, which makes available a large number of the questions asked in economic and social surveys (the data are archived separately, as discussed in **Section 6.1**). Some of these surveys are quite extensive: the National Food Survey has been running since the 1940s.

You may also be able to find a book that provides questions on your research topics. Books that collect together a large number of questions about your topic are known as 'question banks'. These are good sources of questions because experienced researchers will have already tested the questions.

Designing your own survey

If you cannot find a predesigned instrument or questions for your research topic, and you are still interested in designing a survey, we describe some of the major elements of the process below. Because surveys, especially postal questionnaires, are so popular, people have carried out extensive research into survey research and know a lot about what works and what doesn't. We also list some more detailed sources of advice in the

Additional resources at the end of this chapter. However, you can learn some of the tricks of the trade only by hands-on experience with designing and administering surveys. You may want to consult your project supervisor and/or anyone in your university who is expert in survey design before you launch a full-scale effort.

The survey design process

The work that you put into getting your survey instrument right – whether it is an interview schedule or questionnaire – is critical. Software for designing and analysing questionnaires or online surveys, such as SNAP, makes the technical job of developing an instrument much easier. However, this may result in poorer content, because it focuses more attention on the design and layout of the survey than on the content. We receive many questionnaires that look good, but are poorly conceived and designed, with missing or unclear instructions, poor or confusing questionnaire wording and the entire questionnaire being irrelevant because it has been sent to the wrong person. This agrees with the survey expert Oppenheimer (1992: 5–8), who says that the most common problems with surveys are too little design and planning, not asking the right people and not asking the right questions.

How to design a survey

Figure 6.1 presents a simplified overview of the survey design process. The backwards loops are especially important in survey design, because you won't have a chance to revise your structured interview schedule or your questionnaire once you launch into full-scale research mode.

Step 1. Decide what you want to ask
Students often decide to use a survey, without knowing whether a survey can actually answer their research questions and so often end up being limited in what they can study by their research design. Starting with your research questions and conceptual framework, you should see how – and whether – you can capture the information you need using a survey. List the major concepts and relationships you need to measure. Will you need additional sources of data? Is there a better way to capture this information?

Step 2. Decide what respondents you want to ask and how you want to ask them
The next step is to identify the people with the information you need. Who can answer the questions you want to ask? Do the people you want to interview or answer your questionnaire have the information to answer your questions, and answer them accurately? The 'good subject' effect (discussed in **Section 6.3**) may lead them to give an answer, even if they have to guess.

Also, will your proposed respondents actually have any interest in being interviewed or answering your questionnaire? CEOs of Fortune 500 companies are extremely unlikely to answer a student's (or even a professor's) unsolicited questionnaire. What incentives, if any, are there for your proposed respondents to participate in your survey – you are asking for a commitment of their time, which they might use better in other ways. Although this is not a unique problem for questionnaires, it is probably most

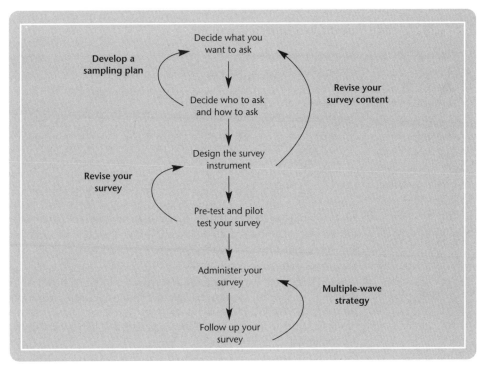

Figure 6.1 An overview of the survey process

critical for them, since you have to provide some incentive for people both to fill in the form *and* to return it.

You might think that your respondents have a duty to fill out your questionnaire, or they will want to just because you have asked, but this is not necessarily true. One of us saw a form letter sent out by a Japanese company's UK site in response to a request to fill out a questionnaire. The company politely returned the questionnaire and explained that it would have to hire a full-time employee just to fill out questionnaires, it received so many of them! On the other hand, other students on your course or in your halls of residence, members of an organisation or society, people you work with and so on will be much likelier to participate because of a shared interest or connection. We will consider this again in this section when we look at sampling and response rates.

You should also think about how you will administer your survey during this step, whether you will collect data using an interview or a questionnaire. Interviews are good at getting answers to questions, but can be difficult to arrange. You can send a questionnaire anywhere in the world, but they typically have low response rates – even as low as 1 in 100. We know of a student group who sent out several hundred questionnaires, including stamped self-addressed envelopes for the replies. They received two responses. This is unusual, but you should calculate the total costs of your research design, including your time and effort, per response. It doesn't make any sense to use a research design whose strengths are large-scale research and only collect a small set of replies. We do not advocate widescale postal surveys for student projects, unless you have managed to secure external funding and sponsorship from an organisation that will give your project the 'stamp of approval' and perhaps even access to a mailing list, as in **Student Research in action 6.2**.

Student research in action 6.2
LIKE THEY DO ON THE DISCOVERY CHANNEL

Five final-year undergraduate students were working on a project sponsored by an animal welfare group, which we will disguise – for reasons that should become apparent below – as the Hamsters and Gerbils Conservation Society (HGCS). The organisation raised money in the UK to fund refuges for hamsters and gerbils that had been abandoned or abused by their owners, and feral colonies of hamsters and gerbils. It also carried out political campaigning to try to strengthen the laws on hamsters and gerbils in the UK and internationally. Some of this it carried out on its own, some of it with similar groups in other countries and some of it with organisations interested in other rodents.

The organisation wanted the group to survey its members to see how satisfied they were with its strategy. The organisation had a list of its members, to whom it sent publications about its activities and requests for funds. It also distributed a monthly newsletter specifically to junior members (memberships were popular as birthday gifts for children aged 12 and under).

The students developed a survey, which the HGCS enclosed with its next newsletter to junior members. The response rate was high, so the students were able to argue that they had a clear picture of what the organisation's current members thought. They would never have been able to capture this information through interviews or observation. Thus, the students believed that they had captured both information of interest to the society (which they had), and information that could help them to solve an academic (theoretical) problem (which they hadn't, as we discuss below.)

Step 3. Design your survey

Once you get the questions themselves right, you can then think about the order you want to present the questions in, which has a surprising influence on your respondent's willingness to answer and the answers themselves. You should also design the instructions carefully. Once you have the content right, you can work on the look and feel of the questionnaire, including the layout and design on the page, which will make it easier for you to conduct a structured interview or observation, or your respondent to fill out a questionnaire. The final step is to think from your respondent's perspective – have you actually created something that he or she can and will answer? We give some pointers on each of these areas below.

Design your questions. Our advice is that you should try to use an existing survey or existing questions wherever possible, because these have already been extensively tested. If you do want to design your own questions, there are two main types of survey question, closed and open-ended.

You can specify the answers to a **closed-ended question** in advance, so that your respondent chooses the most appropriate response from a list. In a structured interview, you would read your question and then the list of answers or prompts. In a structured observation, you might tick a category that you have already defined. In a web-based questionnaire, your respondent might answer a closed-ended question by indicating their response on a tick box, a radio button or a scrolling list, as shown in **Figure 6.2**.

The advantages of closed-ended questions for quantitative research include:

- *Speed* – Interviewers can record the answers and respondents can answer closed-ended questions more quickly.
- *Accuracy* – Interviewers or respondents are less likely to record inappropriate answers.
- *Data entry* – You can enter data from an interview schedule or questionnaire more quickly.

In a closed-ended question, your respondents can only choose from the responses you have already selected. You can also ask an **open-ended question**, where you allow your respondent to give any response. You can ask an open-ended question such as 'Who would you say are your top three competitors?' and record the response directly on your interview schedule or computer, if you are using CAPI. Open-ended questions are often used in structured interviews, since the interviewer is there to provide quality control.

In a web questionnaire, you might ask your respondent to fill in an open-ended answer in a text box. You can make this text box long or short, to give your respondent a clue as to the length of the expected answer. We show some examples in **Figure 6.3**.

You can mix both open-ended and closed-ended questions in a survey. If you are more interested in asking open-ended rather than closed-ended questions, you might consider using a questionnaire, but it might be more appropriate to use an interview (see **Chapter 7**). If you want to ask a large number of questions about a large number of respondents, you should emphasise closed-ended questions. First, since your respondents can only choose from a limited range of answers, you only have to deal with a limited number of different answers per question. Second, you can convert these answers from text into numbers, which makes it easier to record (or 'code') the answers in a computer spreadsheet and analyse them using statistics.

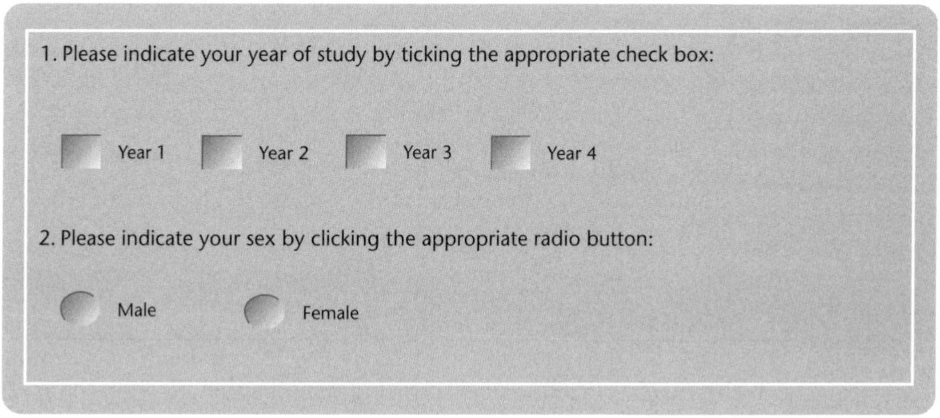

1. Please indicate your year of study by ticking the appropriate check box:

☐ Year 1   ☐ Year 2   ☐ Year 3   ☐ Year 4

2. Please indicate your sex by clicking the appropriate radio button:

○ Male   ○ Female

Figure 6.2 Common formats for closed-ended questions

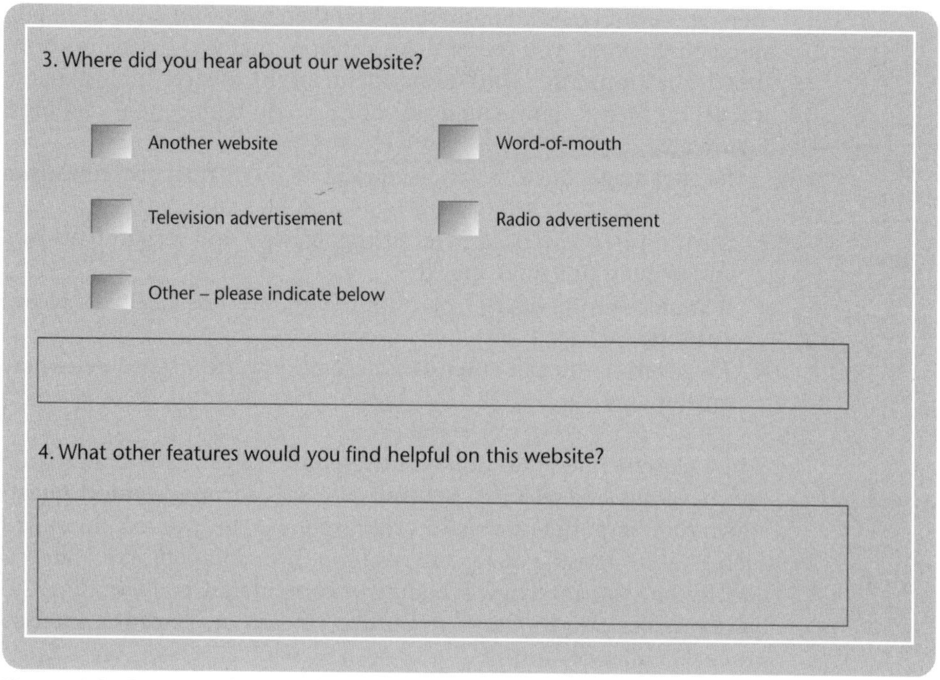

Figure 6.3 Common formats for open-ended and mixed questions

Some common mistakes that students make in designing questions are forgetting about:

1. *Clarity* – if you are using questions whose responses may ask for judgements such as 'seldom' or 'frequently', whenever possible, structure your responses so that it is clear what each response means instead of making your respondent interpret them. How would your respondent know whether 'seldom' means less often than 'rarely'? Why not specify 'Once a month' and 'Once a year' – unless you are actually investigating how people interpret terms such as seldom and rarely.

2. *Simplicity* – avoid questions that are actually multiple questions or general questions. If you ask a double-barrelled questions such as 'How often do you walk or use the bus and train to get to work?', you are losing any information about the individual activities. Don't use technical terms that may be unfamiliar to your respondent: 'Does your manufacturing plant use JIT/TQM/BPR' might be more intelligible as 'Does your manufacturing plant use just-in-time, total quality management or business process engineering?', although it's still not a good question. Check to make sure that each question is only a single question. Even if it takes up more physical space, you might want to rephrase the last question as 'Please place a tick beside each of the following techniques that your manufacturing plant is using' and list each of the options separately.

3. *Brevity* – avoid long questions, in interviews because it is difficult for your interviewee to remember the entire question and answer it accurately, and in questionnaires because your respondent may lose interest and skip the question.

4. *Neutrality* – avoid asking leading questions, such as 'Are you in favour of raising taxes to waste money on able-bodied people who could work but don't?' You are conducting research to find out information, not confirm your own opinions.

Even if your respondent has the relevant information, you might still get inaccurate answers depending on how you ask the questions. Rather than asking your respondent to estimate a figure in response to 'How many times did you go to the cinema last year', it might be better to ask 'On average, how often do you go to the cinema' and give a range such as weekly, monthly, and so on.

Design your instrument. Once you are happy with your individual questions, you need to check the order you are asking them in and how the whole interview schedule or questionnaire flows together. Some tips for smoother flow are:

- Begin with simple questions and put difficult questions at the end of the questionnaire. This keeps you from putting people off at the beginning.
- Put awkward or potentially embarrassing questions last.
- If your questionnaire is long, or covers different areas, divide the questionnaire into sections. This gives your respondents a break and helps to avoid 'respondent fatigue'.
- Make sure that you have provided clear and explicit instructions on how to answer the questions, and what to do when the questions have been answered – especially important for self-completion questionnaires!

Lay out your questionnaire. Finally, once you are happy with the individual questions and overall structure, you should work carefully on the physical design and appearance of your instrument. Good design can substantially improve your response rate. For informal or small-scale questionnaires, a neatly word-processed and photocopied questionnaire (or a web-based questionnaire you have designed yourself) will usually do. For formal or large-scale questionnaires, or where respondents are of high status, you may need to have them professionally designed and printed.

Using a software package such as Snap may make designing the instrument and entering the data much simpler, but the trade-off is the time involved in learning to use the package and the temptation to focus on design at the expense of content.

Check the questionnaire length. Check to make sure that your interview schedule or questionnaire is not too long and you have not asked too many questions. When people get tired, they may give incorrect answers, may not complete all the questions, or may even not fill it out at all.

To maximise your response rate, your questionnaire should fit entirely on one folded A3 page (that is, no more than four A4 pages), including your instructions. You may have to decide whether to drop some questions, or settle for a lower response rate. Using design tricks such as narrow margins or smaller fonts may actually discourage people from answering it. The same principle applies to online surveys – if you try to disguise a long survey by breaking it into multiple screens, people can still get survey fatigue.

If you absolutely must ask a large number of questions for your research, you might divide the questions into two or more questionnaires for different respondents. An example of a project that did this is the World Class Manufacturing Project, where researchers administered 26 separate questionnaires at each plant site, so that no respondent had to answer more than 100 questions. Each questionnaire could thus be answered in a reasonable amount of time, before the respondent got bored or fatigued. If a single respondent had been asked to give all of this information, he or she would have had to answer more than 1500 questions! You should also consider what information you could collect yourself, for example information that is already published in company annual reports or industry publications.

Pilot your survey

If you test your interview or questionnaire using a pilot test before you start using it to collect data from your sample, you are more likely to pick up serious problems with your questions, instructions or survey design. You should:

1. Make sure that people know who you are, why you are asking for their help and that you have dealt with any reservations about providing you with the data (for example, through a statement on confidentiality).
2. Try out your questions – do people understand what the questions mean? Missing or incorrect responses may indicate that people do not understand what you are asking.
3. Time how long it takes for the interview or your respondents to fill out your questionnaire – too short or too long, and you either miss data or people do not complete the forms.
4. See how they deal with the instructions on the forms, including what to do with the completed form.
5. Enter the data – set up the necessary databases or spreadsheets to feed your data into – how easy is it for you to enter data from the spreadsheets?

Revise your survey

Once you have pilot tested your survey, you should revise anything that you identified as a problem. If you make major changes, you should pilot test your survey again before you administer it. Keep doing this for as long as it takes to get it right, no matter how eager you are to start collecting data. Once everything seems to be OK, check it one more time. You will probably find some errors or ambiguities you have not previously spotted. Fix these and then start interviewing people, making observations or sending out questionnaires.

Administer your survey

If you are using a postal questionnaire, you may want to keep track of the response rate to your questionnaires, so that you can take corrective action if necessary. Some researchers follow a multiple-wave strategy, in which they do not leave their project's success to a single mail shot. This might involve following up nonresponses with a letter or polite phone call after a reasonable period of time to remind people to respond. You may need to send out reminder letters after an appropriate period (two to four weeks), and perhaps even send out more surveys to the same sample or a new sample. As we have mentioned above, a lot of research has been done on this method, so you may want to look to the specialist literature for guidance on more complex survey designs.

6.2.3 Sampling

Except for a census, which is administered to every member of a population (or at least as close as possible), surveys gather data from a subset, or sample, of the population, who represent the entire population you want to study. How you select your **sample** is therefore the second key factor for successful survey research besides instrument design. This will determine your ability to draw conclusions about the social units you are studying.

Sampling allows you to make conclusions about the social units you are studying by selecting units that are representative of your population. To sample you need to understand what population you want to sample and what characteristics you want to measure. 'The first step in understanding and representing a population is to be able to name that population' (O'Leary 2004). Your **population** is the set that contains all members of the social units you want to study. A population might consist of all Chinese restaurants in the UK, all university students or all Honda drivers. Your sample is the subset of those social units you have selected to study, for example students at your own university to represent all university students.

Your list of all the units in the population is known as your **sampling frame**, although in many cases it will be difficult to accurately list these units. If you have defined your population as all of O2's mobile phone customers, even if you had access to the company's customer database, this might include customers who no longer have a mobile phone but who haven't cancelled their accounts, or exclude customers who have signed up in the last week.

Your sample must be representative of your population if you want to generalise from your sample to your population (Bryman and Bell 2003: 91); otherwise, your results will be inaccurate because your sample is **biased**. The two main approaches to sampling are probability sampling and nonprobability sampling. In **probability sampling**, the units you study are drawn randomly from your population, whilst in **nonprobability sampling**, you systematically or purposefully select these units.

Activity 3

Nadia and her project group want to collect data for a research project on the environmental effects of low-cost air travel from England to Portugal. They plan to stop students outside the student union and ask them a few questions, which they estimate will take about ten minutes per student. They plan to entice students into answering their question by giving each respondent a chocolate bar.

Do you think that this is a good plan? What issues do you think they should take into account in designing a sampling plan?

Probability sampling

If you want to use statistical tests to measure how likely it is that your findings about your sample are representative of your sample (see **Chapter 10** for more on quantitative analysis), you should use probability sampling. The goal of probability sampling is to make sure that your sample is representative by making sure that each unit in your population has a known and equal probability of being selected. Most probability samples also rely on the units you study being randomly selected. If you want to draw conclusions about household wealth by sampling only footballers' wives, you would be doing journalism or consulting rather than research.

We describe four techniques that you can use for probability sampling below and illustrate them in **Figure 6.4**:

1. *Simple random sampling* – You are equally likely to select any particular member of the population to study. If you want to sample 10 out of 100 employees, you should have a 10 per cent (10/100) chance of selecting any individual employee for your study. If you have access to a spreadsheet or a table of random numbers, you can use random numbers to select the employees from your sampling frame. If you assigned a random number between 1 and 100 to all 100 employees, you might use a rule that you would select any employee whose random number fell between 41 and 50.

2. *Systematic sampling* – Similar to simple random sampling in that you are equally likely to select any member of the population to study, but instead of using random numbers you take a systematic approach. You might decide to study every tenth employee on the list (2, 22, 32, ...). However, if your list is in a nonrandom order, your sample may be biased (for example all women in the first half of the list and all men in the second half).

3. *Stratified random sampling* – If your population is not uniform, you may want to make sure that you select enough members of certain subsets. You may want to make sure that each subset is proportionally represented. If you are trying to sample students from three years of your degree course, you may want to assign each year its own sampling frame and then use random sampling within the subgroup. This helps you make sure that your sample is representative if simple random sampling might not result in equal representation in your study.

4. *Cluster sampling* – If you have a nonuniform population, you may want to select your entire sample from a particular subset that is representative of the entire population. This is known as a cluster. You might choose a particular police station to be representative of all police stations, or a particular house to represent all first-year student houses. Again, unless your cluster is perfectly representative of your population, you risk building sample error into your sampling plan.

Although this does not describe every possible probability sampling plan, these four techniques illustrate two important aspects of sampling. Probability sampling can be random or systematic. You can draw your sample in a single stage, as in simple random or systematic sampling, or in more than one stage, as in stratified random or cluster sampling. We will discuss other issues related to probability sampling when we describe sample bias and error.

Nonprobability sampling

In nonprobability sampling, you have a greater chance of selecting some units to study than other units. Four techniques that you can use for nonprobability sampling are:

1. *Convenience sampling* – You choose a sample because you have access to it, for example all the students who live in your hall of residence. This may get you enough responses, but you will have trouble convincing anyone else that you can draw any sort of general conclusions from it. The best use of a convenience sample is to pre-test or pilot your instruments, and then just discard the data from your sample.

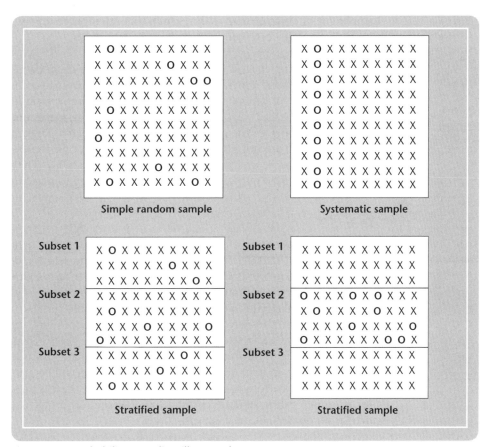

Figure 6.4 Probability sampling illustrated

2. *Volunteer sampling* – You advertise for a sample, for example in a newsgroup or on a bulletin board at school. This pretty much violates all the random sampling rules – researchers have found people who volunteer to be different from the general population. Anyone who watches shows such as *Oprah* or *Tricia*, or reality TV, can vouch for that!

3. *Snowball sampling* – Your sample evolves from a small sample, often a convenience sample, to take in contacts known to or suggested by your original respondents. This is often an effective way to study a social network or otherwise invisibly connected group. Again, you may have problems with drawing conclusions beyond your sample.

4. *Quota sampling* – You choose the characteristics you want your sample to have, and then sample until you have enough representatives of each category. This is not a random or systematic sample, because each unit does not have an equal chance of being selected. However, a quota sample can provide a good approximation to a probability sample. Quota sampling is often used to make sure that you have equal representation of male and female respondents, or respondents by age. If you need, for example, to interview 50 men and 50 women, you would stop interviewing men after you had reached 50, even if you only had 40 women at that point. Quota

sampling is often associated with research that attempts to represent a large population, for example opinion polling for election research.

Each of these techniques lacks one or more characteristic of probability samples that would let us make some general conclusions about the population from the sample. You should be wary of generalising if you use one of these techniques. On the other hand, these can be useful ways to sample when your main goal is not generalisation: you might be sampling for the purposes of qualitative research. Researchers who take a qualitative approach are not interested in how well the sample represents the population, but the lessons learnt from the sample (O'Leary 2004). They describe their samples as theoretical or purposive rather than nonrandom to make this clear.

Sampling error

Using probability sampling allows you to draw conclusions about your population from your sample. The difference between the sample you select and the population you take it from is known as **sampling error**. Sampling error is a threat to generalisability. If you have an accurate sampling frame and you use probability sampling correctly, it is less likely that you will over- or undersample certain members of your population. However, you may still end up with sample error if you cannot contact all the social units you have selected or if some of these refuse to participate. This sampling error is due to **nonresponse**. Selective or systematic nonresponse may skew your sample away from your design, because your findings will be biased towards your respondents and away from your nonrespondents. Even if there is no sampling error, a low response rate can create both practical and theoretical problems for your survey research, as we discuss below.

Response rate

Response rate creates a big headache for students and their supervisors. Students often underestimate how many surveys they will need to administer in order to get a specific number back. (We will describe sample size separately below.) Most surveys are lucky to achieve a 10–15 per cent return rate. Even legally required surveys such as the National Census don't achieve a 100 per cent return rate: you may need to send out 20 or even 100 questionnaires by post in order to get a single survey back. If possible, look at the survey response rates reported in the articles in your literature review. To estimate how many questionnaires you need to send out, divide the number of responses you want by your most likely response rate. So, if you need 100 responses and you estimate your response rate is 10 per cent, you will need to send out 1000 surveys. For interviews, divide the number of interviews you want by the likely conversion rate of contacts to interviews.

As well as reflecting people's dislike of filling out forms or lack of time, a low response rate can suggest problems with your study. This is where good survey design can make a difference. If you plan to use a questionnaire, make sure that it is short and clear, and that you have given people a good reason to fill it out and return it. If there are any serious problems with your survey, then pilot testing, follow-up and multiple-wave survey designs can identify the most serious problems and improve your response rate.

Sample size

'What sample size do I need?' is one question that project supervisors are repeatedly asked. The simple calculations often reported in methods books only apply to some types of surveys such as public opinion polls, where you want to draw relatively simple conclusions about your population, you do not need to investigate differences between subgroups and you only want to know the answer to each question in isolation. You can look up sample sizes on charts or calculate them. The calculation depends only on how confident you want to be that your conclusions accurately represent your sample, and what percentage of the population is likely to give each response to your question. In this case, as Bryman and Bell (2003: 101) point out, the *absolute* size of your sample is more important than the *relative* size. This is due to the statistical properties of sampling – the sample size you need does not increase proportionally with the size of the population you are studying.

In business and management we are seldom interested in questions that are as simple as those posed in opinion or electoral polls, so calculating sample size is rarely straightforward. To estimate the sample size you need, you will need to know not only details of your population and the variables you want to study, but also the precise statistical tests you will use to analyse your data and the confidence level you want to achieve. (We will discuss this further in **Chapters 10** and **11**.) In general, you will need a larger sample size when:

1. you plan to use sophisticated statistical methods
2. you plan to test the relationships between two or more variables
3. your variables can take on more values
4. your data do not follow a normal distribution
5. you are investigating weaker relationships among your variables.

The best advice is to get as large a sample as you can within your time and cost constraints. If calculating sample size is essential to the success of your project, you should probably consult an experienced statistician.

An experienced statistician can also give you useful advice on choosing statistical tests to suit the sample size that you can reasonable obtain. Some statistical analyses cannot be conducted except on very large data sets, whilst some statistical tests can be conducted on very small numbers of responses. As the administrative scientist James March and his colleagues observed, a sample size of one is sufficient, if it's the right one! (March et al. 1991). Sample size is a consideration, as shown in **Student research in action 6.3**.

> *Student research in action 6.3*
> **BACK ON THE CHAIN GANG**
>
> Rob and his project group wanted to show that the more hours per week a full-time student worked in paid employment, the less likely they were to get a good degree. They decided to survey past students to see whether the number of hours that students worked in paid employment affected their final degree classification. So, how many questionnaires to send out? First, Rob and his group needed to think about the likely

response rate to their survey: some students might have moved, some might not reply.

Second, the way Rob and his group defined student work in their hypothesis was likely to have a big effect on the number of cases they needed to collect:

- Students who worked versus students who didn't work
- Students who worked more than eight hours per week
- The number of hours worked
- The definition and distribution of 'good degrees' in the programme, for example, if only 5 per cent of students received a first, versus 20 per cent received a first. On the other hand, if the group defined a 2.1 or above as a good degree and 95 per cent of the class achieved that level, it would be difficult to show that work accounted for the other 5 per cent.

 ## 6.3 DESIGNS FOR EXPERIMENTS

The final research design that we will discuss in this chapter is the experiment. An **experiment** is a structured process for testing how varying one or more inputs affects one or more outcomes. Many people forget to include the experiment as a research design for business and management research, because it is associated in the popular imagination with the natural and applied sciences. However, you are probably already familiar with experiments from everyday life, even if they go under names such as 'taste test' or 'trial offer'.

 ### 6.3.1 Principles of experimental design

An experiment may be your best choice if you want to test hypotheses that concern cause-and-effect relationships. You are interested in such a relationship when a hypothesis states a relationship between two or more concepts, and you propose that at least one concept is an **independent variable** (cause or input) and one concept is a **dependent variable** (effect or outcome). To be able to test this, you must also be able to measure and vary the independent variable, and measure the change in the dependent variable, as well as measuring any other variables that might explain the change in the dependent variable (alternate explanation).

This is one of the major drawbacks of using the experimental design for studying complex business and management situations. In **Chapter 5**, we used the scientist conducting laboratory experiments (perhaps on white mice) as the exemplar of the scientific approach to business and management research. An experiment is often carried out on a limited part of the phenomenon or context that is being studied. Researchers in natural science and engineering fields are often able to study the systems they are interested in studying in controlled settings such as laboratories, and keep most of the aspects of the system and the environment constant whilst varying only one factor at a time. Researchers may study natural or physical systems by breaking them down into smaller systems or parts that can be studied in isolation from the whole system (reductionism). They can study how a car engine works without having to study the entire automobile, or how an artificial hip joint works, without having to study the entire human body.

On the other hand, people who take the ethnographic approach as their model for doing research often regard the experiment as an inappropriate design for studying complex organisations and human behaviours. They argue that the social units and systems that we research in business and management are difficult to reduce to a simple enough system to study in a laboratory. This doesn't mean that experiments are not used in business and management, just that business and management research (with the exception of some subjects) seldom applies the experimental method in the same way and with the same rigour as the natural sciences.

You should be wary of concluding that the experiment is completely out for business and management research. It *is* possible to carry out an experiment by varying one or more aspects of a situation and observing the effect on some outcome, such as sales or customer satisfaction, as shown in **Student research in action 6.4**. In fact, much of what we know about business and management has been learnt from field experiments, starting with Taylor's scientific management experiments and the Hawthorne experiments. You may even have unwittingly participated in quite a few business and management experiments. Fast-food companies often test out new sandwiches in just a few locations before offering them nationwide – the fast-food company McDonald's even has a mock-up of an entire McDonald's restaurant on the campus of McDonald's University, where new menus and new processes can be tried out before they go public (Bradach 1997). Heinz has tried out different colours of ketchup around the world, to see whether total ketchup sales will increase (BBC News 11 July 2000).

Student research in action 6.4
ONE FROM COLUMN A, ONE FROM COLUMN B

Xin decided that he wanted to test David Maister's eight principles for managing service queues in his MSc dissertation.

Xin decided that his summer job in a Chinese restaurant would be a good place to test these principles with real customers. One of Maister's predictions is that 'unexplained waits seem longer than explained waits' (Maister 1993). In order to test whether this was true, one evening he told some groups of customers who were waiting to be seated why they had to wait and told other groups nothing. At the end of the meal, each group of customers was asked to fill out a questionnaire rating their satisfaction with the meal. Xin expected that if Maister's principle were true, those groups who had been informed would be more satisfied with the meal – everything else being equal of course!

It does mean, however, that the conclusions we can draw from an experiment in business and management research are not necessarily as strongly supported as in scientific research.

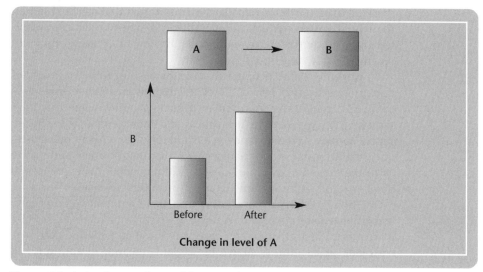

Figure 6.5 A simple experimental framework

Cause-and-effect relationships

An experiment is the strongest method for showing a relationship between two or more concepts, especially if you want to show that a change in one causes a change in another – a **cause-and-effect relationship**. Because an experiment allows you to see what effect varying an independent variable has on the dependent variable, holding everything else constant, it is the strongest design for showing a cause-and-effect relationship between concepts.

As noted above, natural scientists are able to study a system in isolation from the environment and hold everything constant except for the one input or condition they are trying to vary. What you can vary is known as your **experimental treatment**. This means that you have more chance of ruling out the observed change in the dependent variable being due to a factor you have not controlled or observed, rather than the change in the independent variable. For example, a company wants to know why the pay-for-performance programme (A) that it implemented didn't result in higher employee performance (B). We might naively conclude that pay-for-performance didn't work, but if we also knew that the company had laid off a significant number of workers during the same period, we might instead decide that we need to include other things that are going on.

In business and management research, you need to rule out the possibility that your observed outcome B isn't due to the other factor (C) that you have not identified. You need to identify any other factor (C) or factors that could affect the outcome, the relationship or offer an alternative explanation. These factors might include any other potential causes of changes in the results, difference in the people or organisations being observed or even our own expectations about what the outcome of the experiment should be.

The most important step in experimental design is the step where you are deducing your hypothesis or hypotheses from your theory. If you do not identify all the alternate causes and measure or control them, your experiment will be pointless. Being able to identify at least one independent variable and one dependent variable is an impor-

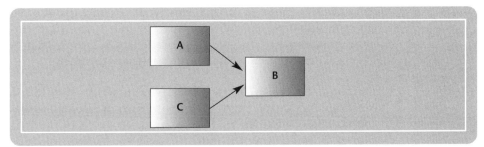

Figure 6.6 Alternate causes

tant aspect of the experimental design, and one that makes it different from secondary analysis and surveys, where we may only study relationships between variables.

An experiment is the best research design if you want to rule out the possibility that any other factors have affected the relationship between the two (or more) factors that you are looking at. If you can systematically examine the relationship between varying your input factor and changes in the output factor you are observing, and you consistently find changes in the outcome, it is easier to propose that changes in A lead to changes in B.

Ruling out alternate explanations for the relationships between two or more concepts is always difficult, especially when you are doing research with people or organisations rather than natural systems. In scientific research, being able to study a small part of a system in a controlled setting such as a laboratory makes it much easier to do this. In business and management, however, when you start considering what else might be going on in what you are studying, the picture almost always becomes more complex.

If you do find that C (or D and so on) has an effect on B or the relationship between A and B, you may need to revise your model or even your theory. You might need to come up with an alternate hypothesis for the role of C. First, A might not really have any effect on B and a variation in the level of C might be causing the change in B rather than A. Second, although A might have an effect, the effect of C might overwhelm or cancel out the effect of A. Alternatively, A and C might both affect B, but it might be difficult to disentangle their relative effects, especially if A and C always occur together.

It is difficult in many cases to show cause and effect, because for one factor to cause another, the factor that we argue is the cause must precede the result in time, consistently. If you can eliminate as many other factors as possible – which we will discuss in more detail below – you can be even more confident that you have found a cause-and-effect relationship. But this is not the same as proving that A causes B. What if it is impossible to show that the variation in A happens before the variation in B? In real life, this is difficult, so usually we can only make statements about associations, or correlations, which are much weaker than statements about cause and effect.

Experimental treatment and control

Scientists have developed a structured approach to ruling out as many alternate causes or explanations as they can in an experiment. This relies on a design that enables you to hold constant those factors you want to rule out as causing the changes in the output variable so that you can maximise your certainty that the changes are due to varying your input. In experimental language, this is known as **control**. Control is essential for examining cause-and-effect relationships. There are four types of variables that you will need to measure and/or control in an experiment:

1. *Experimental variables* are the inputs you intend to vary to see the effects on outcomes, for example varying the drink (water or Red Bull) as the input to see the effects on test performance
2. *Dependent variables* are the outcomes that you predict will vary in response to changes in the experimental variables
3. *Controlled variables* are any elements of the experiment that you will try to eliminate as potential causes of the variation in outcomes by excluding them from the experiment, holding them constant during the experiment or by randomising some element of the experiment
4. *Uncontrolled variables* are variables you do not know about or are unable to control, which might lead you to make mistakes about concluding there is (or isn't) a cause-and-effect relationship.

Developing your conceptual framework thus becomes crucial for the experimenter because you must be able to identify and specify not only all the variables you want to manipulate and observe, but also any other ones that might affect your experiment.

If you are considering using an experiment, you should already realise that it is difficult to control any systems except simple systems, or any human behaviours except basic or readily observable behaviours. You might also be able to observe the behaviour and interactions of two people (a dyad). Large groups, or complex systems, such as organisations, are extremely difficult to manage in an experiment, although it has been done. This means that true (that is, scientific) experiments are difficult to conduct in business and management, and hence rare. On the other hand, business and management research often draws successfully on experiments done in other areas such as social psychology, in drawing up conceptual frameworks and explaining what is observed in organisations.

Control group

Since we can never be sure that we have eliminated or controlled all other alternate causes besides our independent variable, we need to make sure that the change in our dependent variable wouldn't have happened anyway. The second principle of experimental design is the control group. The term **control group** is often used to describe the group that gets no experimental treatment. If we have two groups – one a control group and one a treatment group – we will be more convinced that our independent variable has created our change in our dependent variable if it only happens to the treatment group and not to the control group.

As you can see in **Figure 6.7**, the control group has stayed the same despite the experimental treatment (change in the independent variable A), whilst the treatment group has changed. Thus, we are more confident that our experimental treatment has caused the change in the dependent variable.

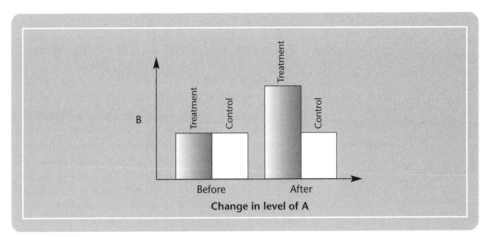

Figure 6.7 Treatment versus control group

Random assignment

Can you really be certain that the experimental treatment has caused the change in the dependent variable, even if you have a control group? Perhaps the two groups would have changed anyway, whether the experimental treatment was applied or not. You need to make sure that there were differences between the treatment and the sample groups that could have caused the change independently of the experimental treatment. This can only be ruled out if you have randomly assigned the experimental participants to the two groups (which you can check by comparing characteristics of the two groups).

Random assignment is the third principle of experimental design, and one that is often violated in business and management experiments. Since people and organisations usually vary significantly one from another, unlike laboratory rats, **random assignment** helps to rule out any variations due to differences between the people or organisations assigned to different levels of your experimental treatment. Random assignment helps you to ensure that differences in your experimental outcomes (dependent variables) aren't due to pre-existing or systemic differences between the people in your groups. We discussed the importance of sampling in **Section 6.2**. Probability sampling is used in the survey design to apply the logic of random assignment.

Statistical analysis

Although it is not a principle of experimental design, you want to make sure that the change you have observed in the dependent variable has actually occurred, and any difference before and after the treatment is not measurement error or natural fluctuations. Ideally, you should design your experiment so that your experimental data provide the strongest empirical evidence (that is, statistical analysis of data) to support (or overturn) this hypothesis. Control, including random assignment, makes the experiments the best method to test an **experimental hypothesis** – what you predicted would happen *before* you conducted the experiment.

You should use statistical tests to make sure that you are not arguing for a cause-and-effect relationship based on a systematic association where this relationship is actually due to change. This is one area where journalism and consulting often fail to measure up to research.

Research shows that people are not very good at actually interpreting results accurately, and without statistical tests they often reach the wrong conclusions. Knowing how to design a statistical test and which statistical test you can use is important to being able to correctly interpret the results of an experiment. However, statistical probability and common sense don't always coincide. This could lead to concluding that there is no relationship when one exists, or that there is a relationship when one doesn't exist. People often overestimate or underestimate the probability that certain events will occur, or the probability that the distribution of events that have occurred differs significantly from randomness, as shown in the activity below.

Activity 4

If you flip a coin 20 times, you expect on average to get 10 heads and 10 tails, if it is a fair coin. If you get 12 heads and 8 tails, you might not be too surprised. If you get 1 head and 19 tails, though, you would probably begin to expect that you might not have an average coin or your flipping technique might be suspect.

Suppose we asked you to mentally flip a penny 10 times and record the number of times it comes up heads and the number of times it comes up tails. How many times would you expect it to come up with no heads or no tails in 10 tosses? 1 or fewer? 2 or fewer? Record your answers in the table below.

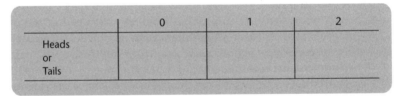

	0	1	2
Heads or Tails			

Suppose you did flip the penny ten times and it came up with zero, one or two heads or tails. Would you think that the coin was dodgy? We flipped a simulated penny 10 times, for 100 trials. The exact distribution is shown in the Postscript at the end of this chapter.

If you thought that it was unlikely that a fair penny would come up heads or tails 0 times, then you are right – this might happen by chance once in less than 1000 times, and it never occurred in our simulated 1000 trials. Coming up with one head or tail is also unlikely – this might happen as often as 1 in 100 times. Once we get to two heads or two tails, this might occur 1 in 10 times. This is well above the level of 1 in 20 times that is the accepted level for statistical testing.

What you are investigating in an experiment may be much more subtle than flipping a coin. This means that you need to be careful so that you do not draw the wrong conclusions from an experiment (or indeed any other relationship). **Chapters 10 and 11** will help you identify some useful statistical tests.

6.3.2 Types of experiments

Although you might think of the stereotypical scientist conducting experiments in a laboratory, an experiment doesn't necessarily have to take place there. Researchers classify experiments as **true experiments** if all the principles of experimental design – experimental treatment, random assignment, control groups, before-and-after measurement – are met. If one or more of these are lacking, but the general design is experimental, these research studies are known as **quasi-experiments**.

Researchers also classify experiments according to the relationship between the experiment's setting and the natural setting of the system or phenomenon being studied. Experiments can take place in any kind of setting, but the amount of control you will have over variables and random assignment will differ.

Laboratory experiments

In a **laboratory experiment**, you are conducting your experiment in an artificial setting, not the natural setting where participants would normally be found. In natural and behavioural sciences, this setting is usually literally a laboratory, as in Stanley Milgram's experiment on people's obedience to authority, described in **Chapter 1**. However, laboratory settings for business and management research can include settings such as classrooms. Many business and management experiments take place in classrooms, for the convenience of the experimenter and the participants, even though classrooms (and students) are not necessarily identical to organisations (and managers). Other artificial settings for experiments include reality television shows such as *Big Brother* or *Fame Academy* where participants are isolated from the world.

The laboratory experiment gives you the most control over your participants, your experimental treatment and the experimental setting. In areas such as medicine, science, engineering or psychology, this setting might well be a laboratory, but it can be any setting where you have a high degree of control. A formal laboratory setting lets you maximise your control over the experimental setting, the experimental treatment and the assignment of your participants to a particular treatment or control group. An extreme example of a laboratory experiment is a computer simulation, where the experimenter can control all aspects of the experiment, and variation in the outcome results from the application of statistical variations (for example Monte Carlo simulation) and rules for the behaviour of the system that is being simulated.

Even in a laboratory setting, there may be factors that you are not testing but you can't control. These variations might be systemic, recurring in some fashion, or they might be extraneous, nonrecurring. If you conduct an experiment where your outcome variable is participant performance, the room temperature might be higher in the afternoon sessions than in the morning sessions, and the heat might negatively affect your afternoon participants' performance by putting them to sleep. This would be a systemic variation. On the other hand, the noise caused by drilling outside the room might be a one-off and hence extraneous, even though it might still affect the participants.

Laboratory experiments are often criticised as unrepresentative of what actually goes on in organisations. The laboratory setting can be artificial and simplified compared with organisations. The treatment may not closely represent people's actual tasks in organisational settings. The experimental participants themselves are often undergraduates, or business/management students, rather than representing typical organisational populations. All this means that laboratory settings are most appropriate when you are investigating basic aspects of how people behave, independently of the setting, rather than complex social and organisational phenomena.

Field experiments

An experiment that takes place in its natural setting is called a **field experiment**. Xin's Chinese restaurant experiment in **Student research in action 6.4** was a field experiment; so were F.W. Taylor's experiments in work methods. Natural settings for business and management experiments include the workplace (office, shop, factory), the classroom, the household and public spaces such as shopping malls or public streets. Although field experiments minimise the artificiality of the experimental setting on what you are studying, you may have less control over your participants, experimental treatment and other factors than in a laboratory experiment.

Laboratory experiments are high in control, but low in realism. In a field experiment, you trade off some control for a more realistic setting. A field setting might be a classroom, a shopping mall, or even a public space such as public transport – the setting in **Research in action 6.7** is a summer camp. However, you typically can exert only a moderate degree of control over the people, conditions and/or environment.

> ### Research in action 6.7
> #### STOP, THIEF!
>
> Sherif (1956) and Tajfel (1970) both tested whether 'simply being a member of a group was enough to cause people to discriminate against members of another group'. Sherif set up an experiment known as the 'Robber's Cave' in a summer camp, where he allocated boys randomly to different groups and got them to compete on different tasks. Even when the boys in different groups had previously been friends, the rivalries grew so intense that the experiment had to be modified!
>
> Similarly, Tajfel found that when boys were allowed to allocate rewards, they discriminated against members of the other group (the outgroup) in favour of their own group (the ingroup). The ingroup–outgroup hypothesis has been widely used in social psychology and organisational behaviour to explain and predict people's behaviours.

Even if you study people in natural settings, experiments can have surprisingly misleading effects on their behaviours and our interpretation of research findings. Soft drink giant Coca-Cola found this out the hard way in the 1980s when it replaced Coke with New Coke, whose taste customers had preferred in market research blind taste tests. People refused to buy New Coke in the supermarkets, and an embarrassed Coca-Cola was forced to bring back Classic Coke (the original, less-preferred recipe) at enormous expense.

Quasi-experiments

A quasi-experiment is not a true experiment but is a naturally occurring situation that you are taking advantage of as a researcher. You can only observe what is going on directly or indirectly but not manipulate it. You have little control over your participants, the experimental treatment or other experimental conditions. You might be interested in a quasi-experiment because you can analyse the data using the same logic as a true experiment. **Research in action 6.8** illustrates how useful a quasi-experiment can be for a researcher.

> *Research in action 6.8*
> **STRIKE THREE, YER OUT!**
>
> Stanford doctoral student Alan Meyer (1982) developed an ingenious quasi-experiment as part of his dissertation research. In the middle of Meyer's research on hospital management, hospital anaesthesiologists in the San Francisco Bay area went on strike. Although this disrupted his data collection, he realised that the strike created 'before-and-after' conditions – in other words, an experimental treatment – and that he could collect additional data after the strike to complement the data he already had before the strike.

Many natural quasi-experiments let you collect useful data and apply the logic of experimental design. Suppose you are interested in studying the provision of online shopping by supermarkets, you should be able to identify which supermarkets have adopted online shopping, and which haven't, even though you have no influence over which ones do or don't. In this case, you will be observing a quasi-experiment. Your ability to support your hypothesis, though, will be weakened because you can neither randomly assign supermarkets to adopters and nonadopters, nor can you rule out as many systemic or extraneous sources of variation.

> ## Activity 5
>
> We described Xin's research study in **Student research in action 6.4** as an experiment. Do you think his study was closer to a true experiment or a quasi-experiment? How much control do you think he had over:
>
> - Queuing time – long versus short wait to be seated
> - Waiting time – long versus short wait to receive meal
> - Number of people in party – couple to group
> - Quality of meal.

6.3.3 Experimental design issues and ethical considerations

The principles of experimental design enable researchers to minimise the risk of mistaking a chance result or spurious cause for the cause-and-effect relationship you are interested in. Other issues might still cause your experiment to lose credibility. We discuss some of these below.

Minimising potential sources of bias

Although the principles of experimental design rule out some sources of error, you need to rule out other sources or error or bias when you are designing and conducting your experiment. Your experimental results will be more believable if you can show that you have minimised potential sources of bias. Social psychologists Rosnow and Rosenthal (1997) list the major sources of experimental bias as experimenter effects, and experimenter expectancies, as well as subject effects.

Experimenter effects are intentional or unintentional mistakes in how you collect, record, interpret or report your data and findings; or interactions between you and the experimental treatment, participants and/or setting, especially **experimenter expectancies** – your expectations about the outcomes of the experiment might influence your design of the experiment to increase the likelihood that that outcome actually occurs.

This isn't the same as deliberate fraud (which has been known to occur in scientific and other experiments). It is sometimes known as a 'self-fulfilling prophesy'. Educational experiments have shown that teachers are more encouraging towards students classified as 'bright', and less encouraging towards those designated 'not bright'. These 'bright' students were actually found to outperform the other students at the end of the year, even though there was no difference between the two groups at the beginning. This is similar to the experiment with 'bright' and 'dull' rats by Rosenthal and Fode (1963) described in Chapter 5.

Another source of experimental bias is **subject effects**, also known as demand characteristics. The **good subject effect** occurs when participants change their behaviours to help (or hinder) the experimenter, thus making the experimental results invalid because they do not represent how people usually behave. The **volunteer subject effect** occurs when people who volunteer to participate in studies differ from the general population, and again the experimental results may not represent how people in general (rather than experimental subjects) usually behave.

When other people assess the quality of your research, any experiment will be measured as to the extent you have designed your experiment to minimise – even if you can't rule out – these potential sources of bias. These biases are the major threats to the experimental design.

Ethical issues in experiments: consent

Many ethical issues have been identified for laboratory experiments, and now these experiments nearly always have to be approved by an ethics committee or board before they are allowed to proceed. One element you must absolutely consider in designing an experiment is any potential harm that might come to participants – even inadvertently – because of your experiment. Any experiment with human participants carries some risk of some temporary or permanent effect, so many institutions require approval to minimise the risk of harm. Field experiments pose many of the same issues, so they are often required to undergo the same approval process. Quasi-experiments may need to be approved, even if you are just observing a naturally occurring process, because of the risk that you might pose to confidentiality. If you are considering the use of an experiment of any kind, besides reading this section carefully, you may want to find out about your university's policy, and read Oliver's book *The Student's Guide to Research Ethics* (2003). You may also want to read **Chapter 9** in this book, where ethical issues are covered further.

In laboratory and field experiments, you are always manipulating some experimental treatment that may affect your participants. One way of minimising risk to

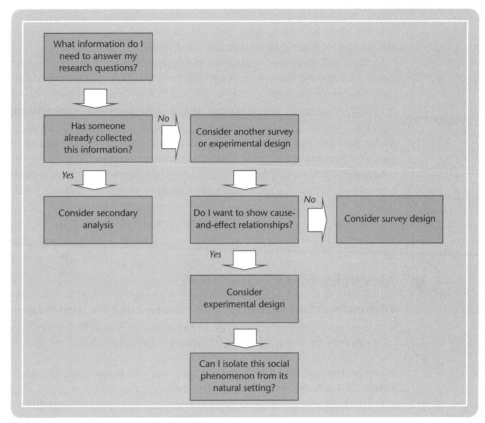

Figure 6.8 A decision tree for this chapter

your participants is by getting their **informed consent**. You will typically need to give your participants information about the experiment before they agree to participate, before you begin the experimental treatment and after the experiment. Especially when you are experimenting on individuals, you will need to give them enough information about the experiment's purpose and content so that they can give fully informed consent to participate. You should also brief your participants at the beginning of the experiment, and give them the opportunity to withdraw from the experiment if they have changed their minds. At the end of the experiment, you should debrief your participants about the experiment – always remember to thank them! – and give them a chance to give you feedback about the experiment.

SUMMARY

In this chapter, we have considered three research designs that are often associated with the scientific approach to business and management research.

Section 6.1 introduced the secondary analysis of data as a research design. Secondary analysis can be used to analyse data that have already been collected, and sometimes analysed, by other people. The sources of this secondary data include archived surveys and proprietary databases. Secondary analysis can also be used to analyse data that you collect yourself from indirect sources, including documents and

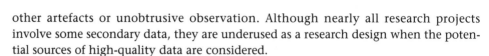

other artefacts or unobtrusive observation. Although nearly all research projects involve some secondary data, they are underused as a research design when the potential sources of high-quality data are considered.

Section 6.2 discussed a familiar research design, the survey, which includes interviews and questionnaires. Surveys can be used to gather information about a sample that can be generalised to the population from which it comes. Survey design needs care and experience, so you should first see whether there is an existing survey or question bank related to your research topic before you decide to design your own survey and questions. You should also think about the trade-off between the cost of information and the quality of information, especially with postal or online questionnaires.

Section 6.3 explained how you can use experiments to investigate cause-and-effect relationships. Laboratory experiments are seldom used in most areas of business and management, but field experiments and quasi-experiments are common designs. In designing experiments, you should try to minimise experimenter and participant effects, and be mindful of ethical issues that you may need to address before you do your experiment.

 ## ANSWERS TO KEY QUESTIONS

What methods for collecting data are associated with the scientific approach?

- A secondary analysis, a survey or an experimental research design for social measurement all provide ways to capture quantitative data

How can I design a research project that analyses documents or databases, conducts a survey or runs an experiment?

- By understanding the advantages and disadvantages of the methods presented in this chapter, I can choose between:
  - Secondary analysis to analyse data that other researchers have already captured, to analyse data from documents and other artefacts produced for purposes other than research by individuals and organisations, or to capture information about distant or historical activities
  - A survey to capture structured information about a sample by asking the same questions of all respondents in a face-to-face or other contact situation, or at a distance from the researcher
  - An experiment such as a true experiment or a quasi-experiment in a natural setting – field experiments – or an artificial experiment – laboratory experiments

How can I use these methods as part of a qualitative research design strategy?

- These methods can be adapted to gather qualitative data
- These methods may be useful in case studies or mixed-method research

 ## REFERENCES

BBC News. 2000. Heinz to launch green ketchup, Tuesday 11 July.

Bradach, Jeffrey L. 1997. Using the plural form in the management of restaurant chains, *Administrative Science Quarterly*, **42**(2): 276–303.

Bryman, Alan and Bell, Emma. 2003. *Business Research Methods*. Oxford: Oxford University Press.

Carroll, Glenn R. and Swaminathan, Anand. 2000. Why the microbrewery movement? Organizational dynamics of resource partitioning in the US brewing industry, *American Journal of Sociology*, **106**(3): 715–60.

Foddy, William. 1993. *Constructing Questions for Interviews and Questionnaires: Theory and Practice in Social Research*. Cambridge: Cambridge University Press.

Gray, David E. 2004. *Doing Research in the Real World*. London: Sage.

Lee, R.M. 2000. *Unobtrusive Methods in Social Research*. Maidenhead: Open University Press.

Maister, David H. 1984. *The Psychology of Waiting in Lines*. Boston: Harvard Business School.

March, James G., Sproull, Lee S. and Tamuz, Michal. 1991. Learning from samples of one or fewer, *Organization Science*, **2**(1): 58–70.

Oppenheimer, A.N. 1992. *Questionnaire Design, Interviewing, and Attitude Measurement*, New edn. London: Continuum.

O'Leary, Zina. 2004. *The Essential Guide to Doing Research*. London: Sage.

Reilly, Michael D. and Wallendorf, Melanie. 1987. A comparison of group differences in food consumption using household refuse, *Journal of Consumer Research*, **14**(2): 289–94.

Rosenthal, R. and Fode, K.L. 1963. The effect of experimenter bias on the performance of the albino rat, *Behavioural Science*, **8**: 183–9.

Rosnow, R.L. and Rosenthal, R. 1997. *People Studying People: Artifacts and Ethics in Behavioural Research*. New York: W.H. Freeman.

Saunders, Mark, Lewis, Phillip and Thornhill, Adrian. 2003. *Research Methods for Business Students*, 3rd edn. Harlow: Financial Times/Prentice Hall.

Sherif, M. 1956. Experiments in group conflict, *Scientific American*, **195**: 54–8.

Stack, Steven and Gundlach, James. 1992. The effect of country music on suicide, *Social Forces*, **70**(5): 211–18.

Stack, Steven and Gundlach, Jim. 1994. Country music and suicide: A reply to Maguire and Snipes, *Social Forces*, **72**(4): 1245–8.

Stack, Steven and Gundlach, James. 1995. Country music and suicide – individual, indirect, and interaction effects: A reply to Snipes and Maguire, *Social Forces*, **74**(1): 331–5.

Tajfel, H. 1970. Experiments in intergroup discrimination, *Scientific American*, **223**: 96–102.

Underhill, Paco. 2000. *Why We Buy: The Science of Shopping*. Texere.

Voss, Christopher A., Roth, Aleda V., Rosenzweig, Eve D., Blackmon, Kate and Chase, Richard B. 2004. A tale of two countries: Conservatism, service quality, and feedback on customer satisfaction, *Journal of Service Research*, **6**(3): 212–40.

Wallendorf, Melanie and Nelson, Daniel. 1986. An archaeological examination of ethnic differences in body care rituals, *Psychology and Marketing*, **3**(4): 273–99.

Webb, E.J., Campbell, D.T., Schwartz, R.D. and Sechrest, L. 1966. *Unobtrusive Measures: Nonreactive Research in the Social Sciences*. Chicago: Rand McNally.

Zeithaml, Valarie A., Parasuraman, A. and Berry, Leonard L. 1990. *Delivering Quality Service: Balancing Customer Perceptions and Expectations*. New York: Free Press.

 ## ADDITIONAL RESOURCES

Aldridge, A. and Levine, K. 2001. *Surveying the Social World: Principles and Practice in Survey Research*. Maidenhead: Open University Press.

Bell, Judith and Opie, Clive. 2002. *Learning from Research: Getting More from Your Data*. Maindenhead: Open University Press.

Blaikie, Norman. 2000. *Designing Social Research*. Cambridge: Polity Press.

Boone, Christopher, Carroll, Glenn R. and van Witteloostuijn, Arjen. 2004. Size, differentiation and the performance of Dutch daily newspapers, *Industrial and Corporate Change*, **13**(1): 117–48.

Dobrev, Stanislav D., Tai-Young Kim and Carroll, Glenn R. 2003. Shifting Gears, Shifting Niches: Organizational Inertia and Change in the Evolution of the US Automobile Industry, 1885–1981, *Organization Science*, **14**(3): 264–82.

Easterby-Smith, Mark, Thorpe, Richard and Lowe, Andy. 2002. *Management Research: An Introduction, 2nd edn.* London: Sage.

Johnson, Roxanne T. 2000. In search of E.I. DuPont de Nemours and Company: the perils of archival research, *Accounting, Business and Financial History*, **10**(2).

Maguire, Edward R. and Snipes, Jeffrey B. 1994. Reassessing the link between country music and suicide, *Social Forces*, **72**(4): 1239–43.

Mauk, Gary W. and Taylor, Matthew J. 1994. Comments on Stack and Gundlach's 'The Effect of Country Music on Suicide: An Achy Breaky Heart' ..., *Social Forces*, **72**(4): 1249–55.

McKendrick, David G. and Carroll, Glenn R. 2001. On the genesis of organizational forms: Evidence from the market for disk arrays, *Organization Science*, **12**(6): 661–82.

Meyer, Alan D. 1982. Adapting to environmental jolts, *Administrative Science Quarterly*, **27**(4): 515–37.

Oliver, Paul. 2003. *The Student's Guide to Research Ethics*. Maidenhead: Open University Press.

Parry, Vivienne. 2004. The panic button, *Guardian*, 29 June, G2: 16.

Snipes, Jeffrey B. and Maguire, Edward R. 1995. Country music, suicide, and spuriousness, *Social Forces*, **74**(1): 327–9.

Webb, E. and Weick, K.E. 1979. Unobtrusive measures in organisational theory: A reminder. *Administrative Science Quarterly*, **24**(4): 650–9.

Key terms

Discussion questions

1. What research designs are associated with the quantitative approach?
2. What is secondary analysis?
3. How can I use secondary data to answer my research questions?
4. What are the main advantages and disadvantages of secondary analysis?
5. Does secondary analysis always mean quantitative data and hypothesis-testing?
6. What reliability and validity issues does secondary analysis present?
7. From a research methods point of view, what might be wrong with the statement, 'I haven't decided what to look at yet, but I will be using a questionnaire'?
8. What are good practices in setting up a survey?
9. How do laboratory experiments, field experiments and quasi-experiments differ?
10. Sherif's experiment (**Research in action 6.7**) was set in a summer camp – literally a field experiment. Although he could control the random assignment of boys to groups, and the boys competed on similar tasks in a similar environment, Sherif couldn't control the boys' interactions with other campers, the weather and so on. What do you think would have been different if the experiment had taken place in a laboratory setting (for example, choosing the group from students in a classroom)?

Workshop

This workshop will give students practice in gathering data using a scientific approach.

Background

Capacity is often a problem for frontline service operations because demand tends to be higher in certain parts of the data and lower in others. For example, a coffee shop, cafeteria, restaurant or other food service facility will probably experience peaks and troughs of demand during the day. The operation needs to collect information on these variations in demand so that it can set service levels and decide how many service operatives it needs to deploy at a given time.

Task

Form into teams of no more than three people. Each team should pick a food service facility to observe and set aside several hours to complete the activity.

1. Decide how you would collect data to determine the number of customers arriving at the facility, how long each customer had to wait before being served, and any other information that you think would be relevant.
2. Decide how you would record and analyse these data.
3. Collect these data. (It is a good idea for each team member to collect data independently for at least part of this exercise, so that you can see how accurately people can collect data.)
4. Analyse the data and present the results to your instructor.
5. Hold on to these data for the workshops at the end of **Chapters 11** and **12**.

POSTSCRIPT TO ACTIVITY 4

Heads	0	1	2	3	4	5	6	7	8	9	10
	0	9	45	131	187	244	223	97	51	13	0

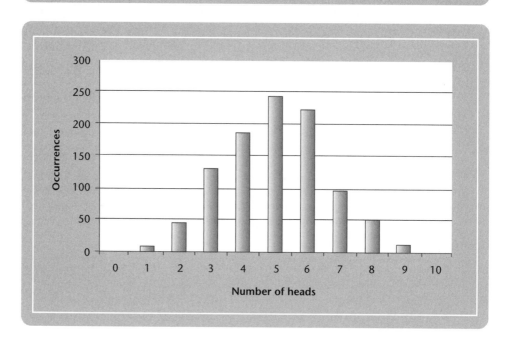

Relevant chapters

13 Answering your research questions
14 Describing your research
15 Closing the loop

Key challenges

● Interpreting your findings and making recommendations
● Writing and presenting your project
● Reflecting on and learning from your research

4

Relevant chapters

1 What is research?
2 Managing the research process
3 What should I study?
4 How do I find information?

Key challenges

● Understanding the research process
● Taking a systematic approach
● Generating and clarifying ideas
● Using the library and internet

1

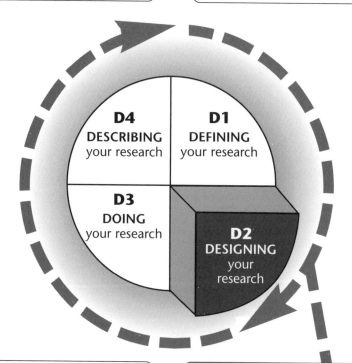

Relevant chapters

9 Doing field research
10 Analysing quantitative data
11 Advanced quantitative analysis
12 Analysing qualitative data

Key challenges

● Practical considerations in doing research
● Using simple statistics
● Understanting multivariate statistics
● Interpreting interviews and observations

3

Relevant chapters

5 Scientist or ethnographer?
6 Quantitative research designs
7 **Designing qualitative research**
8 Case studies/multi-method design

Key challenges

● Choosing a model for doing research
● Using scientific methods
● **Using ethnographic methods**
● Integrating quantitative and qualitative research

2

Designing qualitative research
Using ethnographic methods for uncovering social meaning

 Key questions

- What research designs can I use to collect data to uncover social meaning?
- How can I use remote data collection, observation, interviews or participant observation?
- How can I use these designs as part of a scientific research approach?

 Learning outcomes

At the end of this chapter, you should be able to:

- Decide whether an ethnographic approach is appropriate for your research
- Choose between designs for indirect data collection, nonparticipant observation, unstructured interviews and participant observation
- Evaluate the relative practical challenges associated with each method, and how these might affect your study

Contents

 **INTRODUCTION**

> Words are merely utterances: *noises* that stand for feelings, thoughts and experience. They are symbols. Signs. Insignias. They are not Truth. They are not the real thing. Words may help you understand something. Experience allows you to *know*. Yet there are some things that you cannot experience. So I have given you other tools of knowing. And these are called *feelings*. And so too thoughts.
>
> **(Walsch** 1995: 4)

In **Chapter 5**, we introduced the ethnographer as the second role model for business and management researchers. Many interesting research studies in business and management research use qualitative research designs and methods as part of an ethnographic approach to studying people and organisations. Even in areas we usually think of as mostly quantitative, such as consumer marketing, taking this kind of approach can help us ask – and answer – some interesting questions about how and why people behave in certain ways. For example, why do people take up extreme sports such as skydiving? What explains the revival of motorcycling among middle-aged accountants and other professionals – the born-again bikers known as 'bambis'? Why do secretaries gossip? Does the chatting that goes on during surgical operations help to prevent medical errors (such as leaving instruments inside patients) or contribute to them? Is accounting really as objective as we are led to believe? These kinds of questions occur in many business and management settings.

If your research questions ask 'how?' or 'why?' rather than 'what?', you should consider taking an ethnographic approach, which means that you should consider using one of the qualitative research designs presented in this chapter to gather your data. You can choose from many different qualitative methods that people have used effectively, all justified and supported by guidelines practical tips and tricks. Qualitative methods and data require different skills than do the quantitative methods and data discussed in **Chapter 6**.

If you decide to use a qualitative design after reading this chapter, make sure you read **Chapter 12** on analysing qualitative data before you start collecting data. It is vital that you collect your data with how you will analyse it in mind. You should also be aware of some issues that commonly arise in doing qualitative research.

How qualitative designs differ from quantitative designs

Before we look at qualitative methods in detail, we should revisit the root of this approach. In qualitative research, your research questions will focus on increasing your understanding of a particular issue – and will be 'why?' or 'how?' questions. Although you can also use quantitative research designs to answer 'how' and 'why' questions, they are usually different kinds of how and why questions.

Qualitative methods are important because research in business and management deals not only with organisations but also with the people in them. As the opening passage in this chapter indicates, people can ascribe meanings, thoughts and feelings to the situation in which they find themselves. Organisations are both social systems and the setting for social behaviour. Since people construct and maintain social systems, research on them is different from research on the physical objects and systems that are studied in the natural sciences.

This situation is therefore multidimensional. Your research also has the potential to be far more personal. As we shall see, you can bring in your own views of the world, and make a feature of your interpretation. Such interpretation would not be appropriate in quantitative research designs, especially research where the researcher is presumed to be objective and uninvolved (see **Chapter 5**).

One final word. Many students find the tone of discussion in some qualitative methods texts aimed at more advanced researchers daunting. However, although many authors suggest that there is a degree of 'mystique' surrounding qualitative research, which may put off new researchers, don't let 'dictionary overload' put you off. Qualitative research is actually much more straightforward than you might think. Boiled down to its essentials, qualitative data-gathering is built on skills that we already possess: reading, asking questions, talking to people, participating in everyday activities and observing what is going on around us. Remember from **Chapter 5** that qualitative research draws on the skills of the ethnographic researcher.

Designs for qualitative research

Although there many different tools and techniques you can use as part of a qualitative research design, in this chapter we will concentrate on the main ones you might use for your project. As with quantitative research, you can be creative in your research design. You can combine different qualitative methods, and even combine quantitative and qualitative methods. Indeed, this can be highly desirable, since you can investigate your research problem from multiple perspectives this way. In addition to

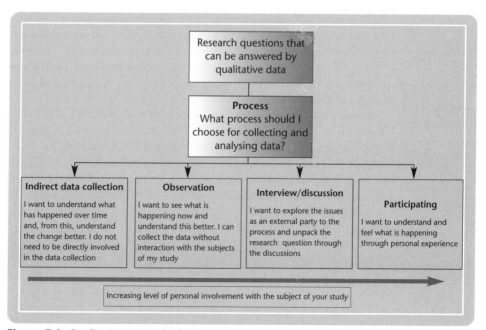

Figure 7.1 Qualitative research designs

suiting your research problem and questions, the particular technique you choose will also be influenced by the practical issues associated with each method.

Figure 7.1 arranges the main qualitative designs by how involved the researcher is with the subject of the investigation. At the left-hand end of the scale, there is little involvement. Remote data collection, as you will see, is close to the surveys, experiments and secondary research designs that we explored in **Chapter 6**. As your design moves to the right, you become part of whatever situation is being investigated – you will explore the issues through your personal experience. Participant observation, where you actually become part of the organisation or other context that is being explored, is the most different from quantitative designs. Below, we will discuss remote data collection, observation, interviews and discussion, and participation in turn.

7.1 INDIRECT DATA COLLECTION

In **Chapter 5**, we introduced the ethnographer as the role model for qualitative research designs. Like the ethnographer, in most qualitative research, you will be present to collect data directly from people or organisations. However, you may sometimes want or need to collect data when you can't be present for various reasons. Sometimes organisations will not give you access to the data you need for your project. Other times, you may need to investigate a particular issue through secondary data, especially if they are the only data available.

To answer your research questions, you may be able to use **indirect data collection**, sometimes called **remote data collection**. Indirect data collection may be your only option if you are studying a historical phenomenon. This was the case for a student who was investigating the spending patterns of people in postwar Europe. He was not able to travel back in time to directly observe people's behaviour, so he had to rely instead on contemporary diary accounts.

This approach has many similarities with secondary analysis, which we presented in **Chapter 6**. However, our focus in that chapter was on data that were already in the form of numbers (for example official statistics or computer databases), whilst in this chapter the focus is on non-numeric data, including words, pictures, sounds and other qualitative data. You can start your data collection by asking the two questions: 'How should I collect the data?' and 'When should I collect the data?'

You can also use the techniques associated with **indirect observation,** discussed in **Chapter 6**, as a way to collect qualitative data. Such indirect data are useful, especially if you combine them with a complementary direct method. As we noted, archaeologists, forensic scientists and garbologists rely mostly on physical clues to our behaviour and may never talk to the people they are researching. They have a well-developed set of tools for compiling these kinds of data. An advantage of indirect observation is that these data are not affected by social pressures for people to give the 'right answers' (the socially desirable responding described in **Chapter 6**).

Finding out what people *really* think creates all sorts of challenges for researchers, as people do not always answer truthfully when questioned. In the UK general election of 1993, the pre-election polls predicted that the Conservative Party would be roundly defeated. They actually won the election by a comfortable margin. The people who had been polled felt under social pressure to say they would vote a particular way, influencing the answers they gave in public, but they actually cast their secret ballots for different candidates. These social pressures affect the responses given by participants in many areas of business and management research.

7.1.1 *How* should you collect the data?

Secondary sources such as publications or web pages can be a good source of qualitative data about individuals and/or organisations. Your challenge here is to identify potential sources of secondary data and gather data from them. You might find the techniques from **Chapter 4** for reviewing the literature, and from **Chapter 6** for secondary data analysis, appropriate for doing this. You might also collect data about individuals and/or organisations directly from their original source in real time, without being directly involved in capturing the data.

For example, suppose you were studying decision-making and in particular the history of a particular kind of decision. Because the decision-making process is usually both confidential and sensitive, you might have difficulty in getting 'real-time' access to observe a decision being made within an organisation. However, an organisation might agree to provide you with access to its archives, for example to see copies of reports and correspondence on past decisions, even if it did not allow you to be present. Company documents such as the minutes of meetings can provide valuable data, especially about the timing of issues and decisions. You could use these documents to track the organisation's decision processes by analysing the minutes from organisational meetings, as they contain the formal records of decisions and notes of the actions that need to be completed prior to the next meeting. (If you are considering doing a project based on this kind of documentary analysis, you should remember that you are relying on the documents providing a faithful record of the discussion, although in practice they may be incomplete as a source. If the minutes of the previous meeting have been confirmed as the first item on the agenda of the subsequent meeting, standard practice for many organisations, at least you have some confidence in their accuracy. Similar concerns apply to other organisational records.)

7.1.2 *When* should you collect the data?

If you are studying a research problem that occurs in 'real time' rather than in the past, ideally you will gather the data directly from organisations or participants immediately as events unfold, with an immediate 'up-link' to your research database. You should try to get your data regularly and quickly. In reality, you may have to keep encouraging (or even nagging) people to provide you with your data, and you may not get it until well after the events they report have happened. Any compromises will undoubtedly affect your data, as people's recollections become far more 'selective' after even a short lapse.

7.2 NONPARTICIPANT OBSERVATION

In indirect data collection, you will have little or no direct contact with the organisation or people that you are studying, and have only their words and other records to speak for them. In **nonparticipant observation** you will actually collect data directly by watching someone doing something, but you will still have little or no direct interaction with them. You might not even be physically present, as we discuss below. Nonparticipant observation may therefore be as simple as watching and noting how people behave under different circumstances, as in the coffee bar case in **Student research in action 7.1**.

Student research in action 7.1
CENTRAL PERK – AND WAIT

For a coursework assignment, a student project group decided to investigate service quality in a local service operation. The group wanted to see how the varying workload caused by changes in customer demand over time affected a local coffee shop. In particular, they wanted to see how customers responded to the queues that built up at peak times and how staff responded.

The students observed that first thing in the morning customers were able to get a seat easily once they had collected their coffee and cakes. Customers seemed happy to sit for a while in the café and enjoy the experience. As the day progressed, particularly at lunchtime, customers had to queue to get served and then were unable to get a seat. Not only was customer satisfaction dropping off, with customers becoming frustrated by trying to get seated whilst balancing their coffee and shopping bags, but the shop also was losing business to less-crowded neighbours.

On several Saturdays, the students recorded how customers reacted to the different queue lengths during the day, including counting the number of people who walked in, looked around and then walked out again. They used this as a measure of the lost business that the shop could have captured, if only it had had the capacity. The study identified the likely 'tolerance' of potential customers to waiting, its cost and its effect on customer satisfaction. As a result, they were able to recommend how the coffee shop should change its layout and process for serving customers.

As well as observing people's behaviour and actions in person, some researchers are starting to take advantage of electronic technologies such as videotaping. If you have an opportunity to do this, you should think carefully about the ethical implications for your participants. If you have obtained permission to video participants as part of a research project, for example the discussion in a focus group, then it is certainly appropriate to use these recordings as a source of data for that particular research project.

It is usually OK to observe people in public settings such as streets or fast-food restaurants, and take notes, but recording them may raise ethical issues. Town planners and store designers frequently use videos as a research tool, for instance to see how people move (speed, direction or what causes them to change direction). You should always seek such permission from people you are observing if you can, especially if it might affect them, as **Student research in action 7.2** illustrates.

> ## Student research in action 7.2
> ### HOW TO WIN FRIENDS AND INFLUENCE PEOPLE (NOT)
>
> A student was undertaking a placement project at a large car factory. As part of his work, he was asked to investigate the practices associated with the assembly of a car door. Taking the initiative, he took his clipboard, stopwatch and white coat, and headed out to the factory floor. He then started observing the work of the people who were assembling the doors, noting the tasks they were doing and the times that each task took.
>
> When the union convenor saw the student and his stopwatch, he jumped to the conclusion that the student was retiming the jobs that people were doing on behalf of the organisation. This was a perennially sensitive issue, as the timing of a job determined an individual's rate of pay, and any retiming had to be pre-agreed with the unions. Since no such agreement was currently in force, the union ordered all work in the factory to stop. Needless to say, our student was not too popular with the factory management after that.

We recommend that you do *not* use **covert observation** in your project, that is, observing people using surveillance technology or in semi-private or private settings. Even though we are used to being observed – there appears to be CCTV on every street corner in many parts of the world, and there are even television shows that use such footage, which may give the impression that it is acceptable to observe anyone at anytime – this contravenes the ethical guidelines that we recommend for your projects, which we cover more completely in **Chapter 9**. You may need to consider other methods of obtaining such data if you need them for your research.

7.3 UNSTRUCTURED INTERVIEW/DISCUSSION

In indirect data collection and nonparticipant observation, you have very little direct contact with the people (and organisations) you are studying. A method that involves more contact is unstructured interviews and/or informal discussions. As noted, interviews are one of the most widely used methods in student projects, not least because they draw on familiar skills of finding out things by asking questions. You can use interviews to collect **non-standardised** data as well as the standardised data described in **Chapter 6**. You can make sure that your study maximises its benefits by carefully considering key issues such as:

- Should I interview individuals or groups?
- How should I choose my interview subjects?
- How should I structure the interview/discussion?
- What sort of questions should I use?
- Should the issues be structured or should I be *led by the data*?
- How should I record the interview data?
- How do I make sure that I avoid possible sources of bias in the interviewing process, both from myself and the interviewee(s)?

We will now discuss each of these in turn.

7.3.1 Should I interview people one by one or together?

The question here is whether you should carry out individual or group interviews. Each has a different purpose and will draw on different data collection and analysis techniques. If you are part of a group project, you should also decide whether you should carry out your interviews singly or in pairs. You will not be able to standardise your interviews as much as in the structured interviews discussed in **Chapter 6**, but you can multiply your efforts by splitting interviews between team members. In **Student research in action 7.3**, the five students in one group conducted ten interviews each, giving them fifty interviews in total to analyse. By carefully coordinating the questions they asked and checking the transcripts (see below), they were able to cover a much wider perspective than five researchers working alone. Although one-to-one interviews are fine, working with another interviewer can generate synergies between researchers, as shown in **Student research in action 7.3**.

Student research in action 7.3
BLAME THE PROJECT MANAGER

In a research project with a major airline to investigate a failed IT project, students were considerably younger than most of the people they were interviewing. Working together in pairs gave them extra confidence. An unexpected benefit was that it allowed their different perspectives on the issue to be brought out when they began to discuss their findings. One student thought, for instance, that the project manager was causing the problem they were investigating. The other argued firmly that it had resulted from cultural resistance within the company. By carrying out the interviews together and discussing the results, they were able to overcome their individual opinions and move closer to the truth.

Table 7.1 summarises some of the strengths and weakness of the various combinations of interviewers and interviewees.

7.3.2 How should I choose my interview subjects?

When you are deciding whom you will interview, you should consider the sampling issues discussed in **Chapter 6**. Quantitative research designs emphasised random sampling as a key to being able to generalise results based on statistics. For qualitative research design, instead of random sampling, you should try to select your sample so that it is represents the concepts, rather than the population, that you want to generalise your findings to. You may want to consider either **theoretical or purposive sampling**. Here, instead of choosing people to interview based on how well they represent the group you are studying, you will select them to create the maximum variety in their responses. However, given the practicalities of arranging interviews, many people use **convenience sampling,** that is, sampling those people to whom you have easy access.

Table 7.1 A comparison of individual and group interviews

Interviewer	Interviewee	
	One	**More than one**
One	Most common type of interview, relatively easy to arrange. Susceptible to the biases of both parties. The most appropriate method for confidential or sensitive subjects	Group interview – such as a focus group. Can generate a large volume of data in a short time. Susceptible to biases and group dynamics. Can be difficult where there is a lack of true consensus in the group. Can be difficult for a new researcher to manage alone
More than one	A panel interview. Can be used to remove the biases of one of the interviewers, but can be intimidating for the interviewee if there is a power differential – unlikely with students as interviewers. Good for building the confidence of novice interviewers and to make sure that all relevant points are covered	Group discussions are used to look for some issues. Due to the limitations of the dynamics of both groups, less likely to be useful for in-depth explorations

If you can use theoretical/purposive sampling, your interviews will provide a range of views about the issue being researched, rather than define what any particular group thinks. This is not a drawback – remember that the standards by which you will assess the quality of qualitative research are different from quantitative research, which we will discuss further in **Chapters 10** and **12**.

You will need to manage access issues if you decide to gather data using interviews. Gaining physical access to your subjects – agreeing to meet or interview them by some other means – is important. This access needs to be arranged in advance. Ideally, you could decide exactly whom you will see and for how long. In most projects, you are using people's goodwill to gain you the interview, so you are at their mercy. You should tell people in advance what you expect to talk to them about, how long it will take and what they might hope to gain from it. It is often tempting to promise a full report to the organisation of your findings. The rule here is that you should always exceed your promises – a good compromise might be to agree to provide some up-to-date articles on what you are researching.

As well as physical access, getting your interviewees to agree to provide information is important. Having arranged all the logistics of the interviews, you will sometimes find that you will not be given full information. These two factors – physical access and incompleteness – will affect how many people you should plan to interview.

7.3.3 How should I structure the interview/discussion?

In a qualitative interview, you do not go in with an interview schedule with precisely worded questions in a strict order. Despite this unstructured format, this doesn't mean you will be going in without a plan or agenda. You might make use of the 7-I structure introduced below:

1. *Introduce* – state who you are, who you represent, your purpose in seeing that person or people and how long you will be (see note on time below). Reassure them about the confidentiality of the information you hope they will give you. Gain agreement to use any recording equipment you intend to use (see below).

2. *Icebreak* – start to establish rapport with the person or people you are interviewing. Don't forget that they might not have a clear idea why you want to talk to them. It is also worthwhile to start with some easy questions to get the ball rolling. Show an interest in what they are doing. Ensure that you appear relaxed about the discussion – people pick up on anxiety very easily.

3. *Increase the intensity of the questioning* – ask the questions either as prestructured or as the discussion leads (see following section).

4. *Intervene* – when a discussion goes off track, you may need to intervene. If you need to be focused because of time constraints, you should politely but firmly refer the person back to the original question. Some interviewees will have prepreprepared speeches of their own, and will 'play their tape' whether it answers your question or not. You might go with the flow for a short while, but when you absolutely must collect specific information and time is limited, simply letting someone ramble on about their favourite topic may be cathartic for them, but of limited use to you. A more extreme experience – but thankfully rare – is described in **Research in action 7.1**. You should think about how you might handle an awkward interviewee – perhaps to thank them graciously for their time and cut your losses and run.

Research in action 7.1
I'LL NEVER BE YOUR BEAST OF BURDEN

Having arranged an interview with the research director of a large multinational company, I went excited about the good material I hoped the interview would yield for my doctoral work. The discussion started with the interviewee asking me about the research I was doing. That was OK, until he stated that this was, of course, 'missing the point'. He then proceeded to tell me what my research should have been about. His opinion was that whilst what I was asking about was interesting, it was all stuff that had been done ten years previously, and was already well documented. He then patted me on the head as I left and said that he hoped his contribution would be recognised in my thesis. Given that I was already established in this area, with a half-dozen books in print, I found this quite ironic. It could very well happen to you, so please don't feel so bad about it when it does!

---

5. *In conclusion* – wrap up the session at the end and thank the interviewee for their time. Check details such as how to get out of the building. Attempting an exit through the broom cupboard at this stage is going to blow any credibility you had with the interviewees!

6. *In case* – always request that you can get back to the person you have just spoken with to clarify any points. This is vital for when you start your analysis. You cannot always cover everything you need to in one session, and there will be some areas

that you will have missed altogether. Don't count on being able to follow up any missed material, though.

7. *Interpret your data* soon after the interview – many researchers do this in the car park before they leave or within a few hours of the event. Otherwise, it is easy to forget that critical point that you didn't note down, or be unable to interpret some ambiguous and cryptic notes you have made to yourself.

7.3.4 What sort of questions should I ask?

Chapter 6 provided examples of open-ended and closed-ended questions. You may want to start out with some closed-ended questions, where you provide your interviewee with a limited set of prescribed answers. For instance, you might start out a discussion on motivation by asking:

Q: Would you say that your motivation level was high, moderate, or low?

You could follow this up with an open-ended question to elicit more detail:

Q: Why was your level of motivation low at this point?

Open-ended questions are more exploratory in nature and can lead to many other questions that cannot always be determined in advance. You may also use them to clarify or probe an issue more deeply, such as

Q: Does your work environment determine your level of motivation?

Q: Would you say that there are any other external factors that affect your motivation?

There are some simple rules for asking questions. Start with easier, closed-ended questions – as suggested in Icebreak above. As you develop rapport with the person or people you are interviewing, seek confirmation or further discussion of key points. This should then lead to your most in-depth questions, but only after the people are comfortable with what you are doing. Even when you have interviewed that person before, start gently and allow the flow of information to be established.

A golden rule of interviewing is to respect the time of the people you are interviewing. More than once, after someone has told me repeatedly they are so busy they can only give me ten minutes, I have offered to close the meeting after ten minutes, only to be told that it is fine for me to continue. The important issue here is that if they say ten minutes, it is *your* responsibility to watch the clock. After that time, offer to go. It is rare that an interview that is going somewhere will be terminated, but your courtesy will be respected.

A final note is that the location is important. If the interview is in someone's office, which often happens when you are interviewing managers, any disruption can prove fatal to the process. A ringing telephone or other interruption can cause a break in the flow that makes it difficult to restart the interview afterwards. Where possible, try to arrange the interview in a neutral location where you are less likely to be interrupted.

Tip. Something that can totally ruin an interview is when *your* mobile phone goes off. Check before you go into the interview that your phone is turned off.

7.3.5 Should the issues be structured or should you be *led by the data*?

In structuring your interviews, beyond the type of questions you use, consider how you intend it to progress. The extremes of your choices are shown in **Figure 7.2**.

If you are asking exploratory research questions, you will probably find it more natural to use the unstructured approach, although an interview doesn't have to be entirely structured or unstructured. In an unstructured interview, you direct your interviewee to the general area you want to discuss, and then allow the issues to emerge from the conversation.

Getting this to happen is a specialised skill that you have to hone over time. If you reflect on the interview process as you go along by analysing your recordings or transcripts, this will greatly help you to improve. If you are planning to use unstructured interviews, it may be useful to look at Glaser and Strauss's (1967) text on grounded theory. We present a simplified version of grounded research in **Chapter 12**.

You should also consider some other issues in unstructured interviewing:

- *Don't* impose your own preconceptions or ideas by the language you use. In discussing the uncertainty caused by a merger of two large companies, an interviewer was trying to determine its effects on workforce morale. If he were to ask the question 'How angry do you feel about the possibility of being made redundant?', he would clearly be imposing *anger* and *redundancy* into the discussion. If the interviewee has not previously mentioned these two ideas, this might well bias the resulting discussion.
- *Do* use the interviewees' language. If they are talking about something you don't understand, clarify what they mean and then use their language. (The technical term for this is 'native categories'.) In most organisations, people have their own codes, or even TLAs (three-letter abbreviations), for most things.

One respondent answered a question with:

> The first stage of the NPI process is to prepare a PID which includes an MRA. We then gate and get all the LUGs to look over the specs before we move to second-stage EDM.

We could translate this as:

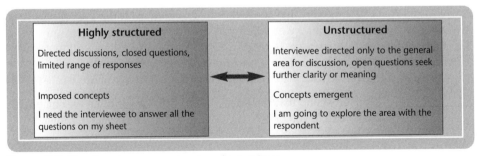

Highly structured	**Unstructured**
Directed discussions, closed questions, limited range of responses	Interviewee directed only to the general area for discussion, open questions seek further clarity or meaning
Imposed concepts	Concepts emergent
I need the interviewee to answer all the questions on my sheet	I am going to explore the area with the respondent

Figure 7.2 Structured versus unstructured interviews

The first stage of the New Product Introduction Process is to prepare a Project Initiation Document that includes a Manufacturing Readiness Assessment (a document reporting on the ability of the firm and its suppliers to actually produce the product being considered). We then stop and have a review of the process so far (gate) and determine whether we continue, and get the Lead Users Group (a group of customers who are prepared to be involved in the new product process) to look over the specifications (product description and technical data) before we move to the second stage Engineering and Design for Manufacture (the part of the process where the technical specification is turned into actual tangible parts for the product).

You also need to think about precisely how you will elicit information and opinions from your interviewees. On the one hand, imposing your concepts on them through the questions you ask is clearly contrary to the spirit of qualitative research. As Whyte (1978: 111) notes:

> The interview structure is not fixed by predetermined questions, as it is in the questionnaire, but is designed to provide the informant with the freedom to introduce materials that were not anticipated by the interviewer ... a genuinely non-directive interviewing approach simply is not appropriate for research. Far from putting informants at their ease, it actually seems to stir anxieties.

Such a naive approach may be inappropriate in a professional setting, such as when you are interviewing managers – see our comments above about respecting their time.

This suggests that, at least in opening the interview, you will need some structure so that you can develop a rapport with the interviewee and establish mutual credibility. When you start discussing the key issues you are investigating, you should follow the guidelines recommended by Whyte (1978) for interviewing, which we have quoted briefly above. You may need to apply these 'rules' flexibly, however, by varying your degree of directness (guiding the respondent in the type of answer) and restrictiveness (guiding the respondent in the length of answer), depending on the situation.

All this should indicate that **qualitative interviewing** is very different from quantitative interviewing, where your goal is to find answers to the questions on your sheet. It does raise the criticism that unstructured data-gathering is 'unscientific' because the content *emerges* as you progress the interview. However, where your objective is to build your understanding, this continual evolution is to be expected. Eisenhardt (1989: 539) warned researchers that:

> This flexibility is not a licence to be unsystematic. Rather, this flexibility is *controlled opportunism* in which researchers take advantage of the uniqueness of a specific case and the emergence of new themes to improve resultant theory.

That controlled opportunism is part of the skill set that you will develop as you use the methods – it takes practice and reflection to make this happen.

7.3.6 How should I record the interview data?

The best method to ensure that you faithfully capture your qualitative data is to record your interviews, wherever possible, and **transcribe** them word for word later on. This is a painstaking process, but it has significant benefits, as we show in **Student research in action 7.4**.

Student research in action 7.4
THE BEST MAN FOR THE JOB?

As mentioned in **Student research in action 3.9**, Anjali was investigating the criteria by which managers were selected for particular jobs. Despite her discussions with both managers and various human resource professionals, she never felt she was making any real progress finding out the criteria or how decisions were made. She had started out looking for a formal, identifiable process, but felt frustrated by the answers she was getting. Going back to the recordings of her interviews, she noticed that when she looked for evidence of a rational selection process, the HR interviewees became more careful and frequently tried to change the subject.

This provided the evidence for one of her findings – there was little to suggest that rational selection processes were taking place in the firms she was investigating, and that whilst they may think this undesirable, it was with the consent of the HR professionals. This was quite a surprise, but one that could not be proved directly in the position she was in – an outsider with the interviews only proceeding out of goodwill. Being seen in that context to be implicitly critical of the interviewees was not going to help her to carry out the project. Instead, she was able to rely on other non-verbal communication signals.

Some dos and don'ts in recording your interviews include:

- *Do* get permission to record the interview.
- *Do* reassure your interviewees about confidentiality.
- *Do* make sure that your recorder is working, including testing in the actual situation to ensure that you can hear what is on the tape. Background noise often makes the conversation inaudible.
- *Do* have a system worked out for keeping tapes – mark those that have been used and those that are available for recording.
- *Don't* use recording equipment that is so intrusive that the interviewees are put off talking openly.

You should never assume that recording takes the place of **taking notes**. During the interview, you should note down any issues that might be worth returning to during the interview, should any topics need probing or the conversation needs more direction.

What should you do if you can't get permission to record your interviews? In a quantitative design where you have a structured interview schedule and mainly closed-ended questions, recording short answers on your interview scripts may be good enough. When you are using mainly open-ended questions, however, to summarise responses you will have to filter the data – decide what is important and what is not. This is definitely something you should avoid: whatever you don't write down, you won't have available to analyse, and you could lose important data because you only realise its significance later on. Furthermore, no matter how fast you can write, you also need to listen to what the person is saying, so that you can seek clarification where necessary or be ready with the next question. Very few people manage both simultaneously. This alone is a good reason to interview in pairs if you are allowed only to take notes.

Transforming verbal data into written form makes it relatively simple to work through and perform the analysis. The usual stage between recording and analysis is **transcription**, where you convert the spoken word into written text, which then becomes your raw data for analysis. Also, transcribed data, if you manage the process carefully, will allow you to trace particular themes or issues back to particular people you have interviewed.

As a rough rule, it will take at least three to four hours of transcription work for each hour of interviews, and may take as much as six to eight hours. Professional typists can work faster, but it does get expensive quickly.

After you have transcribed your interviews, you should check your transcripts, especially of key points, against your recordings to make sure that they have been faithfully reproduced. This will be useful anyway as the first stage of the analysis process – you can use it to refamiliarise yourself with the material you have collected. Try not to summarise or filter your data here. Do not discount any material at this stage, just because it may appear to be out of line with other material. You should wait until the analysis stage to look for the reasons as to why it was different.

 ### 7.3.7 How should I avoid bias in the interview process?

So that you can give appropriate attention to the statements made by interviewees during coding and analysis (see **Chapter 12**), you should think about the kind of data and the source in deciding how much to weight the data. If you are collecting **descriptive data**, for example background or general information, you should include in your notes the proximity of the interviewee to the issue being considered (level and nature of involvement) and the likelihood that it was being faithfully reported.

In the case of **evaluative data** (people making judgement statements about an issue or individual), you should consider (Whyte 1978):

1. ulterior motives for sharing insights, experiences and so on
2. the apparent level of desire to please the interviewer
3. idiosyncratic factors, such as mood, feelings guided by dominant events and so on.

Whyte (1978) suggests that you should use the following steps to ensure that your data are as free from such distortion as possible. The first is to check whether a story seems plausible. The second is to consider the reliability of the interviewee. The third is to list and evaluate obvious influence biases (such as political). These should be supplemented by comparing accounts between interviewees and other observations. Where accounts produce conflicting arguments, you should cross-check them using the process above to detect whether this is likely to be a genuine perceptual difference.

You should also recognise that interviewees may hold simultaneously conflicting viewpoints. They may either not be sure themselves, or be prepared to have a different position on an issue depending on who they are talking to. The viewpoint presented to you is influenced by many factors, including those given above. Good listening, asking follow-up questions and just a small dose of cynicism are useful here.

7.4 PARTICIPANT OBSERVATION

The last design for qualitative research that we will consider is **participant observation**. Participant observation requires personal involvement with the subject of your investigation, with the objective of deriving knowledge from a total experience of the situation. In the study reported in *Street Corner Society* (summarised in **Chapter 1**), researcher William Foote Whyte (1955) joined a street corner group to explore the lives of its members, even going bowling with the out-of-work men he was studying. Whilst most student research projects are not quite so 'hands-on', this illustrates participative research very well. Indeed, many organisations use some sort of participant observation as part of their normal data-gathering processes, as shown in **Student research in action 7.5**.

Student research in action 7.5
SOME PEOPLE HAVE ALL THE LUCK

Mark was working in the IT department of a brewery as part of his course of study. Periodically, office staff members were required to act as mystery customers in the pubs that the brewery also ran. This involved their going to the pub and spending an evening there. The company paid for all their drinks and transport home was even provided at the end of the evening. All the staff had to do was to provide a short report on their experiences of the evening. This helped the firm to understand better the service system that customers required, as well as providing some immediate feedback from a 'customer perspective' of how a particular pub was performing.

Mystery customer studies can be useful for an organisation as a form of short-term participant observation. Indeed, some senior managers have been known to use participant observation to find out what is really going on in their firms. In MBNA Bank, for instance, senior managers regularly spend time answering the phones, as this gets them speaking with customers. The experiences they have are carried back into the decision-making process (this is a key element of the BBC television series *Back to the Floor*, which puts CEOs to work in the front line for a few days).

Participant observation is probably the most classic ethnographic method, which means that it is closest to the 'role model' for qualitative research that we presented in **Chapter 5**. An ethnographic study investigates the culture of a particular organisation or group and tries to make sense of the particular situation. For instance, what are the mechanisms that lead to changes in worker productivity around the times that company bonuses are announced?

The object of using an ethnographic approach is to build the richest possible picture of the *context*, that is, the circumstances surrounding the events and actions you are analysing. This affects both data collection and analysis. The data you collect must provide evidence that the actions you see people taking are connected to the particular events at the time. This is entirely feasible for student projects, and the language, such as that used in the quotation from Rosen (1991: 12) below to describe this kind of research, should not put you off:

> The goal of ethnography in general is to decode, translate and interpret the behaviours and attached meaning systems of those occupying and creating the social system being studied. Ethnography therefore is largely an act of sensemaking, the translation from one context into another of action in relation to meaning and meaning in relation to action.

Participatory action research is participant observation with a twist. An essential aspect of this approach is that you are trying to change the organisation in some way through your involvement as a researcher, not just analysing and reporting the situation. In participatory action research, you are involved in making a change and participating and observing the consequences. For instance, you might use this approach if you were investigating a system for handling customer complaints. Your recommendations for changes are implemented, and you then spend time with the team working in the new system.

In general, action research is associated with research on issues that have a social component, such as equality, fairness or the environment. For example, if you are a participant-observer in a charitable organisation, you might actually try to change the organisation so that it better accomplishes its goals. A real danger here, though, is 'going native' and letting the participation and action aspect overwhelm the research aspect. It also raises some ethical questions, especially if you are participating in an organisation or a context that has legal or moral aspects.

There is much to recommend participant observation as a research method, provided you can manage the risks involved, which we discuss below. This method is often a natural fit with placements or sponsored projects where you are carrying out work for the organisation as well as doing research on it. You can take advantage of this access and the insights gained in doing your research, which would be difficult if not impossible to gain through other types of research. We will cover some other relevant issues such as honesty and confidentiality in **Chapter 9**. You may want to look ahead as they are particularly pertinent here: participation often yields personal insights from the people you are working with.

 ### 7.4.1 Risks of participant observation

Whilst you are unlikely to be allowed to do a student project in business and management that poses as much risk to your personal safety as Whyte's *Street Corner Society* (1995) did to his, you should be aware of several risks posed by participant observation. First, if you are unfamiliar with an organisation, participant observation can take more time than you have available. To gain any real insights, you will need considerable preparation (applying for your project to be supported by an employing organisation, for instance), must collect data over a period usually of months, and then will need time to assimilate and analyse the large amount of data you have amassed. The time requirements mean that participant studies are less often used for student projects than the other qualitative research designs.

Second, you must rely heavily on the organisation you are studying and this creates a significant risk to your project's success. Any organisational changes could mean that your project is no longer supported (it does happen), and you are left exposed, with your data collection only partly completed and not enough time to start again with another organisation.

Finally, in participant observation you must deal with your split role of researcher and participant, and retain some **critical subjectivity** about the situation. You should not become so involved with the situation that you are unable to carry out the reflection necessary for it to be a useful piece of research. When you fail to maintain some separation, you have 'gone native', and your research may only reflect what the organisation thinks and believes, not what is true. This happened to a student project group that spent one day per week for most of a year in their sponsoring organisation (the Hamsters and Gerbils Conservation Foundation mentioned in **Chapter 6**). They lost any critical perspective and, as a result, turned in a poor piece of work from both the supervisor's and the organisation's perspectives, as it was simply market research and a 'puff piece' at that.

7.4.2 Recording observations

When you are doing participant observation, you will usually record your data in a personal **research diary** during the period of the study. You will need considerable discipline to keep a research diary, but you will lose or distort your thoughts and impressions if you do not record them straight away. You will usually need to make time for such recording time away from your research context, otherwise you might compromise your status as a participant.

 ## SUMMARY

This chapter addresses the key question: 'What design should I choose for collecting qualitative data?' You can choose from a large range of methods, depending on your research question and the practicalities of your available time and places to carry out your research. We discussed possible difficulties with access early in the chapter, but this is an issue that is central to all research methods, not just those described here.

We classified qualitative methods according to the level of involvement you would have in each with the subject of your research. You can carry out observation remotely, and collect data collected about what people do. Remote observation is the least involved of the methods and can be either direct or indirect. More involved methods included the direct interview. These are very common and there is much to guide the practices you use to make your study highly effective. You can achieve even higher levels of involvement under the heading of participant observation – there are well-formulated research designs for both ethnographic and action research. Furthermore, you do not have to use any of these methods in isolation, as one method can provide further evidence to support or question the findings of another method.

ANSWERS TO KEY QUESTIONS

What research designs can I use to collect data to uncover social meaning?

- Remote data collection
- Observation
- Interviews
- Participation

How can I use remote data collection, observation, interviews or participant observation?

- To understand how participants view the social world, rather than have your view imposed upon it
- To collect data directly from participants in their own words and behaviours

How can I use these designs as part of a scientific research approach?

- Transform the qualitative data into numbers and analyse the numbers using statistical techniques

REFERENCES

Eisenhardt, Kathleen M. 1989. Building theories from case study research, *Academy of Management Review,* **14**(4): 532–50.

Glaser, B. and Strauss, A. 1967. *The Discovery of Grounded Theory: Strategies of Qualitative Research.* London: Wiedenfeld & Nicholson.

Rosen, M. 1991. Coming to terms with the field: Understanding and doing organisational ethnography, *Journal of Management Studies,* **28**(1): 1–24.

Walsch, Neale D. 1995. *Conversations with God:* Book One. London: Hodder & Stoughton.

Whyte, William F. 1955. *Street Corner Society.* Chicago: University of Chicago Press.

Whyte, William F. 1978. 'Interviewing in field research'. In Burgess, R.G. (ed.). *Field Research: A Source-book and Field Manual.* New York: Allen & Unwin, pp. 300–18.

ADDITIONAL RESOURCES

Denzin, Norman K. and Lincoln, Yvonne S. (eds). 2000. *Handbook of Qualitative Research,* 2nd edn. Thousand Oaks, CA: Sage. See particularly Fontana, A. and Frey, J.H. Chapter 22, Interviewing – the art of science, pp. 361–76.

Gummesson, Evert. 2000. *Qualitative Methods in Management Research,* 2nd edn. Thousand Oaks, CA: Sage.

Lee, R.M. 2000. *Unobtrusive Methods In Social Research.* Milton Keynes: Open University Press.

Mintzberg, Henry. 1979. An emerging strategy of 'direct' research, *Administrative Science Quarterly,* **24**: 582–9.

Rathje, William and Murphy, Cullen. 1992. *Rubbish! The Archaeology of Garbage.* New York: HarperCollins.

Reason, Peter and Bradbury, Hilary (eds). 2000. *Handbook of Action Research: Participative Inquiry and Practice*. Thousand Oaks, CA: Sage.

Richardson, S.A., Dohrenwend, B.S. and Klein, D. 1965. *Interviewing: Its Forms and Functions*. New York: Basic Books.

Strauss, A.L. and Corbin, J. 1999. *Basics of Qualitative Research: Grounded Theory Procedures and Techniques,* 2nd edn. Thousand Oaks, CA: Sage.

Symon, Gillian and Cassell, Catherine. (eds) 1998. *Qualitative Methods and Analysis in Organisational Research: A Practical Guide*. Thousand Oaks, CA: Sage.

Van Maanen, John. 1982. 'Fieldwork on the beat'. In Von Maanen, J., Dabbs, J.M. Jr. and Faulkner, R.R. (eds). *Varieties of Qualitative Research*. Thousand Oaks, CA: Sage.

Key terms

action research, 235
convenience sampling, 226
covert observation, 225
critical subjectivity, 236
descriptive data, 233
evaluative data, 233
indirect data collection, 222
indirect observation, 222

nonparticipant observation, 223
non-standardised data, 225
participant observation, 234
participatory action research, 235
qualitative interviewing, 231
remote data collection, 222
research diary, 236

taking notes, 232
theoretical or purposive sampling, 226
transcribe, 232

Discussion questions

1. What are the main methods associated with a qualitative research design?

2. How can an interview be used in both quantitative and qualitative designs?

3. Think of three examples of data that could be collected by remote observation. What would be the main method of actually gathering the data in each case?

4. Why is it a good idea to tape record unstructured interviews?

5. What is the role of the interview schedule and how does this compare with a questionnaire?

6. How is ethnographic research different from nonparticipant observation?

7. What are the risks involved with participant observation?

8. Why is it a good idea for you to transcribe your own data? What are the drawbacks of this?

9. Are verbal statements really data?

10. What forms of data, other than words, could you collect as part of a qualitative research study?

Workshop

This workshop focuses on how to use unstructured interviews to find out information. At the end of the workshop, you should have a better understanding of what it is like to be both interviewer and interviewee, by playing both roles.

Background

As the **Chapter 2** workshop explained, people have to make significant changes in their lives when they go into higher education. To assist in this process, we need to understand the nature of these changes better.

Workshop cont'd

Task

Conduct interviews in pairs – not necessarily from the same subgroup.

1. Set-up – Two-minute individual preparation (silence) to think about the issues involved.

2. Interview – Spend five minutes with one person interviewing the other on the subject of their experiences of moving into higher education (all aspects of the change – not just educational). The interviewer is responsible for recording the interview – take notes, tape or video record it if possible – it will be used again in the Chapter 12 workshop.

3. Debrief – what types of questions were asked (open/closed, structured/loose) and what was the role of the interviewer (how much did they impose their own views on the interviewee, intervene) and so on?

4. Now change roles – those that were interviewing now become the interviewee – again a five-minute interview and interviewer is responsible for taking a record of the interview.

5. Debrief – what questions were asked this time, how were they put and how did the interviewer ensure that they did not impose their view on the situation? What form did your record of the interview take? What did you write down – everything they said or just what appeared important (to you)?

6. Break into subgroups (four or more usually works well, the key is to have no more than five or six students per group) – collate the information using thematic groupings – combine your interviews with your own experiences in the group (use good processes from the Chapter 4 workshop to ensure that maximum input is achieved). It is suggested that a mind map display may be appropriate here.

7. Debrief the rest of the group – one minute 'show and tell' of what you found about the subject and the process of carrying out unstructured or semi-structured interviews (such as how much of what was said you were able to capture using notes).

Relevant chapters

13 Answering your research questions
14 Describing your research
15 Closing the loop

4

Key challenges

● Interpreting your findings and making recommendations
● Writing and presenting your project
● Reflecting on and learning from your research

Relevant chapters

1 What is research?
2 Managing the research process
3 What should I study?
4 How do I find information?

1

Key challenges

● Understanding the research process
● Taking a systematic approach
● Generating and clarifying ideas
● Using the library and internet

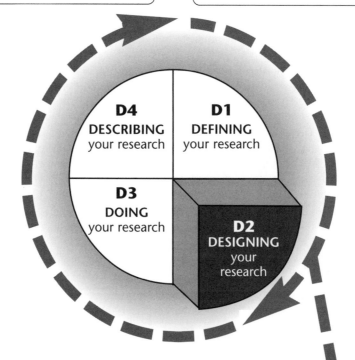

Relevant chapters

9 Doing field research
10 Analysing quantitative data
11 Advanced quantitative analysis
12 Analysing qualitative data

3

Key challenges

● Practical considerations in doing research
● Using simple statistics
● Understanding multivariate statistics
● Interpreting interviews and observations

Relevant chapters

5 Scientist or ethnographer?
6 Quantitative research designs
7 Designing qualitative research
8 **Case studies/multi-method design**

2

Key challenges

● Choosing a model for doing research
● Using scientific methods
● Using ethnographic methods
● **Integrating quantitative and qualitative research**

chapter

8

Case studies and multi-method design

Key questions

- How can I design and conduct a case study?
- How can I design and conduct research studies that use more than one method or approach?
- How can I combine quantitative and qualitative methods to study social phenomena?
- What are the advantages and disadvantages of integrating quantitative and qualitative methods to study social phenomena?

Learning outcomes

By the time that you have completed this chapter, you should be able to:

- Decide whether a case study or other multi-method design is appropriate for your research project
- Design and conduct a case study or other multi-method design
- Incorporate ideas about triangulation into your research design, of any type

Contents

INTRODUCTION

Chapters 6 and **7** introduced you to some common quantitative and qualitative research methods that fit with the scientific and the ethnographic approaches to doing business and management research. Not every research design is based on a single research method, however. Before surveys and participant observation became popular in social research, case studies were the main style of social research (Blaikie 2000). Case studies are still widely used in social research, including psychology, sociology, education and economics, as well as in business and management. This chapter will consider the case study, which is often used in business and management research, and other multi-method research designs. The case study is not really a research method, but it is important enough as a research design to deserve a discussion of its own. Multi-method research combines research methods, which makes it worth considering but particularly tricky to get right. We will also consider mixed-method research, which combines both the scientific and the ethnographic approaches.

As you will see in this chapter, a case study is defined by the boundaries of data collection – *what* you collect data about – rather than research methods or techniques – *how* you collect your data. This is particularly useful when you're not sure where the boundaries between the phenomenon you are investigating and its context should be drawn, or exactly what you will find when you begin to explore the phenomenon. If you organise your research around the social unit you are studying, this will make defining the boundaries of your data collection and therefore your research easier. For example, if you are working on a sponsored project, you might collect data about the organisation that is sponsoring you, using as many different methods as you find appropriate, and use all your information to study the company. Case study designs, because they focus on a 'natural' unit of observation, are popular for student research projects.

This inclusion of many different methods and sources of data makes the case study one of the most powerful, yet challenging, research designs because it comes closer than most other methods to the complexity of real organisational settings and phenomena. A case study can be a good way to investigate a phenomenon in its real-life setting, particularly the dynamics that take place in this setting.

Although the 'case' you study in business and management research will often be an organisation or an organisational subunit, you can study an individual, a group, an organisation or even an industry – the range of case study is unlimited. One case study already discussed in this book is William Foote White's (1955) study of street corner life, where he focused on a particular group of people in society. Other significant case studies include Philip Selznick's (1949) study of the Tennessee Valley Authority and Alfred Chandler's (1962) study of the historical development of American industry. In these examples, the focus of the case study can be large organisations and long periods of time, but a case study can be as small as a single person (Sigmund Freud's psychological case studies) or a short period of time (teaching case studies).

Section 8.1 presents the case study. Our discussion of the case study gives us a natural starting point for discussing multi-method research designs, and triangulation in **Section 8.2**.

After you have read this chapter, you should be able to decide whether you want to use a case study approach or a mixed-method approach in your own research project. You might want to go back to **Chapters 6** and **7** to review the tools and techniques we have presented, to see which might be appropriate for your design.

8.1 THE CASE STUDY

Creswell (1994: 61) defines a case study as a single, bounded entity, studied in detail, with a variety of methods, over an extended period. Compared with the research methods presented in **Chapter 6** and **Chapter 7**, the case study method is not a 'pure' research method, because you will normally collect your data from multiple sources and using several methods such as surveying, interviewing, participant observation and archival research. A case study design does not dictate the use of any particular technique for collecting or analysing data, but it does have definite implications for the choice of the unit of analysis to which you will apply one or more techniques.

The social unit being studied defines your **case study**, whether it is a person, a programme, a company, a situation or whatever. For instance, in a study of management coaching you might collect data about each individual person coached as a **case**, in the way that a case is usually used in quantitative research, but you could also define your case study around a team or the organisation. You could write about the performance of a team following coaching (focused on the team as the case), or the performance of all or part of the organisation under the influence of the coaching (the organisation is the case). Although every research design involves the study of cases, only the case study is defined by the case as unit of analysis rather than the techniques for collecting data.

Just as with any other way of doing research, if you choose a case study you need to show that it is the best way to answer your research questions. A case study is as valid as any other research design we have described in the previous two chapters. There are a number of different ways of carrying out a case study, and you need to justify which particular approach you select.

Business and management researchers carry out case studies for both practical and theoretical reasons. A case study is particularly useful if you want to conduct a limited or exploratory study. A case study, like archival research, may be a good approach if you want to study an organisation or phenomenon that you cannot study directly – you can use a case study when you have no control over the events you are interested in studying *and* the phenomenon takes place at least partly during the period you are doing your research. You may want to select a case study approach if you are conducting an individual research project and you have a limited budget and limited time (Blaikie 2000). Group projects can also take a case study approach. However, good case study research, like surveys, takes careful planning and execution (Yin 1989).

As Yin (1994: 3) comments:

> We were once taught to believe that case studies were appropriate for the exploratory phase of an investigation, that surveys and histories were appropriate for the descriptive phase, and that experiments were the only way of doing explanatory or causal inquiries. [This] view reinforced the idea that case studies were only an exploratory tool and could not be used to describe or test propositions. This … view, however, is incorrect. Experiments with an exploratory motive have always existed. … case studies are far from being only an exploratory strategy. Some of the best and most famous case studies have been both descriptive (for example, Whyte's *Street Corner Society* 1943/1955) and explanatory (see Allison's *Essence of Decision: Explaining the Cuban Missile Crisis*, 1971).

If you are not overly limited by practical considerations, you should consider a case study approach if your research questions lend themselves to this approach – specifically if the unit of analysis is right. A case study can answer either exploratory and descriptive or analytic research questions – 'how' and 'why' research questions. A case study can explain, describe, illustrate, explore or evaluate the social phenomenon you are interested in (Yin 1994). You can use a case study approach to test theory as well as to build theory.

Many groups find that the case study approach is a good approach for their research project because of this diversity. If more than one person in your group is doing research (multiple investigators), then each person may pick up aspects of the case that the others have missed. This is especially useful when you can conduct site visits in pairs or teams. Splitting the group, then comparing and contrasting experiences can be an excellent way of gaining insights from multiple perspectives.

If you decide to use a case study, you should note that research case studies are usually more complex than teaching case studies you have encountered in textbooks and in class. These teaching case studies are usually prepared to illustrate part of a situation for specific teaching purposes. Even if they are based on case study research, they have usually been simplified. So, we recommend that you do not use a teaching case study as the model for investigating and/or writing up your research.

8.1.1 Designing and conducting case studies

The key elements of a case study design are:

- defining the case to be studied
- determining what data to collect and how to collect them
- deciding how to analyse and present the data.

We will consider each of these in turn.

8.1.2 Defining the case to be studied

Issues for getting started on your research design include:

- how you will identify the case or cases you plan to study
- where you will draw the empirical boundaries of the case
- whether you will assign cases to pre-existing theoretical categories.

When you identify the case (or cases), you decide what you are going to study, as shown in **Student research in action 8.1**. If you are doing a sponsored or placement project, then the general setting of the case is usually obvious. You will still need to decide what the boundaries of the case will be. Is it your work group, department, business unit, organisation or industry? If you are free to choose the context of your research, then you need to decide what you are going to study, which gives you both more freedom but also less guidance than for a research project linked to a particular business sponsor.

Student research in action 8.1
THE BIGGER THEY ARE

Rebecca wanted to do her MSc dissertation on why English biotech firms survived or failed. Since she only had three months to design, conduct and write up her research and she didn't already have access to any biotech firms, she decided to do a comparative case study of two firms – one which had survived and one which had failed – to see if she could identify factors that contributed to these outcomes. She selected her two cases to create the maximum contrast between firm success in the biotech field; she could thus test various propositions about what factors, for example early venture capitalist involvement, influential people sitting on the corporate board, differed between the two.

Determining the boundaries of the case means deciding what is relevant and what is not to your case. Although this sounds simple, it's a lot more difficult in practice. It is sometimes difficult to separate the case, or social unit, that you are studying from its context. Ragin and Becker (1992: 6) suggest that 'A researcher probably will not know what their cases are until the research, including … writing up the results, is virtually completed'. You may need to describe the department you are working in so that your reader understands the context of your work group. So is the department or the work group the focus of your case?

This also brings in some issues that relate back to **Chapter 5** and the scientist/ethnographer distinction. Quantitative and qualitative researchers may define cases differently. If you take more of a quantitative perspective, you will probably perceive cases as 'out there', existing independently of you as a researcher. Once you have identified a case, then you will assume that its boundaries are set by the case you have defined. For example, if your case is a company, then you will not need to investigate the industry as part of the case, although it may be relevant to the overall research in describing the context and so on. You will probably identify your cases using pre-existing categories based on general or conventional social units such as individuals, teams, families, organisations, cities and nations. You main task is to identify these cases and investigate them.

On the other hand, if you take more of a qualitative perspective, you might be interested in investigating cases that are theoretical constructs created by investigators, which are specific to a piece of research and are developed during the research itself. The boundaries of the case you are studying do not exist until you have defined them – they are not set by the definition of the case (the 'object' you are studying). The 'type A personality' or the 'newly developing country' did not exist before someone defined them. As you accumulate empirical evidence, your cases will emerge. Therefore, your task is not only to identify and investigate cases, but also to bring them into being.

Single versus multiple case studies

Another important issue in designing your research project is whether to study a single case, an in-depth case that includes more than one 'sub-case', or more than one (independent) case. A **single case study** focuses on a single unit of analysis, such as a corporation. A single case study may naturally occur when you are studying something that is unique – such as the Enron scandal. Students often conduct a single case study when they are working in a company and using it as their research setting, or when they are working to a project brief and their sponsor has asked them to focus on a single internal problem. Note that, although you might find that someone doing question-naires might scoff at you for having only a single case, rather than many, as we have noted above many classic examples in business and management research have been single case studies.

Not every case study is a study of a single case (which is a major difference between a teaching case study and a research case study). You can also study multiple units of analysis, or cases, in a single case study. A **multiple case study approach** is useful if you want to identify which features are unique to a case and which are common across cases. You might decide, for example, to study corporate scandals by doing case studies on both Enron and Parmalat. This replication and contrast provide a significant advantage over the single case study design when you are building and testing theory. You can test or build theory by looking for patterns across cases, use individual cases to support or disconfirm your propositions or develop a more complete theoretical picture. However, you will have less time and effort to spend on each case than if you were doing a single case study.

When you are reading research reports, you may sometimes find it difficult to tell whether a case study is a single case study, a multiple case study conducted within a single setting, or a multiple case study conducted within multiple settings. The multiple case, single-setting design described in example 2 in **Student research in action 8.2** is an **embedded case study**. An embedded case study might involve the study of multiple divisions within a single company, or multiple project teams within new product development. By holding the setting or context constant, you can elimi-nate external sources of variation and look systematically for patterns of actions, behaviours or practices. You can also use an embedded case study to investigate multiple hierarchical levels within a single study, for example, industry, firm and divi-sion level as in example 4.

We are often asked by our students how many cases they should do in a multiple case study design. Whilst there is no way of calculating sample size, as there is for more quantitative methods such as surveys, a good rule of thumb is that you should do between two and eight case studies, given of course that each case study is to an adequate depth. You might also consider doing a single in-depth case study as your main study, and then collect a number of shallower and smaller contrast case studies.

Deciding whether you should study one or several cases in your case study will usually require you to think about whether you are more interested in depth or breadth. **Student research in action 8.2** illustrates student projects that used different forms of case study design.

Student research in action 8.2
EXAMPLES OF CASE STUDIES

Example 1: Strategy implementation
Derkhart was working for a large German bank, and was interested in how the bank implemented its stated corporate strategy. Specifically, his research question concerned how the bank controlled the many activities

that were concerned with this strategy implementation. This is an example of a single case approach – he considered many examples of the activities within the one organisation without focusing on any specific activity, group or part of the organisation. He mixed his insights as a manager in this organisation with some survey work of the organisation and interviews with individual senior managers to provide a rich picture of this issue in the organisation.

Example 2: Programme management

Liz was working with a large public sector organisation, looking at how they implemented organisational change projects. The total number of projects carried out at any one time was over 100, so she decided to consider some key cases that would illustrate her research question – 'what would constitute "best practice" in such an organisation?' Specifically, she considered a small number of cases that had been successful and some that had failed. The key aspects of the successful projects could then be compared with those aspects of the failed projects, and allow further comparison with the best-practice literature in the area. This is a good example of an embedded case study, because she sampled more than one case from the same organisation.

Example 3: Capacity and capability management at a county council

Ian's project was set in a county council where there had been some problems – notably that it had been audited and labelled as a failing council. A key aspect of this failure concerned its ability to deliver services and make changes. Ian's project was to consider the way the council managed the capacity and capability – literally to find whether it had the workforce or ability to deliver all that it was required to do. He soon found that nobody really knew how much work the organisation was capable of doing. The result was that the organisation regularly took on far more work than it could handle, resulting in chaos. Having spent the majority of his available research time with the council exploring the project in depth and identifying his key findings, he then contacted local organisations from both the public and private sectors to provide contrast cases – and explored each of his key issues at those organisations. In this way, he was able to gain insights into those specific issues of importance. This is an example of a multiple case study, because Ian's other cases came from outside his original case study site (compare with Liz's selection of cases in example 2).

Example 4: Empowerment in construction

Ann's study of empowerment practices in the construction sector investigated the research question, 'what is the policy and reality of empowerment in the construction sector today?' In answering this research question, she looked at the overall patterns of empowerment, as cited in various reports on the sector. She then looked at one firm thought to be 'typical' of the sector. Here she considered the firm's policies on empowerment and how these fitted with the overall managerial philosophy of the firm. She also considered what really happened in the enactment of that policy, by considering examples from a division within the firm – again through management statements such as policy statements, and then particular projects – by short site visits conducting interviews of site personnel. This multi-level approach was particularly good at providing a contrast between policy and practice in empowerment – as she did find that there was considerable variation between the views at different levels. This is another example of an embedded case study, where the cases are selected vertically, rather than horizontally as in example 2.

Compare examples 2 and 3 with examples 1 and 4 in **Student research in action 8.2**. If you take a quantitative research approach (as in example 1), identifying common patterns will help you show that your findings are valid and reliable. This does not mean that the quantitative approach to the case was necessarily better than that adopted in the other examples – which were more qualitative – it just answered a different type of research question.

Activity

Fast-food corporations have a choice between franchising new units and opening these units themselves. This decision has obvious financial implications. A less obvious implication is the opportunity to use a company-owned site for getting closer to customers and creating learning, and trying out different policies and procedures, and new products.

Suppose you were interested in how a fast-food corporation changed its advertising and product offerings in response to government initiatives on obesity, and changes in public opinion due to anti-fast-food films and campaigns. How might you develop a case study to investigate this? Try to think about how you would:

- Define the case and its boundaries
- Decide how many cases and what sort of sampling logic to use to select cases.

How would these decisions affect what you find out in your research? Does it make a difference?

The logic of multiple case studies is similar to the logic of qualitative research – you don't need to go on adding cases if you find the same results in all cases, that is, you are not adding any new information. In a multiple case study approach, you should review the contribution each new case is making, rather than wait to the end of your study to note that the findings were the same in all cases.

If you do start to find great consistency in areas where you didn't expect to find it, perhaps it is time to investigate the reasons behind this consistency, rather than simply continue with the same research questions. In this kind of situation, you will find that the case study design is often more evolutionary, and therefore akin to qualitative research.

Logic of sampling

If you decide to investigate more than one case, you will need to think about how you will choose your cases. Whether you take a quantitative or qualitative perspective, you will probably *not* make your case selection based on the principles for probability sampling presented in **Chapter 6**: this is actually the opposite of what you need to do. In most cases, you will want to generalise the findings from your case study to theory, not to a population of similar cases.

There are two ways to think about choosing your research cases. One is to choose either an extreme situation (for example a 'best-practice' or 'worst-practice' company), or a set of cases that varies widely on one or more aspects of either the setting or the main variable you are interested in researching (the 'theoretical variable'). For instance, if your research question was 'what effect does firm size have on the nature of marketing activity carried out?', you may wish to select one small, one medium-sized and one large company as cases, and investigate what 'marketing' constitutes in each case. This theoretical (or purposive) sampling will allow you to select your case or cases so that you can study one or more theoretical propositions. Once you have completed your research, you will be able to draw some conclusions about the effect of size on marketing, rather than what small companies do in marketing, what medium-sized companies do and so on.

The second way to choose your cases is to take a replication approach – choose a set of cases that are similar to each other and look for differences and what causes those differences. For example, you could select a set of small companies to investigate that use similar marketing strategies. You could then try to tease out differences within that similarity about marketing. How robust is the association between marketing and size, for example?

8.1.3 Determining what data to collect and how to collect it

So why haven't we included the case study in either **Chapter 6** on quantitative methods or **Chapter 7** on qualitative methods? In a case study, you may collect quantitative data (numbers), qualitative data (words) or both, using any of the methods discussed in previous chapters (except experiments). Most case studies use more than one technique for collecting data. Nearly all case studies rely on some archival or indirect methods of collecting information. Some stop there, but many go on to use various direct methods, including interviews, questionnaires and nonparticipant observation.

Although case studies always involve a real-life context, in student projects you would not necessarily be limited to using only the ethnographic and participant obser-vation methods described in **Chapter 7**, even though researchers using these two methods describe what they are studying as cases. If you are an undergraduate or taught master's student, you will probably have too little time to conduct your project using ethnography or participant observation. You will probably combine survey methods such as questionnaires and interviews with participant or nonparticipant observation and archival research. You can use these different methods to collect different information, or you may use them to collect information on the same issues so that you can triangulate your findings, as we describe in **Section 8.2**, rather than using each technique to collect different information.

To see where the case study fits with quantitative and qualitative research methods,

Table 8.1 Typical quantitative versus qualitative research designs

	Quantitative approach	Qualitative approach
Number of observations	Many	Few or single
Research questions	Who, what, when, where	How, why
Variables	Specified ahead of time, based on theoretical concepts	Emerge from study, based on grounded research
Collection of information	One variable at a time	One case at a time
Analysis	Level of variables and relationships among them; statistical analysis	Finding patterns of events or processes
Goal	Generalisable to observations or contexts beyond sample	Generalisable to theoretical concepts

you should think about the points discussed earlier in understanding research approaches (**Chapter 5**) and research designs (**Chapters 6** and **7**). These are summarised in **Table 8.1**.

As you saw in **Chapter 5**, quantitative research follows a characteristic pattern where the researcher relies on random sampling, a priori (before data collection starts) definitions of constructs and their measures, specification of research questions, multiple respondents, previous literature, a priori development of research instruments and protocols. The final argument is often structured around producing statistics about the observations. Because of the focus on a single social unit, the case study doesn't fit neatly with quantitative research designs.

On the other hand, qualitative case studies usually begin with loosely defined research objectives and evolve according to the data that are collected. They are often single case designs, involving only a single informant and methods such as ethnography, participant observation or action research. They usually start without any theory in mind and no hypotheses to test: since only the most naive or inexperienced researcher will not have been exposed to some theoretical thinking, this means having a research problem and perhaps some key variables in mind, but not any specific relationships between variables or a theoretical perspective.

The logic of the qualitative case study design is thus closer to a qualitative research design than a quantitative design; however, you may rely on quantitative or qualitative methods for gathering your data. The case study doesn't always fit with qualitative research designs either, because case study researchers may also draw on quantitative approaches, especially in multiple case study research designs. Most case study designs in study projects involve collecting quantitative data using the methods described in **Chapter 6**.

Nevertheless, most case studies will draw heavily on the methods for analysing qualitative data in **Chapter 9** to support their interpretation. **Figure 8.1** illustrates how the case study as a design integrates aspects of both quantitative and qualitative designs.

Whether the case study takes more of a quantitative or qualitative perspective depends on how the researcher designing and conducting the case is guided by the relative methodological perspectives and assumptions and practical considerations.

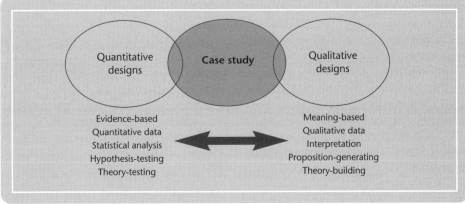

Figure 8.1 Case study as research design

Student research in action 8.3 shows how qualitative data were turned into quantitative data, as a pragmatic approach to dealing with a large data set.

> *Student research in action 8.3*
>
> Although it was a bigger project than most undergraduate or master's student projects, this is a good example of a case study that relied heavily on quantitative analysis to identify key findings, which then fed into the further analysis. Peter, a Swedish research student, spent several years immersed in a company making office products. He made notes of every conversation or meeting he observed on the days he was present at the company. At the end of his three-year observation period, he had over 6000 observations saved on his computer. Peter used content analysis to identify key themes in his data, then plotted the frequency with which those themes came up over time.

8.1.4 Deciding how to analyse and present the data

Although using multiple methods and multiple data sources improves the quality of case study data and analysis, this can make deciding how to present your case study data tricky. In quantitative research designs such as surveys, reporting your findings is usually straightforward – you can analyse your data statistically and then present them in tables and charts, and structure your discussion around these exhibits. In a case study, you first need to decide how you will analyse and present your results. There are many different ways to do this, depending on whether your research perspective is aligned more with a quantitative or qualitative methodology, which will influence how you develop a coherent analysis and present and organise your data. If your research is more oriented towards the scientific approach, you should try to be consistent with the style and content of a scientific analysis and report; if more ethnographic, with the style and content of an ethnographic analysis and report.

Either way, the first step in most case study research is to develop a coherent narrative that tells the story of your case study. This still leaves the question open of exactly how you will do it, since you can usually identify many possible themes around which you could organise your story, including chronologically, around actors (such as people, groups or organisations) or around processes (such as work activities or technologies). Once you have developed your story, you can use guides to qualitative analysis such as Miles and Huberman (1984) to identify the techniques you can use in analysing your case study data.

How to analyse individual cases

You should write a detailed case study for each case, for example each plant site you have visited. This is usually a descriptive write-up, although you can also provide quantitative information such as graphs and tables to illustrate your case. At the end, your reader should understand the detailed and unique features of each case by itself. Tracy Kidder's *The Soul of a New Machine* (1981), for example, describes how Data General developed the Eclipse computer by telling it as a story in more or less chronological order from the founding of the company through to the introduction of the new computer. This is often the easiest way to organise your narrative, especially if you are telling the story of a company or a person. The most common way that student projects report case study research is to arrange the narrative around a timeline. **Within-case analysis** is the process by which you focus your analysis only on an individual case, without trying to bring in the findings or lessons from any other cases you might have been investigating.

How to analyse multiple cases

When you have conducted multiple cases or have used an embedded case design, you should next search for patterns across cases. This process is to conduct within-case analysis, followed by cross-case analysis if you have multiple cases. When you have conducted within-case analysis on each of your cases, then you should analyse all the cases simultaneously, which is known as **cross-case analysis**, to look for common patterns or significant variations across your cases.

One way of doing this cross-case analysis is to select a number of categories and see how each case fits into that category. Are different cases more similar or more different? Another way to do this is to identify common themes across all the cases, and then see which individual case best illustrates each of those themes. In *Microsoft Secrets*, for example, Michael Cusumano and Richard Selby (1995) organise their story around the key themes they identified in their study of Microsoft:

- organising and managing the company
- managing creative people and technical skills
- competing with products and standards
- defining products and development processes
- developing and shipping products
- building a learning organisation.

They then bring in different aspects of the organisation to illustrate each of them.

You can also analyse multiple cases using a **paired-case analysis**, as illustrated in

Student research in action 8.4, where you list the similarities and differences between pairs of cases. This can help you to identify new concepts and categories from the data. People who feel more comfortable with the scientific approach may find the paired-case analysis a more natural way to analyse their findings, because it draws more on the scientific reasoning described in **Chapter 5**.

Student research in action 8.4
WHY CAN'T WE BE FRIENDS?

Teh-Yuan's project was concerned with the management of science and scientists in collaborative biotech research projects. He wanted to establish how such projects could be managed well, in particular focusing on the exploitation of the knowledge produced during the research. His work was to take place partly in the UK and partly in his home country – Taiwan. He chose two cases – one in each country.

Initially he noted the difference in productivity between UK and Taiwanese researchers in terms of their key outputs – specifically papers in scientific journals, where UK researchers were at least twice as productive (in terms of papers per researcher) as their Taiwanese counterparts. The difference in terms of patents registered was similar, with the UK researchers being more than twice as productive.

His paired-case analysis would establish some of the differences in the way that scientists worked – by looking at comparable cases from the UK and Taiwan. His work showed that there were many similarities in the motivations of scientists, but that the need to 'publish or perish' was much stronger in the UK. It became clear that the UK researchers were given more time for this activity and when they didn't get it as part of their working hours, they would put in more of their own time to complete the writing tasks.

Grounded case study designs

Many business and management researchers have found the procedure for grounded case study research presented by Kathleen Eisenhardt (1989) helpful. Since in a case study you are often analysing multiple sources of data and multiple methods, you may find that you can best capture the evolving insights and determine your evolving research design using a grounded research approach where data collection and data analysis overlap. Here, grounded refers to a weaving back and forth between theory and data (for example Bryman and Bell 2003), which is different from the deductive (theory determines what data you collect) and the inductive (data determine what theory you develop) that we described in **Chapter 5**.

A grounded approach can be extremely helpful when you haven't started with a particular theory (or conceptual model), and when trying to induce theory from your observations is difficult. In some case studies, you may be examining a phenomenon that no one else has studied before, so it may not be clear before you start your research either what models are relevant or what data you need to collect. For instance, you might be the first person to do research in a particular type of firm, or on a particular practice. In this case, you might not be able to identify what sorts of things you need to be looking for, or even what sorts of things you might expect to find. This grounded approach will help you to capture both theoretical and empirical insights in such situations.

Eisenhardt (1989) presents an extremely useful road map for using a **grounded case study** research approach to build theories from case study research. This road map is appropriate for research that combines both quantitative and qualitative approaches. The steps she suggested are as follows:

1. *Getting started* – problem definition
2. *Selecting cases* – theoretical sampling
3. *Crafting instruments and protocols* – preparing multiple data collection methods
4. *Entering the field* – collecting data
5. *Analysing data* – within-case analysis followed by cross-case analysis
6. *Shaping hypotheses* – building evidence and explanation
7. *Enfolding literature* – comparing findings with the literature
8. *Reaching closure* – knowing when to stop.

Steps 1–4 of the grounded case study design are common to all case study research. However, whilst you can use the same methods to collect data for a grounded case study and a case study from the scientific approach, typically you will need much more time to interpret the data and understand what they mean.

Steps 5–8 are worth looking at in more detail. Teh-Yuan's project given in **Student research in action 8.4** illustrates the data analysis – within-case followed by cross-case analysis. First, Teh-Yuan analysed each of his UK cases and Taiwanese cases using a within-case logic. Next, he compared pairs of similar cases using cross-case analysis, based on the case's background (for example size of project, type of technology being worked on (predominantly biotechnology) and stage in the research (basic research or commercial development). Teh-Yuan used this to examine whether how the research process was managed had an impact on its outcome.

Based on this, Teh-Yuan could then use speculations about the differences between cases that he found in his cross-case analysis to develop his propositions. For instance, if he found that a key difference between the projects was the presence of a scientist-manager – someone with the specific remit to manage the project – he could propose that 'the presence of a scientist-manager in such research projects is associated with higher productivity'. He would only need to show that this proposition was reasonable based on the case study data – it need not hold for cases outside the sample. This proposition would then give him something to add to his section on 'areas for future work' in his final research report, and a point for discussion and comparison with the literature.

This is where Step 7, **enfolding the literature**, comes in. Eisenhardt's seventh step is completely in line with the second reason for the existence of the literature review – once a researcher has analysed and speculated from the cases, he or she can now turn to the literature to find vital points of reference and comparison. For example, Teh-Yuan could use the literature to find support for his proposition about the importance of the role of the scientist-manager. If your findings are outside the scope of your previous literature review, you may need to conduct a mini-literature review to find relevant research. Your work can be used to reinforce key findings and provide evidence for the need for research to be carried out to explore the areas of difference further.

Step 8 – **closure** – comes when you are confident that if you stop gathering data you will not miss anything new. This is a powerful reason for closely linking your data collection and your data analysis. You will have reached conceptual saturation when relatively few new concepts are coming out of your cases. At this point, you should be working on the further analysis of the data, through coding and testing out different propositions on the data you have collected. You may need to return to the field later to collect specific data about issues that have emerged from your work, and check that the scope of the work you had envisaged has or has not changed.

Presenting the case study

As we mentioned above, even if you take a quantitative approach to your case study, the design and outputs of a case study are considerably more complex than projects based on research methods such as experiments or surveys and are closer to qualitative research. This can present a challenge when you start writing up and presenting your findings.

There is no 'one best way' to present a case study. During your literature review, look at how case studies are presented in the literature on your research topic, which should provide you with some good examples. For instance, if your evidence is mainly:

1. *questionnaire or other quantitative data* – present the case study evidence as statistical summaries and tables, using the case study detail to illustrate or explain the findings
2. *archival* – present the case study evidence as a narrative, often in chronological order
3. *interview* – present the case study evidence around themes, illustrated with quotes
4. *ethnographic* – present the study as a narrative, often around themes, illustrated with quotes.

Remember that as well as using the literature to support your findings, you can also use the literature to show how your findings have filled a gap in the existing literature or how they challenge existing theoretical explanations.

The following example illustrates how one student chose to present his work at this stage. Sam's project considered the failure of a major new product development project, despite the application of conventional and accepted methods for managing project risks. Sam identified eight key issues that emerged from his analysis – these were concepts that emerged consistently during discussions with people at many levels in the organisation and in his analysis of company documents. Having considered all the options for presentation, Sam used a basic table to present his findings and reintegrate them with the literature. (We will discuss this method of presenting your results in detail in **Chapter 13.**) A summary is given below in **Table 8.2**.

Assessing the quality of a case study

The criteria that may be used to judge your case study include:

1. Have you conducted your research in a systematic way?
2. Does the story that you tell make sense?
3. Does your evidence support your story?
4. Is there any other story that could equally well be told?
5. Have you shown something new?

Table 8.2   Sam's findings table

Issue	Theory/best practice	Case findings
Use and deployment of risk management systems	If you use a formalised risk management process, it is likely that you will avoid costly problems during the project	Despite the use of formalised risk management systems, problems emerged, particularly during the early stages of the project
Project complexity	Even complex projects can succeed if formal risk management is used	Clear evidence that project managers underestimate risk and complexity so there was no clear view of what the project really entailed
Organisational structure untested	Insufficient organisation will have serious consequences	It did have serious consequences
Senior management interference	Senior management intervention should be minimal once the project has started	Senior management interfered and increased project complexity
Reporting of 'bad news'	Communication channels should be open and used with a no-blame system	People afraid of passing on bad news as management and customers tended to 'shoot the messenger'
Proactive risk management	Formal risk management minimises risk exposure	Risk management seen as secondary and not implemented effectively
Attitudes to risk	Attitudes towards risk should be based on individual experience and training	Attitudes to risk based on overoptimism and wild guesses
Risk deferral	Effective risk management avoids crisis management	Management almost always by crisis, but could have been avoided if addressed early

8.2 MULTI-METHOD RESEARCH AND TRIANGULATION

The case study is probably the most well-known example of a research design where you employ multiple methods for collecting and analysing your data. However, the case study is not the only example of a multi-method research design. For example, in marketing, studies often employ focus groups, interviews and questionnaires in a single study. Focus groups are used to capture what respondents think are the most important issues or aspects of an issue, usually in a fairly nondirective way. These issues or aspects can then be used to shape a structured interview or questionnaire as the next stage of the research process.

There are three situations where you might want to use multiple methods in a single research project. First, in some projects you won't be able to capture all the information you want to find out using a single method. For example, if you are on a placement project, you might be able to interview managers in your local department about the issues you are investigating. However, if you need to find out information about past decisions, you may need to rely on secondary sources if no one has the relevant knowledge. In this case, you are using different methods to investigate a single issue or a single aspect of that issue. This pluralism in your choice of methods is very much 'horses for courses', so you can usually justify each method you use.

A second reason for using multi-method research occurs when you find out different answers depending on what method you use, and no one method reveals 'the truth' you want to get at. This is why researchers may come up with different findings about the same issue or phenomenon – the answers are method-dependent. For example, in the garbage study described in **Chapter 6**, researchers were interested in whether people could accurately report their use of packaged foods. What people reported they had consumed in their weekly surveys was significantly different from the evidence provided by what they discarded in their rubbish. If the answers you get from different methods converge, even if they are not identical, then you should have more faith in the conclusions you draw from the different methods. For example, even if the amounts discarded in the rubbish varied, if you found that consumers in neighbourhoods with an active recycling programme discarded less waste than those in other neighbourhoods, whatever method you used, you would be more confident in arguing that recycling programmes were effective in promoting desirable behaviours.

Different methods are especially likely to result in different answers when you are asking sensitive questions. People will often give the answers they think are socially appropriate in face-to-face interviews, they are slightly more likely to be honest in telephone interviews, since they can't be seen, and much more likely to be honest in anonymous surveys or computer-based questionnaires. We have already mentioned the differences between people's reports on how often they wash their hands after going to the loo and direct observation. You may be interested or appalled to find out that socially desirable responding makes it difficult for toilet paper manufacturers to find out how people actually use toilet paper – fold or crumple – despite significant consumer research budgets.

You might also consider using different methods when you are asking people to recall or estimate behaviours for which recall may not be accurate. Perhaps the people in the garbology study weren't trying to mislead the researchers, they might actually not have had accurate recall of how much they discarded (how much attention do you actually pay to your rubbish?). Here, the more methods that you can bring to bear, the more chance you have at finding a reliable set of answers.

If you have the time and resources, you may want to experiment with different methods to find out how the information you find out differs according to what method of data collection you use. You can then select the best method – or combine information from the different methods – in answering your research questions. You can capture information about the same issue or aspects of that issue using different methods to see if the information is consistent or inconsistent. The principle of using different methods to collect information on the same thing, rather than on different things, is known as 'triangulation', and is so important for doing research that we will return to it below.

A final reason for using more than one method in your research project is when you want to conduct your research in stages, and different methods are appropriate for each stage of your research. This would actually be a series of linked mini-research projects examining the same research question. For example, you might identify a general topic and conduct a few pilot case studies to identify the important characteristics of the topic. The outcomes of the case study analysis could be used to generate input to interviews, and interviews to surveys. Over time, the research methods could be used to converge progressively on more detailed refinements of your investigation.

At this point, you might be asking yourself whether using multiple methods doesn't conflict with the differences between the scientific and ethnographic approaches. However, these tools and techniques are extremely flexible. You can use a questionnaire to collect unstructured verbal data about why people attend *Star Trek* conventions, if you like. You can use observation to collect detailed measurements on how people navigate through particular websites, if you would rather. At this level, you need to consider the differences between the scientific and ethnographic approach to choose the best set of tools and techniques for what you want to find out, but the 'research methods police' will not hunt you down and arrest you for 'mix-and-match' violations.

Differences between the scientific and ethnographic approach become important when you consider the sequence of activities in the research process. Remember that one of the emphases in the scientific approach is deduction, where you draw on theory to determine what data you collect, whilst the ethnographic approach emphasises the role of data in guiding what theory you choose to explain your observations. It should be obvious that you cannot conduct a research study using the scientific and the ethnographic approach simultaneously, because you cannot let theory determine your observations without selecting a theory, or data determine your theory if you haven't collected data. (The grounded research approach described in **Section 8.1** is a way of 'bootstrapping' your way if you want to choose the middle ground – you are going back and forth between theory and data.)

This also ties into our discussion in **Chapter 5** on the underlying world-views associated with the scientist and the ethnographer. It would be quite a juggling act to believe that we can simultaneously research the social world as real, objective and independent of us, and constructed, subjective and dependent on us. Thus, we argue that it is not possible to conduct mixed-approach research – at least within a single stage of multiple-stage research – even if we can mix tools and techniques. (We will also allow that researchers can mix approaches across stages of multiple-stage research, even if this requires some major flexibility on the researcher's part.) For now, though, you should set this discussion in the context of using multiple tools and techniques.

The contradictions between the process and the world-view associated with each approach may, paradoxically, explain why you can also observe mixed methods across some subjects if you look across researchers, or at the stream of research projects conducted by an individual researcher. This reflects the way that research methods change as a topic moves from being new and not well understood to being established and fairly well understood.

Quite commonly, the methods that people use to investigate a particular topic or phenomenon vary over time across different research projects in predictable fashion. Some researchers even argue that there is a hierarchy, or natural cycle of methods, starting with case studies and ending up with large-scale surveys. However, this has been argued to be a quantitative way of thinking: from a qualitative viewpoint, it may be that any sequence of methods might be valid in investigating a phenomenon.

8.2.1 Triangulation

When you are studying the same phenomenon from several perspectives, for example using more than one method or more than one source of data, this is known as **triangulating** your research. As you might remember from basic maths, the triangle is the strongest and most stable geometry. Some of the different approaches to triangulating your research include:

1. multiple methods
2. multiple sources of data
3. multiple measures
4. multiple viewpoints.

Multiple methods

As mentioned above, you can use multiple methods for collecting your data to strengthen your conclusions. This is especially important when what you find out using one method conflicts with another method, or where you can't capture the information you want using a single method.

Multiple sources of data

Most data are inherently unreliable. If you collect data about the same thing from different sources, you are more likely to spot data that are unreliable. To take a trivial example, imagine reading the same news story in a tabloid, a conservative broadsheet and a liberal broadsheet. How many of the facts and opinions will be consistent? How many of the facts and/or interpretations will differ? You may need to collect some data from only one source, for example the country where the firm's headquarters are located.

Multiple informants

A special case of multiple data sources is asking several people the same question. Many research projects rely on just one person – a single informant – as the source of data about an organisation, work group, household or other group of individuals. Obviously, you need to choose someone who is well informed! Single-informant designs, especially in strategy research, have been widely criticised (for example Van Bruggen et al. 2002). Multiple informants are particularly desirable when you are asking opinion or other subjective questions. For example, if you are studying new product introduction, you could ask the same questions of both marketing and manufacturing managers and see how consistent their answers are.

Multiple informants can be especially useful when you are asking questions for which there is no 'right answer'. You are more likely to reveal a diversity of opinion, if there is one, than if you sample only one person and take their response as representative of the whole. For example, it has been our experience that if you ask a range of people in an organisation what the corporate strategy is, you will get a range of answers – when presumably there is just one corporate strategy being pursued. The marketing manager will see it differently from the manufacturing manager and so on.

If the different responses converge, then you can have more confidence that you have the right answer – at least for that organisation and set of respondents. Opinion polls, especially electoral polls, go to great lengths to get multiple informants so that the answers to the questions they ask are as representative of the whole population as they can possibly be.

Multiple measures

Another way of triangulating is to collect more than one measure for each significant concept (or aspect of an issue) you are investigating. Again, you are trying to get convergence, and divergence between the measures may signal that you need to pay careful attention to some problem.

In attempting to assess, for instance, the level of motivation of a group of employees, you could think of many different measures that can be applied. For instance, you could assess the amount of their own time they were prepared to invest in their work, the level of excitement they felt on a Monday morning going to work and the number of sick days they took off when they weren't really ill.

A word of caution here on developing multiple measures. It is easy to assume that different measures are of the same aspect, but you might well be measuring different aspects that aren't related. For example, absenteeism might reflect employee motivation but lateness to work might reflect extra-work responsibilities that have nothing to do with motivation. If you are taking a scientific approach to measuring intangible aspects such as emotions or beliefs, you may need some expert help in devising multiple measures for the same emotion or belief. You may want to read ahead about measurement scales, which contain a number of different items that (at least in theory) measure the same underlying aspect. We will discuss these in **Chapter 11**.

Multiple viewpoints

A final way to triangulate is to think about what you are researching from as many different angles as you can, and try to include as many possible explanations for what you have found out as you can. If you would arrive at the same conclusions from different perspectives, this should give you more confidence in your results than if a 'scientist' might interpret your research in one way and an 'ethnographer' might interpret it in another.

If you are doing a group project, this sort of triangulation of multiple viewpoints may come naturally. Try to make sure that your group is receptive to these different perspectives, and that 'groupthink' or premature convergence doesn't keep you from being as creative as you can be.

If you are doing a placement or sponsored project, you may find it helpful to have a discussion with your co-workers or your manager to get different perspectives and make sure you haven't missed anything out. Of course, if you get agreement, you need to make sure that you have not gone native – you might try consulting with someone outside the company, within the limits of confidentiality. You should also try to make sure that the received 'company line' does not overwhelm your own findings if they are not what the company wants to hear. You might want to read ahead in **Chapter 10** if this seems to be happening.

If you are doing an individual research project, it may help to discuss your research and findings with someone else, to make sure that it is making sense. If you have kept a research diary along the way, as we recommend, go back and read through your emerging thoughts. Have you left out some promising insights by focusing on the major themes, which you can recapture now? It might also be useful to try to see your

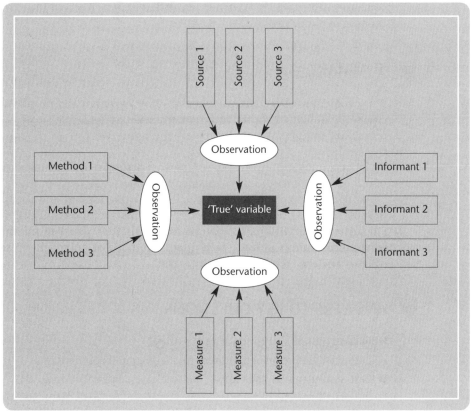

Figure 8.2 Triangulation

research from a different perspective – how would this look to me if I were a scientist/ethnographer? **Figure 8.2** summarises the discussion of triangulation.

 ## 8.2.2 Advantages and disadvantages of mixed-method research

If there are so many advantages to doing mixed-method research, why don't all researchers use mixed-method research in every research project? Some of the reasons include:

- you must invest more time and other resources in doing mixed-method research
- you may have difficulty in reconciling the answers from different methods
- different methods may not give you additional information
- only a single method (or narrow set of methods) may be considered appropriate in your research area or subject
- different methods may reflect different and incompatible research approaches (at the process and world-view levels).

Despite these potential disadvantages, however, we suggest that you consider a mixed-method design if you have the time and resources to carry one out. The advantages that you will gain in terms of confidence in your data, your interpretation and your conclusions may well make a mixed-method approach worth the extra investment in carrying out your research.

 ## SUMMARY

This chapter presents some guidelines on how to design and execute a case study. The case study design combines both quantitative and qualitative research designs, whilst remaining unique. We briefly review the grounded case study approach proposed by Eisenhardt.

The case study is only one type of research design to use multiple methods. The logic of using multiple methods is explained in **Section 8.2**.

Triangulation explains how you can combine quantitative and qualitative data, techniques, methods or approaches with multiple methods and other approaches to strengthen your findings. Triangulation, whether you use multiple informants, researchers, sources of data, techniques, methods or approaches, can increase your insights and the credibility of your research.

 ## ANSWERS TO KEY QUESTIONS

How can I design and conduct a case study?

- Cases can use predefined issues or take a grounded approach
- Case studies can be single cases, multiple cases, embedded cases and paired cases

How can I design and conduct research studies that use more than one method or approach?

- Similar to the logic of the case study, different methods can be combined to answer different parts of a research question and provide different insights into a research problem

How can I combine quantitative and qualitative methods to study social phenomena?

- Case studies allow the application of multiple methods in the design, collection and analysis of data
- Multiple methods can be used at different times and on different aspects of a case

What are the advantages and disadvantages of integrating quantitative and qualitative methods to study social phenomena?

- Advantages include the generation of a greater insight into the phenomenon being studied
- Disadvantages include more work and the need to reconcile often conflicting data

REFERENCES

Blaikie, Norman. 2000. *Designing Social Research*. Cambridge: Polity Press.

Bryman, Alan and Bell, Emma. 2003. *Business Research Methods*. Oxford: Oxford University Press.

Chandler, Alfred D. 1962. *Strategy and Structure: Chapters in the History of the American Industrial Enterprise*. Boston: MIT Press.

Creswell, John W. 1994. *Research Design: Qualitative and Quantitative Approaches*. Thousand Oaks, CA: Sage.

Cusumano, Michael A. and Selby, Richard W. 1995. *Microsoft Secrets: How the World's Most Powerful Software Company Creates Technology, Shapes Markets, and Manages People*. London: HarperCollins Business.

Eisenhardt, Kathleen M. 1989. Building theories from case study research, *Academy of Management Review*, **14**(4): 532–50.

Kidder, Tracy. 1981. *The Soul of a New Machine*. New York: Avon Books.

Miles, Matthew B. and Huberman, A. Michael. 1984. *Qualitative Data Analysis*. Beverly Hills, CA: Sage.

Ragin, Charles and Becker, Howard S. (eds). 1992. *What is a Case?* Cambridge: Cambridge University Press.

Selznick, P. 1949. T*VA and the Grass Roots*. Berkeley: University of California Press.

Van Bruggen, Gerrit H., Lilien, Gary L. and Kacker, Manish. 2002. Informants in organizational marketing research: Why use multiple informants and how to aggregate responses, *Journal of Marketing Research*, **39**(4): 469–78.

Whyte, William Foote. 1955. *Street Corner Society*. Chicago: University of Chicago Press.

Yin, Robert K. 1994. *Case Study Research: Design and Methods*, 2nd edn. Thousand Oaks, CA: Sage.

 ADDITIONAL RESOURCES

Eisenhardt, Kathleen M. 1991. Better stories and better constructs: The case for rigor and comparative logic, *Academy of Management Review*, **16**(3): 620–7.

Glaser, Barney G. and Strauss, Anselm L. 1967. *The Discovery of Grounded Theory: Strategies of Qualitative Research*. London: Weidenfeld & Nicholson.

Gomm, Roger, Hammersley, Martyn and Foster, Peter (eds). 2000. *Case Study Method: Key Issues, Key Texts*. London: Sage.

Jick, Todd. Mixing qualitative and quantitative methods: Triangulation in action, *Administrative Science Quarterly*, **24**: 602–11.

Kanter, R.M. 1983. *The Changemasters*. New York: Simon & Schuster.

McClintock, C., Brannon, D. and Maynard-Moody, S. 1979. Applying the logic of sample surveys to qualitative case studies: The case cluster method, *Administrative Science Quarterly*, **24**(4): 612–29.

Schroeder, R.G. and Flynn, Barbara B. 2001. *High Performance Manufacturing: Global Perspectives*. New York: John Wiley & Sons.

Stake, Robert E. 1995. *The Art of Case Study Research*. London: Sage.

Strauss, Anselm L. and Corbin, Juliet. 1999. *Basics of Qualitative Research: Techniques and Procedures for Developing Grounded Theory*. London: Sage.

Travers, Max. 2001. *Qualitative Research Through Case Studies*. London: Sage.

Yin, Robert K. 2002. *Applications of Case Study Research*, 2nd edn. London: Sage.

Yin, Robert K. 2003. *Case Study Research: Design and Methods*, 3rd edn. London: Sage.

Discussion questions

1. What is a case study?
2. Why are case studies so popular among student research projects?
3. What are the different forms of case research?
4. How many cases are enough?
5. Can you use questionnaires and ethnography in the data collection of one case study?
6. What does triangulation mean and how might it be applied in other (non-case) areas of research?
7. Surely cases are just like journalism and consulting?
8. How can having multiple researchers be helpful to the quality of your research?
9. How do you know when to stop collecting data?
10. Can you do a case study on an organisation without visiting it?

Workshop

Task

You have been asked to demonstrate how you would use a case or multi-method research design in the project to find the changes that people experience as they move into higher education. Using the results of the previous workshops on this, or starting afresh, identify:

1. Opportunities for using cases – what questions might cases be good at answering? What types of case analysis could you use here, for example would an embedded multiple case design be appropriate?
2. Opportunities for using triangulation – again, what questions might such an approach be good at answering?
3. Choose a main research question from this work and construct a research design that will enable you to answer this in detail.

3 Doing your research

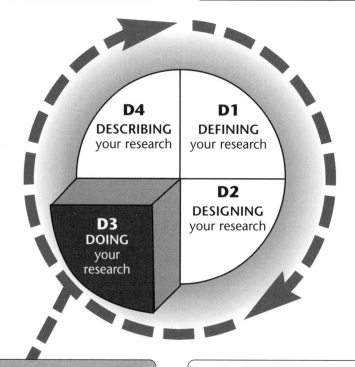

Relevant chapters

13 Answering your research questions
14 Describing your research
15 Closing the loop

4

Key challenges

- Interpreting your findings and making recommendations
- Writing and presenting your project
- Reflecting on and learning from your research

Relevant chapters

1 What is research?
2 Managing the research process
3 What should I study?
4 How do I find information?

1

Key challenges

- Understanding the research process
- Taking a systematic approach
- Generating and clarifying ideas
- Using the library and internet

D4
DESCRIBING
your research

D1
DEFINING
your research

D2
DESIGNING
your research

D3
DOING
your
research

Relevant chapters

9 **Doing field research**
10 Analysing quantitative data
11 Advanced quantitative analysis
12 Analysing qualitative data

3

Key challenges

- **Practical considerations in doing research**
- Using simple statistics
- Understanding multivariate statistics
- Interpreting interviews and observations

Relevant chapters

5 Scientist or ethnographer?
6 Quantitative research designs
7 Designing qualitative research
8 Case studies/multi-method design

2

Key challenges

- Choosing a model for doing research
- Using scientific methods
- Using ethnographic methods
- Integrating quantitative and qualitative research

chapter 9

Doing field research
Practical and ethical considerations for conducting research

 Key questions

- How can I gain access to the organisations and people I want to study?
- How can I manage the expectations of different project stakeholders?
- How can I balance academic research and consultancy in a sponsored project?
- What ethical issues should I consider in managing my project?

 Learning outcomes

At the end of this chapter, you should be able to:

- Identify strategies for gaining access to organisations you are interested in
- Manage multiple stakeholders for your project outcomes
- Balance the different aims of research and consulting
- Identify the ethical issues concerned with carrying out field research

Contents

INTRODUCTION

With this chapter, you begin the third major stage of your project – 'doing your research'. Your hardest decisions, which concern how you define and design your research, have been made, so the time for agonising is past. However, you should always be open to issues that arise during your research, as these may present exciting and unexpected possibilities.

In our experience as supervisors, in-company research is especially challenging for students. In this chapter, we will offer you some tips and strategies for doing **field research** in **natural settings**, especially if you are doing research in organisations or will be in extended contact with them. Many research challenges only arise when you are in direct contact with organisations, either gathering data or actually working temporarily or permanently in an organisation.

Many students find one of the biggest challenges in doing field research is gaining access to the organisations and/or the people in them who you want to study. Even experienced researchers find this difficult. In **Section 9.1** we present some strategies you can use to gain access to organisations.

Working for or with an organisation, rather than just using it as a source of information, comes with its own set of challenges. Field research will be most involving when you are working in the setting that you are investigating as during an internship or a placement. This is the focus of **Section 9.2**. You should carefully consider how the organisation's goals and expectations might conflict with your research project, without letting it dictate the direction of your research. You may be pulled in many directions – not least by your academic supervisor and your business sponsor. You will also need to determine actively how much of your role is *researcher* and how much *consultant*. Balancing research and consulting can be crucial to your project's overall success. Students who 'go native' seldom turn in good research projects, because they have lost the ability to see the organisation and issues from a critical perspective.

We conclude with **Section 9.3**, which discusses some ethical issues that apply to all research. Even if you are doing desk research, and not in direct contact with organisations or people, you may be faced with some decisions that involve judgements about right and wrong or potential harm to other people. This is likely when you are in direct contact with or working in an organisation and have to deal with issues such as confidentiality. We introduce some general principles for ethical research in business and management projects, including some guidelines on doing ethical research. Ethics used to be on the 'nice to cover' list for student projects, but now is on the essential list. Your institution may have its own ethical policies on research that you need to know and follow.

After you have read this chapter, you may want to revisit your research design. If you can make sure that you have thought about access, responsibility and ethics before you go into the field, you are more likely to be able to deal with any unexpected or difficult problems you find.

9.1 GAINING ACCESS TO ORGANISATIONS AND PEOPLE

Unless your research projects are based only on indirect contact with organisations and people, and you obtain your data from the library and the internet, you will need to gain access to people and/or organisations. Usually, you are responsible for arranging this access and establishing your contacts on your own. Even where your university or project sponsor arranges access to organisations or your project site for you, for a successful project you will still need to establish your credibility with the people you will be working with.

This section will cover some of the golden rules for doing field research including:

1. *Put your project requirements first when choosing what project to do.* Work-based projects are only attractive when they allow you to pursue the qualification you have been working for.
2. *Don't leave your success in other people's hands*, particularly when it comes to gaining access or data. Get agreements in writing. This can be just writing down what has been agreed and getting people to initial it, confirming that this is what has been agreed, or a formal agreement. Some business schools have their own forms, especially for placement students or sponsored projects, which formally commit the organisation to providing access and data for the purposes of the project. Some organisations have their own forms, which specify what you will and will not be able to do. Always investigate this before you commit too much time or resources to a particular project design.
3. *Don't overpromise or overcommit just to get a project.* You must always follow the highest ethical and legal standards when you design and do your research project. (More about this in **Section 9.2** when we discuss how to manage competing demands.)

9.1.1 Using contacts to gain access

To gain access to any organisation, you must start by making contact. There is no one best way to do this. Sometimes it will be worth approaching organisations with a well-worked proposal, stating exactly what you intend to do. A simple expression of an interest in working with them on any interesting project and a summary of your project guidelines may be enough at this stage.

Given the large number of requests that firms receive to become involved in different types of research, you may need someone to vouch for you, sponsor or champion your project for it to be agreed to go ahead. Such contacts are key to moving forward the project. You may need to cultivate your personal contacts or networks to find such a champion. Even though networking is promoted actively in business and management, if you are starting your project, you may not find advice such as 'you should always be developing your networks' very useful. However, think about the many networks of people you have to tap into:

- *Professional associations* related to your area of interest or the trade association of particular organisations – most are keen to gain student members and be seen to be assisting in the development of the professional community
- *Alumni networks* of your academic institution – most institutions have become far more aware of the potential of their alumni in recent years – this is now a good source
- *Attendees* at a relevant public event (for example an evening talk related to your area of interest) – even better to meet people in person, rather than have to 'cold-call'
- *Sporting or interest groups* (a club or church, for instance) where social contacts could be made

● *Families and social contacts* – you should not underestimate these, as in our experience, this is the prime source for collaborative projects.

Your best starting point is a **warm contact**, that is, someone with whom you have a connection (family, acquaintance, sporting or professional associations). Warm contacts are people who at least know of you and will probably find the time to pass you on to the right person to talk to. The business cards you have collected over time can be a valuable source of warm contacts.

If you don't have any warm contacts, you can use your **personal networks** to gain access to organisations that would otherwise ignore or turn down your request out of hand. Personal networks give you access to people with contacts in the organisations – 'friends of friends'.

The type of network that you can build to try to get your main contacts is shown in **Figure 9.1**.

Having to try to negotiate access through **cold contacts**, people who do not know you personally and with whom you have nothing in common, is the hardest way to gain access, but it still worth trying. These contacts might be 'friends of friends of friends', but at least you will have a name within the company, who may be willing to give you details of more promising contacts. If you can mention the name of the person who gave you the name of the cold contact, this might help warm them up a bit.

Getting in touch with even the coldest of contacts is usually more successful than random approaches to organisations, which we might describe as 'ice-cold' contacts. Many researchers have found that company receptionists serve as an effective barrier to contacting anyone within the company, although web pages and databases may provide a way around this. In our experience, though, calling up an organisation and asking to be touch with 'the guy (or gal) who knows about ...' just leads to frustration and few good leads.

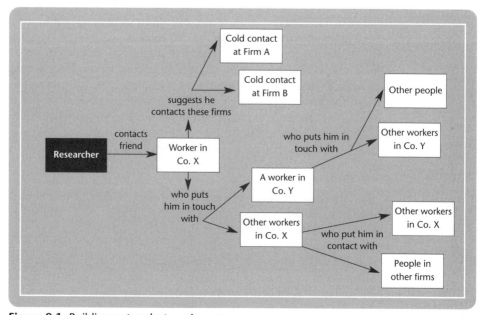

Figure 9.1 Building networks to gain access

9.1.2 Making contact

Contacts and networks are only useful if they come through for you. This at least partly depends on your convincing them of your project's potential benefits for them and why you deserve access to their organisation. You can improve your chances by giving them the necessary information, illustrated in **Student research in action 9.1**. This might be a copy of your project proposal (**Chapter 2**) or a one-page précis of your research that you can fax or email to the organisation. Be sure to highlight any key 'selling points' of your research.

Student research in action 9.1
A FRIEND IN NEED

Bill was due to start a project on customer relationship management (CRM) practices in fast moving consumer goods (FMCG) firms. He knew someone who worked for the marketing department of a large FMCG firm, so Bill asked him to arrange for him to interview appropriate people in the organisation. He gave his friend a brief verbal outline of the project and waited for his call. Nothing happened for weeks.

When Bill called his friend to find out what was happening, he was told that the firm had decided not to implement any more software solutions for the rest of the year, due to a freeze on IT spending, and therefore nobody was interested in talking to him. This seemed bizarre to Bill, who had only mentioned IT in passing as a potential enabler of CRM – IT was not central to the project, yet this is what his friend had focused on.

If only Bill had put together a short written proposal for his friend, there might have been a chance that the firm would have been interested in his work. As a result of this falling through, he ended up changing his project.

As well as deciding what information you will give to contacts about your study, you need to make sure that you have it available promptly when it is needed. A clever student will already have it ready, just in case. This is important because once you have managed to gain entrée through a contact, your potential project sponsor will typically want to know:

- What are you investigating?
- How many people do you need to speak to?
- How long will you need to speak to them?
- Can you guarantee confidentiality?
- What's in it for the firm?

Make sure that you can answer all these questions.

9.1.3 Gaining deeper access

The guidelines above apply to any field research, whether you need access for an hour or several months. In some situations, you will want to arrange deeper access to an organisation, perhaps by doing a paid or unpaid internship. If you hope to study or work in the organisation for an extended period, you will probably need to provide more information about yourself and your research project than your project brief or proposal. At a minimum, you are likely to be asked for your CV, so have it ready.

Unless a company has already arranged the work you will be doing and is looking for someone to do it, you will almost certainly be asked:

- How much time do you plan to spend in the organisation?
- What facilities will you need to do the work?
- What is it going to cost?

You should have an initial discussion with the person in the firm who makes the decision to set your project parameters and decide what you can reasonably ask for. What you cost the organisation is not trivial, whether you are asking the organisation to be paid a salary, to be reimbursed for expenses, or simply to do an unpaid internship for the period of your research, particularly if someone has to justify it. If you find out that the person you are talking to doesn't have the authority to make this decision or perhaps to make any commitments, you are not talking to the right person to get the project rolling, so check to see to whom you should be talking, and set up a meeting or phone call.

In any meeting with potential sponsors, you should take notes. Afterwards, you should summarise the meeting, and, provided that you have received a positive response, put your understanding of your project and the organisation's commitment in writing. This is the first part of scope management (discussed in **Chapter 3**). It also provides some momentum to your project, always helpful if you want it to proceed. Levels of access have been discussed in **Chapter 8**. This is where the network approach to research really comes into its own.

Students often ask whether they should go to an organisation with a well-worked out strategy, or approach it with something looser and try to find areas of mutual interest for a project. The best answer is most likely to be 'both' – the more ways you try to gain access to different organisations and the more organisations you try, the luckier you will get.

9.2 MANAGING COMPETING DEMANDS

If you are doing a field project, you will have two customers for your project – your examiners and your project sponsor. Each will have different expectations of your project and your research process, so you will need to manage both relationships as well as your research project. Balancing the academic requirements of your work and the practical output that the organisation is interested in can be a challenge. Understanding this tension and managing both parties to the process is the first step towards successful field research. Ignoring this, or getting it wrong, can have disastrous consequences, as demonstrated by **Student research in action 9.2**.

Student research in action 9.2
A BUNCH OF COMPLETE BANKERS

Jie was a very determined student, and had a number of options open to her when she came to considering subjects for her master's project. The two most attractive projects were one on human resource management policies in her native China (her preferred choice) and a paid project looking at investment policies for a bank in the City of London.

Jie chose the banking project, but right from the start her supervisor was concerned about the amount of time that she could give to her project. The bank were paying her very well, but also demanded that she fulfil a significant operational role within the organisation. She ended up working nearly 60 hours a week on this role, leaving little or no time or energy for her project. The bank also reneged on promised data to enable her to complete her project. In the end she was unable to submit a piece of coursework of sufficient quality to enable her to complete her course.

Your academic institution will require you to turn in a project that is sound and satisfies the assessment guidelines. In some instances this will require you 'to apply theory to the solution of a practical problem', whereas in others, it will be 'to demonstrate knowledge and ability to design a study, collect appropriate data, analyse that data and present suitable recommendations'. These are different requirements – the latter puts far more emphasis on the research aspects than the former. You should be visualising how you will satisfy your particular requirements long before you start writing up your research.

Again, in our experience as supervisors, we have found that students either take this requirement too seriously and start getting stressed out – how can I complete my practical project for the project sponsor and make a great theoretical discovery in the area of organisational behaviour? – or fail to take it seriously and deliver a project that only hits the mark on one of the two criteria. It's probably better to get a little stressed early on, discuss this with your supervisor, and sort out clearly what you need to do on both the theoretical and the practical side. If you think you have it sorted without having discussed it with your supervisor, all we can say is you are probably heading for disaster, and your supervisor has probably been giving you a lot of clues that you are focusing on the wrong thing. If so, we will probably see you again in **Chapter 15**, when we describe the most common reasons that projects fail.

Here it might be useful to reflect on what your different stakeholders might be expecting from your project. If you have forgotten who these stakeholders are, you might flip quickly back to **Chapter 1**. An organisation is interested in solving a particular practical problem rather than creating new management knowledge, therefore it will be more concerned with your recommendations, rather than how you get there, although it will need to be confident that you have got there the right way. It is here that you need to actively manage the situation. In our experience, students who have created expectations that they cannot meet are the major cause of dissatisfied project sponsors. They promise an elephant and deliver a mouse.

An awareness of the basics of customer satisfaction can be useful. Maister's first law of customer service (Maister 1993) states that: Satisfaction = perception – expectation, that is, the level of satisfaction is determined by the difference between what the organisation expected and what you delivered. You must manage both the expectations and perceptions of the people you will be working with. We will explore how to manage the scope of your project in **Section 9.2.1** below.

9.2.1 Managing scope

The first step in managing the expectations for your project is to define the scope of your project clearly. As we explained in **Chapter 2**, **project scope** describes 'what is included in the project and what is excluded'. The three important aspects of scope that you need to manage are:

1. *Initiation:* identifying your assumptions and constraints
2. *Planning:* providing a statement for agreement of your work
3. *Change control:* seeing how changes made to the scope either deliberately or through circumstances will affect the end result.

During the initial stages of your project, your assumptions will include what you will study. Your constraints include the availability of resources, data in particular. If you assume too much, you risk having to change your project, as **Student research in action 9.3** shows.

Student research in action 9.3
WHAT THE HECK IS GOING ON?

Paul wanted to study whether what the people of a company spent their time doing and the corporate strategy were related. He assumed that there would be data or the possibility for data collection as to what diverse groups of people (the firm was spread over 30 locations) spent their day doing. He also assumed that there was an explicit statement of corporate strategy that would allow the comparison to be made.

This assumption was never challenged until a few weeks into the project, when it became clear that neither assumption held. Fortunately, he was able to look at how such a system could be constructed, and the type of data that he might record, and start to implement it. This changed the focus of the project, but was not fatal in this instance.

An essential part of planning your project will be to generate a written scope. The **scope statement** is a document of what is included in the project and what is excluded. Usually one page of description will do. This statement becomes a vital tool for managing expectations, since it clarifies what the organisation should expect from you. As **Student research in action 9.4** illustrates, you should always get a scope statement agreed with your sponsor.

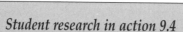

Student research in action 9.4
SCANTY BRIEFS!

Pascal gained sponsorship for a project with a large financial institution. The firm gave Pascal a verbal brief for the project, which he noted during the original discussions. Pascal interpreted this for the university and the project started well.

His first meetings with the main person responsible for his project went less well. The sponsor was always late or simply agreed to meet with him in the presence of others at lunch. Promised data were not forthcoming and contacts and meetings that had been suggested never materialised. He was left with a fairly 'thin' project, but one that he could salvage into a report for the university that met all the necessary criteria.

The firm was not so happy. It threatened court action if its criteria (which Pascal had never seen but which differed significantly from the brief as he understood it) were not met. He had little choice but to go back to the firm after the project was supposedly completed and try to rescue something.

Pascal could have avoided this fiasco if he and the organisation had agreed on the project scope. As he reflected later: 'I wish that I had put in place all the CYB (cover your back) stuff, it would not have taken long and would have saved a whole pile of trouble later on.'

We want to make it clear that project disasters such as John's are mercifully rare. However, what you should note about this one is how preventable the problems were. If John had spent a few minutes documenting the scope at the outset, and regularly reviewed it as he went, he would have saved this particular 'pile of trouble'.

Gaining early commitment from key individuals is a vital part of success in projects being undertaken in organisational settings. You should always get a signed, written agreement from your project sponsor (preferably the person who will be paying for it and the person who will be making sure that you get your work done). In addition, you can use the scoping process to set out what the firm and, in particular, key individuals are prepared to do. You should secure written agreement early on for the time and access necessary to do your work. If this is not forthcoming, you can demonstrate how they have not 'met their side of the bargain'. **Student research in action 9.5** demonstrates the effective use of such agreements in making a project successful.

Student research in action 9.5
HOW GREEN WAS MY VALLEY

A group of undergraduates was asked by a large energy company to consider the market for green power in the UK so that the firm could start to tap this market. The brief provided by the firm was contained in an email. Wisely, before going any further with the project, they interpreted this brief in the form of a scope statement. In the scope statement they:

● Defined the terms to be used – including how they understood the concept of 'green power'.

- Set out that they would be prepared to carry out primary research with existing customers of the firm, provided they were given details of relevant contacts and meetings were arranged through the firm. Expenses would be provided for such visits and any wider-scale survey of firms was outside the scope of the work.

- Confined the project to the commercial energy sector, as this was the implied area of interest in the original brief. They could exclude the domestic sector from consideration.

- Agreed to carry out case-based analysis of firms and also investigate the regulatory aspects of a green power company. They would not be responsible for starting to 'build a brand' around the concept of green power.

The group presented a one-page statement of what they would do and received the necessary signatures to allow them to move the project to the first stage. By interpreting the brief in their own words and limiting what they would do, the students found that the project, which had originally looked too large for them, became far more manageable. Moreover, they found out through this scoping process that two key players in the firm wanted different things from the project. Once this was identified in advance, they were able to resolve what would otherwise have been an inevitable conflict.

Limiting project creep

You can also use your statement of project scope to prevent **project creep**, which occurs when you are asked to accommodate changes to the project. These changes are often innocently disguised as 'just do this bit as well'. 'Just this bit' usually turns out to be a large piece of work that takes up valuable time, usually at the end of the project when you can least afford it.

Your logic should be simple. Until the project is complete, if additional work is added, something must be taken away. The scope statement provides you with a tool for managing the performance expectations of the project – you can evaluate any changes against it to show the impact on other performance aspects. This is vital particularly where the project is emergent, that is, only planned as far as the next milestone (see **Chapter 2**).

 9.2.2 Am I a researcher or a consultant?

The seeds of disaster are sown for many students when they go native and adopt the perspective of the organisation, or perhaps never have an independent view to start with. One way to avoid this kind of disaster is actually to visualise and manage your role in the organisation, ideally from the start of the project. This will help you design your project so that you are doing the right things, always a good idea. Even more importantly, it will help you manage your approach to the organisation, and your role with relation to the organisation, which is usually where things start to get sticky.

Any field research can lead to conflicts between academic and practical expectations, but when you are employed by an organisation to conduct your research and feed back the findings, they are inevitable, although of more ethical concern. A researcher is free to gather any data that illuminates the project and draw any conclusions that are justified by the evidence (informed by theory if appropriate). A consultant may feel constrained in gathering data (don't try to find out what is hiding under that huge lump in the middle of the carpet, it could be an elephant, which would be extremely awkward!) and in the conclusions that he or she draws from the evidence. You need to be clear on the difference between your role as a researcher and your role as a consultant.

Consultancy was defined as 'giving advice to an organisation' in **Chapter 1**. Many researchers conduct consultancy projects for organisations, and many consultants engage in research projects. However, the two types of project and person are distinguished by a number of characteristics, as shown in **Table 9.1**.

Company-sponsored field research projects fall between research and pure consultancy, as shown in **Figure 9.2**. The starting point for research and consulting differs, with the consultant defining and *bounding* the areas for investigation at an early stage. This is vital, as the discussion on scope management showed.

Table 9.1   Differences between research and consultancy

Issue	Research	Consultancy
Strategic purpose	Investigate an area of interest	Solve a problem
Motivation	Personal interest in the area	Improve the organisation in some way
Research object	As defined by the research questions in the study	Usually a bounded problem
Research question viewpoint	Ontology defined explicitly	Functional standpoint more relevant
Subject originality	Some element of novelty usually required	Rarely totally original; perceived novelty to the organisation important
Quality control	Process control through use of recognised and appropriate methodology executed in recognised ways	Little on the process, focused on the outcomes
Assumptions	All assumptions, including those of your research approach, must be clear from the outset	Usually focused on the assumptions of the prevailing 'business model'
Research audience	Assessors and possibly wider community	People from the organisation
Idea, pedigree, information basis	Based on identification of needs through analysis of extant literature	Based on perceived needs
Resource–quality trade-off	More likely to be quality-focused	More likely to be resource-focused
Presentation style	Formal academic, focus on the process and discussion	Formal, business-speak, focus on the 'bottom line'

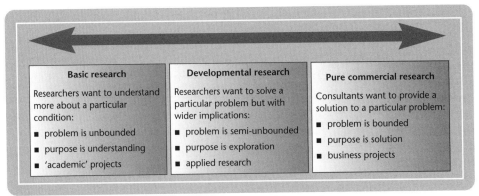

Figure 9.2 Differences between research and consulting projects

As we noted in **Chapter 1**, researchers and consultants often conduct projects for different purposes. The consultant looks for solutions to a particular practical problem, and the researcher is more interested in finding out more about the area they are looking at. They are fundamentally different, not least because the consultant may be far less involved in 'pure' research.

The role of the consultant

A cynical definition of a consultant is 'someone who asks for your watch, and tells you the time'. Consultants do not always have the best reputation. Most organisations can tell stories of the consultant who ran off with both their watch and their fee. The credibility of an assignment that is seen as consultancy by an organisation will therefore need to be justified.

A consultant can take one or more of the following roles:

- *an honesty broker* – providing an external 'independent' viewpoint on a situation, which can be immensely beneficial. As one consultant commented, 'Sometimes people get too close to the coal face to see the wood for the trees!' People working within an organisation can be more inclined to accept the views of an outsider on changes, than to move from entrenched positions at the behest of a colleague. As importantly, such a solution may allow individuals to 'save face'.
- *a change agent* – providing the focus for activities, while keeping an overview of what is happening.
- *an integrator* – taking responsibility for a particular piece of work that needs inputs from people from different parts of the organisation.
- *a knowledge provider* – providing expertise in one or more specific areas or techniques.
- *a resource provider* – facilitating tasks to be carried out that people from within the organisation claim they do not have the time or capability to do (certain documentation activities or specialist technical knowledge).
- *a checker* – inspecting the way in which the process is being carried out.
- *a trainer* – rather than doing the job for the organisation, imparting the knowledge to the members of the organisation through training.

Students make take any of these roles, although the role of trainer is less common, particularly where there is a research objective. Each role comes with its own challenges, and this list is useful when discussing with an organisation which they expect you to take (see Block 1981 for further description of the roles of consultants).

If you run through the list above, none of these roles involves generating knowledge specifically. This is one of the ways in which not explicitly managing your dual roles as researcher and consultant can get you into trouble – you can get so involved in the consultant role that the researcher role falls by the wayside.

Organisations will clearly have different expectations as to how you would conduct yourself during a student project and how a professional consultant would behave. A student will not necessarily have all the answers, but should know either where to get them or when to say that there are not answers. As demonstrated by **Student research in action 9.6**, you will also occasionally have to say 'no' to organisations.

Student research in action 9.6
DON'T LEAVE ME THIS WAY

As part of his placement project, Ivan developed a spreadsheet to measure the effectiveness of his sponsor's advertising across different media. Because the sponsor was a small company, when Ivan's placement was over, the company kept calling him up and asking him to do just a little more work on the spreadsheet. Ivan, however, needed to do his coursework and study for his final exams – besides, he was no longer getting paid and the updating of information wasn't very exciting. After a couple of months, he saw through the flattery and politely told the company that he was unable to provide further support.

Whilst you should always maintain the general ethical standards discussed in **Section 9.2.3**, there are also particular codes for consulting, such as those available through the Management Consultancies Association and the Institute of Management Consultants. The effort of the student-consultant is only one part of the puzzle, however. A 1995 UK government report cited by Lynch (2001) concluded that 'it is difficult to do good work for a bad client, and it is difficult to do bad work for a good client'. The organisation therefore has to take part of the responsibility for the outcome of the work. In particular, the discussion in **Section 9.2.3** on sponsors who have a secret agenda may be worth reviewing.

9.2.3 Sponsors and coercion

Manipulative and determined sponsors can make your job difficult if you start to diverge from their plan for your project. Doing research is rarely dull; people are likely to surprise you. There is always risk involved when you are working with people, and a key skill is recognising this and learning how to deal with it.

People agree to sponsor a research project for many reasons, but often they will have an agenda – personal, political or other – they want to promote through your research project. They may try in different ways to influence your research to fit this agenda, including trying to control your research question, limiting your access to sources of information (for instance limiting the people you could talk to) and systematically controlling your findings, including limiting your report's content and scope. Early warning signs include not disclosing why the study is being undertaken or explanations that don't appear to make sense. It is quite possible that you will get some indication of problems through your interactions with people in the organisation, particularly if you tell them who is sponsoring your research.

This is unethical behaviour on the part of the sponsor. You should discuss your project with your academic supervisor if you think this is going on. You might need to consider withdrawing from the study. This is part of the challenge of real-world research. You still need to manage your dual roles as researcher and consultant, and part of your write-up should reflect any influence the sponsor has had.

9.3 ETHICS

Ethics concerns the moral principles that determine how we think and act in particular situations. Even though you will rarely have to deal with the kinds of ethical dilemmas that face medical researchers, you will have to deal with many philosophical and practical issues in organisational settings. We are not talking here about researching ethical issues in companies (for example 'Do banks have ethical investment policies?'), but how you are going to run your research project. Research ethics is the ethics of how you carry out your work.

In a book such as this, it is impossible to give advice on every ethical issue you might come across. Instead, we will cover the basic principles you should consider and encourage you to refer elsewhere to sources of guidance and advice – particularly your academic supervisor. You should be aware of the implications of research ethics for your research project. In the past, research ethics has been treated as a kind of 'disaster aversion', that is, avoid unethical behaviour or your study will be seen as below par or unacceptable. Ethics ensured that nobody is actually or potentially harmed as a result of your work (see for example Cooper and Schindler 2001). This is a very minimal goal, given the potential for good that a study can have.

In recent years, organisational ethics has moved from a 'nice if we've got time' to a 'must do' issue. Ethical behaviour will not necessarily improve your study, but behaving unethically will certainly adversely affect your work. At a minimum, you should make sure that you conduct each aspect of your research to the highest ethical standards possible.

A minimum ethical standard is to do no harm. A higher goal is to find a way that your research project can benefit the organisation and individuals involved.

In addition, you may like to consider your personal ethics, for instance would you be prepared to carry out work with a company that produced military weaponry or had a poor record on environmental or human resource issues? Your beliefs and the moral code that you subscribe to influence your research approach. Amongst other factors, national culture influences this, so it is important you determine the principles that are relevant to your particular context. These personal ethical issues are outside the scope of the discussion in the rest of this section, but are ones that you need to consider.

The ethics of a particular research method or situation are most important for this discussion. **Research in action 9.1** describes the reactions to a particular piece of research.

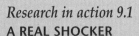

> ### *Research in action 9.1*
> ### A REAL SHOCKER
>
> In the Chapter 1 workshop, we reviewed some classic research studies. Each study raised ethical issues, but Stanley Milgram's (1974) social psychology experiment on obedience to authority, experimenting on people in a laboratory setting, raises some particularly interesting issues.
>
> How ethical do you think it was for Milgram to deceive participants into believing that they were really administering electric shocks to his confederates? Could these participants have potentially suffered some trauma? The immediate consensus (for example Baumrind 1964) was that the experiments went 'too far'. However, Milgram's finding that under orders people are prepared to be systematically cruel to others was significant and provided a building block for psychological knowledge and research for many years. The ethical committee of the American Psychological Association investigated Milgram's research and decided that it was ethically acceptable. The American Association for the Advancement of Science awarded him a top prize for the research in 1965.
>
> Do you think that, faced with the same situation today, these two organisations would arrive at the same answers? Did the end (a fundamentally important piece of work) justify the means (the potential for people in the study to be traumatised)? The ethical hurdle has undoubtedly been raised over time.

How do we assess the ethics of a research situation? To answer this, we need to consider the nature of the ethics and develop a generic framework for their description. The overriding principle that we advocate should govern how you deal with people or organisations is:

> Treat others as you yourself would want to be treated and provide benefit to the organisation and individuals involved in your work.

If you stick with this principle, stay open to the concerns of both individuals and organisations and keep focused but flexible with your research questions, you should be able to identify areas where you need to address ethical concerns.

In **Chapter 7**, we proposed a scale of involvement of the researcher with the subject of their research. At one end was the secondary analysis design, where researchers are only indirectly involved with their subjects. At the other, researchers have extensive direct involvement with the people and organisations they are studying. These two extremes and the ground in between provide us with ethical challenges – as to how data were collected, analysed and reported.

Many of the codes of ethics have been developed for experiments, where people are subjected to some sort of experimental treatment, rather than for less involved methods such as surveys or observation. If you are manipulating people's behaviour or environment in some way, you should investigate further your university's code of ethics, including whether you will need consent from a human subjects board, and whether you need participants to sign explicit consent forms (see, for example, www.scholari.com/toolchest and the **Additional resources** at the end of this chapter).

9.3.1 Ethics and research design

Guidelines for experiments

As noted above, many of the ethical issues associated with business and management research were first raised by field or laboratory experiments. If you are conducting an experiment, you should be especially aware of the extensive guidelines for ethical issues. The American Psychological Association publishes a clear set of guidelines, which have become the basis for similar guidelines used by many organisations. These principles include:

1. Establish a clear and fair agreement with research participants before their participation that clarifies both your and their obligations and responsibilities. Stick to this agreement. (This is covered further in the following section.) You should include the policy of your organisation on this kind of research.
2. Inform participants of all aspects of the research that might reasonably be expected to influence their willingness to participate and explain all other aspects of the research about which the participants enquire. For instance, if you are working with one organisation, it is not ethical to work with a competitor by using your academic institution as a 'cover' and not informing it. You should always disclose to the company that you are working with its competitor.
3. If achieving the purpose of your study makes concealment or deception necessary, you should make sure that this is unavoidable and debrief the participants afterwards. This is less likely to be applicable to student projects but this does occur where, for instance, you want to distract participants from the main issue you are researching, so that you get a natural view, rather than what people think you might be looking for. This was certainly an issue for Milgram's experiment.
4. Respect the fact that people may not want to participate in your research, or may want to stop participating during the study. You should obtain 'informed consent' for participation if there is any level of intrusion into people's lives. This is linked to the previous point. Consent may be difficult to obtain from certain groups – for instance children or other people with limited powers of reasoning.
5. Clarify any issues that may have arisen during the study with your participants post-completion by debriefing them.
6. Respect confidentiality – particularly of the individual, but also of the organisation. Any quotations in your project report should not be traceable to individuals by someone reading your report. Certainly, don't pass on negative comments during interviews or discussions.

Informed consent

Gaining informed consent is highly desirable. However, making someone fully aware of the objectives of your study, or who is paying for it, may bias the data you collect, as discussed in **Chapter 6**. To overcome this problem, particularly where 'natural responses' are required from participants, some approaches that have been suggested include:

● 'be truthful, but vague and imprecise' (Bogdan and Taylor 1984)
● get consent after the study (post hoc)
● avoid the issue by using the credibility of your institution or supervisor ('they wouldn't allow me to do anything unethical').

Going back to the suggestion that a minimum goal for your research project is to do no harm, but a higher goal is to provide positive benefit, how consistent with the highest ethical standards do you think these suggestions are? Always beware of anyone who asks you to compromise your ethical standards, even if it doesn't seem important at the time. You never get a second chance to go back and put things right if they go wrong. If an aspect of your research seems to entail some ethical compromise, try to figure out a way to change the research design, rather than thinking it's OK.

It's also important to realise that ethical standards change over time, so that what you read in the research literature may no longer be acceptable. For example, the acceptability of deception has changed. An Ivy League researcher decided to investigate the customer complaint handling and recovery procedures of a number of famous local restaurants. The researcher sent letters claiming to have contracted food poisoning from a meal eaten at the restaurant, to see what response the restaurants would make. Several restaurants were extremely concerned and took drastic action, only to find that the meal (and the complaint) was fictitious. The researcher, alas but quite rightly, found himself on the receiving end of a quite stringent complaint process.

Institutional credibility has been raised in connection with several famous experiments. Participants may believe that they will be protected from harm or potential harm by the university. In the obedience to authority experiment we discussed, Milgram (1974) was conducting his research at Yale University, an Ivy League university. Similarly, the famous prison simulation by Haney et al. (1973) took place in the basement of the psychology department at Stanford University. Neither experiment would be permitted today.

Ethics and the internet

If you are collecting data from people through questionnaires, interviews or observations, you will not usually need to be quite so formal, but you should always think through and, if possible, discuss with your supervisor the ethical implications of your research in advance. You should be aware of organisational constraints on the use or publication of data. Again, practice is evolving rapidly over time, so you should consult with key stakeholders, including your supervisor and manager as appropriate. In the UK, for example, there are many restrictions on the data you can collect and store, which might affect how you handle the recording and analysis of, for example, survey data. Pay attention when you read **Section 9.3.3** if you are collecting data that identify individuals.

Needless to say, the internet has created new ways for researchers to be unethical in conducting their research. Researchers have found many benefits from using email and online surveys in their work. You should think through the possibilities for harm or deception if you use email or the web in doing or disseminating your research.

You could be considered to be using unethical means if:

- you 'spam' by sending unsolicited emails to a large number of individuals or organisations
- you collect data on individuals through tracking devices, if you do not get explicit consent
- you use the internet to conduct research on behalf of an organisation and do not identify your sponsor
- you hack into an organisation's website or servers to download information.

9.3.2 Ethics and the research report

Ethics and writing up your project report

Three further ethical issues need to be discussed in the context of the write-up:

- *Maintaining privacy* – make sure that the confidentiality of individuals and, where necessary, organisations is preserved in reporting your research.
- *Representation and misrepresentation of data* – report and analyse your data honestly, regardless of whether it fits in with your prior expectations or the pressures that may be applied on you to obtain a particular answer.
- *Taking responsibility for your findings* – delivering an unfavourable report and running away is not a grown-up way to behave.

Maintaining privacy

When you report your research, you should be able to trace where comments or particular pieces of data have come from. However, it is important, particularly in qualitative research, that potential readers of your reports cannot do the same unless you have explicit permission to identify the source by name. This is a non-negotiable feature of reports and you must always check that any quotations you use will not breach confidentiality by being identifiable. For instance, the following appeared innocuous enough:

> To illustrate the tensions that were present in the call centre, one female middle manager stated: 'The management here is isolated in all ways. We have all the responsibility but little way to make sure that people do what they are supposed to. They just don't care, so we end up having to work long hours to put right all the mistakes that the operators make. We get no real support for this from the board members. Every time we ask for something to help prevent problems, they turn it down.'

This would have been fine except that there was only one female middle manager in the group of companies in the study. Careful writing, and sometimes creative editing, is needed to make sure this doesn't happen to you. This is not a licence to be unsystematic or avoid justifying your findings. You should provide as much evidence in the form of quotations and insight from your work to demonstrate that you did carry out this research. This theme will be developed further in the following chapter.

Many companies ask for nondisclosure agreements to be signed and the name and company data to be disguised. There are many levels of disguise. These include renaming individuals and organisations, and disguising details about either that might lead them to be identifiable. Referring to the firm as 'Company A' or giving them a representative name (for example, giving a brewer the name 'Beer') is one way to disguise firms. This is especially sensitive where there are few individuals or few organisations. For instance, Kate worked on a survey of service management practices where one respondent rightly pointed out that, in a global industry with only four key players, anyone would be able to guess his organisation if his organisational segment were mentioned.

Of course, above all else, you must make sure that you will be able to complete your project before you give any assurances, whilst balancing this with the principles of doing no harm and providing positive benefits. Make sure that you consult your supervisor before you negotiate any confidentiality agreements or agree to disguise aspects of your research. You need to make sure that your academic supervisor is aware of any restrictions and that they will not affect your ability to turn in a good project.

Don't misrepresent your data

An interesting aspect of research is the presumption of researchers' personal integrity. There have been many notable cases, especially in scientific research, where researchers have misrepresented their data, although in many cases they were eventually found out, as reported by Bell (1992). In one case, a leading scientist painted his lab rats' fur to support his theories! Whilst few researchers go so far, there are other ways of cheating, including being selective about how you analyse your data, which data you include/exclude from your analysis, how you report your results and so on.

All these undermine the personal integrity required of a researcher. As you will probably have gleaned already, few supervisors or markers have the time to replicate your study or otherwise verify that you have actually carried out the research you say you have. However, it is easier than you think for an examiner to spot faked research, not least because of inevitable inconsistencies between what you report and what they know about the world, for example results that are too statistically 'good to be true', or that contradict the results of other studies they are aware of or have even conducted.

Take responsibility for your findings

Becker (1972: 113) said of sociological research that 'A good study will make somebody angry.' According to Becker, educational institutions often grant access to researchers in the hope that the research will show that the government, society, parents or students themselves are why students don't learn anything in schools. They seldom expect to have their educational practices questioned and often react badly when this happens.

Your research has an equal opportunity to make someone angry. Organisations or managers often sponsor research that they hope will make them look good or will point the finger of guilt at someone else. Provided that you have carried out your research diligently and reported it faithfully, this is an occupational hazard and you should not avoid reporting bad news. However, you do need to manage how you report it.

This is not only an ethical matter but also a pragmatic one. Some information needs to be handled sensitively. Presenting figures in isolation with no point of reference or benchmark, as shown in **Student research in action 9.7**, can provoke this kind of reaction. If you are around to defend your work, this may be justifiable. If you drop or dump your findings on the organisation, you only avoid the initial confrontation about the findings. This does not fit with the main principle of research advocated in this section – ensuring that there are benefits of your research to the organisation and the individuals involved.

> *Student research in action 9.7*
> **HASTA LA VISTA, BABY**
>
> Stephanos carried out an excellent study to provide the cost justification for improvement activities in an organisation. He began by estimating the cost of failure of critical aspects of the business and presented his figures to the board of the firm. One of the directors was threatened by this and said, 'If that is what you really believe, you can leave now, and clear your desk on the way out.' Luckily, this reaction did not undermine the quality of the work he had already done, which had been based on data gathered from a representative range of the firm's activities. Nor, as it transpires, did it cause him any long-term career damage.

You should also think through the consequences of your project report falling into the wrong hands. What you put in writing cannot be dismissed like a verbal comment, and it lasts a lot longer. For this reason, you have a **duty of care** in the language you use. This does not mean that you should completely sanitise your work, just beware of provocative statements that could be taken out of context and used against anyone you have been working with.

Activity

Conflict: What would you do?

Two students were working in an engineering firm over a period of several months, looking at methods of working, but focusing on ergonomics in particular. One area of the production floor particularly interested them, as it contained many identical machines. They analysed the machines and spent some time with the operators. They realised that there was a high absentee rate, and lower back problems were often cited. This led them to consider whether the physical environment around the machines or the materials handling might be causing this, or whether, as the managers they interviewed suggested, there was simply poor morale amongst those operators, resulting in absenteeism.

Given that the managers were in a position of some power over the study, the students had to tread carefully when considering that there might be something wrong with the working environment. Indeed, it quickly became apparent that the way the workers were having to use the machines was central to the problems and for some workers the long-term effects of using the machines were disabling.

Considering what they had found – that people were being asked to work in an environment that was likely to cause them physical harm – how should the researchers present the findings to management? As far as the educational institution was concerned, they had done an excellent piece of work. The firm was not so impressed when the findings began to emerge. Admitting that it had a problem with these machines would not only leave the firm open to a bill for having them amended, but could open the way for a flood of litigation from the machine operators, for having failed to protect their physical welfare while at work. The firm was also very busy and any changes were certain to cause disruption and loss of business. The students had also interviewed union representatives at the plant, who had insisted that they also be provided with a copy of the report.

The students faced a dilemma. Releasing a full report, as they wanted to do, would cause all sorts of problems for the firm. Not publishing their findings would be to condemn the operators to more years of back problems.

Which of these options would you choose, or can you come up with an alternative?

What the students actually did is revealed in the Postscript at the end of the chapter.

Ethics and supervision

The issue of reporting your work has been covered above. However, as part of the assessment process, there are several further issues we need to cover. First, you need to make sure that your supervisor can assess your work on its merits and isn't influenced by any other criteria.

In commercial organisations in many countries, it is no longer acceptable for suppliers to give their commercial customers gifts (for a sample written statement, see www.cips.org). This is so that purchasers are not influenced, even unconsciously, in favour of those suppliers. In many cultures, it is traditional for students to give presents to their supervisors. In English-speaking countries, the dividing line between thoughtfulness and attempted bribery is not written down, but the boundary between what is acceptable and what is not is set at a low monetary (or other) value. Whilst this genuine and largely innocent tradition is still generally acceptable, you should bear in mind that your supervisor will probably be the first examiner on your work, and he or she clearly needs to assess your work without bias or favouritism. It is worth being 'nice' to your supervisor however, as illustrated by **Student research in action 9.8**.

> *Student research in action 9.8*
> **HAVE ANOTHER PAVLOVA, TEACHER?**
>
> David, one of Kate's MBA students, brought coffee and a chocolate-chip cookie to each one of their tutorials. Whilst this did not influence the project mark Kate gave him, it did make her look forward to Tuesday morning meetings.

You should also distinguish ingratiating behaviour from 'What would it take for you to give me an A grade on this report?' The student who asked this question was apparently unaware of the implications of what he was asking. It was culturally acceptable for this to happen in the student's home country, but most institutions have harsh penalties for this kind of behaviour. Ethically and legally, this was not acceptable in the institution where the student was studying at the time.

9.3.3 Ethics and the law

Making sure that you appropriately attribute other people's work is a major ethical concern. As we saw in **Chapter 4**, plagiarism is a perennial problem so it is vital that you understand your institution's rules on plagiarism. While you may not plan to publish your project report, you must show what your original contribution is, and what you are taking from other people, including unpublished internal company reports. This becomes a particular issue in group projects, or where you are drawing on a previous project.

You also need to recognise that there are legal constraints on research beyond the issues of plagiarism and copyright. Over recent years, legislation that affects research has increased dramatically. In this section, we will highlight some important legal issues for student research projects, but this is only the tip of the iceberg.

Most countries including the UK (1998) have adopted a **Data Protection Act**, which restricts what data you can collect about people and entitles the people named in any electronic database to find out what information you are keeping about them on file and obtain a copy of that information. Previously confidential data such as medical records and credit ratings are now available for scrutiny.

Although the law does permit some exceptions for education and research purposes, you should think about why you need each piece of data you are collecting, and whether it is really necessary. You should only collect data that are strictly relevant to your project, rather than going on a 'fishing trip', where you collect data that aren't relevant to your research questions just because they are there. Few student projects will require you to collect **sensitive personal data** such as someone's political opinions, religious beliefs or organisational memberships. If you wanted to explore the relationship between a person's religious beliefs, sensitive personal data, and days off sick you would need explicit written consent to collect, analyse and report these data, even if your report does not make people individually identifiable.

Furthermore, you shouldn't keep data relating to people any longer than you need to complete the project, unless you are required by your project guidelines to keep it. You should never make the data you have collected available to anyone else who does not have the same legal duty of care to the people in the database. If you want more guidance on these issues, ask your supervisor, or consult your manager if this is work-related data rather than externally collected data.

Although we have only covered some ethical and legal issues in this section, you should make sure that you have, and can show that you have, considered the most likely ones in advance. You should also show that you have dealt with any that have emerged during your project before they become critical or threaten the project objectives. Whilst you will not get a high mark just for having managed your project with ethical and legal issues in mind, it is almost certain that you will be severely penalised or even failed if you have not.

 ## SUMMARY

In this chapter, we have considered issues that arise when doing field research, where you are collecting data from organisations and/or individuals in their natural setting.

These issues included how to gain access to organisations, conduct your research ethically, balance organisational and academic expectations and requirements and balance research and consulting.

Although it is possible to gain access to organisations by presenting them with a project proposal, you will often need to gain access through the agency of a person, including your personal contacts and/or the contacts of people in your personal networks. Organisations will expect you to provide them with information about your project, and about yourself, so that you have credibility.

When you have responsibilities to both your academic institution and your project sponsor, conflicts will almost inevitably arise. These may be particularly difficult if your project sponsor has a hidden agenda and tries to influence your research.

Finally, some research is closer to consultancy than to research, in that the organisation expects you to give them advice, rather than simply reporting on a state of affairs. In this case, you should behave ethically and professionally, but remember your academic responsibilities.

A number of professional organisations have codes of ethics for conducting research that you can consult for guidance. You should also let the golden rule – do unto others as you would have done unto you – guide you in your research design and data collection and reporting.

ANSWERS TO KEY QUESTIONS

How can I gain access to the organisations and people I want to study?
- Warm contacts are usually more successful than cold contacts for gaining access, but either can yield the access that you require
- Personal networks are usually most effective in gaining initial points of entry to organisations, and from there to find the relevant people to talk to
- You will need to be prepared, with project ideas and CVs ready, and flexible to find avenues that will yield benefits for both you and the organisation

How can I manage the expectations of different project stakeholders?
- We advocate putting your academic requirements as the highest priority in your research
- A managed scope statement will greatly assist in providing the basis on which expectations of your work will be set

How can I balance academic research and consultancy in a sponsored project?
- Give explicit thought up-front to which roles you are playing and manage those roles carefully
- As part of your research design, recognise that research is the opportunity to investigate a topic of interest, whereas consultancy is giving advice to an organisation. You will need to have elements of both in your work and manage expectations accordingly

What ethical issues should I consider in managing my project?

- The prime ethical consideration is that your project does not result in any harm to individuals or organisations
- There are many professional guidelines for particular research approaches (for example experimentation) that must be observed, in addition to legal requirements and requirements of your organisation for conducting research
- Ethical issues apply to both the conducting of the research and the way it is reported

What is the difference between research and consultancy?

- Research is usually carried out to learn more about a particular issue
- Consultancy is more likely to involve solving a particular problem
- Researchers are paid badly, consultants earn loads!

 ## REFERENCES

Becker, Howard S. 1972. A school is a lousy place to learn anything in, *American Behavioral Scientist*, **16**(1): 85–105.

Bell, Robert. 1992. *Impure Science: Fraud, Compromise, and Political Influence in Scientific Research*. New York: John Wiley & Sons.

Block, P. 1981. *Flawless Consulting*, Austin, TX: Learning Concepts.

Bogdan, Robert and Taylor, Stephen J. 1984. *Introduction to Qualitative Research Methods: The Search for Meanings*. New York: John Wiley & Sons.

Cooper, Donald R. and Schindler, Pamela. 2001. *Business Research Methods*. New York: Irwin.

Haney, C., Banks, W.C. and Zimbardo, P.G. 1973. A study of prisoners and guards in a simulated prison, *Naval Research Review*, **30**: 4–17.

Lynch, P. 2001. 'Professionalism and ethics'. In Sadler, S. (ed.). *Management Consultancy*, 2nd edn. London: Kogan Page.

Maister, David H. 1993. *Managing the Professional Service Firm*. New York: Free Press.

Milgram, S. 1974. *Obedience to Authority*. New York: Harper Perennial.

 ## ADDITIONAL RESOURCES

Buchanan, D., Boddy, D. and McCalman, J. 1988. Getting in, getting on, getting out and getting back. In Bryman, A. (ed.) *Doing Research in Organisations*. London: Routledge.

Russ-Eft, D., Burns, J.Z., Dean, P.J., Hatcher, T., Otte, F.L. and Preskill, H. 1999. *Standards on Ethics and Integrity*. Baton Rouge, LA: Academy of Human Resource Development.

The Institute of Management Consultants. 1994. *Code of Professional Conduct*. London: IMC.

Web resources

The Academy of Management (US) – www.aomonline.org. The current code is online at http://www.aomonline.org/aom.asp?ID=53&page_ID=54.

The American Psychological Association – www.apa.org.

British Academy of Management – www.bam.org.uk.

The Chartered Institute of Purchasing and Supply – www.cips.org. The current code is online at http://www.cips.org/Page.asp?CatID=31&PageID=116.

Institute of Management Consultants – http://www.imc.co.uk/. The current code is online at http://www.imc.co.uk/our_standards/code_professional_conduct.php.

The Market Research Society – www.mrs.org.uk.

A repository of useful resources for research – www.scholari.com.

Key terms

cold contacts, 270
Data Protection Act, 288
duty of care, 286
ethics, 280
field research, 268
natural settings, 268

personal networks, 270
project creep, 276
project scope, 274
scope statement, 274
sensitive personal data, 288
warm contacts, 270

Discussion questions

1. What is the difference in the nature of the activities you will be doing in D3, compared to the other phases of the project?

2. What problems would you expect in gaining access to individuals and organisations for the purpose of carrying out your research?

3. A friend has suggested that you join a marketing project, looking at the marketing strategies of Virgin, The Body Shop and Apple. The project requires you to have access to the organisations. Do you envisage any problems with this?

4. Investigate the ethical requirements of your organisation. How do they compare with the general principles set out in this chapter? How do they compare with the requirements of one of the organisations listed (for example American Psychological Association)?

5. Would it be ethical for you to do a research project with a tobacco company? Would a financial incentive help you to make the decision?

6. You have been working in a team within an organisation, looking at how they have adapted to new hours and methods of working over a period of several months. During an interview with the plant manager, you see a note on her desk that has asked her to nominate groups who could be eligible for redundancy under a new cost-cutting drive. She has pencilled in the name of the team you have been working with. Do you tell them?

7. What are the ethical challenges that your project is likely to face?

8. Who are the customers of your project? What are the requirements of each and how will you go about managing them?

9. Imagine you were taking the role of consultant in one project and researcher in another. What differences would you expect in the way you would carry out the work? Are there any inherent conflicts between these two roles?

10. You are carrying out a project in an organisation in order to obtain an academic qualification. How would you resolve the conflicts between the requirements of the organisation and your academic institution?

Read the following case study prepared by a student, and presented here in summary form.

New Product Development at Big Car Company
Background

Big Car Company (BCC) is one of Europe's larger mass producers of vehicles. The decision was taken in 2000 that it would belatedly enter the market for mini MPVs, and this case refers to events surrounding the development of the powertrain for this vehicle. Powertrain development includes the design and alignment of the engine, transmission, exhaust, cooling, mounts, air induction, clutch and drivelines. The product was launched late in 2003, three months behind schedule.

The process

The overall time frame for a development project from concept to mass production within the car industry is between 18 and 42 months. The duration is set at the beginning of the project. Powertrain is just one of the divisions involved in the process – the others being responsible for other systems that go to make up the car.

The first stage in the process for the powertrain people is agreeing the basic parameters of the powertrain design, including engine power, transmission options (for example manual, auto, steptronic, CVT), vehicle weight and likely sales volume. The budget for the development is also fixed at this stage and often has to go through several iterations, as specification issues impact sales projections, and marketing requirements influence design issues. As one manager commented on this process:

> Price, target and volume assumptions for the new product directly depend on the powertrain line-up. Adding or deleting one powertrain line (for example by changing the choice of engines available) will affect the price of each component, as the production is very sensitive to any volume or complexity changes. This negotiation is a time-consuming process. Over and over again, current assumptions about required design, projected component quantities, product targets and programme budget are rejected. In many projects it can be observed that this iterative loop becomes a never-ending process. Given that this time is part of the already fixed development time, time lost today will cause losses on cost and/or quality at the other end of the programme.

Even once agreement is reached internally at BCC, each of the teams then has to do its own negotiation on pricing, design and volume with various suppliers. These in turn have a similar process to go through with their suppliers. The theoretical procedure versus the reality is illustrated in **Figure 9.3**.

The overall effect of the above was that BCC did launch three months late. This meant that they lost three months at 500 vehicles per day of sales. The firm do recognise that a lost sale is a lost customer to the organisation for many years. The losses were huge and the knock-on effects to other programmes have been significant.

The resourcing profile on this project is shown in **Figure 9.4**.

Workshop cont'd

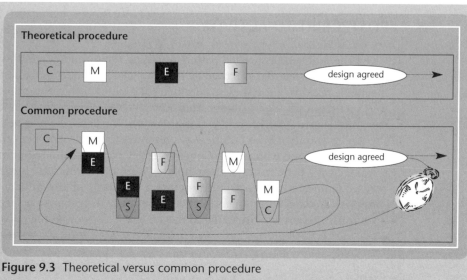

Figure 9.3 Theoretical versus common procedure

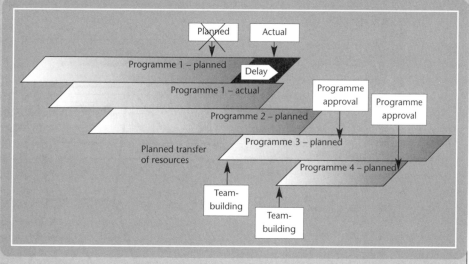

Figure 9.4 A resource profile

Discussion questions for Chapter 9 Workshop

Discussion

1. What type of case study is this?

2. What data collection methods were used?

3. What practical and ethical concerns would you have about researching this case?

4. As an employee of the company, as well as a researcher, how would you feel about this case being made publicly available? Practically, what would you do about this?

POSTSCRIPT TO ACTIVITY

Given the problems associated with redesigning the machines and the view that their report would be rejected as flawed by the management (they were told that this was an inevitable response), the students decided they had no other option but to rework the job description for the operators. This, in effect, redesigned the operator. The result is shown in **Figure 9.5**. This stroke of genius saved the day – the managers did not reject the report as only a brief outline was presented to them, focusing on the benefits of such a change, and with such a conclusion they had little choice but to act on it – but it was seen as a benefit, rather than 'holding a gun to their heads'. Indeed, the management committee made a commitment on the basis of the project to replace the machines and for other amendments to be made as a matter of urgency. The full, anonymised report was presented to the students' assessors at the university.

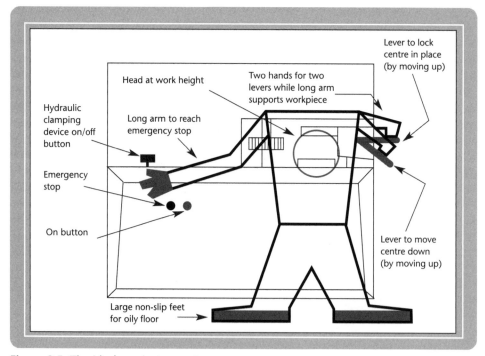

Figure 9.5 The ideal maxicut operator
Source: Courtesy of Wendy Bourne and Susan Myers

Relevant chapters

13 Answering your research questions
14 Describing your research
15 Closing the loop

Key challenges

● Interpreting your findings and making recommendations
● Writing and presenting your project
● Reflecting on and learning from your research

4

Relevant chapters

1 What is research?
2 Managing the research process
3 What should I study?
4 How do I find information?

Key challenges

● Understanding the research process
● Taking a systematic approach
● Generating and clarifying ideas
● Using the library and internet

1

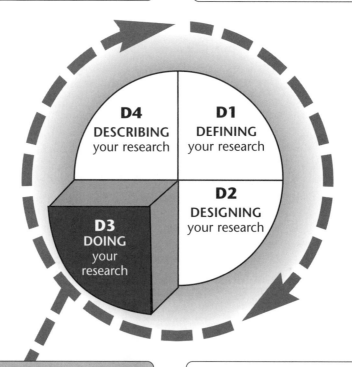

D4
DESCRIBING
your research

D1
DEFINING
your research

D2
DESIGNING
your research

D3
DOING
your
research

Relevant chapters

 9 Doing field research
10 **Analysing quantitative data**
11 Advanced quantitative analysis
12 Analysing qualitative data

Key challenges

● Practical considerations in doing research
● **Using simple statistics**
● Undertanding multivariate statistics
● Interpreting interviews and observations

3

Relevant chapters

5 Scientist or ethnographer?
6 Quantitative research designs
7 Designing qualitative research
8 Case studies/multi-method design

Key challenges

● Choosing a model for doing research
● Using scientific methods
● Using ethnographic methods
● Integrating quantitative and qualitative research

2

10 Analysing quantitative data
Using simple statistics

 Key questions

- How can I record and manage quantitative data?
- How can I describe my quantitative data using statistics?
- What computer programs can I use to analyse quantitative data?
- How can I test relationships between variables or differences between groups using statistics?

 Learning outcomes

At the end of this chapter, you should be able to:

- Record quantitative data in a data matrix
- Describe the distribution of variables using statistics
- Analyse relationships between pairs or variables using statistics

Contents

INTRODUCTION

Whether you have taken the scientist or ethnographer as your role model, you will probably end your research with some numbers you may want to analyse. If you have taken a scientific approach to doing your research study, especially if you have used a survey, experiment or secondary analysis, you will usually end up with some – or a lot of – data that you need to analyse to see whether your evidence supports your hypotheses. This evidence will then help you to answer your research questions. Scientists, as noted in **Chapter 6**, rely on statistics to measure concepts and relationships and see how much confidence they should have in those concepts and relationships as truly representing the reality they have measured.

In **Chapters 5** and **6** we described an essential feature of quantitative research as the extensive planning that goes on before you start collecting data. You might decide what data to collect, how to collect it, how to analyse it and how to present it in your project report even before you started collecting data. Before you analyse your data, you must record them, enter them into a data set in a format you can use for analysis and check for any errors and missing data.

Although the ethnographic approach de-emphasises quantitative measurement or statistical testing, for some aspects of ethnographic data having a feel for numbers can be helpful. Ethnographers still formally or informally apply some sort of quantitative yardstick to their data, even if just terms such as 'most' or 'usually'. As we noted in **Chapter 6**, people's intuitive interpretation of probabilities, especially rare events, is often faulty, so being able to verify that your statements are true can be useful even for ethnographers. Even if you have not planned to do statistical analysis, the emergent nature of qualitative or mixed-method research designs means that some opportunities may arise.

Section 10.1 will review some useful ways to record your quantitative data and prepare them for further analysis. We briefly introduce the four measurement types. It will also discuss types of software you can use for quantitative analysis, including spreadsheet programs such as Microsoft Excel, and statistical programs such as Minitab and SPSS. Although many people think that analysing quantitative data requires powerful statistical packages, complex statistical texts and large data sets, properly organised, simple statistics can be effective for analysing and presenting data from small-scale social research (Denscombe 2003: 236). The emphasis in this chapter is on statistical analysis that you can do in a spreadsheet such as Excel, with a calculator or by hand if you need to.

Once you have processed your raw data, you will want to understand them better. This chapter presents simple statistical techniques for analysing quantitative data, whether you have collected it using the quantitative methods presented in **Chapter 6** or the qualitative methods presented in **Chapter 7**. **Section 10.2** will show you how to summarise and present your data using simple descriptive statistics such as measures of frequency, measures of central tendency and measures of dispersion that describe how each of the variables is distributed. The section will also describe how you can understand which statistical tests are appropriate, given the type of design you have used.

If you have used a quantitative research design, you will probably want to examine relationships between variables, as well as the variables themselves. **Section 10.3** presents some simple statistics – inferential statistics – that you can use to measure the relationships between pairs of variables. We briefly discuss chi-squared tests, t-tests,

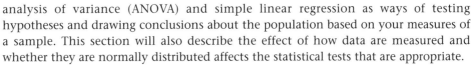

analysis of variance (ANOVA) and simple linear regression as ways of testing hypotheses and drawing conclusions about the population based on your measures of a sample. This section will also describe the effect of how data are measured and whether they are normally distributed affects the statistical tests that are appropriate.

This chapter is important whether you plan to analyse your data using statistics or using thematic analysis, which we discuss in **Chapter 12**. After you have finished this chapter, you should be able to analyse quantitative data, whether they originate as numbers or words, using simple statistical tests. You should also understand which tests are appropriate for a particular type of data.

Moreover, no matter what research problem you are investigating or which research design strategy you have selected, you will probably collect some quantitative data as part of your research project, or read other people's research findings that have been based on them. Reading about these techniques will help you to make sense of qualitative and quantitative research findings and judge the findings of other people's research, as well as journalism and consulting.

MANAGING YOUR QUANTITATIVE DATA

If you feel comfortable with the scientific approach, you may also feel comfortable with numbers and statistical analysis, and already have some practice and skills in working with numbers. Even if you prefer the ethnographic approach and feel a bit apprehensive about statistical analysis, computer technology has made it painless to record, organise and analyse numerical data. It is even possible to collect and analyse your data completely on your computer – using techniques such as computer-assisted interviewing (CAI). There are many cookbook type guides – and even some computer programs – that let the most confirmed number-phobe do simple statistics.

A systematic approach to quantitative data

Before you can use the data you have gathered, you need to process them so that you can use them to answer your research questions. The first step is to write them down or enter them electronically so that they are in the same place and in the same format.

A key success factor in analysing quantitative data is to think about how you will record, manage and analyse your data before you start collecting them:

- Decide what variables and what characteristics of your respondents (the social units you are studying) you will capture as data
- Decide how you will measure for each variable or characteristic
- Decide how you will record each measure.

The process is shown in **Figure 10.1**.

Recording and managing your data

You will usually need to process your data in their original form, or **raw data**, before

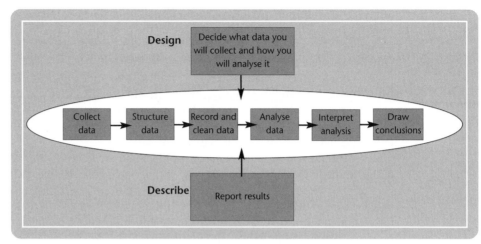

Figure 10.1 A structured approach for analysing quantitative data

you can use them in any analysis. This processing includes coding the data, entering the data into a format you can analyse and checking for errors or missing data.

Your first step is to develop some sort of system for capturing your raw data, which may be numbers or words or even pictures or sounds. You need to decide how to end up with numbers. Depending on the research design you select, your data may be stored or recorded:

- in a data archive or database of secondary data (**Section 6.1**)
- on a questionnaire, structured interview schedule or structured observation log sheet (**Section 6.2**)
- in an experimental logbook (**Section 6.3**)
- in a transcript, document or other unprocessed form (**Chapter 7**).

Your first step is to combine the raw data from your individual records into a single, common format. We recommend that you develop the format for recording your raw data early in the research process, especially if you are collecting data from a large number of respondents or on a large number of variables. If possible, you should also have a 'dry run' of entering your data into your spreadsheet before you start collecting them, and analysing your data using the statistical tests you plan to use but with 'made-up' data. Doing this will reveal many design problems while you can still fix them.

Once you have collected your data, we recommend that you spend some time getting to know them, even if you have collected your data electronically. As in **Student research in action 10.1**, understanding your data thoroughly before you start analysing it can be key to success. There is no substitute for a creative and intuitive feel for your data rather than just 'number-crunching' (O'Leary 2004: 184).

> *Student research in action 10.1*
>
> **DOWN THE TUBE**
>
> Charles was working on a placement project in which he needed to analyse data from every station in the Paris Metro. Before getting too deep into the technical details of how he would analyse the data, he looked at creating a database to hold the details of each station – which had never before been combined in a single place. As he set up the database, it became obvious that the same information was not available for each station and the accuracy of the data varied wildly. This ruled out some methods for analysing the data, so he didn't waste a lot of time chasing down blind alleys by choosing the wrong methods.

10.1.3 Organising your data

Before you analyse your data, you must put your raw data, however you have collected and recorded them, into a format suitable for analysis. Depending on how much data you plan to collect and how you plan to analyse it, you can tabulate your data:

- By hand
- In a table in a word-processing document such as Microsoft Word
- In a spreadsheet such as Microsoft Excel
- In a specialised program such as Minitab, SPSS or SNAP.

Two factors you may want to consider when you decide which to use are:

1. How much data will you collect? Multiply the number of respondents by the number of measures to get a rough idea of the size of your data set.
2. How do you plan to analyse the data? Unless you are going to use advanced statistics to analyse your data (more about this in **Chapter 11**), you may find that learning a specialised statistical program may cost you too much time and effort. **Student research in action 10.2** introduces an example that we will return to several times during this chapter.

> *Student research in action 10.2*
>
> **GOODNESS GRACIOUS ME**
>
> Natalia was investigating whether women entrepreneurs from South Asian backgrounds found it difficult to get financing from high-street banks. She decided to interview a number of women about their experiences in starting up businesses, which ranged from florists to nurseries. She also collected data from a number of banks about their lending policies. After several months, Natalia had enough data to start her analysis. She decided to use a spreadsheet to record and analyse the

> data she had collected, since that would help her get to know the data and see whether she was ready to stop collecting data and get on with the final parts of her research.

Manual

Most people find it easiest to use a table, or **data matrix**, for this. A simple format for a data matrix is to use rows to represent your cases (each separate organisation, household, individual or other social unit) and columns to represent each variable or characteristic of the case you have recorded. **Table 10.1** shows an example data matrix.

If you only have a small quantitative data set, you could draw a simple data matrix by hand and fill in your responses, which you can analyse by hand or with a calculator. This is unlikely if you have a large sample or many questions, but it might be true if you have a small sample or are analysing only a small part of your data quantitatively. An advantage of this method is that you understand your data much better. You might find this useful when you are developing your research design (for example what will the data matrix for the data I collect in this field experiment look like?), or when you are recording your first few cases. A slightly more sophisticated version of this is recording your data using a word-processing program such as Microsoft Word.

Spreadsheets

Whilst recording data by hand is a good way to start organising your raw data, and may be all that you need if you have fairly simple questions and few responses, you will usually need to use more sophisticated methods if you have more than a little data to record and analyse. Doing it by hand gets tedious and if you make a mistake, you need to Tippex it out or start over again.

Most students are already familiar with a computer spreadsheet program such as Microsoft Excel, a logical step up from hand tabulation. A spreadsheet allows you to enter both quantitative and qualitative responses (verbal data or observation) which is useful if you have included open-ended questions or responses, as shown in **Student research in action 10.2**. A spreadsheet can deal with a large number of responses and

Table 10.1 An example data matrix

Student	Date	Sex	Age	Course	Bank	Credit cards	Overdraft
John White	10/9	Male	19	ENGR	HSBC	No	No
Sara Jones	10/9	Female	20	SOC	HBOS	Yes	No
Amit Chaudhari	11/9	Male	19	BUS	Abbey	No	Yes
Om Puri	11/9	Male	21	ENGR	NatWest	No	Yes
Saffi Walden	12/9	Female	28	BUS	IF	Yes	No

a large number of variables, although some large social surveys would exceed a spread-sheet's capabilities.

> ### Student research in action 10.2 (cont'd)
>
> Natalia set up one spreadsheet so that she had a row for each person she had interviewed and a column for each variable or other issue she had collected data on. She set up another spreadsheet so that she had a row for each high-street bank and a column for each aspect of its lending policy.
>
> She carefully labelled each column with a name for the variable, a description of the units (if any) that the measure had been collected in, and a brief explanation of the variable. Then she entered the data in the form of numbers or words as appropriate. For example, in the column Age (years at last birthday), she entered the appropriate figure. In the column Reason for starting own business (early experience), Natalia summarised any critical incidents that the women entrepreneurs had mentioned from their own childhoods. She carefully entered the data from each interview until the spreadsheet was complete.

Like Natalia, you may find it convenient to use a row for each respondent and a column for each question, although you can also use a row for each question and a column for each respondent instead. **Table 10.2** shows the first few rows of a sample data matrix.

Coding your data

Something that you might note in **Table 10.2** is how compact the data entry is when you represent qualitative data using numbers compared with recording qualitative data. In the table, we used a numerical **code** to represent each possible response to each question. Your codes should be complete (one for every response) and unique (each code is assigned to only one response).

Substituting numbers for words makes data entry much quicker (and potentially more accurate), for example instead of typing in 'strongly agree' each time it has been circled by your respondent, you can type in '1'. Assigning numbers to verbal responses is known as **coding**, and, somewhat confusingly, entering the codes associated with responses is also often called coding. (Coding is also used for one of the main steps in

Table 10.2 A sample data matrix

Respondent	Library	Residential	Catering	Parking	Social	Sports
001	3	4	4	2	4	5
002	2	5	3	2	3	3
003	4	4	3	3	4	4
004	2	3	2	2	1	3

Figure 10.2 Examples of a coding scheme

4. Sex:	❑ Male [1]	❑ Female [2]		
5. Country:	❑ Denmark [1]	❑ Finland [2]	❑ Norway [3]	❑ Sweden [4]

thematic analysis of qualitative data, but in that sense it refers to processing words (or images) into other words. We will clarify this in **Chapter 12**.)

If you decided on a coding scheme when you designed your questionnaire or other data collection instrument, you will be well ahead at this point. Experienced researchers often design questionnaires or interview schedules to show the codes as well as the responses, as in **Figure 10.2**.

Recording open-ended questions and blank responses

You will seldom collect data using only closed-ended questions: you will usually provide some opportunities for open-ended responses. It is up to you whether you record the answers to open-ended questions in your data table. In some cases, it may be useful to list all the responses to an open-ended question or response (such as 'other – please specify') and then convert the most frequent responses to numerical codes. In other cases, you might want to use the techniques for qualitative data analysis presented in **Chapter 12** instead.

Items that respondents have skipped or incorrectly answered present more of a problem. There are several ways to deal with blank responses. In some cases, it might be possible to follow up with the respondent and obtain the correct data. Obviously, if you have not obtained permission to follow up a questionnaire or interview, or have used anonymous respondents, this won't be possible.

In other cases, other pieces of data may help you to predict what the response probably would be. For example, if someone omits to answer whether he/she is single or has a partner, but later responds to a question that asks for information about his/her partner, you might be able to go back and enter data for the earlier question.

If you get more than a few blank responses, this often signals problems with your sample or instrument or protocol. Missing data can create significant problems, especially when you have a smallish data set and are trying to use advanced statistical techniques. You may want to consult the research methods literature for ways to assign values for missing data, if they would substantially reduce your effective sample size. You should always analyse both your questionnaires and raw data to look for patterns in nonresponses. If many respondents are only filling out the first part of a questionnaire and leaving the rest blank, it's probably too long. If many respondents refuse to answer a particular question, you may be asking for information they don't have, or it may be too sensitive to answer. If the omissions are intentional rather than inadvertent, this might bias your findings.

In any case, if there is a clear pattern of missing data, you may run into problems later on. If an individual respondent has omitted to answer many items in a questionnaire (for example answered the first page and no more), it's probably best to omit that whole questionnaire. If there are many nonresponses to a questionnaire item, you may have to omit that item from further analysis, as they usually indicate a serious problem with that item. Either way, this will reduce your sample size, but increase the quality of your findings.

Types of quantitative data

Part of getting to know your raw data is understanding what type of measures each type of data you have collected belongs to, before you start focusing on the magnitude and patterns in the numbers. There are four types of quantitative data, and understanding the differences between these is important, because it affects what they mean and what you can do with them.

The first type is **nominal**, or 'in name only'. Any number you assign to a nominal variable is arbitrary, rather than an essential aspect of that variable. Many qualitative variables are converted to nominal values in scientific research. For example, you might record the sex of a respondent as a 1 if your respondent is a man and 2 if a woman. The choice of 1 and 2 is arbitrary. You could choose 0 and 1 instead without affecting your data. The number is for convenience in data reduction. Similarly, in measuring customer satisfaction, you could represent 'satisfied' as a 1 or a 100.

The second type is **ordinal**, or, 'in order from high to low (or vice versa)'. Again, you are representing a variable as a number, but rather than the number being arbitrary, it represents more or less of some quality that can be placed in some order. For example, you might assign numbers to your respondent's level in the organisation: 1 = plant manager, 2 = supervisor, 3 = direct labour. This does not imply that a direct labour employee has three times as much 'levelness' as a plant manager, or that a supervisor has exactly half the 'levelness' of the other two, but that you can rank them in some consistent order. However, we cannot do familiar types of arithmetic, such as calculate averages, on ordinal measures. (We will discuss other issues related to ordinal measures in **Chapter 11**.)

Ordinal measures are often associated with attitude measures, such as the familiar ranked-order responses known as a Likert-type scale illustrated by two items shown in **Table 10.3**. Since the numbers only represent moreness or lessness, rather than a definite quantity, this often tempts even experienced researchers who know better into making mistakes. Someone who circles 5 (strongly agree) is not 5 times as satisfied as someone who circles 1 (strongly disagree), and the distance between 3 (neutral) and 1 or 5 is not necessarily the same.

The third type of quantitative measure is **interval**, where the interval (or distance)

Table 10.3 Examples of ordinal measures

Please circle the number that best represents your response	Strongly disagree	Disagree	Neutral	Agree	Strongly agree
1. I am satisfied with the university's library facilities	1	2	3	4	5
2. I am satisfied with the university's residential facilities	1	2	3	4	5

between numbers is constant and corresponds to the numerical difference between the numbers. Examples of interval measures include the year and the temperature in degrees Farenheit (or Centigrade). Here, the distance is constant and corresponds to the numbers we have assigned. In the ordinal example above, we could not say that the distance between 'strongly disagree' and 'disagree' is the same as the distance between 'agree' and 'strongly agree', but we can make this argument for interval measures. The difference between 32°C and 40°C is the same as the difference between 40°C and 48°C. Hence, we can perform familiar arithmetic such as addition and subtraction on interval measures. However, we cannot do all arithmetic operations on interval measures, because they do not include an absolute 'zero' point. We cannot argue that 64°F is twice as warm as 32°F, because 0°F (or 0°C for that matter) has been arbitrarily chosen.

The final type of quantitative measure is **ratio**. Ratio measures have all the properties of interval measures, plus having a zero point. An example of a ratio measure is salary or number of employees of an organisation. We could argue that £20,000 is half the salary of £40,000, or that 500 employees is twice as many as 250 employees. We can thus perform any reasonable mathematical operation on ratio measures.

So why do you need to know that there are four types of quantitative measure? This is essential because it determines how you can analyse or interpret it. The key point to remember is that even though you can stick any number into any statistical analysis and get an answer, those that you can use appropriately will depend on measurement properties.

Statistical programs

We recommend you enter your data into a spreadsheet, since most of the data analysis and statistical tests described in this chapter can easily be done in a spreadsheet, and a spreadsheet can usually be read by a statistical program if you want to do more sophisticated tests. However, you can also enter your data directly into many specialised statistical programs.

Many statistical analysis programs, such as SNAP and SPSS, even use a spreadsheet format for data entry, usually rows for respondents and columns for questions, but they may represent blank data in different ways than a spreadsheet. These programs do vary in their ability to record qualitative data (that is, data presented as words), so you might want to consider the balance between quantitative and qualitative data that you want to capture. However, both spreadsheets and statistical programs make it easy to manipulate or transform the data, such as recoding data.

If you aren't familiar with statistical software or don't need its advanced statistical analysis and graphical presentation capabilities, you might choose a spreadsheet program such as Excel. Most statistical software packages will let you import data from popular formats such as Excel. Spreadsheets such as Microsoft Excel offer a variety of built-in statistical functions, but if you know you will be using advanced statistics or have an extremely large data set (more than 16,000 responses or more than 256 variables), you may want to enter your data directly into an advanced statistical software program.

10.1.4 Cleaning your data

You should find and correct any errors that have occurred in collecting or entering your data. You will catch more errors if different people do the checking and enter the data. You might start by randomly checking to see how many errors you have made during data entry, for example working in pairs to check every tenth response. Depending on the number of errors you detect, you may want to check more thoroughly. The quality of your analysis can never be better than the quality of the raw data.

If you are using a spreadsheet or statistical program, you can take advantage of the program's mathematical and statistical functions to identify coding errors where the numerical response is out of range. For example, if you have a series of items where responses have been made on a 1–5 scale, you can check for responses that lie outside that range, for example, 6 or 55, by writing a formula rather than having to check every response.

DESCRIPTIVE STATISTICS: SUMMARISING AND PRESENTING RAW DATA

Once you have recorded and cleaned your data, you can start to analyse them. You can analyse your quantitative data:

1. by hand/eye
2. using a general purpose program such as Microsoft Excel
3. using a specialised statistical software program.

You should start by looking at your individual measures. This will help you to get a good feel for your data and identify any potential problems or unexpected findings.

Frequency counts

Once you have created your data tables and are ready to start making sense of your data, a good place to begin is by summarising the raw data question by question. You can compute a frequency count for the individual responses to each question. A **frequency count** is a total for each individual response to a question. Frequency counts are a compact way of presenting the information from a questionnaire or structured interview in summary form, and anyone reading the table can start to draw some conclusions from the summarised raw data.

Hand tabulation

Hand tabulation is often appropriate for small or simple data sets. All you need is a sheet of paper and a pen or pencil, hardly high-tech, but quick, dependable and reliable. It does give you an excellent feel for your data, especially nominal and ordinal data, but not ratio data. On the other hand, it does get tedious, especially where there could be many possible responses to a question, for example annual income.

To tabulate data by hand:

1. For each variable or characteristic of your respondent, set up a data matrix with a single row and a column for each possible response to that question. For example, from **Table 10.1**, you might want to hand tabulate which courses our student

respondents were studying and whether they had an overdraft. The result looks like **Table 10.4**.

2. As you go through each of your responses, record it in the appropriate category, as shown in **Table 10.5**.
3. Once you have recorded all your responses, sum the numbers for each category and total them. This is shown in **Table 10.6**.

You could do the same for the ordinal data in **Table 10.3**. Here, this hand tabulation would let you start to see some patterns immediately.

The other problem with hand tabulation is that you lose any sense of relationships between variables, which we will discuss in **Section 10.3**. For example, you would have a hard time seeing whether there is a relationship between whether a student has a credit card and an overdraft, unless you cross-tabulated the data as shown in **Table 10.7**. This table suggests there might be a relationship between whether a student has a credit card and whether they also have an overdraft. This wouldn't be obvious from hand tabulating credit cards and overdrafts alone. However, cross-tabulating every pair of measures would be pretty boring!

Table 10.4 Simple data matrix – step 1

Course	ENGR	SOC	BUS
Overdraft	NO	YES	

Table 10.5 Simple data matrix – step 2

Course	ENGR	SOC	BUS
	XX	X	X
Overdraft	NO	YES	
	XX	XX	

Table 10.6 Simple data matrix – step 3

Course	ENGR	SOC	BUS	TOTAL
	XXXXX	XX	XXXXX X	
	5	2	6	13
Overdraft	NO	YES	TOTAL	
	XXXXX XX	XXXXX X		
	7	6	13	

Table 10.7 Relationship between credit cards and overdraft

Credit cards	Overdraft		TOTAL
	YES	NO	
YES	*XXXXX*	*X*	6
NO	*X*	*XXXX*	5
TOTAL	6	5	11

If you have entered your data into a matrix on a spreadsheet or statistical program, you can use built-in program functions to compute frequency counts. (These tables are then ready to be incorporated into your project report or presentation if necessary, as discussed in **Chapter 13.**) You may want to summarise these as percentages out of 100 or raw counts. You can also present this information in graphical form such as a pie chart or a **histogram** as in **Figure 10.3**, since many people find charts easier to read and interpret than frequency tables. Both frequency counts and histograms are useful for getting an overall perspective on your data, for example details of the individuals and/or organisations you studied. You probably won't include them in the main body of your report for your other questions, but they might be included in an appendix.

10.2.2 Measures of central tendency

Frequency counts are useful for summarising your data, especially the characteristics of your sample or other aspects of your research setting. The next step is descriptive statistics, which provide information about the shape of your response. The two most popular descriptive statistics are measures of central tendency and measures of dispersion. **Measures of central tendency** describe the central point of a measure, for example the familiar average. **Measures of dispersion** describe how widely your data are spread around this central point, for example the standard deviation. You can compute various measures of central tendency and dispersion by hand, or using the handy built-in functions on your spreadsheet or statistical program.

By computing these two measures, you can describe your data with just two numbers, instead of the entire raw data or the frequency counts. This ability to summarise a large data set is useful.

Suppose the number of women sitting on each board of directors of 500 companies could be described using the frequency distribution shown in **Table 10.8**. You might want to describe the typical or average board. Although people commonly refer to the average as a single figure describing any set of numbers, there are actually three

Table 10.8 Frequency distribution – number of women

											Total
Response A	1	2	3	4	5	6	7	8	9	10	
Frequency B	3	18	67	96	120	107	61	23	4	1	500
C	3	36	181	384	600	642	427	184	36	10	2523

A – Number of women on board of company   B – Number of companies with that number of women on board
C – Number of women on boards in those companies

different averages: the mean, median and mode. The **mean** is the arithmetic average (the sum of values divided by the number of observations) of the values in a data set, and is what is commonly meant by the 'average'. The mean for the data in **Table 10.8** would be 2523/500 or 5.046. This agrees with what you can observe from the frequency distribution.

Many kinds of data have a central point roughly halfway between the minimum and maximum values, for example the average temperature in London. However, there is no reason that this central point has to be there; more data may lie to the left or the right of the arithmetic mean. If so, the mean may give a misleading estimate of the central point of the data. The **median** describes the midpoint of a data set, that is, the place where an equal number of values lie above and below that value. For example, if in Natalia's sample (**Student research in action 10.2**), 95 per cent of the women entrepreneurs were aged between 35 and 40, but two were aged over 60, these two women would shift the mean – perhaps misleadingly – towards the right. A more accurate measure of central tendency here would be the median. A spreadsheet calculates the median by ordering all 500 responses (1 to 10) and then picking the middle response. Here, the median is 5, again which you could predict from the frequency counts. You cannot decide this without looking at the symmetry in your data set.

The mean and the median are not necessarily always the same. Let's look at the histogram for our numbers in **Figure 10.3** to see why the mean here is above the median. Although the distribution of responses (number of women on the board) is more or less symmetric, the responses are slightly weighted towards those above 10, so the mean is greater than the mode and median. When the distribution of data is not skewed, for example in a normal distribution, the mean and the median will be the same.

Suppose that your responses had been distributed according to the histogram in **Figure 10.4**. The median is still 5, and the mode is still 5, but the mean is less than 5 because there are more responses in the lower numbers (towards the left). Thus, the mean is not always the best measure of central tendency, because it can disguise this asymmetry.

The mean and the median both measure a single central tendency of the data.

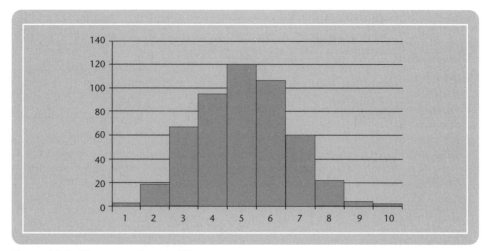

Figure 10.3 Women on boards (1)

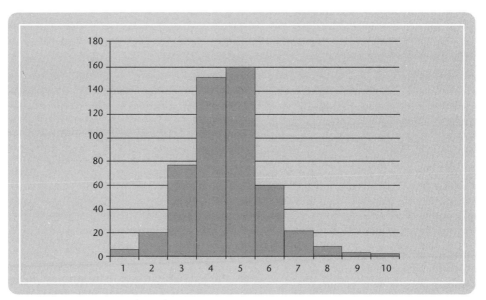

Figure 10.4 Women on boards (2)

However, your data need not be distributed so that there is only one most frequently occurring answer. A third measure of central tendency, the **mode**, indicates the most frequently occurring value or values within a data set. The mode describes the answer(s) given the most frequently, which can be seen in your frequency count or histogram. This can be at the centre or shifted above or below the centre. Here, the median is 5, which we can see from the frequency counts, but it is not necessarily so. You can even have more than one mode – some data are bimodal, with more than one peak in the data. For example, a fast-food restaurant might serve more customers between 12 and 2 and 6 and 8.

The normal distribution

The mean, median, and mode will all be the same in data that are normally distributed. The **normal distribution** is sometimes called the 'bell curve', because its shape resembles the cross-section of a church bell. More data lie halfway between the maximum and the minimum, and are symmetrically distributed around that point, so that the mean is also the median and the mode (see **Figure 10.5**). Many data are normally distributed, for example the time it takes to serve customers at a supermarket till. (On the other hand, not every data set will follow a normal distribution, for instance the time between customer arrivals does not usually follow a normal distribution.)

To see if your data are normally distributed, start by looking at the frequency distribution or histogram. Are the data symmetrically distributed on both sides of the mean? If your data are asymmetrically distributed, or **skewed**, more data will lie below the mean if they are negatively skewed, and more data will lie above the mean if they are positively skewed.

So why is it critical to know whether your data are normally distributed? This information is required in order to use many common statistical tests. Tests that assume your data have a certain distribution such as normally distributed are known as **para-**

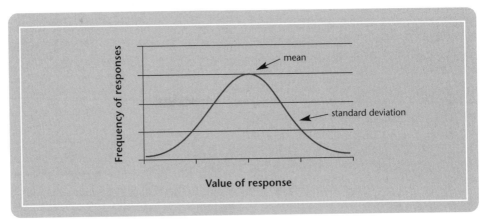

Figure 10.5 A bell curve

metric tests (in some cases they assume other distributions). If your data are not normally distributed, you may need to use **nonparametric tests**. You can check to see whether your data are normally distributed using a spreadsheet or statistical program.

When you examine bivariate relationships, you need to make sure that your data meet the assumptions about normality of the test you want to use. For bivariate tests, this usually means that each variable must be at least interval and normally distributed, and your two variables are jointly normally distributed. You should ask your project supervisor or consult a statistics book if you need further guidance. If you want to test relationships between variables that are nominal or ordinal, or that are not normally distributed, you will need to use different tests.

Measures of dispersion

As well as seeing where the centre of your data lies, you will be interested in how widely your data are spread around the centre. For example, if Natalia (**Student research in action 10.2**) measured the number of children the women in her study had, she might find they all had the statutory 2.4 children (low dispersion), or the number of children could vary from none to many (high dispersion). This would be important to know if she wanted to understand how family size affected entrepreneurial behaviour.

Some common measures of dispersion include:

- *maximum* – the highest value in a data set (10 for our board members example)
- *minimum* – the lowest value in a data set (1 for our board members example)
- *range* – the distance between the maximum and the minimum (1–10 for our board members example)
- *percentage rank* – the percentage of responses lying below a specified value (the median value always has a percentage rank of 50 per cent)
- *percentile or quartile* – the value below which a given percentage (or quarter of the data) lie below (for example 20 per cent of the data fall below 37)
- *standard deviation* – the variation around the mean, computed as the square root of the mean of the squared deviations of the observations from the mean

- *variance* – another measure of the variation around the mean, which is the square of the standard deviation (or the standard deviation is the square root of the variance).

As the measure of dispersion increases, the spread of your data around the mean increases, as it decreases, the data are closer to the mean. The **standard deviation** is one commonly reported measure of dispersion, because the central tendency and dispersion are the only two numbers you need to know to describe the data that are normally distributed. By knowing the mean and the standard deviation you have a complete picture of how those data are distributed as a normal distribution curve: how close or how far away data are from the mean.

A less than normal distribution might have more responses at the mean (centre) or close to the edges (or tails), so that they are bunched more closely in or spread more widely out than a true normal distribution. This is described as **kurtosis**. If your normal distribution curve looks 'tall' because more of your data lie close to the mean, and fewer in the tails, then your data have positive kurtosis, whilst if your normal distribution looks 'squashed', more data points lie in the extremes, then your data have negative kurtosis.

Thus, after you describe the frequency distribution of each variable, you can describe the central tendency and the dispersion for each variable (remembering that this is not appropriate for nominal and ordinal data), and start looking for patterns and trends in your data. You might want to prepare a summary table or set of tables that shows the frequency distribution and/or measures of central tendency and dispersion for each of your key variables, before you go on to the next step of your analysis. These can be useful in presenting your data to other people, for example an interim report on your research to your supervisor or your manager.

So where do you go next? The measures we have described above are useful in summarising your raw data and giving you some insights into your data. The frequency counts, tests of central tendency and tests of dispersion are **univariate tests**, because they only look at one variable at a time. This is useful information, and you need it before you do any more sophisticated statistical tests, but univariate tests do not usually answer research questions, except in the most basic descriptive research. The only research questions that this level of analysis really answers is 'how many?', not a very sophisticated research question. Here, we will introduce some simple **bivariate tests**, which test the relationships between pairs of variables.

 ## 10.3 BIVARIATE STATISTICS AND SIMPLE HYPOTHESIS-TESTING

To answer most research questions, we are interested in looking at more than one variable at a time. Most hypotheses are based on a relationship between at least two concepts – there is a relationship between variable A and variable B. (We will describe tests of the relationships between more than two variables – multivariate tests – in **Chapter 11**).

You can use a number of simple statistical measures and tests to look at bivariate relationships, including measures of association, such as correlation coefficients or simple regression analysis, and measures of difference such as t-tests. Measures of association show the strength of the relationship between two variables, a common concern of business and management. 'Do men have more automobile accidents than women?' is an example of a question about the relationship between the variable of biological sex and driving performance. You may be interested in showing that there is a relationship, perhaps to justify lowering insurance rates for women, or there is not a relationship. This is a simple form of hypothesis-testing.

Statistically analysing bivariate relationships might also be useful in showing that there are significant differences between two or more categories in your data, as shown in **Student research in action 10.2** below.

Student research in action 10.2 (cont'd)

As Natalia's research project progressed, she became interested in seeing whether the barriers to the success of Asian women entrepreneurs mentioned in the popular press really existed, and if they existed, did they have an effect? For example, studies of women entrepreneurs often suggested that taking time out early in your career to have children was incompatible with becoming successful, yet most of the women she interviewed had had children at an early age and were also successful. Were there significant differences in the two groups, she wanted to know?

As you decide how you will test your data, you may want to ask yourself some of the questions suggested by O'Leary (2004: 192):

1. How does my sample compare to the larger population?
2. Are there differences between two or more groups of respondents?
3. Have my respondents changed over time?
4. Is there a relationship between two or more variables?

These questions often concern researchers. See, for example, **Student research in action 10.3**, where Costas was interested in two different groups of customers.

Student research in action 10.3
TAKE A LETTER, MARIA

Costas, an MSc student, was interested in the effect of queuing on customer satisfaction. He designed a study to test the relationship between queuing times and customer satisfaction, using structured observation and a questionnaire rather than an experiment. He used the Greek post office as the setting for his field research, timing the length that customers waited in line, and using a questionnaire to collect information such as their satisfaction with the service.

Costas wanted to examine whether there was indeed a negative relationship between the length of time customers had to wait and their satisfaction with the service. He measured both the length of time and a Likert-type scale for customer satisfaction, and found that customer satisfaction was indeed lower when customers queued longer. The Pearson correlation of 0.77 also supported there being a relationship, and provided more support.

Correlation

You may want to investigate the strength of the relationship between pairs of variables in your data set, often reported in the descriptive statistics as the **correlation** between these variables. Researchers often compute correlations for survey data or secondary data. For example, suppose you had measured the size of each corporate board and the number of women sitting on the board. You could plot the two measures against each other, as shown in **Figure 10.6**. From the figure, you might expect that there is some relationship between the size of the board and the number of women who sit on it, and in fact the correlation is 0.462, indicating that there is a moderate relationship.

It might help if you can think of the values of one variable being plotted against the values of another variable as in the figure. How much one variable's values increase or decrease with a corresponding increase or decrease in the other variable's values indicates a stronger positive or negative relationship between the two. If for every one-unit rise in Variable A, there is a corresponding one-unit rise in Variable B, for example every time a respondent answers '3' for statement 1, he or she answers '4' for statement 2, every time a respondent answers '4' for statement 1, the answer for 2 is '5', then there is a perfect positive correlation.

Interpreting correlations is fairly straightforward. The correlation between two variables will always fall between 1 and −1. The three possibilities are:

● *Positively correlated* – correlations that are close to +1 mean that there is a strong, positive linear correlation between two variables. In the example, the size of the board increases as the number of women increases, so they are positively correlated.
● *Uncorrelated* – correlations that are close to 0 indicate that there is no significant relationship between two variables. If there were no relationship between the size of the board and the number of women, you would expect a correlation of 0.

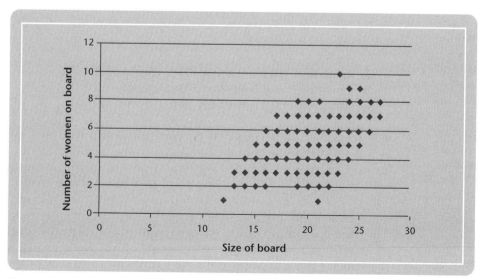

Figure 10.6 Data on board size and number of women board members

- *Negatively correlated* – correlations that are close to –1 indicate that there is a strong, negative linear correlation between two variables. If the number of women actually decreased with board size, the correlation would be negative.

The most common correlation is Pearson's product moment correlation coefficient, which describes the strength of the linear relationship between two variables, and is usually what is meant if you see the term correlation. (Pearson's product moment correlation is appropriate for items that are interval or ratio measures, whilst Goodman-Kruskal's gamma, Guttman's mu2, Spearman's rho or Kendall's tau are more appropriate for ordinal measures.)

Even a simple statistical procedure such as correlation requires some understanding of statistics: knowing the assumptions of the test is important. If your data are correlated, but not linear, you might be misled by a Pearson correlation of 0. The results of correlation are also affected by missing data – whether you choose pair-wise deletion (computing the correlation on the largest set of data) or list-wise deletion (computing the correlation on the most complete set of data) will significantly affect what you find.

Statistical significance

As well as reporting the strength of the correlation between any pair of variables, you should also report whether it is significant or not. In most research reports, and the outputs of most statistical software, you will see statistical significance reported. This shows the probability that the results you have found are due to chance, rather than a real underlying relationship or difference between variables.

Statistical significance ranges between 0 and 1. The closer it is to zero, the less chance there is that we have been misled into believing we have found support for our hypothesis when we have actually not. The accepted level of significance for business and management studies, as in most other disciplines, is .05 (or 1 chance in 20 that we are mistaken). Although you might sometimes see someone claim that a level above .05, say .10, is acceptable, it is not.

Because reporting statistical significance is integral to reporting statistical analysis results, instead of reporting the exact significance level, the following scheme is used to highlight different levels:

*   the significance level is less than .05 (1 chance in 20)
** the significance level is less than .01 (1 chance in 100)
*** the significance level is less than .001 (1 chance in 1000)

Most spreadsheets will report only the correlation coefficient, but a statistical program such as SPSS will report both the correlation coefficient and the statistical significance. If you try to interpret statistical significance only by looking at the correlation coefficient, you may be misled, especially if you are working with a small data set.

If you calculate the correlation coefficient between all the pairs of variables in your data set simultaneously, you have a good chance of accepting a relationship as significant when it is due to chance. For example, if you calculate the correlations between 20 variables, you are calculating 20 correlations. If you accept an individual correlation as significant if $p < .05$, then you have a good chance of accepting a spurious (false) correlation. Most statistical programs will let you correct your significance tests if you want to compute multiple correlations.

10.3.2   Simple linear regression

If we know that two variables are related, we may want to use our knowledge of that relationship to predict a future behaviour. If two variables are significantly correlated, you should be able to use information about one variable and the relationship to predict the level of the other variable. You can use **simple linear regression** to see how variable B (customer satisfaction) increases or decreases with changes in variable A (queuing time). Linear regression attempts to find a linear (that is, straight-line) relationship between two variables by minimising the **sum of squares of the errors**, the squared distance of each data point from the line for all the values in the data set. (Although the mathematics of linear regression are somewhat complicated, you can ignore them and use Excel or a statistical program to compute the relevant coefficients.)

Using simple linear regression to compute the relationship between variables represents this relationship between two variables to a line that can be expressed with the y-intercept (b) and the slope (m) of the line (y = mx + b). You can then substitute any x into this equation to see what y would be at that level of x. For example, if you knew that customer satisfaction decreased with queuing time, you could predict the level of customer satisfaction for various queuing times, which could help you set service standards. You should note that even though you specify an independent variable (x) and a dependent variable (y) in linear regression, linear regression does not demonstrate that a cause-and-effect relationship exists, just that the two variables are related. For example, you could equally use the same method and data to predict the relationship between customer satisfaction and queuing time, even though it is not logical that customer satisfaction causes queuing time.

You can also compute measures of how well a line fits the relationship between the variables. These measures include the **goodness of fit** terms for the intercept, slope and the entire equation. This is important to know because the goodness of fit terms tell you how much confidence you should place in the results being real rather than chance. The **coefficient of determination** (R^2) measures the proportion of the variation in the dependent variable that is explained by the independent variable. R^2 is like the correlation coefficient, except that it varies between 0 (there is no relationship between the independent and dependent variable) and 1 (the independent variable perfectly explains the dependent variable). (In fact, R^2 *is* the square of the correlation between two variables.)

10.3.3   T-tests and ANOVAs

To answer many research questions, you will need to use statistical analysis to find out whether there are differences between one or more subgroups in your data, such as different categories of your respondents. The simplest statistical test that measures differences between two groups is the **t-test** (as discussed later, the ANOVA is a t-test for more than two groups).

Suppose Costas also wanted to test whether tourists would mind waiting in the post office queue less than residents. The data he would need to test this hypothesis include information about each respondent (whether a local resident or a visitor to the area) and the respondent's level of customer satisfaction with the post office transaction. By computing the means and standard deviations of the two groups, Costas found the following results, shown in **Table 10.9**.

The t-test looks for differences between the means of the two groups. Costas could use the statistical functions in Excel to find the probability that the two groups have the same mean.

The number that the t-test returns reflects the probability that a statistical difference between the two groups is due to chance rather than actual. For example, if the number (p) is .04, we would expect once out of 25 times that the difference is not statistically significant, or 24 times out of 25 it would be. Since the usual standard for business and management research is a $p < = .05$, then Costas should accept the t-test as showing a statistically significant difference between the two groups. If the difference had been .10, or 1 out of 10, he would have to reject this as showing a statistically significant difference in their level of customer satisfaction with the post office, even though there is a difference between the two means.

Although the t-test is a simple test, there is a little more you ought to know. An important assumption is that the data are normally distributed within each subgroup. It also requires a minimum sample size. If the two groups you are comparing come from different samples, you should use an **independent t-test**. For example, Costas cannot assume that locals and visitors are alike in other ways, so he should use an independent sample t-test. Costas does not need the same number of visitors and locals, because the t-test only uses the mean and standard deviation in its calculations. However, he does need to ensure that the standard deviation is not different for both groups.

If Costas knows that he has carefully matched the locals and the visitors, he can use a paired t-test. The **matched pair t-test** compares the scores of the two different groups (pair-by-pair) on the same measure. The difference between the matched pair and independent t-test is that there is more information available in the matched pair t-test, so the results are more likely to be significant if there actually is a difference. **Table 10.10** shows the results.

Table 10.9 Costas's results

	Number (N)	Mean	Standard deviation
Visitors	35	16.27	6.25
Locals	40	14.35	6.25

Table 10.10 Matched pair t-test

	Satisfaction	
Pair	Visitor	Local
1	19	23
2	15	22
3	11	7

The **paired t-test** compares the scores of the same respondent on two different measures. For example, Costas might have measured both the customer's satisfaction with the length of time he or she had to wait and their satisfaction with the service at the window. In this case, this extra information again gives a more precise test, as shown in **Table 10.11**.

A final variation on the t-test is the **one sample t-test**, which is used when the mean for your sample group varies from a constant value, for example zero. Costas might have been interested in whether the difference between the customer's estimate of the time they had to wait and the time they actually waited was consistently overestimated, underestimated or neutral. He could test the differend versus a constant value of zero to see whether this was true, as given in **Table 10.12**.

You can use an **analysis of variance (ANOVA) test** when you want to test the difference in the means between more than two groups. Suppose Costas had studied customers at three different post offices (PO). He might then analyse his data set to see whether there were differences in queuing times and customer satisfaction between the three different samples. A one-way ANOVA is a better test here than three t-tests (PO1 versus PO2, PO1 versus PO3, and PO2 versus PO3), because it takes the data from the three sites into account simultaneously.

When an ANOVA is used as above, it is classified as a one-way test because only one way of splitting the sample is being used at a time. Although we won't discuss it here, the two-way ANOVA allows you to consider more than one way of splitting the sample at a time, for example testing the effects of post office location and time of day simultaneously.

Table 10.11 Paired t-test

	Satisfaction	
Respondent	Queue	Window
1	19	23
2	16	21
3	14	9

Table 10.12 One sample t-test

	Satisfaction	
Respondent	Wait	Window
1	0.52	0
2	0	0
3	−0.37	0

Table 10.13 Chi-squared example: internet purchases by sex

	Books	DVDs	Clothing	Sports	Total
Male	9	12	7	22	50
Female	21	8	15	6	50
Total	30	20	22	28	100

 10.3.4 **Chi-squared test**

The bivariate statistical tests we have described in this section are only appropriate for seeing whether two variables are significantly related if the variables are interval or ratio. But what if you want to test relationships between variables that do not meet this criterion? A useful test is the **chi-squared test**, which works with nominal, ordinal, interval and ratio data. You can compute the chi-square for any two variables that you can put into a 2 × 2 (or higher) table.

Most spreadsheets and statistical programs will perform a chi-squared test and return a figure for the level of statistical significance, which you can interpret in the normal way. The chi-squared test is based on the expected distribution of the frequency counts if there is no relationship between the data and the actual distribution of the frequency counts.

Suppose you had been studying what people buy over the internet. You expect that there is a relationship between the sex of the consumer and the category that he or she has purchased items from, in other words, men and women have different internet purchasing habits. Suppose you have observed 100 internet purchases and come up with **Table 10.13** for your data. If there were no relationship between sex and what people bought, you would expect to see no differences in the purchases by category between men and women. The chi-squared test returns a probability of .0005, or a chance of 1 in 2000 that this is due to chance.

If you want to use a chi-squared test, like any other test, you should read more about it in a quantitative methods book. One restriction on the chi-squared test is that every cell should have a minimum of five observations. Although it is possible to achieve this by combining cells with low frequencies, this is not always theoretically justified. There are some other restrictions, such as degrees of freedom and the need to correct a 2 × 2 table, so you might want to ask an expert in statistical analysis or look in a good stats book if you want to use this test to test hypotheses.

 SUMMARY

This chapter has provided an overview of the basic techniques associated with analysing quantitative data. You should think of them as a way of starting to understand your quantitative data. This chapter will help you to understand the relationship between how you record the data and how you can analyse them. In **Chapter 11**, we will introduce some more sophisticated ways to analyse quantitative data than those presented here.

ANSWERS TO KEY QUESTIONS

How can I record and manage quantitative data?
- You can record quantitative data by hand, in a spreadsheet or in a statistical program
- You can proactively manage your data by taking care with the coding and cleaning of your data set so that you do not make assumptions based on faulty data

How can I describe my quantitative data using statistics?
- You can describe your quantitative data using descriptive statistics such as frequency counts, measures of central tendency and measures of dispersion
- You can present them using tables, charts and graphs
- You should make sure that you understand the implications of types of measures – nominal, ordinal, interval and ratio – and the normal distribution for what you can do with your data

What computer programs can I use to analyse quantitative data?
- You can use a calculator, a spreadsheet or a specialised statistical program to analyse quantitative data
- A spreadsheet is adequate for descriptive statistics and basic inferential statistics
- A statistical program is useful for more sophisticated statistics and provides more guidance on the assumptions, limitations and other issues associated with a particular test

How can I test relationships between variables or differences between groups using statistics?
- You can test the bivariate relationships between variables using measures of association such as correlation and simple linear regression, and measures of difference such as t-tests or ANOVAs and chi-squared tests

REFERENCES

Denscombe, Martyn. 2003. *The Good Research Guide for Small-Scale Social Research Projects,* 2nd edn. Maidenhead: Open University Press.
O'Leary, Zina. 2004. *The Essential Guide to Doing Research.* Thousand Oaks, CA: Sage.

ADDITIONAL RESOURCES

Bryman, A. and Cramer, D. *Quantitative Data Analysis with SPSS Release 10 for Windows.* Routledge.
Bryman, Alan and Bell, Emma. 2003. *Business Research Methods.* Oxford: Oxford University Press.

Oakshott, L. 2001. *Essential Quantitative Methods for Business, Management, and Finance*, 2nd edn. Basingstoke: Palgrave.

Swift, L. 2001. *Quantitative Methods for Business, Management and Finance*. Basingstoke: Palgrave.

Key terms

analysis of variance (ANOVA) test, 319	interval scale, 305	ordinal scale, 305
bivariate tests, 313	kurtosis, 313	paired t-test, 319
chi-squared test, 320	matched pair t-test, 318	parametric tests, 311
coding, 303	mean, 310	ratio scale, 306
coefficient of determination, 317	measures of central tendency, 309	raw data, 299
correlation, 315	measures of dispersion, 309	simple linear regression, 317
data matrix, 302	median, 310	skew, 311
frequency count, 307	mode, 311	standard deviation, 313
goodness of fit, 317	nominal scale, 305	sum of squares of the errors, 317
histogram, 309	nonparametric tests, 312	t-test, 317
independent t-test, 318	normal distribution, 311	univariate tests, 313
	one sample t-test, 319	

Discussion questions

1. When should you start planning your data matrix and your data analysis in a quantitative research project?

2. Why are missing data a problem in quantitative research?

3. Many researchers treat ordinal responses as equally spaced. What would be the implications of this practice for a linear regression?

4. 'It is always better to use the most sophisticated software package and the most advanced statistical tests on your data if you want to get a good mark.' Discuss.

5. Is it true that managers don't need to know about statistical significance because you can tell the answer to most practical problems simply by 'eyeballing' the data?

6. If you have gathered data about a large number of variables from a large sample, why shouldn't you try to induce your hypotheses from a matrix of correlation coefficients?

7. Why should you always be sceptical about the statistical significance reported for a test? Doesn't it mean that a relationship must exist (or not exist)?

8. What might happen if you skip univariate analysis of your variables and go straight to bivariate analysis?

Workshop

Find a dataset that you can use for analysis or use the data in the workshop in Chapter 6.

1. Set up a spreadsheet or data matrix by hand.
   - What are the major decisions that you have in doing this?

2. Enter the data.

3. Have someone else check it.
   - What kind of error rates have you found?
   - What would this mean for the final analysis?

4. Discuss with your project team or another student what kind of tests for this chapter you would use for testing these data.
   - Use frequency counts, histograms or other statistics to show the distribution of at least *2* variables.
   - Conduct at least *1* test of association and *1* test of difference in these 2 variables.

5. Assess the results in terms of what you have learnt in this chapter.

Relevant chapters

4

13 Answering your research questions
14 Describing your research
15 Closing the loop

Key challenges

- Interpreting your findings and making recommendations
- Writing and presenting your project
- Reflecting on and learning from your research

Relevant chapters

1

1 What is research?
2 Managing the research process
3 What should I study?
4 How do I find information?

Key challenges

- Understanding the research process
- Taking a systematic approach
- Generating and clarifying ideas
- Using the library and internet

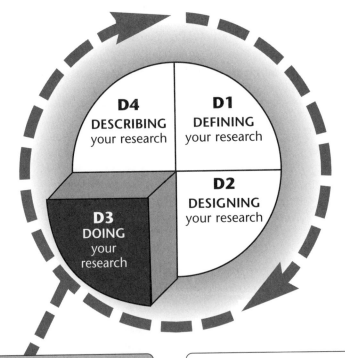

Relevant chapters

3

9 Doing field research
10 Analysing quantitative data
11 **Advanced quantitative analysis**
12 Analysing qualitative data

Key challenges

- Practical considerations in doing research
- Using simple statistics
- **Understanding multivariate statistics**
- Interpreting interviews and observations

Relevant chapters

2

5 Scientist or ethnographer?
6 Quantitative research designs
7 Designing qualitative research
8 Case studies/multi-method design

Key challenges

- Choosing a model for doing research
- Using scientific methods
- Using ethnographic methods
- Integrating quantitative and qualitative research

chapter

11

Advanced quantitative analysis
Multivariate analysis

 Key questions

- What happens if I want to analyse relationships between more than two variables?
- How can a third variable influence the relationship between two variables?
- What statistical techniques can I use to analyse multivariate relationships?

 Learning outcomes

At the end of this chapter, you should be able to:

- Describe how multivariate analysis can help you to understand complex relationships
- Understand what kinds of questions multivariate statistics can help you to answer
- Identify the most common multivariate statistical techniques

Contents

INTRODUCTION

Rugg and Petre (2004: 162) described an agricultural student who studied the growth of mushrooms for his doctorate. From the student's observations, he concluded that mushrooms grew in four-hour cycles. He found this exciting, because he would be the first person to observe such variation. The student made it all the way to his viva before his examiner pointed out that, instead of making a revolutionary finding about growth cycles, he had actually spent several years measuring the effect of the on/off cycle of central heating in the mushroom sheds. Not only had he failed to find anything, he overlooked one of the most obvious things he should have been studying. He also forgot one of the basic principles of experimental designs – eliminating extraneous variables (see **Section 6.3**).

Our experience as supervisors is that many student research projects, whether they take a quantitative or qualitative approach, have an overreliance on bivariate relationships and ignore the true complexity of reality. This is a threat to every single research design, quantitative or qualitative. Even experienced researchers may not always be able to identify every variable they need to include.

In **Chapter 10**, we looked at how to analyse quantitative data using univariate and bivariate statistics. The student above applied bivariate analysis to the relationship between time of day and mushroom growth; however, he ignored a second and equally important bivariate relationship between time of day and central heating cycles. Many interesting research questions involve the relationship between more than two variables, which leads to the study of multivariate analysis. This chapter will briefly introduce the principles of multivariate analysis, illustrate some techniques for analysing data and help you to understand the statistical analysis you might have been reading about.

Whether you are doing quantitative or qualitative research, understanding the basic principles of multivariate analysis is useful because it helps to illuminate both ways of thinking and particular statistical methods. Whilst we can only provide a brief overview of multivariate statistical techniques, we will explain how you can apply multivariate logic to understanding your data and conceptual model so that, even if you do not become an expert, you can ask someone else for help in doing multivariate statistical analysis and interpret the results. This understanding is especially helpful when you are trying to relate your research findings to your conceptual framework.

This chapter is expecially useful if you are analysing qualitative data. Qualitative research is naturally multivariate, even if qualitative researchers seldom use multivariate statistical techniques to analyse their data formally.

Section 11.1 explains why you might be interested in multivariate research. Although you could use bivariate analysis to analyse the relationships among three variables one by one, such bivariate analysis is often not enough to adequately test your hypotheses or understand a complex data set.

Section 11.2 explains a logic for analysing multivariate relationships. You must make sure that you have included the right variables in your research design in order to be able to do multivariate analysis. This means including every variable you want to investigate, and excluding those you do not want to investigate. You should draw the boundaries of your conceptual model based on theoretical considerations, rather than on data or practical considerations. However, as shown in the example at the beginning of the chapter, this is easier to say than to do.

Section 11.3 provides a brief overview of statistical techniques for analysing multivariate data. Whilst many undergraduate and master's level students do not consider using multivariate analysis, modern statistical software has greatly simplified the technical aspects of working with quantitative data, so these techniques have become more accessible.

After you finish this chapter, you should be able to look at your conceptual framework and data set – whether quantitative or qualitative – and decide whether to consider multivariate analysis. This analysis might be formal and statistical, or it might be informal and conceptual. This chapter's goal is for you to understand the logic of multivariate analysis, so that you can apply it to understanding possible relationships in your data. Once you understand this, you can get help in analysing these data from an expert, or take a 'cookbook' approach to perform multivariate analysis yourself using a user-friendly statistical program.

11.1 UNDERSTANDING MULTIVARIATE RELATIONSHIPS

Plausible findings from good research often fail to hold up when they are re-examined by other studies because the original findings were based on too-limited an analysis. This often occurs when the research study is based on examining the relationship between only two variables and failing to consider what other variables might have an effect, or examining the relationships between two or more variables but only considering the relationships pair-wise so that the simultaneous effect is ignored.

Deciding whether a bivariate relationship is credible is critically important if we want to make policy decisions or take other actions based on someone's research findings. For example, if we decided that there is a credible link between listening to country music on the radio and suicide, we might propose that country music stations should be banned or run public service announcements advertising the Samaritans' telephone counselling services. On the other hand, we do not want to take hasty action based on a spurious relationship. For example, if research suggests that there is a link between playing video games and violent behaviour, we might decide to ban violent video games. If this decision is not based on reliable evidence, we might reduce people's freedom to play games without reducing the incidence of violence.

If we could use the scientific approach to test critical research findings, for example experiments as explained in **Chapter 6**, we could more rigorously test cause-and-effect relationships. However, researchers might not have the time to conduct an experiment if decision-makers need to take urgent action, or might not be able to conduct an experiment for various practical or ethical reasons. It would probably be both impractical and unethical to ask men to carry mobile phones in their pockets to see if their sperm counts are damaged by radiation, and it might be difficult to find a control group (outside the Amish) who could be convinced to completely avoid carrying phones. Another example of ethical concerns was reported by the *Guardian* in July 2004, in an article reporting that studies of whether aspirin was effective against a myriad of health problems could no longer be ethically conducted because the proven benefits of aspirin against heart disease meant that giving someone a placebo instead of an aspirin might put his/her health at risk.

Even if we could conduct experiments when we need to test cause-and-effect relationships, the need in business and management research to investigate topics in their natural rather than laboratory setting might make it impossible to do convincing experimental research. We simply might not be able to include enough factors, control the environment sufficiently or gather data from a large enough sample for statistically significant results. If we want to maximise the probability that we reject spurious relationships and accept valid ones, rule out alternate causes and strengthen the credibility of our findings, then we should use a multivariate approach to extend our analysis beyond bivariate relationships. When you read a research report that reports that a significant relationship has been found between two variables (or, on the other hand, that no significant relationship has been found where there ought to be one), the question you should immediately ask is: What other relationships might explain this significant relationship (or lack of one)?

11.1.1 Multivariate analysis

Multivariate analysis is a method for analysing multiple variables simultaneously (Dillon and Goldstein 1984: 1). Bryman and Bell (2003: 24) describe three situations in which multivariate analysis is useful to researchers:

1. Establishing whether the relationship between two variables is spurious or nonspurious
2. Establishing whether there is a third variable that intervenes between the two variables you have studied
3. Establishing whether there is a third variable that affects the relationship between the two variables that you have studied.

Multivariate analysis is more credible than sequential bivariate analysis of multiple relationships for ruling out spurious relationships. Further, multivariate analysis lets us describe the structure of a data set in a more efficient way than multiple bivariate analyses. If you look back to the discussion of correlation in **Chapter 10** it should be obvious why this is so.

Spurious versus genuine relationships

Understanding the logic of multivariate analysis is especially critical for researching organisations and people, because many research projects fail to include all the relevant variables and end up making misleading conclusions. The problem usually starts with an incomplete conceptual framework, so that the researcher leaves out one or more important variables. The most serious challenge to any bivariate relationship is that we have not accounted for the effect of one or more other variables which might affect the relationship between these two variables. This may be because the theory guiding the research is incomplete or the research design has failed to include enough variables in the conceptual design or qualitative data-gathering.

Chapter 6 described a study by Stack and Gundlach (1992) that argued that country music and suicide were linked: higher audiences for country music radio stations were linked to higher rates of suicide amongst audiences not composed of people of colour. Other researchers, however, argued that differences in suicide between metropolitan areas were explained by poverty, gun ownership, divorce and living in the south. In particular, Snipes and Maguire (1995) argued that the relationship between country music and suicide was **spurious** because the suicide rate in each metropolitan area

could be explained equally well if you did not include the information about country radio listenership.

Unobserved variables

The original researchers on country music and suicide above failed to consider whether some general underlying factor – perhaps southern rural culture – might create the same relationships between a number of variables (such as poverty or gun ownership) and suicide, as well as country music listenership. This is an **unobserved variable** in this study. Researchers sometimes think that they have found a relationship between two variables when the relationship is actually caused by the relationship of each variable (A and B) to some unknown variable (C) that has not been observed – such as the heating cycle in the mushroom sheds mentioned earlier. C causes A, and C causes B, as shown in Figure 11.1, but A and B are only related through C, which hasn't been observed. The relationship between A and B is spurious because A and B are related to C and not to each other.

Intervening variables

You might need a third variable to explain a bivariate relationship when your two variables are indeed related, but you have omitted a relevant third variable that affects the relationship between them (rather than causing the covariation). One case is when the third variable intervenes between the two variables you have studied. We show an example of an **intervening variable** in **Figure 11.2**.

For example, many best-practice studies measure the adoption of specific techniques such as kaizen or six sigma and the firm's performance. They argue that adopting such best practices should improve the firm's performance. However, many variables might intervene between practices and performance, for example changes in market conditions. Failing to include intervening variables might make you conclude that no relationship exists when one actually does, or accept a spurious relationship. It might not be enough to adopt best practice – the firm might not see any benefits without top management leadership or employee commitment.

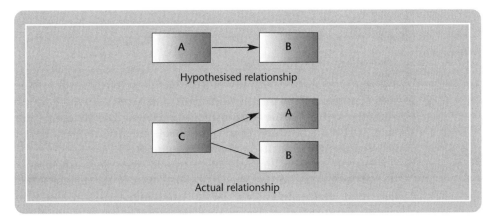

Figure 11.1 A spurious relationship

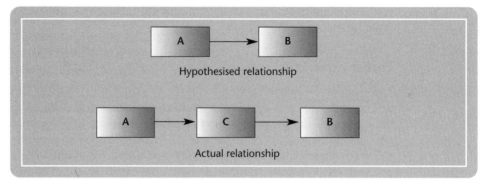

Figure 11.2 An intervening variable

Activity

In the UK the value of expanding higher education has been hotly debated over the past few years. An argument in favour of higher education is that graduates' lifetime earnings tend to be higher than nongraduates. However, some studies have failed to show a relationship between the two and you can find plenty of anecdotal evidence that some graduates earn less than some nongraduates (plumbers and other trades being a highly visible exception in these reports, where they are shown to earn considerably more on average than, for example, academics or social workers).

If you were designing a study of the relationship between level of education and earnings, what kinds of factors would you consider as intervening variables?

1.

2.

3.

Moderating variables

The third threat to the validity of a bivariate relationship that you might consider in your conceptual framework is whether there is a third, unidentified variable that might affect the strength of the relationship between your two variables – a **moderating variable**. Rather than intervening, this variable intensifies or weakens the relationship between the two variables, as shown in **Figure 11.3**.

This type of moderating variable is true for many research areas. In public health studies, social class (or income) moderates most of the relationships between behaviours and health, including obesity, smoking, fast-food consumption, fruit and vegetable consumption, exercise or dental care, and intervenes in many others. So if you fail to include social class in public health studies, you are likely to come up with an incomplete explanation. Similarly, in business and management studies, bivariate

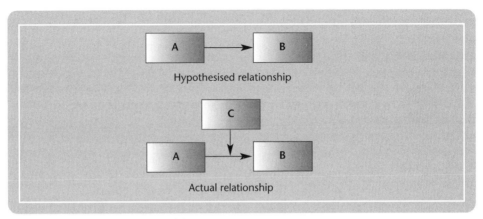

Figure 11.3 A moderating variable

relationships are often affected by characteristics of the members of the sample, for example age or gender for people, and industry or size for organisations. Failure to take account of these demographic characteristics can lead to misleading results.

Multivariate predictor or criterion variables

The final and perhaps most important reason we recommend a multivariate rather than a bivariate explanation in designing and doing your research is that bivariate relationships don't reflect the complexity of social reality very well. Two or more independent variables may contribute to one or more dependent variables, as shown in **Figure 11.4**. If you don't take account of these variables in designing your conceptual model, data collection and analysis, or when you are doing your statistical analysis, you are likely to come to misleading conclusions.

If you analyse each of these relationships separately using bivariate analysis, you are likely to end up making conclusions that leave out the simultaneous relationships between variables. For example, how would you know which variable is more strongly related to E, B or C? What is the true relationship between B and F?

We are not trying to *force* you to do multivariate statistical analysis on your data. In

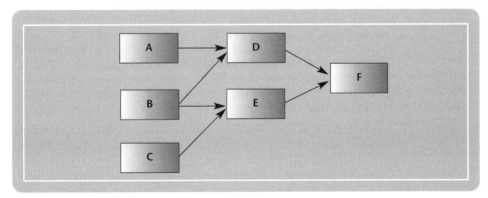

Figure 11.4 More multivariate relationships

fact, students often use this as an excuse for fishing, or data-gouging. We believe, however, that all research projects can benefit from multivariate thinking in the design and interpretation stages. This is equally important when you decide what you will or won't investigate.

 ## 11.2 ANALYSING MULTIVARIATE RELATIONSHIPS

As noted above, few relationships in business or management – or life itself – are simple and bivariate. In most research projects, you need to consider whether multivariate relationships might exist and might be relevant when you are defining your research questions and designing your data collection.

If you don't recognise that you might have a multivariate relationship before you analyse your data, it is often too late to do anything about it. If you haven't measured an important variable, you cannot see if it affects your significant bivariate finding. You should try to identify a comprehensive (but not exhaustive) set of variables in the research design stage. On the other hand, each variable you collect has a cost in terms of time and effort. The worst-case scenario is that you present your research and someone points out that you have left out a key variable – perhaps one already identified in the literature. The example at the beginning of this chapter illustrates a situation where this had a huge impact.

> ### Activity
>
> If you wanted to open an ice cream stand, in predicting your daily sales, what different variables would you consider? First, there is undoubtedly a relationship between ice cream sales and ambient temperature – people eat more ice cream in hot weather than cold weather. Is that enough?

 ### 11.2.1 Have I included all the right variables?

In your research design, you should collect information on any relevant variables. You can seldom go back and collect additional data to clarify those issues, especially in field studies. Cook and Campbell's (1979) threats to research validity identify some of the variables you might want to take into account, so any serious researcher might want to read what they have to say. Some threats are discussed below.

Time

As noted above, many researchers claim to have discovered a relationship between two variables, when both of them are related to a third, underlying variable that has not been investigated. This underlying variable is often time. Many factors vary predictably over time – hours, days, month or years. Others change predictably over the course of time. The science of forecasting explicitly recognises the importance of time to business and management activities.

Characteristics of your sample

One principle of experimental design is the use of random assignment and control groups. Where you cannot use this, and you cannot show that any two or more groups you are studying are absolutely equivalent, you need to use multivariate analysis to account for differences between groups. In **Chapter 6**, we mentioned some researchers who conducted a survey and concluded that the use of mobile phones was associated with lower sperm counts. This bivariate relationship may actually exist. However, the study failed to show that the men they classified into low/none, medium or high usage groups were similar enough for these conclusions to be valid. If the authors had designed their study taking into account other studies that have suggested factors associated with lower sperm counts, including occupation, stress, underwear and age, and taken these other factors into account, they might have explained the contribution of mobile phones to lower sperm counts, if such a relationship did exist.

11.2.2 Have I included some unnecessary variables?

Some students take the opposite view and try to collect as much data as they can, even if they don't know whether or why they might be important. **In Chapter 9**, we described this as 'going on a fishing expedition'. But data are not free, each variable you collect has a cost to your project in time and effort.

Many students are tempted, especially if they are using a program such as SPSS, to try to examine all possible relationships in their data simultaneously. These students set up a regression equation (for example) including all their independent variables at once to explain their dependent variable. So what's wrong with this?

Well, first, unless you have a large data set, you probably have too few observations per variable to get significant results. One author once had to explain to a management consultant that setting up a regression equation with 80 variables and 150 respondents (roughly two respondents per variable) was unlikely to result in significant results. In fact, he would have needed a minimum of 10–15 respondents per variable (or 800–1200 respondents) to test this model. This would have been several times larger than the complete population he wanted to sample!

Second, if you try such an approach, the relationships between the independent (predictor) variables (*collinearity*) may hide which variables are contributing significantly to the dependent (outcome) variable(s). This may be a bit more difficult to see, but if you have independent variables that are closely related it can happen. For example, suppose you wanted to see what factors affected a child's weight. Children's age is significantly and positively correlated with weight: children put on weight at a more or less continuous rate over their childhoods, and few children get lighter as they age. You might also expect children's weight to vary with their height, since taller children tend to be heavier. If you ran a regression equation with age and height as the independent variables, you would probably find that age, height and weight are all positively and significantly correlated. Logically speaking, however, age and height are the most likely independent variables (being taller or heavier is unlikely to make you older, and people do not get taller as they get heavier). Since age and weight are so highly correlated, it is difficult to separate each one's contribution for weight. A statistical analysis might show age as explaining all the variance and height none, height explaining all the variance and age none or a split between the two, making the relationship seem much weaker than it actually is.

This illustrates the fact that each variable you include in your multivariate analysis has a statistical cost as well as the cost of data collection. Adding more variables will increase the explanatory power of your equation only up to a point, after that point it will decrease. If you have experience with multivariate regression, this explains why we look at adjusted R^2 statistics as well as plain R^2.

 ### 11.2.3 Are my data appropriate for multivariate analysis?

To be analysed using most multivariate analysis techniques, your data need to meet fairly restrictive assumptions about data type and distribution, as noted in **Chapter 10**. If you remember our discussion of ordinal data, you may be surprised that researchers who use the familiar agree/disagree or other five-point items are among the biggest users of multivariate statistical techniques. What gives? In **Chapter 10**, we explained that ordinally scaled questions could not be analysed in the same way as interval or ratio-scaled questions, because we could not show that the distance between the numbers assigned to categories was proportional to the distance between categories. Some researchers combine several ordinally scaled questions to create a composite variable that is approximately normally distributed and can then be used in multivariate analysis. (It is also possible to use the same logic to combine nominally scaled items into new variables using techniques such as Guttman scaling; however, this is beyond the scope of this book.)

First, though, a brief note on terminology. From this section on, we will refer frequently to the data you have collected using the terms items, responses, and scales. What we mean by this is:

- *Question* – a question or statement on a questionnaire or structured data collection instrument such as an interview schedule that asks respondents for data.
- *Item* – a single question or subpart of a multiple question on a questionnaire or interview schedule. A simple item might be Gender: M or F.
- *Response* – the range of possible answers to an item, including responses predefined by the researcher (closed-ended) and those not predefined (open-ended). Attitude questions commonly rely on responses of 1 = Strongly disagree to 5 = Strongly agree.
- *Scale* – a single item or group of items that relates to a single underlying variable.

A **scale** is made up of multiple items that all measure different aspects of the same variable. An example might be happiness – you could measure different behaviours or aspects that each relate to some aspect of happiness rather than the single question 'How happy are you?' However, some variables are measured by a single question or item, which can be confusing, as this is often referred to as a scale.

Figure 11.5 might help you understand how this might be useful. Many aspects of organisations are associated with organisation size, for example structure. One measure of organisation size is number of employees. However, you might expect some difference between a pizzeria with 15 employees, a high-tech start-up with 15 employees and a seasonal business with 15 employees. In this case, you might want to collect several measures each relating to organisation size. These measures can be combined

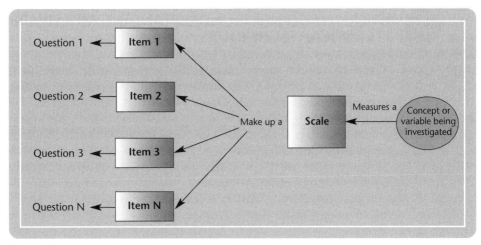

Figure 11.5 Relationship between items and scales

to form a single, more accurate measurement of the underlying variable you are interested in.

So far we have talked about items as though descriptive statistics can be applied equally well to any measure. However, descriptive statistics other than frequency counts are more appropriate for interval and ratio measures rather than nominal or ordinal measures. Try to imagine interpreting the average response for sex, for example. The same is true for ordinal measurements: could someone be 50 per cent in agreement and 50 per cent neutral?

Unfortunately, many people don't think about the appropriateness of statistical measures before they calculate statistics using their spreadsheet or statistical analysis package. In particular, people often report means, standard deviations and other measures for ordinal measurements as though they were really interval and could be meaningfully analysed.

So when can you use statistics to analyse ordinal measures? Probably the best-known way is to use the method proposed by Rensis Likert as a new way to measure attitudes. Likert suggested the following process:

1. Develop multiple items measuring the same underlying attitude
2. Use the same set of responses (graded response) to measure all items in a set
3. Combine the responses from the multiple items to give a single indicator of the underlying item.

By combining the responses from multiple items, the score for a well-designed variable approaches the normal distribution. If you have 5 items and your responses are coded 1 to 5, the range of responses for the scale will be 5 to 25, with a midpoint of 15 if it is normally distributed.

You may sometimes see a *single* item referred to as a Likert-type scale, but a true Likert scale is composed of multiple items. The term is sometimes used loosely to describe graded responses. Researchers who specialise in attitude measurement have developed a number of techniques for determining what items do and don't belong in a particular scale, along with how to develop the graded responses to be used in the items.

11.3 WHERE TO GO NEXT: UNDERSTANDING MULTIVARIATE STATISTICAL TECHNIQUES

O'Leary (2004: 187) suggests that the best way to learn about statistical methods is to 'get your hands dirty' using statistical programs. It is true that you can get good results from these programs without knowing much about the underlying details of different statistical techniques. As a result, most students don't have problems with the mechanics of data analysis, but with understanding the data and the logic of the relationships they are trying to test.

If you want to analyse your data using multivariate statistical techniques, but you haven't studied multivariate methods, you may want to get advice from your project supervisor or someone with experience before you decide on a particular test. This chapter's **Additional resources** lists several books you might find helpful.

 ### Multivariate data analysis methods

The two main types of multivariate analysis are dependence methods and interdependence methods. In **dependence methods**, the goal of multivariate analysis is to establish relationships between independent and dependent variables (that is, the kinds of cause-and-effect relationships examined in **Chapter 6**). In **interdependence methods**, there are no assumptions about independent and dependent variables – all the variables are equal.

Dependence methods include:

1. **Multiple regression** – examines the relationships between one dependent variable and multiple independent variables.
2. **Canonical correlation** – similar to multiple regression but there is more than one dependent variable.
3. **Multiple analysis of variance (MANOVA)** – similar to the ANOVA technique presented in **Chapter 10**, but examining the relationship between more than one independent variable and the dependent variable. Often used in analysing experiments or quasi-experiments.

Interdependence methods include:

4. **Principal components analysis** and **factor analysis** – the goal is to reduce the number of variables into a smaller set by grouping them into factors or categories.
5. **Cluster analysis** – variables are assigned to groups based on similarity of features.

Multiple regression

Multiple regression is a popular method for multivariate analysis, because multiple regression is logically clear if you understand simple regression. For example, suppose you wanted to examine the relative contributions of the use of just-in-time, total quality management and supply chain management to manufacturing performance in terms of plant on-time delivery. Your conceptual model might look like the one in **Figure 11.6**.

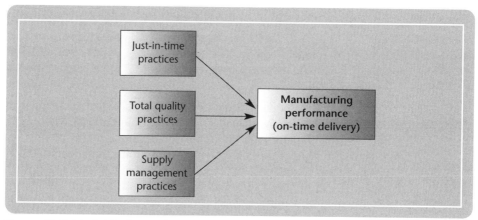

Figure 11.6 Model A of manufacturing performance

If you didn't know about multivariate analysis, it would be easy to analyse the bivariate relationships in isolation and conclude that each of them contributed significantly to on-time manufacturing performance. (In fact, this kind of analysis is typical of journalism and consulting.) On the other hand, most researchers (and managers) would want to know, when we consider all three practices together, which contribute most and least to manufacturing performance.

If you used linear regression, you might find that when you include all three variables in a multiple regression equation, only supply management practices are significant. This is very different from finding that all three are significant. On the other hand, if you stop there, you might be making the same kind of conceptual error you made in using bivariate analysis. Suppose you couldn't implement supply chain management until you had implemented just-in-time, and you couldn't implement just-in-time without having total quality management in place? While you have treated the three practices as independent variables in this model, they are not necessarily independent of each other. In fact, the conceptual model might look like the one presented in **Figure 11.7**.

An experienced researcher could probably pick out a structure like this from analysing the relationships between the independent variables as well as the relationship between the independent variables and the dependent variable. However, the real

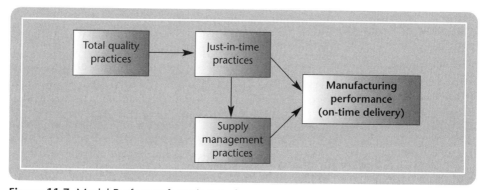

Figure 11.7 Model B of manufacturing performance

lesson is that our ability to perform multivariate statistical analysis usually outstrips our ability to relate it to conceptual models. Don't let the data or statistical methods drive your analysis; your conceptual model should drive it.

Cluster analysis

Cluster analysis is popular because it lets us reduce data and thus manage complexity. Cluster analysis identifies a smaller number of groups in data, where multiple respondents and multiple variables are being measured. You can cluster your data by cases (for example people or organisations), variables (your measurements) or both simultaneously. It is not a statistical technique, but an empirical one. People like cluster analysis because they often think using informal cluster analysis. For example, 'Men are from Mars, women are from Venus' clusters people by sex to predict a substantial amount of behaviour based on this one characteristic. Similarly, demographic classifications such as ABC cluster people on social class, occupation and other variables in order to make predictions.

Suppose you wanted to see what types of consumers eat in McDonald's restaurants. If you prefer quantitative research, you might start with a conceptual framework such as Gabriel and Lang's (1995) catalogue of consumer types – consumer as chooser, communicator, explorer, identity-seeker, hedonist or artist, victim, rebel, activist and citizen. You could develop measures based on this catalogue and then classify the actual consumers you study into each of these types.

On the other hand, if you wanted to let the types emerge from the data rather than imposing them on it, you could decide what data you want to collect and then use cluster analysis to identify clusters of consumers based on the data you have collected. Based on the aggregate characteristics of consumers in your clusters, you could assign each cluster a name or identity. (To complete the analysis, you could compare your clusters with those identified by Gabriel and Lang to see whether your findings are similar or different.)

The two main approaches in cluster analysis (there are many) are:

1. Start with all your data and split them into successively smaller clusters until each cluster has only one member
2. Start with one member in each cluster and create clusters until you have one big cluster that includes every data point.

Which method – and statistical technique – you use for clustering should be theoretically driven (based on your conceptual model) and not by trying all the methods and deciding which output you like the best.

If you decide to use cluster analysis, remember that it is a descriptive technique. Although cluster analysis may reveal clusters that occur naturally in your data, it is more likely that you are imposing (somewhat) arbitrary clusters on messy data. If you identify clusters based on a set of variables, and then apply statistical tests to show that clusters differ on those variables, you are not actually testing anything worthwhile. You should also remember that the number of clusters is arbitrary.

11.3.2 Software for multivariate analysis

Many software packages such as Minitab, SAS and SPSS will let you analyse your data set using multivariate statistics. An advantage of using one of these packages is the number of help texts that have been written to go along with them, for example the excellent guides to SPSS by Bryman and colleagues that you can find listed by Amazon or in your bookstore. There are also many specialised packages such as LISREL.

SUMMARY

This chapter has introduced the logic, analysis and techniques associated with multivariate analysis. Understanding the logic of multivariate analysis can help you to identify avenues in your data that you should explore, and potential threats to the credibility of your results. You can use the logic of multivariate analysis to identify unmeasured variables that might explain, intervene between or moderate the significant (or nonsignificant) bivariate relationship you found in your data.

If you suspect you might have multivariate relationships in your data, you should consider using multivariate analysis of your research problem and data so you can formulate some questions which you can answer statistically (or ask someone else to investigate statistically).

Finally, we have described some of the more common or more important multivariate statistical techniques that you might want to learn to use or you might read about in your literature search.

ANSWERS TO KEY QUESTIONS

What happens if I want to analyse relationships between more than two variables?

- You should use multivariate analysis
- You should start with the conceptual framework and then use the techniques outlined here to determine if the hypothesised relationships exist

How can a third variable influence the relationship between two variables?

- *Underlie* – where the variation in both observed variables is caused by a third, unobserved variable (mushroom study)
- *Intervene* – where there is a variable that comes between the two variables you are considering
- *Moderate* – there is another factor or factors that alter the effect of one variable on the other

What statistical techniques can I use to analyse multivariate relationships?

- Dependence techniques – including multiple regression analysis
- Interdependence techniques – including MANOVA and cluster analysis

REFERENCES

Bryman, Alan and Bell, Emma. 2003. *Business Research Methods*. Oxford: Oxford University Press.

Cook, T.D. and Campbell, D. 1979. *Quasi-Experimentation: Design and Analysis Issues for Field Settings*. London: Houghton Mifflin.

Dillon, William R. and Goldstein, Matthew. 1984. *Multivariate Analysis: Methods and Application*. New York: John Wiley & Sons.

Gabriel, Yiannis and Lang, Tim. 1995. *The Unmanageable Consumer*. London: Sage.

O'Leary, Z. 2004. *The Essential Guide to Doing Research*. London: Sage.

Rugg, Gordon and Petre, Marian. 2004. *The Unwritten Rules of PhD Research*. Maidenhead: Open University Press.

Snipes, Jeffrey B. and Maguire, Edward R. 1995. Country music, suicide, and spuriousness, *Social Forces*, **74**(1): 327–9.

Stack, S. and Gundlach, J. 1992. The effect of country music on suicide, *Social Forces*, **70**(5): 211–18.

ADDITIONAL RESOURCES

Bryman, A. and Cramer, D. 2000. *Quantitative Data Analysis with SPSS Release 10 for Windows*. London: Routledge.

Oakshott, Les. 2001. *Essential Quantitative Methods for Business, Management, and Finance*, 2nd edn. Basingstoke: Palgrave – now Palgrave Macmillan.

Swift, Louise. 2001. *Quantitative Methods for Business, Management and Finance*. Basingstoke: Palgrave – now Palgrave Macmillan.

Key terms

canonical correlation, 336	multiple analysis of variance (MANOVA), 336	spurious, 328
cluster analysis, 336		unobserved variable, 329
dependence methods, 336	multiple regression, 336	
factor analysis, 336	multivariate analysis, 328	
interdependence methods, 336	principal components analysis, 336	
intervening variable, 329		
moderating variable, 330	scale, 334	

Discussion questions

1. What should you take into account when you are deciding whether to accept a causal relationship based on bivariate data?

2. How does an intervening variable differ from a moderating variable?

3. 'It's not necessary to understand how multivariate statistics work, so long as you have a user-friendly statistics software package.' Discuss.

4. What problems might you experience in trying to use nominal or ordinal data in multivariate analysis?

5. Where do you think most spurious relationships come from, faulty statistical analysis or faulty conceptual models?

6. What would happen if we included every possible variable in a conceptual model? What are the implications for research design?

7. Should you leave multivariate analysis to the experts?

Find a quantitative study related to your research topic. Outline the theoretical framework based on the text. Compare this with the model in the figures (if provided).

1. What direct relationships are there among variables?
2. What indirect relationships are there?
3. Are any of these moderating/mediating?
4. Is the model/explanation/findings plausible?

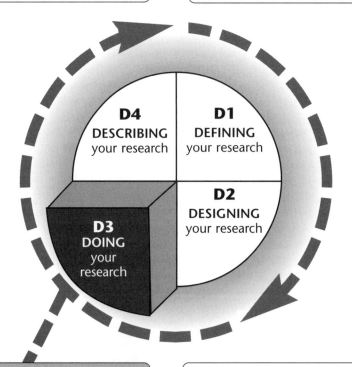

Relevant chapters

4

13 Answering your research questions
14 Describing your research
15 Closing the loop

Key challenges

- Interpreting your findings and making recommendations
- Writing and presenting your project
- Reflecting on and learning from your research

Relevant chapters

1

1 What is research?
2 Managing the research process
3 What should I study?
4 How do I find information?

Key challenges

- Understanding the research process
- Taking a systematic approach
- Generating and clarifying ideas
- Using the library and internet

D4
DESCRIBING
your research

D1
DEFINING
your research

D2
DESIGNING
your research

D3
DOING
your
research

Relevant chapters

3

9 Doing field research
10 Analysing quantitative data
11 Advanced quantitative analysis
12 **Analysing qualitative data**

Key challenges

- Practical considerations in doing research
- Using simple statistics
- Undertanding multivariate statistics
- **Interpreting interviews and observations**

Relevant chapters

2

5 Scientist or ethnographer?
6 Quantitative research designs
7 Designing qualitative research
8 Case studies/multi-method design

Key challenges

- Choosing a model for doing research
- Using scientific methods
- Using ethnographic methods
- Integrating quantitative and qualitative research

Analysing qualitative data
Interpreting interview and observational data

 Key questions

- How should I prepare my qualitative data for analysis?
- What are the main strategies for analysing qualitative data?
- How can I identify concepts and conceptual frameworks in my data?
- What qualities should I aim for in my analysis?

 Learning outcomes

At the end of this chapter, you should be able to:

- Decide whether to analyse your qualitative data in a structured or unstructured way
- See if your data analysis is consistent with your research design
- Assess the quality of your data and analysis

Contents
Introduction
12.1 Managing your qualitative data
12.2 Analysing your qualitative data
12.3 Assessing your analysis
Summary
Answers to key questions
References
Additional resources
Key terms
Discussion questions
Workshop

INTRODUCTION

> Just as painters need both techniques and vision to bring their novel images to life on canvas, [qualitative] analysts need techniques to help them see beyond the ordinary and to arrive at new understandings of social life. (**Strauss and Corbin, 1996: 8**)

If you have collected all your qualitative data and are sitting in front of a significant pile of transcripts, notes and other documents from your interviews or observations, you are probably wondering: 'What do I do with all of this? Where do I start?' Our advice is actually 'Don't start here!' To analyse qualitative data, you need to analyse your data as you go along, not wait until the end.

Once you start collecting data using a qualitative research design, you will see the major difference between the deductive approach taken in quantitative research and the inductive approach taken in qualitative research. In a qualitative research design, you continually refine your data collection and analysis as you investigate your research problem, opening up new areas and closing off other ones. Your qualitative research design will evolve throughout the research process; a quantitative research design is 'frozen' once your data collection has started.

Because of this evolution and flexibility, you need to approach qualitative research as a creative process that requires your intuition and insight. This is one of the key skills associated with the ethnographer rather than the scientist as a role model. The scientist's creativity comes before and after the data analysis (for which there are strict rules), whilst the ethnographer's creativity is especially important in analysing and interpreting the evidence. This might be new to you, particularly if you come from a technical background where research follows the deductive logic. Although you may find this much less structured than statistical analysis, the procedures you can use for identifying themes in qualitative data are as rigorous, well developed and credible as statistical methods for analysing quantitative data.

This chapter presents the two main approaches to analysing qualitative data, one structured and the other unstructured. Which one you choose will depend on how you collected your data. The four qualitative research designs introduced in **Chapter 7** varied by how involved the researcher was in the research setting and with the research participants. For more detailed guidance, refer to the **Additional resources** at the end of this chapter.

In **Section 12.1**, we deal with some issues you must address before you even start analysing your qualitative data. You must organise your data, decide the general approach you will take – structured or unstructured – and whether you will analyse your data by hand or use specialised computer software.

In **Section 12.2**, we discuss key principles of qualitative analysis. We introduce methods for unstructured data analysis. We begin with Kolb's cycle, which is a general approach to analysing qualitative data. We then discuss principles of coding, concept extraction and framework-building. In **Section 12.3**, we describe the criteria by which you should assess the quality of your analysis.

After you have read this chapter, you should be able to plan how you will analyse your qualitative data. This makes it easier to collect data in a systematic way and analyse them. Since a major advantage of qualitative research design is that it enables you to look for unexpected or counterintuitive patterns in your data, you should make sure you capture as many of these insights as you can. Taking a systematic approach is especially important for an open-ended process such as qualitative analysis.

12.1 MANAGING YOUR QUALITATIVE DATA

Whether you used one of the quantitative research methods presented in **Chapter 6**, the qualitative research methods presented in **Chapter 7**, or the case study/multi-method designs presented in **Chapter 8** to collect qualitative data, you will end up with data that are quite different from quantitative data. Ultimately, you can transform all quantitative data into numbers, which can then be treated the same, no matter what they represent. However, qualitative data have no such common ground.

12.1.1 Managing qualitative data

As we saw in **Chapter 10**, you can easily record quantitative data in a data matrix by hand, in a spreadsheet or a statistical program. You can keep track of and analyse them relatively easily. Managing qualitative data presents more of a challenge because qualitative data:

- *Are not processed or transformed*. You must start your analysis with data in their raw form rather than in processed form. This is a major difference from quantitative research, where you might analyse secondary data from a database where someone has already transformed the raw data into numbers.
- *Take many forms*. Qualitative data include interviews, personal statements, opinions, impressions and recollections, along with documents and other artefacts.
- *Are not standardised*. Each piece of qualitative data will be presented in its own way.
- *Are voluminous*. Because they haven't been transformed or processed, qualitative data cannot be expressed as concisely as quantitative data. It is not unusual for qualitative analysis, for example of the results of a participant observation study, to start with hundreds or even thousands of pages of notes and transcripts.

Before you start analysing your qualitative data, you will need to put them in a form that you can work with. This will be much easier if you have taken a systematic approach to collecting, handling and storing these data.

We start with some simple tips for managing your qualitative data. In working with qualitative data, you must make sure that your data are:

- **Traceable**. You must be able to demonstrate where a particular piece of data came from. Who said (or wrote) it? Which organisation or field setting did it come from? When was it collected? Who collected it? See **Student research in action 12.1** for an example.
- **Reliable**. Your transcripts or other records must faithfully record your discussions or observations. Always write up your notes and impressions within 24 hours – we recommend immediately, if you can. This might even be before you leave the interview site – some researchers have even done this in the toilets for privacy.
- **Complete**. You should keep all your field notes, tapes and transcripts. **Student research in action 12.1** shows how a student did this for a project where she collected data in several different ways and from several different sources.

> **Student research in action 12.1**
> **HANNAH AND HER CISTERNS**
>
> As part of a wine-marketing course, Hannah was investigating how market information gets up the supply chain from the sellers to the wine producers and finally the growers. She arranged to interview people at different stages in the supply process.
>
> Following her interviews, Hannah logged her data sources as shown in Table 12.1. Hannah identified each different data element she collected using a simple system. She used a four-digit code to classify each interview or document according to its source and type. Each code contained information about the category of the organisation, the organisation, the individual who was interviewed and the type of data that were collected. She also kept careful track of the dates of the interviews.
>
> These simple codes helped Hannah keep track of interviews and documents. By organising her data systematically, Hannah made sure that she could trace all her data back to their source. She could easily include the table in her research methods chapter in her project report, so that she could refer to them systematically. Also, since Hannah disguised the firms and individuals before she reported her findings, this table helped her keep track of the disguises she used for her firms.
>
> Finally, during her analysis and reporting, she used these codes to compare the views of participants located in different parts of the supply network.

Table 12.1 Hannah's list of contacts and documents

Place in supply chain	Company	Person interviewed	Date(s) of interview	Code(s)
Retail outlet	A	Store manager	7/12/2001	1–A–1 T (transcript)
		Beverage manager	7/12/2001	1-A-2 N (notes only – recording declined)
	B	Regional manager	14/12/2001	1-B-1 T 1-B-1-D (documents)
Distributor	C	Marketing manager	22/11/2001	2-C-1-T
	D	Category manager	18/12/2001	2-D-1-T
Producer	D	Marketing manager	19/12/2001	3-D-2-T
	E	Brand manager	7/11/2001	3-E-1-T 3-E-1-D
Grower	F	Vineyard owner	12/1/2002	4-F-1-T
		Vineyard manager	12/1/2002	4-F-2-T
	G	Planning manager	25/11/2001	4-G-1-T

12.1.2 Software for qualitative analysis

As part of your research design, you should decide early on whether you will analyse your qualitative data by hand, using a word-processing program or a specialised computer program. This will affect not only your analysis, but also how you collect and record your data. If you make this decision early in the research process, you will avoid having to convert your data to a new format before you can analyse it or, more disastrously, having to type it all in at the last minute.

We recommend that you collect and analyse your qualitative data using a simple word-processing program such as Microsoft Word, unless you are collecting a lot of data, working in a team or doing a complex analysis. Even though qualitative research designs usually collect data from a small sample compared with quantitative research designs such as surveys, they result in as much or even more data. As we noted above, you may record or transcribe thousands of words, especially in a long or group project: a doctoral student who takes this approach may often transcribe more than a thousand pages of interviews or observations.

Just as you can use statistical software to manage the complexity of statistical analysis, you can use ethnographic software to manage the complexity of qualitative analysis. You may hear this software generically referred to as **computer-assisted qualitative data analysis software** (CAQDAS). Specialised software such as Ethnograph, QSR NVivo, and winMAX are all available for the qualitative researcher (see www.scolari.com). Although experienced qualitative researchers have differing opinions about CAQDAS software (Bryman and Bell 2003: 446), you may find it useful if you have the time to spend learning to use it. Professional researchers use this software for the routine mechanical work of coding data and finding all the instances of a particular code so they can concentrate on interpreting the data. As O'Leary (2004: 203) points out, the researcher still needs to 'strategically, creatively, and intuitively analyse the data'. **Table 12.2** summarises the arguments for and against using CAQDAS software.

Table 12.2 The advantages and disadvantages of using qualitative analysis software

Pros	Cons
Ease of document management – particularly for very large amounts of data Traceability of concepts ensured Does allow you to demonstrate your methods and obtain high-quality output	Doesn't do anything that cannot be done by other means Can result in loss of contextual information Significant learning curve – takes time to get to be proficient with the software Doesn't do the analysis for you May deter you from using more effective graphical means Requires all data to be entered in the same format – can be highly time-consuming where you have nonstandard data

12.2 ANALYSING YOUR QUALITATIVE DATA

Compared with quantitative data analysis, where only your interpretation cannot be predicted in your research design, the analysis of qualitative data can be complex and open-ended, so new researchers sometimes find this frustrating. In **Chapter 5**, we characterised the logic underlying quantitative research as deductive and qualitative research as inductive. As we have noted, quantitative research (at least in the abstract) is a more or less linear process. Qualitative research, however, is usually much messier. Research design, data collection and data analysis may overlap; you may even cycle back and forth between them repeatedly. As a result, you may not be able to tell how you will analyse your data until you have collected them. You may not even know what data you will end up collecting.

This has a significant impact on this stage of the research process, because you do not know how much time and energy you will spend analysing your data. This stage may be very time-consuming, but skimping on it will mean that you don't find out anything worthwhile. Worse, if you rush your analysis, even if you do find out something interesting, you may not be able to support your findings.

A fundamental strength of qualitative data analysis is its ability to evolve during the study. We will describe a simple technique – based on Kolb's learning cycle – and a more complicated technique – concept extraction – for this.

12.2.1 Using Kolb's learning cycle for qualitative data analysis

A good model which many researchers use to analyse qualitative data is based on **Kolb's learning cycle** (Kolb, 1985), and is shown in **Figure 12.1**. Kolb's cycle starts with what he terms **concrete experience**. Your concrete experience may be very personal, such as a series of feelings or memories, or research-based, such as transcripts of interviews. Your analysis is based on this concrete experience.

The second stage of **reflective observation** involves three separate activities. The first activity is **familiarisation**, becoming intimately familiar with your data. This is particularly important for group projects or where you are analysing your data after a

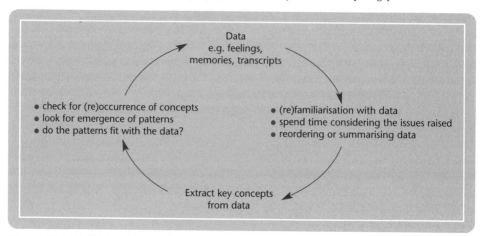

Figure 12.1 Kolb's learning cycle applied to qualitative data analysis

time lapse. Many researchers believe (re)familiarisation to be key to high-quality qualitative analysis.

The second activity is **spending time with the issues and the data**. You are not specifically looking for anything, but unhurriedly reflecting on what is happening. The final activity is **reordering**, or summarising the data to reflect the patterns you see in the data.

Once you have reordered your data, you should spend some time in **abstract conceptualisation**. This sounds horrendous, but it is actually very simple. You extract concepts (or the key themes) from your data. A **concept** is 'a descriptor for an issue, movement, thought or pattern of words that would be recognisable particularly to the researcher'. A simple example of the identification of what became a very important concept in a piece of research is described in **Student research in action 12.2**.

Student research in action 12.2
FLUFFY THE VAMPIRE SLAYER

A student group was interviewing people in a firm about benchmarking. They noticed that they would start talking about benchmarking but become very vague once they had got beyond a simple statement of the word. The students identified this vagueness as 'going fluffy'.

Once they had identified 'going fluffy' as a concept, the students marked the occasions in their transcripts where they thought respondents had 'gone fluffy'. They were then able to relate where this occurred to people's experiences with the benchmarking initiative, and later to its relative success.

By identifying episodes of 'going fluffy' in the transcripts, the students saw that vagueness was associated with low levels of application, and even lower levels of benefits being achieved. They concluded that there were significant pockets within the organisation where knowledge levels were low ('being fluffy') and that if the firm wanted to gain greater success from its initiative, these knowledge deficiencies would have to be addressed.

The final stage of Kolb's learning cycle is **active experimentation** with your data to see where a concept or group of concepts occurs. In this stage, you can see whether any patterns are emerging from your data, or whether your data are starting to fit with theories, models or concepts suggested in the literature. A concept can include actions, so you can analyse actions using Kolb's learning cycle, as illustrated in **Student research in action 12.3**. You will then need to see if these patterns fit with the reality of your data – do they really fit your concrete experience? We will discuss how you can do this in **Section 12.2**.

Student research in action 12.3
PLEASE DON'T SQUEEZE THE KIWIS

A team of students were investigating whether people would purchase fresh vegetables over the internet and what kinds of customers were likely to use internet shopping. They decided to investigate buyer behaviour and spent a considerable amount of time lurking round the vegetable counters of a major supermarket observing and recording the behaviour of different customers. As this was a nonparticipant observation study, they had to unobtrusively record their observations of the movements and actions of shoppers to avoid alerting customers to the fact that they were being watched.

The students started their data collection by observing how people selected fresh produce. These differences included how the person looked for items (browsers versus list shoppers) and how they then selected the actual produce to buy. They noted the process of produce selection by using a series of symbols (as described in **Chapter 6**) for structured observation. They modified a standard set of symbols to include special activities that emerged from their analysis – specifically 'squeeze', 'sniff' or 'tap and listen'.

For each observation they carefully noted the shopper's characteristics. This included whether the shopper was a man or a woman, whether they had a basket or trolley (small or large shopping expedition), their apparent age and their appearance. This provided background information for later analysis.

Once they had observed a sufficient number of shoppers, they examined the sequence of actions by each customer and compared these sequences across the range of shoppers. As part of the abstract conceptualisation stage, they classified shoppers into the following three behaviours:

- *Pickers* – Pick the first thing that they see
- *Lookers* – Have a perfunctory look to check that it is OK before confirming their selection
- *Squeezers* – Do a thorough analysis, including one or more of the special activities listed above.

They then tried to see whether each behaviour could be associated with a particular category of customer. Some of the propositions they identified were:

- Older people are more likely be squeezers
- Younger people are more likely to be pickers.

They tested these propositions by going back to their original data set. They then hypothesized that the main group of prospective purchasers via the internet would be pickers, shoppers who were less discriminating about their vegetables. These would most likely be younger shoppers (under 40). Older people, who checked out their vegetables more thoroughly, were less likely to spend their 'grey pound' via the internet, at least on vegetables, since they would not be able to do a thorough analysis.

By examining how people select fresh produce, the students could understand some general principles of shopping behaviours after observing a small sample of buyers in one store. Since the students hadn't started with any particular hypotheses to test, such as 'Older shoppers are less likely to buy vegetables via the internet', they were free to let the findings emerge from the data they collected rather than imposing an interpretation on it (and making it less likely that they would recognise any unexpected or counterintuitive evidence). They might have missed these different behaviours if they had administered a survey and statistically analysed the data. However, they could argue that their findings were equally as generalisable as survey data, since there was nothing special about the store, its location or the customers). As part of their 'areas for further investigation', they suggested that the findings could be further tested through a survey of a wider population.

12.2.2 Unstructured versus structured analysis

As described above, Kolb's cycle is an unstructured approach to finding out the meaning of your qualitative data. In an **unstructured analysis**, you let meanings and themes emerge from your data, rather than you imposing them on the data. You can then look for conceptual frameworks that help you to understand and explain these themes.

Unstructured approach to qualitative analysis

Although an unstructured approach is excellent for maximising the creativity you can bring to interpreting your data and the chances that you may develop some new and unique insights from your evidence, it can create real challenges for student researchers. An unstructured approach takes no account of deadlines – it is done when it is done and not any sooner. This means that it is open-ended, and that you may take weeks, or even months, to do a thorough job of your data analysis and interpretation.

At this point, you can really start to see the differences between a scientific approach, where considerable project time needs to be spent in planning your research before you start collecting data, down to the statistical tests and tables, and the ethnographic approach, where you can start collecting data almost immediately, but the milestones for analysing and interpreting your data are much fuzzier. This is not to say that we recommend a scientific approach, only that you need to take this difference into account when you are planning and doing your research.

Structured analysis of qualitative data

If you are collecting qualitative data, but you have to meet a project deadline, you might want to consider taking a more structured approach to analysing your qualitative data. Instead of trying to induce everything, up to and including your conceptual framework, from your data, you can use concepts and/or conceptual frameworks from the literature to structure your data analysis and interpretation.

In a **structured analysis** of qualitative data, you compare your findings to a conceptual framework you have developed or found in the literature. This will help to guide your analysis and interpretation, but still allow you to identify those aspects of your evidence that differ from what other researchers have previously found.

Some researchers use pre-existing concepts and frameworks to apply even more structure than the comparative method we have just described. That is, they analyse their qualitative data through the lens of a conceptual framework they have already selected. This process is similar to the 'classical' scientific approach, but substitutes thematic analysis for statistical analysis. If you take this approach, you should realise that this is a quantitative approach, but you are using qualitative rather than quantitative data. The steps in the process are similar to the statistical techniques for analysing quantitative data described in **Chapters 6, 10** and **11**.

Since the structured approach is so similar to the analysis of quantitative data, we will not focus on it in this chapter. Instead, the following considers how quantitative techniques can be applied to qualitative data.

Statistical analysis of qualitative data

You should realise that if you are more aligned with a scientific approach there is nothing to prevent you from statistically analysing data you have gathered using a qualitative research method such as participant observation or unstructured interviews. Indeed, quantitative research is often based on quantitative data that started out as qualitative data. We often reduce the complexity of qualitative data, such as attitudes, opinions or behaviours, to numbers by quantification so that we can analyse them more conveniently using the statistical methods described in **Chapters 10** and **11**. You are likely to be familiar with these shortcuts. For example, many questionnaires ask you to quantify an opinion on a scale of 'completely disagree' to 'completely agree', or a behaviour on a scale of 'rarely or never' to 'frequently or always' by circling a number.

You can analyse any qualitative data set – for example the thousand-page interview transcript or notes based on participant observation – in a quantitative way. If you want to analyse your qualitative data statistically, you will need to make sure that you meet the other requirements for quantitative analysis. Qualitative research designs often involve in-depth investigation of a small number of cases. You will have to make sure that you have a large enough sample to analyse statistically. Small sample sizes and other factors may make it difficult for you to use the inferential statistics described in **Chapters 10** and **11**. Since many qualitative research designs do not meet minimum sample sizes, continuous measurements or normal distributions, you may need to use special techniques, known as nonparametric methods.

However, the main objection to analysing qualitative data statistically is not small sample size. The complexity of the conceptual frameworks (theories and models) that people investigate in qualitative research designs means that multivariate thinking (if not statistical techniques) may be useful in developing and evaluating your findings. If you reduce qualitative data to categorical data, you risk losing much of the data's richness and any unique insights. For example, if you classified people as only 'satisfied' or 'dissatisfied', you might miss out on insights from your data that reveal why they were dissatisfied or whether all dissatisfied customers are alike – are there different kinds of dissatisfaction?

Which approach should you take?

Figure 12.2 shows how the unstructured and structured approaches to analysing qualitative data fit with the different research designs discussed in **Chapter 7**, where we classified quantitative research designs by how close the researcher was to the subject of the research. Your approach should match the data you have collected. Where you

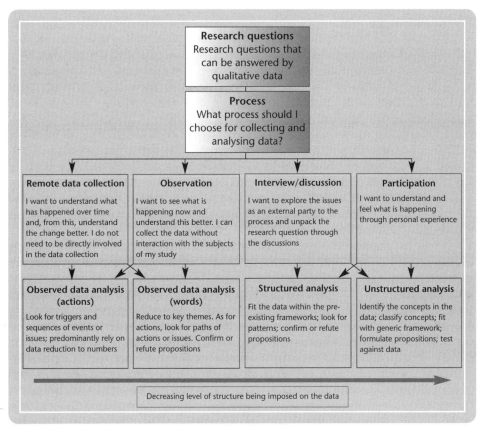

Figure 12.2 Methods for collecting and analysing qualitative data

position your data analysis depends on your research problem and questions, and on the data you have collected. Research questions that ask 'why?' and look for underlying meaning in situations suggest unstructured techniques, whilst research questions such as 'what?' suggest more structured techniques.

In an unstructured approach to analysing your qualitative data, you will not have a predetermined structure, as in structured qualitative or quantitative analysis. As you analyse your data and collect more data, you will change the methods and perhaps even the questions you are asking. You still need to take a systematic approach to managing the analytic process, no matter what technique you decide to use.

12.2.3 Extracting concepts from your data

A more complex technique for identifying concepts and developing or testing conceptual frameworks is **concept extraction**. Concept extraction is often used in analysing structured and unstructured interviews and participant observation. In concept extraction, your concepts emerge from your data, rather than from your literature review. This can be used in either the structured or unstructured approaches described above.

Concept identification

The first step in concept extraction is to identify the key issues, ideas or other meaning units in your data. Many people find this easiest to do manually, by going through a transcript line by line and marking each occurrence of a potential concept. (You can also do this on the computer or using specialised software.) You should try to summarise each concept in a word or a short phrase. You may want to play around with different ways of expressing a concept.

If you have found the concept expressed in different words by different interviewees or sources of data, you may want to call the concepts by slightly different names. This might be easier to see in an example where two interviewees were discussing change in their organisations. They frequently mentioned the measures being applied to the individuals and teams during the interviews, but they focused on different aspects such as those measures that had an impact on pay systems. The researchers identified measures as a concept, but showed the different measures as 'Measures1' and 'Measures2'. You should also note the context in which these issues are being discussed, and any other issues associated with (discussed before or after) them.

Open coding

A systematic process for identifying concepts is **open coding**. Open coding starts with codes that emerge when the researcher highlights the key ideas.

Table 12.3 presents a detailed example of how you can change your raw data – words – into concepts, based on a transcript of an actual interview. The study addressed the research question 'Where do new ideas for changes to new product development processes come from, and how are they implemented?' After some structured questions, the interviewer asked the respondents more open-ended questions about how new ideas came into the department to find out how innovation was being applied to NPD. The table shows how the researcher has highlighted those concepts in the transcript associated with where product ideas come from.

The researcher has identified the exact words used by the manager with **codes** in the right-hand column. Remember that the term 'coding' is used differently in qualitative analysis, which is the first step in building theory, whereas in quantitative analysis, it is purely about 'coding' the data in a way that makes it easier to compare data from different respondents and measures, and also to create the raw material for the next stage.

Coding starts to translate raw data (in this case the manager's words) into your own language or ways of talking. You are looking to link concepts, particularly if they are loosely or poorly described, for instance where the manager describes what goes on in some linear sequence. You therefore turn his words into more abstract codes for concepts that make sense to you. For example, one code refers to the pull of ideas, where someone in a place wants something; push is where someone from outside the place wants it incorporated. You can identify two examples of the pull of ideas in the transcript in Table 12.X.

You will also find that your own questioning may have made perfect sense at the time, but when you read it on the page, it may not be what you intended, or certainly nowhere near as clear – this is the wisdom that comes with time and reflection on the transcripts. The transcript therefore is a substantially different data source than a report, for instance. You may have some challenges decoding what respondents were talking about

Table 12.3 Transcribed interview

Interviewer's question	Manager's answer	Code/concept
I was just wondering how you find out about other things that are going on in the company?	We used to find out about these things **through colleagues,** and curiously enough it often comes from one particular area of the firm – that of silicon chip design. These chips are at the heart of all our products and are highly complex. The guys working down there tend to generate very quick processes for what they do, and they are then taken up by other parts of the design process, so **they tend to lead the way.**	Internal sources

Perceived excellence |
| So they've got something different going on there? Do they have different pressures on the process that means they have to innovate more quickly? | I think that what is different there is that we do our bit first. They are then under pretty **severe schedule pressure.** It is also a fairly deterministic part of the product in that if you get it right, it stays right. | Time-driven |
| Is that because it's too expensive to change it? | No, it's because of the nature of the design – it's digital design. Once you've come up with the digital design, you can make a million of them. From the point of view of the rest of the product, there's a lot more to do after you've come up with the design. For some reason, it does generate an immense amount of schedule pressure on those guys up front and as a result of that there is a strong recognition that it is necessary to get the chips right first time, and that's **fundamental to the health of the overall development programme.**

So they tend to **invest more in novel techniques** to make it happen right and quickly. They do all sorts of things like they'll think nothing of buying some sort of simulator package that we use that costs say a quarter of a million pounds, to save three weeks on a project. They'll probably only use it for a few weeks, but the **payback is in time, so it's worth it.** To kind of complete that, what happens is that **those guys tend to find out new techniques,** then it kind of **seeps out** if you like. **They start talking about it, you go along, you review it. You think this looks good – I can apply it some way; then you do it yourself.** What does not happen and perhaps ought to happen is we don't get ideas coming from the corporate HQ. They have teams of people studying the product development processes. They then come round and say, **'we've got a great new technique for you,'** and **you don't go to the seminar** because we've discovered in the past that what they've really got is something that | Critical

Investment

Time-driven

Pull of ideas – chance

External push – rejection |

	invariably you were doing a lot of years ago, because they're actually going round polling all of us and getting the best practices from us; **it doesn't help**.	Evaluation – ineffective
Is there any other help from the corporation?	No – they are just playing at it really. We just have to do it as well as we possibly can.	
Are there any other sources that you use to find new ideas?	Often from **best practice within the corporation** rather than corporate HQ telling you. This is a good way of doing it. Often at the beginning of a programme, you might find yourself, you get this **breathing space when you are planning**, you use this time to go and visit other parts of the corporation that you know are being successful. So you've got the Laser Printer people who have gone and seen what the disk people are doing, what techniques they are using and seeing if there is anything here we can use?	Pull of ideas – Opportunity available
That would be an informal process then?	Yes, it would be up to the **initiative** of the people involved in the new programme. They'd want to go and find out that stuff. For instance, we wouldn't use universities or educational establishments. I can't remember any times when we do.	Individual initiative
Just as a matter of interest, is there any particular reason for that?	**We don't tend to look outside these walls.** Specifically, why we don't go to academia I couldn't tell you, other than whenever something like that happens, often they're not well engaged; you get the impression they've read every book there is but they haven't actually done any of this stuff. There's an element of having to **win your spurs** here.	Internal sources Credibility

before you can do the analysis. Beware here that you don't impose an interpretation – if there is ambiguity, either go back to them to seek clarification or treat this with care.

Bryman and Bell (2003: 435–6) suggest that you:

- Code as soon as possible, preferably as you are going along, to make sense of your data and avoid being swamped at the end
- Read through all your materials before you start coding or interpreting them
- Read through once and generate your basic codes
- Review your codes to see whether you can group codes into common categories
- Start to look for more general theoretical ideas
- Don't worry about generating too many codes, finding a single interpretation of your data or analysing your data.

Classification

Once you have coded your data, you can start to group together the concepts you have identified. Numbering or otherwise identifying your concepts (as in **Table 12.1**) will let

Table 12.4 Organising concepts by themes

Category	Property	Dimension
Source of ideas	Location Mechanism Perception of source	Internal/external Push/pull Excellence/ineffective Credible/not credible
Drivers for ideas	Criticality of process	Time-driven High/low
Idea-searching process	Involvement in searching Type of searching process Instigation	Active/passive Planned/chance Individual/corporate initiative
Implementation	Opportunity	Available/not available

you track where your data came from. You may want to write down each code or concept on an index card or Post-it note and group them physically, or list them on the computer and start rearranging them. You may see hierarchical patterns in the concepts (concept, subconcept, sub-subconcept and so on).

Table 12.4 shows one possible arrangement of the concepts from **Table 12.3**. As you can see, each significant group of concepts, such as source of ideas, drivers for ideas, search process and so on, defines a **category** representing a real-world phenomenon (Bryman and Bell 2003: 430). A category has **properties**, which are aspects or attributes. Each property has one or more **dimensions**, representing the range of values it can take on, which are derived from your original concepts. For instance, in the transcript, ideas were noted to come from either inside the firm (internal) or outside (external). So, internal and external become the two dimensions of the property 'location'.

Conceptual framework

Once you have developed categories, you can start to develop a conceptual framework and develop propositions about the relationships between concepts, or compare your findings with a pre-existing framework, for example a conceptual framework you have identified in the literature. This provides the input into the next stage of qualitative analysis. **Student research in action 12.4** illustrates how such a framework can emerge as you explore the relationships between concepts.

> ### *Student research in action 12.4*
> **BUDDY, MY BUDDY**
>
> Suzie was considering the role of networks between individuals in knowledge transfer within and between organisations. She focused on the social aspects of knowledge management – she proposed that the more socially active a member of staff was, the more likely he or she was to share knowledge with others. Suzie developed a conceptual framework to show the concepts and relations that she wanted to develop, as shown in **Figure 12.3**.

At the start of her study, Suzie did not know how she would identify socially active employees or measure their behaviour. As she collected and analysed data, she started to see patterns emerge. A concept that consistently emerged during the interviews and observations was the number and duration of non-work-related discussions that took place, either directly or by phone or email. These were often wrapped around discussions of work-related issues. Suzie's analysis suggested that there was a link between nonwork discussions and work-related discussions that was worth investigating further.

Axial coding

Strauss and Corbin (1999) present a method for putting the codes back together in a new way once you have completed your open coding, They explain how you can experiment with your codes and categories, so you can test out different scenarios to explain what you think is happening. This approach is helpful if your goal is to build a conceptual model based on your qualitative data.

This process of building up a conceptual model from your open codes and categories is called **axial coding**. Axial coding lets you elaborate each of your data categories in terms of the relationships that may exist between properties and their dimensions. You can use axial coding to figure out what is going in each of these conceptual categories: what it is, when it happens, when it doesn't happen, what are its consequences. Strauss and Corbin suggest that you link your categories to the causal conditions, contexts, intervening conditions, actions/interactions and consequences of the phenomenon you are investigating, as shown in **Figure 12.4**.

For example, you might be interested in whether there is any relationship between playing video games frequently and failure in exams. You could use the process of axial coding to examine the conceptual category of video game-playing. The **phenomenon**

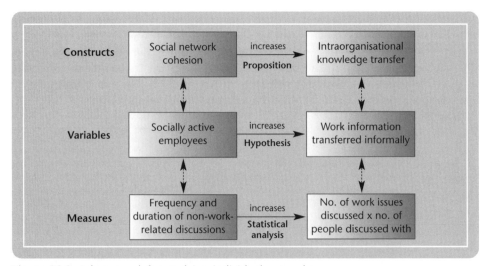

Figure 12.3 A framework for studying individual networks

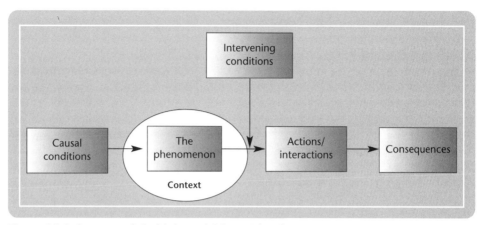

Figure 12.4 Strauss and Corbin's model for axial coding

is the behaviour you are actually studying, whether it is solitary game-playing or group game-playing. You might want to distinguish between high and low levels of game-playing. Is four hours a day a high, moderate or low amount? Does this vary depending on whether it is a school day or a holiday? Finally, you would want to see what consequences game-playing has for study, social activities and so on.

12.2.4 Mapping concepts

Some qualitative researchers find it easier to explore qualitative data using graphical techniques rather than verbal ones such as the axial coding process described above. You could experiment with mind maps, influence diagrams and logic diagrams as ways of identifying patterns in your qualitative data. Mind maps have already been shown in **Chapters 3** and **4** and you might find them useful for graphically displaying and linking the concepts that have emerged from your study.

Influence diagrams

An **influence diagram** not only shows the concepts and whether there are relation-ships between them, it also shows the proposed cause-and-effect relationships. You can use an influence diagram to show where different forces may be acting in a particular situation (see Coyle 2001). An example influence diagram is shown in **Figure 12.5**.

Logic diagrams

Logic diagrams show the logic or preconditions for an event or set of circumstances to occur. Logic diagrams (see also Schragenheim 1998) provide the ability either to struc-ture the logic of the current situation, or to indicate the necessary conditions for that situation to arise. The example shown in **Figure 12.6** enabled the researcher to deter-mine the root causes of particular phenomena. The basis for the figure is the logic that IF the first condition arises, THEN it will logically lead to those that are indicated by the arrows.

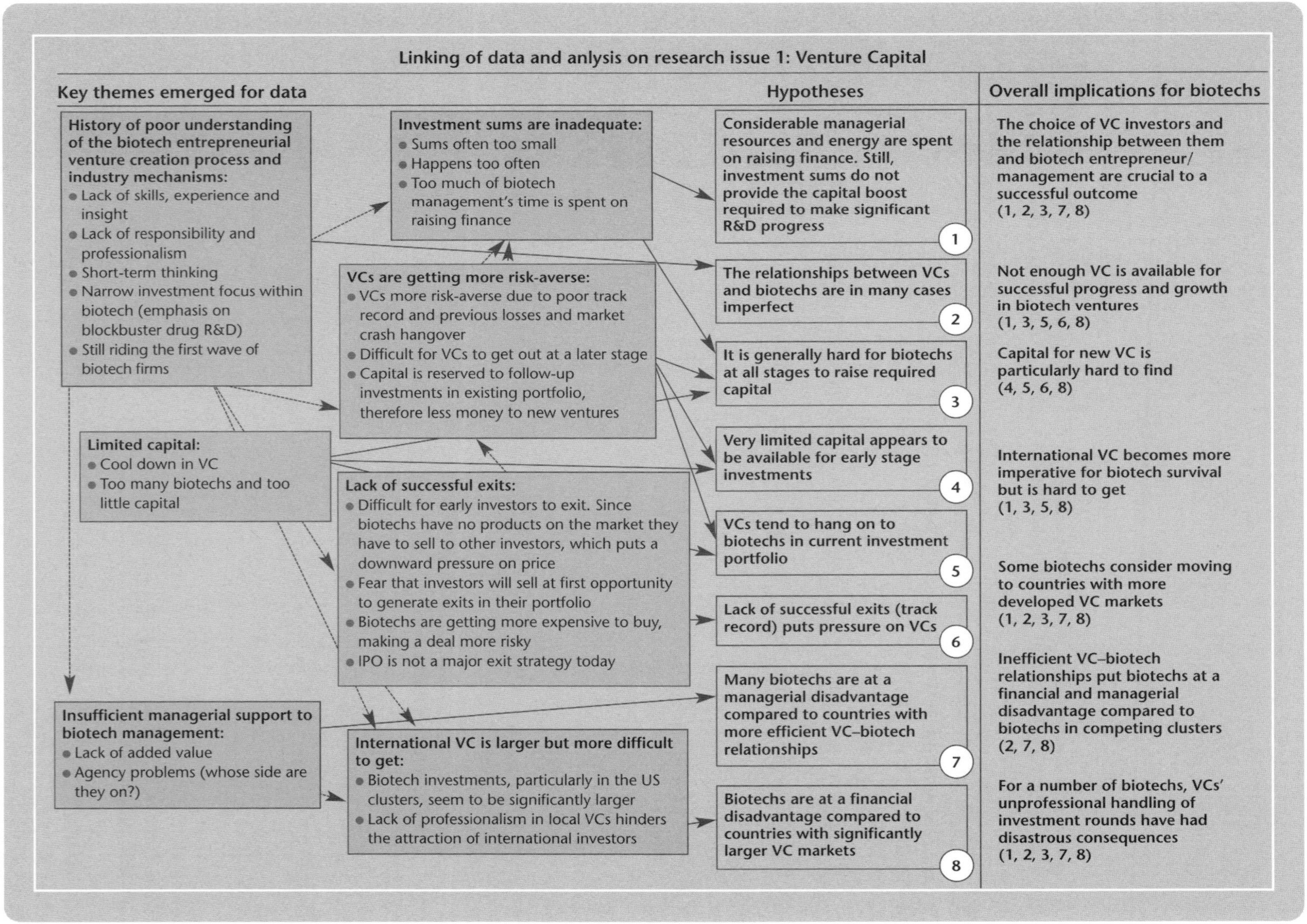

Figure 12.5 An example of an influence diagram

Source: Courtesy of Jes Batting

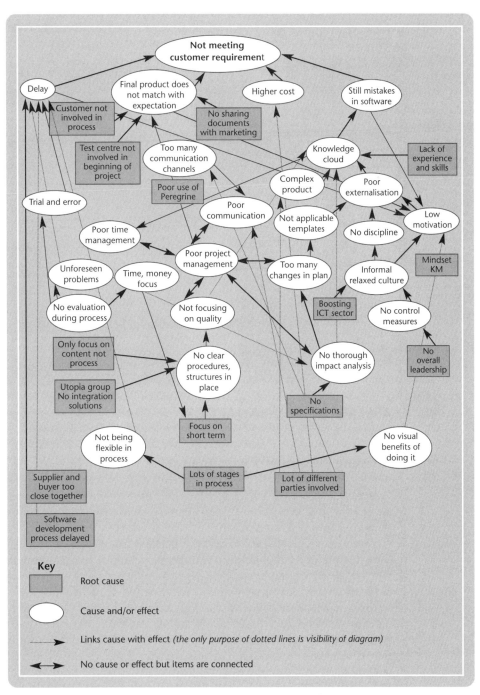

Figure 12.6 An example of a logic diagram

12.2.5 Finishing your analysis

Students frequently ask how they will know when their analysis is complete. Unlike quantitative research designs, where you can determine the sample size required for your statistical data analysis before you start collecting data, in qualitative research designs, it may be difficult to tell when you can stop collecting data and when your analysis is complete. In qualitative research, the term that is often used is **theoretical saturation**. You have reached theoretical saturation when additional data no longer add extra information to your concepts, when you are no longer getting any new insights from coding your data or reviewing your concepts or categories.

You have done enough when you have achieved your goal, which might include:

- *Description*. A better description of a particular phenomenon, the elements that constitute it and its dynamics, for instance how a situation changes over time.
- *Categorisation*. A classification of elements of an issue of interest, for example how people behave or perform particular tasks.
- *Inter-relation*. Establishing relationships between concepts, for instance as described in **Table 12.4**.
- *Explanation*. Explaining a particular action or behaviour by describing what caused it or the circumstances in which it occurred.
- *Prediction*. A better prediction of the circumstances under which some action may work, for example the produce-buying case in **Student research in action 12.3**.

12.3 ASSESSING YOUR ANALYSIS

12.3.1 Assessing the quality of your findings

Figure 12.7 shows the key elements of this assessment and the questions you should ask of your work before, during and after you have analysed your qualitative data. Each element is now discussed in turn.

Is your research **reliable**? Whilst the detailed specification of the conceptual framework and methods of quantitative studies are assumed to lead to higher levels of reliability, qualitative studies – particularly those that are unstructured – would be difficult to repeat exactly. If you were to do a short period of participant observation, it would be unlikely that someone else could go and join the same group and achieve exactly the same findings. Situations, people and dynamics change over time, resulting in this being more of a theoretical question – 'if I went back and did this study again, would I get the same results, and if it had been done by someone else, would they have got the same results?' In a qualitative study, it is unlikely that the results would be the same in either case, but the main points and conclusions should be fairly robust rather than fragile. Both of these questions force reflection on your own interaction and influence with the system you are researching.

Is your research **valid**? Validity refers to the extent to which you have captured the underlying truth of the situation and not been misled by particular influences. Student projects can be biased by the views of key individuals – maybe someone who has been closely associated with the project and who may have his/her own agenda to press.

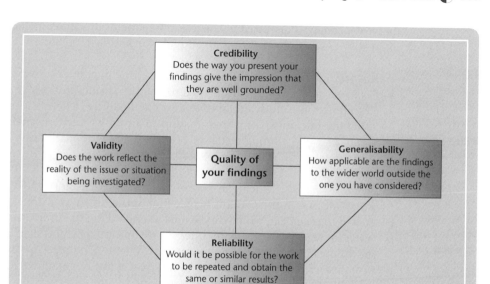

Figure 12.7 A framework for assessing the quality of qualitative research

Furthermore, there is always the issue of whether you have been *rigorous* in your analysis, or succumbed to a shallow *impressionistic* analysis of your data. Whilst there is ample space in the scope of methods used here to allow you to form impressions from your data, you should be able to demonstrate how you got from there to your findings. Documenting and explaining how you got from your data to your conclusions, using strategies such as those described in this chapter (which are explored in more depth in **Chapter 13**), is one way to show this.

Is your research **generalisable**? This is very difficult to get right. Many projects over-state their findings (this is what we found in this organisation/place and therefore it is true for all organisations/places/the entire world) or understate them (these findings are only true in the situation we investigated and have no relevance anywhere else). In qualitative research, particularly in single case studies, you might think that you have a sample of only one, which makes issues unrepresentative. It is possible to learn from a sample of one (or even fewer) by thinking about areas where the findings of a similar piece of work may be similar, and where its particular circumstances would make it different (for example different competitive/legislative/geographical environment).

Is your research **credible**? This was included by Shipman (1982) and is a vital factor – how you present your findings and your research. It is important that you present evidence to support any contentions made, including key quotations and evidence from numerous sources (see the discussion of triangulation in **Chapter 8**). In analysing your qualitative data, you should identify suitable key pieces of data that can be presented in your report. This is discussed further in **Chapter 13**.

12.3.2 Where to look for more information

In this section, we have only looked at structured and unstructured techniques for analysing qualitative data. However, you will find many different approaches to qualitative data analysis discussed in the research methods literature, including those high-lighted by O'Leary (2004: 199–200) and Bryman and Bell (2003):

- *Analytic induction*, a rigorous approach to testing hypotheses from qualitative data
- *Content analysis*, which can be used to identify themes in texts or other materials. Researchers use both qualitative content analysis, where the emphasis is on searching out underlying themes, and quantitative content analysis, where the emphasis is on counting instances of these themes for quantitative analysis
- *Discourse analysis*, which can be used to interpret language in its social and historical context
- *Narrative analysis*, which can be used to interpret the stories told by individuals, which focuses on the patterns people find in their lives over time
- *Conversation analysis*, which can be used to understand the structure of conversations
- *Semiotics*, which can be used to interpret the meaning behind signs and symbols, to show how messages are communicated as systems of cultural meaning
- *Hermeneutics*, which can be used to interpret texts, originally sacred texts such as the Bible, but today applied to both documents and social actions
- *Grounded theory*, which can be used to generate theory directly from data (which we briefly discussed in **Chapter 8** in the context of grounded case studies).

You may want to look at the **Additional resources** at the end of this chapter if any sound interesting. You can find many articles and even entire books written on these approaches.

 ## SUMMARY

This chapter introduces methods for analysing qualitative data. These methods range from highly structured, which are close to quantitative analysis, to highly unstructured, which are not. Which method you should choose depends on how involved you are with the data source, whether you have started with a theoretical framework or expect one to emerge from your analysis, and your research questions.

Many studies start with a conceptual framework, but it is also possible to let the structure emerge, using a grounded theory approach such as that of Strauss and Corbin (1999). You can use various graphical techniques to experiment with your concepts as suggested by Kolb, including mind maps, influence diagrams and logic diagrams, which help you to formulate propositions that can be compared with the data you have collected.

The data analysis process will pass the findings to the discussion and reporting stage of the project in a range of forms. The quality of this outcome is evaluated in terms of reliability, validity, generalisability and credibility. The use of IT support in your process may provide benefits but, for short projects where the volume of data is limited, may take more time to learn how to use than will provide benefit to the project.

 ## ANSWERS TO KEY QUESTIONS

How should I prepare my qualitative data for analysis?

- Verbal data should be transcribed and put in order, with a reference for each piece of data

What are the main strategies for analysing qualitative data?

- Use structured analysis to fit your data into a predetermined framework
- Use unstructured analysis to let your framework emerge

How can I identify concepts and conceptual frameworks in my data?

- Start by coding
- Look for categories
- Elaborate your categories and look for relationships between them

What qualities should I aim for in my analysis?

- Reliability
- Validity
- Generalisability
- Credibility

REFERENCES

Bryman, Alan and Bell, Emma. 2003. *Business Research Methods*. Oxford: Oxford University Press.

Coyle, R.G. 2001. *Systems Dynamics Modelling: A Practical Approach*. London: Chapman & Hall/CRC.

Kolb, David A. 1985. *Experiential Learning*. Englewood Cliffs, NJ: Pearson.

O'Leary, Zina. 2004. *The Essential Guide to Doing Research*. London: Sage.

Schragenheim, E. 1998. *Management Dilemmas*. Boca Raton, FL: St Lucie Press.

Shipman, M. 1982. *The Limitations of Social Research*, London: Longman.

Strauss, Anselm L. and Corbin, Juliet. 1999. *Basics of Qualitative Research: Grounded Theory Procedures & Techniques*, 2nd edn. Thousand Oaks, CA: Sage.

ADDITIONAL RESOURCES

Bryman, Alan and Burgess, R.G. (eds) 1994. *Analysing Qualitative Data*. London: Routledge.

Buzan, A. 2000. *The Mind Map Book*. London: BBC Books.

Cameron, S. 2001. *The MBA Handbook*. Harlow: Financial Times/Prentice Hall.

Denzin, Norman. 1970. *The Research Act: A Theoretical Introduction to Sociological Methods*. Chicago: Aldine.

Denzin, Norman and Lincoln, Y. 1994. *Handbook of Qualitative Research*. Thousand Oaks, CA: Sage.

Dubin, Robert. 1978. *Theory Building: A Practical Guide to the Construction and Testing of Theoretical Models*, 2nd edn. New York: Free Press.

Gahan, Celia and Hannibal, Mike. 1998. *Doing Qualitative Research Using QSR Nud*IST*. London: Sage (Nud*IST is now renamed QSR NVivo).

Gibbs, Graham R. 2002. *Qualitative Data Analysis: Explorations with NVivo*. Maidenhead: Open University Press.

Glaser, Barney G. and Strauss, Anselm L. 1967. *The Discovery of Grounded Theory: Strategies of Qualitative Research*. London: Wiedenfeld & Nicholson.

Guba, E. 1985. The context of emergent paradigm research. In Lincoln, Y. (ed.) *Organizational Theory and Inquiry: The Paradigm Revolution*. Thousand Oaks, CA: Sage.

Gummesson, Evert. 2000. *Qualitative Methods in Management Research,* 2nd edn. Thousand Oaks, CA: Sage.

Kolb, D.A., Rubin, I.M. and MacIntyre, J.M. 1984. *Organisational Psychology*. Harlow: Prentice Hall.

Reason, Peter and Bradbury, Hilary. (eds) 2000. *Handbook of Action Research*. London: Sage.

Symon, Gillian and Cassell, Catherine. (eds) 1998. *Qualitative Methods and Analysis in Organisational Research*. London: Sage.

Web resources

QSR International: http://www.qsr-software.com/

Scolari: Sage Publications Software. Resources for qualitative analysis software: (http://www.scolari.co.uk/).

Key terms

abstract conceptualisation, 349
active experimentation, 349
axial coding, 358
category, 357
codes, 354
complete, 345
computer-assisted qualitative data analysis software, 347
concept, 349
concept extraction, 353
concrete experience, 348

credible, 363
dimensions, 357
familiarisation, 348
generalisable, 363
influence diagram, 359
Kolb's learning cycle, 348
logic diagrams, 359
open coding, 354
phenomenon, 358
properties, 357
reflective observation, 348

reliable, 345
reordering, 349
spending time with the issues and the data, 349
structured analysis, 351
theoretical saturation, 362
traceable, 345
unstructured analysis, 351
valid, 362

Discussion questions

1. How is qualitative analysis different from quantitative analysis?
2. What techniques for analysis are usually associated with which research methods?
3. Why should you try to capture data as close to the source as possible, for instance by recording all notes within a short time of an interview?
4. What is the role of a learning cycle approach in analysing data?
5. What is coding?
6. What research philosophy might be associated with structured data analysis?
7. Do codes exist in the data or should you impose them?
8. What is the difference between a construct, a variable and a measure?
9. What is the end point of qualitative analysis?
10. How would you assess the quality of the research you have carried out and that reported (for example in journals) by others?

Background

In previous workshops you have conducted interviews on the subject of the changes that people go through when they move into higher education.

Task

1. If you did not record the interviews in Workshop 7, in pairs, conduct an interview on the subject of the changes that each other has experienced in their move into higher education. Each interview should last no more than 10 minutes. Use this time to explore any particular issues that the interviewees found challenging and what it was that made the issue challenging or important to them. Record the interviews, if at all possible (computers, some mobile phones, i-Pods and other devices can be used for recording purposes, if you do not have a tape recorder handy).

2. Relisten to the interview and transcribe the most important two minutes (this is not a general practice, but is used here for pragmatic purposes).

3. Use the coding procedures shown in Table 12.3 to identify the key concepts that emerged from the interviews.

4. How would further data (interviews) help here?

5. If you had many more interviews (say 100), how would you handle the data? Describe a process for storing, retrieving and analysing such a large volume of data.

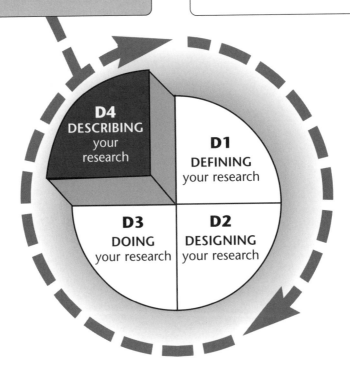

Relevant chapters

13 Answering your research questions
14 Describing your research
15 Closing the loop

4

Key challenges

- Interpreting your findings and making recommendations
- Writing and presenting your project
- Reflecting on and learning from your research

Relevant chapters

1 What is research?
2 Managing the research process
3 What should I study?
4 How do I find information?

1

Key challenges

- Understanding the research process
- Taking a systematic approach
- Generating and clarifying ideas
- Using the library and internet

Relevant chapters

9 Doing field research
10 Analysing quantitative data
11 Advanced quantitative analysis
12 Analysing qualitative data

3

Key challenges

- Practical considerations in doing research
- Using simple statistics
- Undertanding multivariate statistics
- Interpreting interviews and observations

Relevant chapters

5 Scientist or ethnographer?
6 Quantitative research designs
7 Designing qualitative research
8 Case studies/multi-method design

2

Key challenges

- Choosing a model for doing research
- Using scientific methods
- Using ethnographic methods
- Integrating quantitative and qualitative research

chapter 13

Answering your research questions
Interpreting your findings and making recommendations

Key questions

- How can I turn my analysis into answers to my research questions?
- How can I present my analysis?
- How do I use the literature to support my findings and discussion?
- How do I discuss my findings?

Learning outcomes

At the end of this chapter, you should be able to:

- Interpret your data and analysis with respect to your conceptual framework and theory
- Develop interim findings and recommendations from your research
- Use your data and analysis to support your findings, discussion and conclusions

Contents

 **INTRODUCTION**

After you have collected and analysed your data, you need to relate your data and analysis back to your research questions to see whether you have answered them. If you have taken the scientific approach as your model, this usually means comparing what you have found out with the conceptual model you started with and then your research questions; if you have taken the ethnographic approach as your model, this usually means comparing the conceptual model you have developed with your research questions. You will also need to compare the answers to your research questions with the theory in your topic area, and consider alternate explanations and unexpected findings from your research.

In many cases, you will need to do this before you write up your final research report. You may need to present interim results to your academic supervisor and/or business sponsor. You may need to understand what you have found out in one stage of your research before you proceed to the next, especially if you have taken a multi-method or multi-stage approach. Most students find interpreting their data and the results of their data analysis a challenging task, especially closing the loop back to their conceptual framework, research questions and theory, with respect to the theoretical problem, and in developing recommendations, with respect to the practical problem. It is difficult to find specific guidance on how to do this. It is tempting to just forge blindly ahead.

In this chapter, we present a systematic process for interpreting your data and your analysis with regard to your conceptual framework and your research questions. If you follow this process, you should be able to identify your findings, discussion and conclusions for your academic report, and identify an implementation plan and recommendations for your report, if you are writing one, to your sponsor. One of your key tasks is to make sure that you have answered your research questions. It may seem far-fetched to you that someone might present research that does not do this, but people often get sidetracked during their project and end up doing research that is unrelated to their research questions. In fact, we have read many project reports and reviewed many articles for conferences and journals, some by experienced authors, where the research questions are mentioned in the introduction and never heard of again.

Section 13.1 explains how to interpret the data and statistical tests associated with a quantitative analysis to see whether you have answered your research questions. We describe some useful ways to present your data and your statistical analysis to help you with this interpretation. We also point out some common mistakes you should try to avoid. If you have interpreted what you have found out, you will find it easier to turn your numbers back into words – or at least describe them in words – when you present your research. In interpreting what you have found out, you should also keep in mind the criteria by which the quality of quantitative research is judged.

Section 13.2 examines how to interpret the data and the themes associated with a qualitative analysis to see whether you have answered your research questions. Since qualitative research does not necessarily start with a conceptual framework, and one may emerge from the unstructured or structured analysis, this may be more complex than in quantitative research. However, you still need to relate what you have found out back to your research questions, so that you can see whether you have answered them. We point out some useful strategies and common mistakes associated with this stage of doing your research. The experimenting that you do in this stage can help you see how to present your research in your project report, which is often tricky for qualitative research. As with quantitative analysis, you should compare your findings with the criteria for qualitative analysis.

Section 13.3 describes how you can develop what you have found out into your recommendations and implementation plan if you are conducting in-company research. You should consider alternate solutions to your practical problem in this stage of your research, and be able to explain why your solution is the most appropriate one.

This chapter will also help you to develop the core elements of your project report – your findings, discussion and conclusions – which we discuss in more detail in **Chapter 14**. Many student projects fail to achieve high marks because the students see presenting their data and analysis as the end point of their research, and fail to develop a link back to the theoretical and practical problems they set out to investigate. Your data do not have any value until they have been interpreted and measured against the quality standards for the kind of research you are doing. When you understand what you have found out, you will also be in a much better position to present it to your readers, including your academic examiners and project sponsors.

13.1 INTERPRETING YOUR QUANTITATIVE RESULTS

The reader of a research report is usually at least as concerned with how you arrived at your findings (your process) as with what your findings are (your content). Academic readers are interested in how you have translated your research questions into a research design, and how your evidence answers those research questions. In other words, their focus is on the generalisability of your report, which requires validity. Practitioners, on the other hand, will be interested in how you propose that your answers might solve a practical problem. In other words, their focus is on the relevance of your recommendations, which requires rigour. As you will see in **Chapter 14**, this may lead you to write two separate reports, one for each audience, although you may be able to include common material in both. Before you start the writing-up process, however, you need to interpret what you have found out. It is not enough to present your raw (or summarised) data and hope that your reader can (or will) make sense of it for him or herself.

Once you have collected and analysed your data, you have three key tasks:

1. *Interpret your data* – Understand what the data mean, with respect to your hypotheses
2. *Interpret your analysis* – Understand what the analysis means with respect to your conceptual framework
3. *Interpret your empirical research* – Understand what your findings mean for your theoretical and practical problem.

If you are doing your research from a quantitative perspective, once you have completed your statistical analysis you should ask yourself some tough questions about what you have found out (for example O'Leary 2004: 186–7). These questions include:

1. Do my data adequately capture the concepts and relationships I want to investigate?
2. Have I adequately measured these concepts and relationships with my statistical tests?
3. Do my data and statistical tests support or not support my hypotheses?

4. How does this analysis fit with my conceptual model?
5. Have I answered my research questions?
6. Do I need to go back to the literature to explain my findings from another perspective? Are there other ways I can interpret my findings? What did I not find out that I expected to find out? What did I find out that I didn't expect to find out?
7. Do I need to do further research to answer my research questions?
8. What have I learnt about my research setting, research methods, research questions or theory? What can this contribute to future research?

Along with your data and your analysis, the answers to these questions will provide the basis for your findings, discussion and conclusions when you present or write up your research.

 ### Interpreting your data

Your first key task is to relate your data to the research questions you set out to investigate – making sure that the data you have collected are relevant to your research questions; as mentioned in the introduction, this is not always the case in research. **Chapters 10** and **11** presented a number of statistical techniques you can use to interrogate your data, ranging from simple descriptive statistics to advanced multivariate techniques. Applying these techniques rigorously, however, is no guarantee that your data have construct validity – they measure the concepts and/or relationships you set out to investigate – or face validity – they measure what you think they measure. This is a matter of judgement and hence research skill, rather than number-crunching.

You will also need to think about how you will identify the most important and relevant data to support your arguments. This can be a problem in both quantitative and qualitative research, because you will have usually gathered a lot more data than you can make sense of. If you have used a quantitative approach such as secondary analysis, survey or experiment, you are likely to begin your interpretation swamped by numbers – many numbers, raw data, tables, statistical formulae, statistical outputs. This may be too many numbers for you to be able to see the forest for the trees, when you are writing up your research report or presenting your findings. Your reader will have no chance.

No matter how interesting you think each piece of data is, do not become a train spotter. The data are nothing – your interpretation is everything. Try to focus first on those data that will help you to answer your research questions. A good way to get started on this is to reduce your data so you can identify the most *important* patterns in your data, not every possible pattern. One of Kate's former colleagues called this 'holding down the data and torturing it until it surrenders'!

Since most of us find visual data easier to interpret than numbers, you might try converting your raw data into charts, graph, figures and tables. You can present many data more clearly in the form of charts or graphs, tables and figures. Most computer software, whether specialised statistical software, spreadsheet software or word-processing software, lets you create illustrations from your data. These should relate back to your conceptual framework and hence back to each of your research questions. You should generally present your data in the same order as your research questions (**Chapter 3**), which will determine the structure of your literature review, conceptual framework and so on.

The main dangers of this for students are that they waste too much time trying to get things to look 'just right', for example three-dimensional charts when two-dimensional would do, and they try to create a graph or chart for every possible aspect of the data, so inducing 'graph fatigue'. Try to create just the right amount of graphics to identify the story your data are telling. These are like the illustrations in a book – try to make 'your book' relatively grown-up rather than a children's picture book.

Tables

A **table** presents data in rows and columns of numbers and/or words. It is the most basic form of exhibit. 'Tables communicate precise numerical information to readers' (Dunleavy 2003: 165). You should organise the layout of any table systematically, with the columns and rows in some logical order such as largest to smallest or most important to least important.

You can usually find many uses for tables in your project report. Tables seldom show raw data; they usually show data that have been processed in some way, for example to summarise or describe data or findings in compact form. Tables of raw data are rarely helpful in interpreting your data with respect to your research questions. If you look at academic research reported in high-quality academic journals such as the *Academy of Management Journal* or the *Administrative Science Quarterly*, you will see that the first table in most of these articles presents an overview of the key concepts and the relationships between them. This is a good idea for you when you are interpreting your data, before you start looking at the results of any statistical tests. The three things commonly reported in such a table are:

1. A measure of central tendency, such as the mean
2. A measure of dispersion, such as the standard deviation
3. A measure of bivariate relationships, such as Pearson's product moment correlation.

Such a table is invaluable to an experienced researcher, since he or she can often predict the significant findings and potential problems with the data based on this table alone, even before you present the results of any statistical tests. **Table 13.1**, from a project investigating the link between communication and group conflict, shows the means, standard deviations and correlations.

Table 13.1 A descriptive table for your variables

	Variable	Mean	SD	Pearson's product moment correlation					
				1	2	3	4	5	6
1	Face-to-face contact	13.4	3.1	1.00					
2	Telephone contact	10.2	5.1	.56	1.00				
3	Email contact	18.1	3.5	−.21	−.31	1.00			
4	Liking	4.5	1.01	.47	.20	−.36	1.00		
5	Preference	3.2	.87	.36	.33	.21	.39	1.00	
6	Attachment	3.5	.98	.09	.15	.22	.56	.37	1.00

In fact, when you look at **Table 13.1**, the data suggest that face-to-face communication and telephone communication are associated with lower group conflict, but email communication is a bit more ambiguous. Perhaps this is because in the group studied, people who talk to each other face to face tend to talk to each other on the phone as well, but people who email do not communicate in other ways.

Charts and graphs

Charts and graphs present numeric data effectively, especially if you want to look for patterns that tell a story. A **chart** is the term typically used for a figure that presents relationships among two or more independent variables. A **graph** is the term typically used for one that presents relationships among one or more sets of independent and dependent variables, especially where data follow a linear pattern. Microsoft Excel and other statistical programs make it easy to explore a range of charts. You should avoid 'dumbing down the data' too much (for example endless pie charts) and making it look like the front page of *USA Today*. Dunleavy (2003: 173) lists eight types of charts and graphs commonly used in research, which are shown in **Table 13.2**.

When you create your graphics, you should follow good practice (for example Dunleavey 2003: 163–4):

1. Label each exhibit with a heading or caption that clearly describes what is being shown.
2. Number each exhibit uniquely and systematically, preferably with a chapter number and unique figure number, for example **Figure 4.1**, **Table 17.2**.

Table 13.2 Some common charts and graphs

Type	Use to present	Example
Scatterplot (X-Y) chart	The relationship between an independent and one or more dependent variables	Ice cream sales versus average monthly temperature
Line graph	The relationship between time and one or more dependent variables	Sales of Maylor's *Project Management* by month
Vertical bar chart	Discontinuous time-series data	Monthly sales of male deodorants
Horizontal bar chart	Non-time-series categorical data	Amount of time taken to complete activities
Grouped bar chart	Several discontinuous time-series data	Sales of the top three management books by month
Stacked bar chart	Relative shares of multiple categories	Share of grocery spending by different food categories by year for ten years
Pie chart	Shares of a single overall category	Companies by number of employees in your sample
Layer chart	Several continuous time-series (or other continuous) data	Aggregate sales in three industrial sectors over the past 100 years

3. Label the elements of the exhibit clearly, for example table columns, chart legends and the units of measurement. Make sure that each exhibit is self-explanatory.
4. Give brief details of where the data come from.

This systematic approach will make your life a lot easier when you present your graphics or incorporate them into your final project report. You must also make sure that you refer to each exhibit and explain it in words in your main text.

 ## 13.1.2 Interpreting your analysis

Your second task is to interpret the results of your statistical analysis. The goal of interpretation is not just to present your data and statistical test results, but to tell the story of how these data and tests relate to your research question. The structure of this story is determined by your research questions.

If you have analysed your data using statistical techniques, you need to interpret the results of your statistical analysis and turn this interpretation into your findings. This means not only reporting key data and key aspects of your statistical analysis, but also explaining them with respect to your hypothesis (or whatever statement is driving your research).

For each statistical test, you should always make sure that you describe:

1. *Your data* – What data you are analysing, where they come from and any data reduction or other transformation that you have applied to the data.
2. *Your tests* – What statistical test you have used to analyse your data, any important assumptions and what software package you have used in the analysis. If you are using a statistical test that is unlikely to be familiar to your reader, you may need to include details in an appendix.
3. *Your results* – In enough detail so that your reader can interpret them for him or herself, but not so much detail that it is overwhelming. Include the key details, not every number reported in the analytical results. (If you don't know what those details are, you probably shouldn't be using that test.) You may need to include details of equations or outputs in an appendix if your reader might need to consult them in more or full detail.

As we mentioned above, this is where students often lose all sense of proportion. The purpose of gathering data is to answer your research questions, not to gather as much data as you can. Elegance is better than overkill. Similarly, the purpose of using statistical tests is not to test data in as many ways as possible, nor is it to apply as many different statistical tests as you can. One point in **Chapter 5** about the scientific approach was that ideally you would be able to specify the data and tests in advance of collecting data, to the point that you could mostly write up your project report before you ever started collecting data. Gathering a lot of data and testing it to death is an inductive strategy; data-mining has its place, but usually as the prelude to organised research rather than as part of it (it is sometimes referred to as 'data-gouging' for this reason).

What statistics should I be looking at?

A key part of interpreting your statistical tests will be to figure out what the most important and relevant statistical tests are, what they mean and how to present them. The statistics and statistical tests you are most interested in are those that help you to decide whether you have answered your research questions. If you have been following our advice for a systematic research process, you have translated your research questions into your research design by means of a conceptual diagram.

How you actually report your data and the story you tell will depend on your research project. If your research is mainly descriptive, you will present descriptive statistics, often in reduced form, and explain what they mean. If your research is more analytical, you need to present details of your analysis and relate it to your hypotheses. If your research is explanatory, you need to link it to the literature as well.

Figures

A good way to present your statistical tests (especially if you have more than one) is to integrate them with your conceptual model. Drawing your conceptual model and then showing which concepts and/or relationships you have tested and what the results are is a good way to do this. It is definitely a helpful way to begin visualising the story emerging from your research project.

Figure 13.1 illustrates a simple conceptual model with a single independent and a single dependent concept. Suppose you were investigating the link between communication and group conflict. You want to see whether the frequency with which people communicate with others in the same group, by face-to-face contact, telephone contact and email, affects intragroup contact. Your participants have kept a diary recording the number of contacts with other group members per week. You want to see whether the type and frequency of communication affect how much people like each other, who they prefer to work with on projects and how attached they feel to the group. For this study, you might present the conceptual model in a figure and indicate the results of the hypothesised relationships and the direction of those relationships.

Figure 13.1 shows that your main hypothesis is that the more frequently members of a group communicate with each other, the lower the amount of group conflict. An

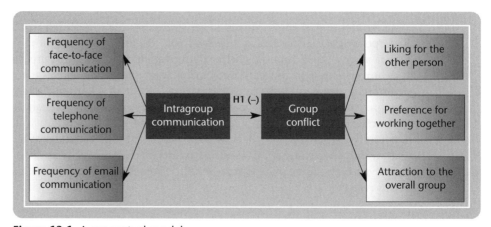

Figure 13.1 A conceptual model

experienced reader will also be able to tell from your figure what kind of data you have collected and what kind of statistical analysis you are likely to have used. Figures such as this are especially useful in showing relationships, which become essential when you have a complex conceptual model that your readers might find difficult to follow if you present it only in words. You can think of a good figure as being a road map for your audience.

Statistical significance

A word to the wise. The ways in which students interpret statistical significance (p) is a source of endless hilarity to examiners and gnashing of teeth by quantitative methods teachers. Do make sure that you understand what a test of statistical significance means and how to interpret the level of statistical significance. The 'golden rule' in business and management research for determining whether a result is statistically significant is $p < .05$, or a 1 in 20 chance that we are falsely accepting a relationship when one does not exist. Any test where the result is $p < .05$ is significant; any test where the result is $p > .05$ is not significant. There is no such thing as almost or nearly significant.

You should also make sure that you are following the conventions for highlighting statistical significance in tables, which we show below:

* $p < = .05$
** $p < = .01$
*** $p < = .001$

13.1.3 Interpreting your empirical research

Once you have interpreted your data and your statistical tests, you have started to create the most important elements of your findings. Your findings are a central element of your research project and hence of any presentation or report. Your third task is to 'close the loop' between these findings and your research questions, to see how well you have done your job as a researcher. This will lead to a discussion of what your empirical research means in light of your research questions, and, usually, the theory that informs and supports those research questions. Remember that your data illustrate those questions and that theory in a particular research setting and sample.

One important aspect of interpreting your findings is to see how well you have done against the criteria on which the quality of your research will be assessed. It is not enough for research to be provocative or interesting; it needs to be done in an appropriate way. One criterion is whether you are able to express your results in the context of the existing knowledge in your area of interest. Your combination of your results with this knowledge makes your research interesting – as demonstrated in **Chapter 8**. It also links with earlier parts of the study – the literature review in particular. You should also demonstrate how you have systematically addressed your research questions.

Although you will show most of the links to your literature in your discussion chapter, in the findings chapter you may need to briefly summarise relevant items to remind your readers what your hypotheses are and why you are predicting a relationship and its direction. In a quantitative research project, you will have started with a theory or conceptual framework that applies to your research topic and develop one or

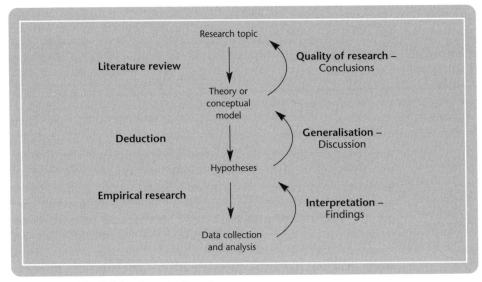

Figure 13.2 The link back to the literature

more hypotheses to test. Since you must find your theory somewhere, you have a link back from data to hypotheses to theory to your research problem. **Figure 13.2** is a simplified description of this process.

In order to close this loop, you need to see how the findings from your secondary analysis, survey or experiment fit with your literature. We described how to interpret the results of your statistical analysis above, to see whether your hypotheses are supported or not supported by your data. Since your hypotheses were deduced from your theory or conceptual framework, then you need to link this back to your research questions and the relevant theory (literature). This can help you to show that your data and analysis support your original framework, and whether you should explore any alternate frameworks to explore what you actually found out. You may need to conduct additional research – or at least identify the need to conduct additional research – as a result of this.

13.1.4 Quality in quantitative analysis

The final task in interpreting your evidence is to think about the quality of your research, primarily in terms of what you set out to do, but also with reference to the standards by which research is judged. The two lenses through which you might view your research are:

- *Scientific* – has it increased the reader's knowledge about/of the research problem and/or the method?
- *Advice* – what can the reader do/what is the reader empowered to do now that he/she has read the report?

Compared with qualitative researchers, quantitative researchers have a good deal of consensus on the scientific, or technical, criteria for judging quantitative research. In **Chapter 12**, we described the four criteria by which quantitative research is judged as:

1. *Validity* – are your results accurate?
2. *Reliability* – are your results repeatable?
3. *Generalisability* – do your results have meaning beyond your data set?
4. *Credibility* – does the 'story' that your results tell appear plausible?

You should also highlight any actual or potential problems with the research you actually did, versus the research you planned to do (especially deviations from your research design). These deviations, which might include problems with missing data, sample size, violation of statistical assumptions or your instrument, might affect what you found out. You should also reveal anything that might influence your interpretation of your findings. Perhaps you should have used a different statistical test or added (or taken away) variables to (from) your model. These sorts of issues become important in drawing conclusions from your research.

INTERPRETING YOUR QUALITATIVE RESULTS

In **Chapter 12**, we described a process for thematically analysing qualitative research. In qualitative analysis, you are inevitably interpreting your findings as you are analysing your data, because you need to build codes and categories from the raw data. This means that the interpretation aspect of this stage of your research process differs from this stage of a quantitative research project, where you can separate analysing and interpreting. As with quantitative research, the main issue you need to address is linking what you have done with your research questions.

13.2.1 Interpreting patterns

In interpreting qualitative research, you will need to link your data with a theory you have identified because of doing your research. This means that you will find it difficult, if not impossible, to adopt the same structured approach to interpreting your research as you did for quantitative research. In qualitative research, your main goal is to weave together a convincing narrative from what you have done. A major task in interpreting is to identify the data that support this story, so that it is grounded in your empirical data as well as in your thematic analysis (for example your use of Kolb's cycle or concept extraction, as described in **Chapter 12**).

As the qualitative research process is usually iterative, cycling back and forth between processes of conceptualisation, data collection and data analysis, you will need to combine these in your interpretation of what you have found out. In qualitative research, you end up creating a conceptual framework, rather than starting with one. Your conceptual framework will emerge from your data, rather than being 'borrowed' from the literature. This means that interpreting your qualitative research report can be difficult because you can identify many different ways to make sense of it. Two different ways for organising emerging ideas and themes are (Figure 13.3):

- *categorical* – reporting your categories and progressively focusing in or out. These categories can be predetermined or emerge from your data analysis
- *thematic* – presenting your overall conceptual framework, then reporting each theme.

Many students find it useful to refer to examples of qualitative research to see how other researchers have induced themes and conceptual frameworks from their rich, qualitative data. It is even more important to understand the 'story' emerging from your research, even if it is not the only story that could emerge. You are depending mainly on the story you tell, or the narrative you create, to communicate the essence of the research you have done, and tables and figures are not as much a part of that story.

Students usually find Miles and Huberman's *Qualitative Data Analysis* (1984) useful, because it presents many different ways to organise the interpretation of qualitative data. You should be able to find a good model for your own research among the many examples they present. You might also go back to an article or book you have consulted in your research project, and map how it structured its discussion.

Instead of basing your interpretation on data summarised in the form of tables and charts, as in quantitative research, you will usually need to work with the critical incidents, concepts or themes that emerge from your data. Many students have found it useful to use physical methods of working with keywords or phrases. For example, market researchers have developed sophisticated ways of sorting ideas written on

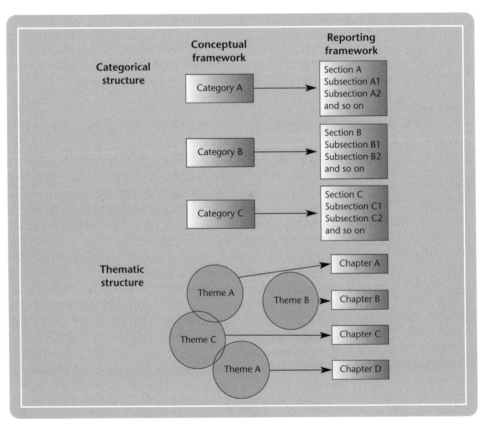

Figure 13.3 Categorical and thematic organisation

index cards, using either R-sort or Q-sort procedures. (The main differences in sorting approaches tend to be whether you start with every idea in the same structure and split them progressively into smaller and smaller groups, or whether you start with individual ideas and combine them progressively into larger groups.) Other qualitative researchers have found it useful to use whiteboards or Post-it notes at this stage.

Kate Fox's *Watching the English: The Hidden Rules of English Behaviour* (2003), an ethnographic study of the 'everyday' behaviour of English people, provides a good full-length example of organising around themes. Fox identifies two main themes from her investigation, which she describes as 'conversation codes' and 'behaviour codes'. These are then used to organise all subsequent subthemes, for example conversation codes start with 'the weather' and end with 'pub talk', while behaviour codes start with rules that apply at home and take in sex, food and work along the way. Conversation codes and behaviour codes represent 'meta-themes'.

Either way, it may be useful to refer back and forth to 'verbatim quoting' from your transcripts and observation notes, comparing them with your argument, and interpreting and commenting on that evidence as you go along. (You need to have carefully catalogued your data, as recommended in **Chapter 12**, to be able to trace your quotes back to the interview or observation they came from.)

13.2.2 Interpreting qualitative data

Qualitative research is also challenging for students who are using this approach for the first time, especially if this is their first major research project. The outcome of interpreting the qualitative research you have done is another story! If the role model for the quantitative researcher is objective, independent scientist, then the role model for the qualitative research as ethnographer has clear implications for how you interpret qualitative research. Your major task is to develop this story, or narrative, and figure out the best way to tell it.

Reading an account of qualitative research is much closer to reading a work of fiction, such as a novel, than reading a scientific report. You would probably be surprised to read the following in a quantitative report:

> As a single, 30 year old woman, I could uninhibitedly ask other women to go to lunch; however, asking the men, most of whom were also older than me, was not as comfortable and seemed to require more of a justification. (**Schultze** 2000)

Although all qualitative reports have more in common with each other than they do with quantitative reports, there are three important models of how to interpret and present your qualitative evidence:

- as a narrative
- as thick description
- as a personal journey.

Narrative

The narrative form is probably the closest that qualitative research comes to the quantitative approach, and may be a good choice if your research is more structured than unstructured. If you have used a relatively noninvolved qualitative design for your research such as indirect observation or secondary source data, your story may be a chronological story, which relates events – both in what you have studied and your research process – as they happened over time. If you develop your interpretation as a narrative, you may focus mostly on the factual details of what you observed and what it meant.

Thick description

If you have been more involved in your research setting, for example as a participant observer, you may want to include more of your own experience in interpreting your research. The style that is often associated with the more participative types of qualitative research is **thick description**, which incorporates how it felt for you to be doing research as well as what you observed. Thick description comes from the tradition of ethnographic research in anthropology (Geertz 1973), where researchers were describing people and contexts, such as the Pacific Islanders studied by Malinowski and Mead, with whom their readers were unfamiliar. Business and management researchers who are influenced by this tradition use thick description to describe less exotic situations, such as police patrols (Van Maanen 1982), scientific laboratories (Latour and Woolgar 1986), artificial intelligence research (Forsythe 2001) or even retirement homes (Ehrenreich 2002). Even though they are observing cultures much closer to home (for example Po Branson's *Nudist on the Late Shift*), they interpret the setting and events for their readers in much the same way.

The goal of thick description is to make your reader feel as though he or she is actually present in the research setting, and perhaps even as if he or she is doing the research. John van Maanen's *Tales of the Field* gives a number of vivid examples from his own experience as an ethnographer. You may describe the physical situation in detail, for example how it looked, felt, smelt and so on. For example, Diane Forsythe (2001: 170) was a participant observer in a computer lab where several incidents had occurred that made the atmosphere a bit tense for the women in the lab. In her discussion of how the women in the lab reacted to the installation of sexist screensavers, Forsythe describes how she herself reacted to the screensavers, eventually bringing the matter up with the head of the lab. She discusses the feelings and reactions not only of the people she was observing, but also her own reactions, and what these might mean in a wider context.

The reader might also note that Forsythe's work is vividly descriptive. When you read it, you can place yourself in the scene it describes: this style of writing could just as easily come from a novel or short story, and is completely different from the factual description found in a quantitative research report. Another difference is that Forsythe puts herself into the story as a major character and takes part in the action. This is a major break with quantitative research, where the researcher writes as an omniscient, neutral 'we', if at all. Especially in direct observation and participant observation, the researcher becomes an active character in the story being told in the research and, to some extent, your reader does too.

Personal journey

As noted above, some forms of qualitative research include the researcher as a major actor, rather than as an observer who mainly observes and reacts. In some forms of qualitative research, for example participative action research or cooperative inquiry, the researcher becomes as much an object of the study as the people in the organisation or context being studied. In this case, your interpretation of what you have done may focus on reflections on how you felt or changed during the research, as well as what you learnt/observed from the field study.

As in the study quoted above, Ulricke Schultze (2000) incorporated her experiences as a researcher into her description of what she saw. Like Forsythe, Schultze's report is vividly descriptive. She presents her reflections on what is going on (how can I interpret this, how does it make me feel) and her reflections on this reflection – a kind of hyperreflexivity that she describes as 'ex-pressing'. To give her reader a feel for reflexive research as a process rather than an outcome, she presents excerpts from her research diary in her report so that the reader gets a sense of the progress (or lack of progress) she was making at various points in the project. Again, this is very different from the mostly retrospective sense-making imposed on research done from a scientific perspective. (This is not to say that scientists never write in an ethnographic style. James Watson, for example, describes the discovery of the structure of DNA in very much this way. But scientists do this outside reporting research, usually in biographies written for popular audiences.)

You may want to talk to your project supervisor, and look at some previous project reports, before you decide how much of your own experience and reflections you need to incorporate when you are interpreting what you have done. Some academic supervisors will expect and/or encourage it, but some may find it inappropriate.

If you are using this as the basis for a report to your business sponsor, you should tread carefully! Your business sponsor may be completely uninterested in this aspect of your placement or sponsored project (although it is not completely unknown), and it can be politically risky for both yourself and the people in the organisation to reveal detailed information. The major exception would be, obviously, situations in which you were explicitly engaged to do action research or other similar research.

13.2.3 Linking your results to the literature

Because you are not basing your research plan on a deep exploration of the literature, in interpreting your qualitative research it is especially important to link what you have found to the literature. One criticism of qualitative research as currently practised is that too little of this linking is done, so there is very little accumulation of knowledge and much repetition. On the other hand, since you are inducing a conceptual model from your data whilst doing your research, as a qualitative researcher you should be in an excellent position to do a wide sweep for relevant literature, since you will have 'already found out what you are going to find out'.

Your interpretation may point towards particular themes or strands in the literature that might explain your findings or your findings might help to explain. You are moving in the opposite direction of the relationship between theory and data found in quantitative research. Again, it may be helpful to look at some examples of qualitative research on your topic for guidance in this area. There is no reason that a qualitative research project cannot be theoretically rich and use this richness to make sure that it is robust.

13.2.4 Quality in qualitative analysis

The last task in interpreting qualitative data is to assess your research against the standards you have set for your research project and the standards for qualitative research. There is much debate over whether qualitative research should be judged by the standards for qualitative research or those for quantitative research. The description in **Chapter 12** may be useful here.

One aspect of the scientific approach is that there is very little room for innovation or improvisation in the way you interpret and present your research. How you present your data and statistical analysis needs in some ways to stand by itself. On the other hand, the actual style of the writing – the aesthetic effect – matters little as long as you get the job done. Whilst there are wide variations in writing ability among quantitative researchers, this has little effect on the credibility of what they say (although it may affect the willingness of other people to read it in the first place). The scientific style intentionally effaces the researcher – rather than highlights his or her role in the research – the findings are what counts.

In qualitative research, especially in thick description or research as personal journey, the aesthetics of the writing style and presentation play an important role in how the quality of your research is assessed. If you are writing a report using qualitative research, you usually mean your reader to take it seriously as a narrative and as a text. You are also being assessed on the additional criterion – how well is this project report written? This includes the quality of your writing, as well as its effect on your reader. Some of the criteria applied to assessing qualitative research, as well as validity and reliability, may be:

- *Aesthetic* – what reactions does it arouse in the reader?
- *Moral* – does the research raise or clarify any moral issues relating to the research problem and/or the reader him/herself?
- *Activist* – what can the reader do/what is the reader empowered to do now that he/she has read the report?

13.3 DEVELOPING FINDINGS AND RECOMMENDATIONS

We advocate that you articulate what you have found in your research so that you have a firmer basis for your findings and recommendations. Here we present a structured way of doing this which will be useful for presenting interim findings and writing up your research.

13.3.1 Summarising what you have found

A good way to make sense of what you have found out, both at the level of your practical problem and the higher level of your theoretical problem, is to summarise what you have found out through your research. We first need to differentiate between the different elements of the process – expectations, findings, discussions and conclusions. An example is given in **Table 13.3**.

Your **expectations** come from the objectives you have defined for your research

Table 13.3 Outcomes of your project

	Quantitative study	Qualitative study
Expectations	Over 60% of people will be aware of the regulations concerning the labelling of GM foods	People will be keen to know about what their food contains and will actively seek out information about it
Findings	32.5% of people were aware of the regulations concerning the labelling of GM foods	The behaviour of the people we interviewed differed from their stated intentions, in that they did not actively seek out information, yet claimed to do so
Discussion	Considerably less people than expected were aware of the regulations concerning labelling. The reasons could be …	Despite the apparent importance to people of GM issues, they do not reflect this in practice. The reasons could be …
Conclusions	Awareness campaigns on food labelling have been less successful than claimed	The effort needed to gain information is more than the perceived benefits. Information needs to be more readily available

project. These are formed primarily from theory, literature or, in many business cases, documented best practice. These provide the basis or first point of reference against which you are going to be making comparisons. The literature may include similar studies that you are replicating, or inference from theory. For instance, studies have shown that in the absence of major inertia effects (such as with personal bank accounts), retail customers will change their buying habits if they are dissatisfied. Grounding your work on this is a good starting point. You will then conduct your study to determine whether, in the particular circumstance you are considering, this is true.

Your *findings* focus on your data and analysis. For example, in a quantitative study, your findings chapter will present your data and show whether they support or do not support your hypothesis. You should make sure that you have interpreted your findings with little editorial (that is, personal opinion rather than supported comment) – they should not require elaboration at this point. When you write up these findings in your project report or present them to an audience, you will need to use signposting and other assistance to help your reader through them.

Part of your task is to speculate on why you found what you did or offer an alternate explanation. This is the job of your *discussion*, not your findings. Your discussion places your findings in the context of your expectations, highlighting similarities and differences. That is, where your findings support your initial expectations or existing theory, they should be noted as such. Where there are differences, these should also be noted and, where possible (as shown in **Table 13.3**), an attempt at some explanation provided.

The discussion needs to be well structured, and you should focus on:

● Areas of weakness and opportunities for improvement in the situation you have studied, for instance if your study indicates that a firm has not identified particular market sectors of interest, your comments, based on the literature, could show how its processes could be improved to make sure that these opportunities are not missed in future.

● Areas where the theory or best practice does not appear to work, for instance one student project commented that the application of ISO 9000 in a small firm led to a massive increase in bureaucracy that was in danger of putting the firm out of business. The literature appeared almost universally to suggest that ISO 9000 was a good thing, with very few authors identifying the major downsides or how these could be avoided. The student was able to provide a critique of the literature on this basis – that the 'theory' was deficient in some way.

These plus the main issues that can be claimed directly from your results are then fed into the conclusions of your work. Your *conclusion* then takes these discussions on a stage further, with the implications of your findings being stated.

13.3.2 Preparing a summary table

Many students find having to summarise their discussion in the form of a table most helpful, as it is easy to drown in the apparent complexity of the issues being dealt with. **Table 13.4** shows the format for the summary table – as used to reintegrate the findings of the case with the literature in **Chapter 8**. The process is summarised in **Figure 13.4**.

13.3.3 Problems with interpretation

Students who have an easy time collecting and analysing data often have a hard time with making sense of it relative to their conceptual framework and research questions, and vice versa. This may be because some people are more comfortable with fact and others with speculation. You should strive, however, for a balance of the two in your research.

The main problems that examiners find in project reports usually happen when students fail to assess the business and management research on the topic, fail to take a critical perspective on this work or fail to take a critical perspective on their own work. We summarise these problems below:

Table 13.4 A summary table

Issue		Theoretical view/best practice/ expectations	Empirical view/reality/findings
1			
2	List the main	For each issue provide	For each issue provide
3	issues that have	a very brief summary	a very brief summary
	arisen from	of what you expected	of what you found
4	your work	to find, based on the	
5		literature	

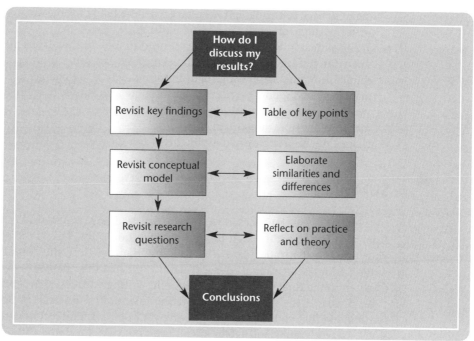

Figure 13.4 Tasks and outputs for your discussion chapter

- *'Told you so'* – examiners find little more annoying than someone starting off with a (usually overgeneralised) hypothesis, and then attempting to prove this is correct, without any critical analysis of either the idea or the alternatives. This is a solution in search of a problem and rarely makes for good research. It usually happens because a student has fallen in love with a concept, idea, method, model or practice and then looked for a situation in which to apply it. It is much better if you investigate the practical or theoretical problem, identify a number of solutions, evaluate these solutions, and then recommend a particular solution based on your work, even if you do have a particular solution in mind when you start.
- *'Everybody else is stupid'* – where a very limited literature review has been carried out, it is easy for critical analysis to consist of personal opinion. This can occur when commenting on the behaviour of individuals, for example, and then relating this to the expectations you had of their actions. Similarly, for literature, it is always worth considering the context of published work, the associated methods and using these as points for comparison, to gain more insight into the findings.
- *'I'm confused'* – where an author does recognise his/her own confusion over an issue, and presents two sides of an issue, whilst appearing to support both. Where there is no clear preference, this is of interest in itself, provided you recognise it and state why this is so.
- *'Therefore, the world is flat'* – the danger of overgeneralising findings has already been discussed in **Chapter 9**, but is bad for the student, as it shows a lack of understanding of the limitations of whatever method set they are using.
- *'We found nothing of interest'* – often after spending a long time with a project, some of the more interesting findings are lost, as individuals cease to treat them as novel any more. This can result in your work not representing the true value of your find-

ings. Go back to the data, if necessary with the help of someone who is not familiar with the study, and re-evaluate the findings.

- *'It's so obvious'* – well if it is, then you need to look further. If the answer is obvious, was your research question worth asking? Whilst some findings are wonderfully simple in nature, expressing them in terms such as 'all change initiatives need top management support to succeed' has become a truism. It is at times like this when you need to look beyond these basics and be more specific. Who in top management? What does support in this context really mean? What are the cases where change has been successful despite this or not successful even though it was in place?

SUMMARY

In this chapter, we have described how to finish 'doing' your research project by going from your data back through to your research questions. This is the opposite journey you took to get to your data and it is important to close this loop before you start writing your research report. After you have finished this chapter, you should be ready to go on to the final phase of your research, writing your research report.

We discussed the model for interpreting quantitative research in **Section 13.1**. We recommend that you start by interpreting your data with respect to your research questions. Charts, graphs and tables are all useful devices for doing this. You should then move on to interpreting your statistical analysis, perhaps by mapping your results against your conceptual model to see what parts of it your empirical research supports and which parts it doesn't. You should then compare your research with the theory that surrounds your research questions. What did you find that you didn't expect, what did you expect to find that you didn't? You should conclude this stage by considering the quality of your research project. What is good about it? What could be improved?

In a qualitative research report, on the other hand, your focus will be on organising and structuring your words, so that your reader can follow your analysis and to demonstrate the dependability of your research process. You need to decide how to organise your report, identify any schematic presentations of your analysis and tie your findings to your research topic. You will also need to decide how you will communicate your research, whether you present your research as a relatively straightforward narrative, thick description or a personal journey.

Finally, we described the chapter in your project report in which you make sense of your findings, which is your discussion chapter in quantitative research but may be integrated into the description of your research in a qualitative report. We suggest some areas you might want to cover and present some strategies for presenting your discussion chapter.

ANSWERS TO KEY QUESTIONS

How can I turn my analysis into answers to my research questions?

- Turn data into findings by comparison with prior expectations (quantitative research) or other scenarios (qualitative research)
- Interpret your findings in your discussion

How do I present my analysis?

● For quantitative data and analysis, use graphs, charts, figures and tables

● For qualitative data and analysis, use stories and pictures

How do I use the literature to support my findings and discussion?

● Link key themes back to your literature review to provide points of contrast and similarity

● Link forward to new questions raised by your study that have not been answered by the existing literature

How do I discuss my findings?

● By provision of points of similarity and difference between the findings and the expectations

REFERENCES

Dunleavy, Patrick. 2003. *Authoring a PhD: How to Plan, Draft, Write and Finish a Doctoral Thesis or Dissertation*. Basingstoke: Palgrave Macmillan.

Ehrenreich, Barbara. 2002. *Nickel and Dimed: Undercover in Low-wage America*. London: Granta Books.

Forsythe, Diana E. 2001. *Studying Those Who Study Us: An Anthropologist in the World of Artificial Intelligence*. Palo Alto, CA: Stanford University Press.

Fox, Kate. 2003. *Watching the English: The Hidden Rules of English Behaviour*. London: Hodder & Stoughton.

Geertz, Clifford. 1973. *Interpretation of Cultures*. New York: Basic Books.

Latour, Bruno and Woolgar, Steve. 1986. *Laboratory Life: The Construction of Scientific Facts*. Princeton: Princeton University Press.

Miles, Matthew B. and Huberman, A. Michael. 1984. *Qualitative Data Analysis*. Beverly Hills, CA: Sage.

O'Leary, Zina. 2004. *The Essential Guide to Doing Research*. London: Sage.

Schultze, Ulrike, 2000. A confessional account of an ethnography about knowledge work, *MIS Quarterly*, **24**(1): 213–42.

Van Maanen, J. 1982. 'Fieldwork on the beat'. In Von Maanen, J., Dabbs, J.M. Jr. and Faulkner, R.R. (eds) *Varieties of Qualitative Research*. Thousand Oaks, CA: Sage.

ADDITIONAL RESOURCES

Bell, Judith and Opie, Clive. 2002. *Learning from Research: Getting More From Your Data*. Maidenhead: Open University Press.

Bryman, Alan and Burgess, R.G. (eds) 1994. *Analysing Qualitative Data*. London: Routledge.

Denscombe, Martyn. 2003. *The Good Research Guide for Small-Scale Social Research Projects*, 2nd edn. Maidenhead: Open University Press.

Denzin, Norman and Lincoln, Y. (eds) 1994. *Handbook of Qualitative Research*. Thousand Oaks, CA: Sage.

Eisenhardt, Kathleen M. 1991. Better stories and better constructs: The case for rigor and comparative logic, *Academy of Management Review*, **16**(3): 620–7.

Locke, Karen D. 2000. *Grounded Theory in Management Research*. London: Sage.

Discussion questions

1. Why shouldn't you assume that your data will 'speak for themselves'?
2. Is it a good idea to present quantitative research in a nonstandard format?
3. Are all numbers forbidden in a qualitative research report? Even page numbers?
4. How should you present case study or mixed-method research?
5. Why should you separate the findings, discussion and conclusions in a quantitative report? Can you separate them in a qualitative report?
6. What should you talk about in your discussion chapter?

Workshop

Task

Choose one of the core articles from your literature review.

Read through the article.

Now read through it again and:

1. draw a square around key terms
2. underline key themes
3. circle key transition words

which relate to the analysis of data.

Copy these onto Post-it notes and stick them onto the wall.

- Can you identify the structure?
- Can you rearrange them into another, better structure?

Relevant chapters

13 Answering your research questions
14 **Describing your research**
15 Closing the loop

4

Key challenges

- Interpreting your findings and making recommendations
- **Writing and presenting your project**
- Reflecting on and learning from your research

Relevant chapters

1 What is research?
2 Managing the research process
3 What should I study?
4 How do I find information?

1

Key challenges

- Understanding the research process
- Taking a systematic approach
- Generating and clarifying ideas
- Using the library and internet

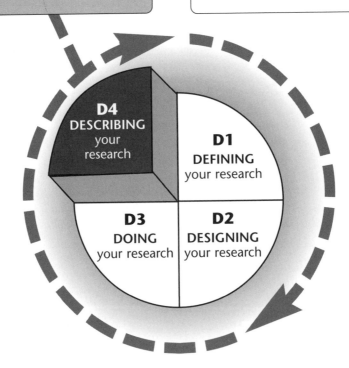

Relevant chapters

9 Doing field research
10 Analysing quantitative data
11 Advanced quantitative analysis
12 Analysing qualitative data

3

Key challenges

- Practical considerations in doing research
- Using simple statistics
- Undertanding multivariate statistics
- Interpreting interviews and observations

Relevant chapters

5 Scientist or ethnographer?
6 Quantitative research designs
7 Designing qualitative research
8 Case studies/multi-method design

2

Key challenges

- Choosing a model for doing research
- Using scientific methods
- Using ethnographic methods
- Integrating quantitative and qualitative research

Describing your research
Writing up your project report

Key questions

- How should I report my research?
- What are the differences between a report on quantitative research and one on qualitative research?
- What are the differences between an academic and a business report?
- How can I manage the writing process effectively?
- How do I write and edit the project report?
- How do I prepare for an oral presentation or viva?

Learning outcomes

At the end of this chapter, you should be able to:

- Prepare your project report, and deliver a written report, oral presentation or viva
- Understand how to vary the project structure and style to suit a particular audience
- Develop a detailed writing plan

Contents

INTRODUCTION

Once you have collected and analysed your data, you may feel as though your project is practically complete, but – don't relax just yet! Writing up your research project is equally as important as actually doing the research. Leaving enough time to write up your research is critical to satisfying your stakeholders and getting a good mark. No research project is really finished until other people know what you have found out; they won't know until you tell them. 'Research is judged not by what you did, but by your ability to report on what you did'(O'Leary 2004: 205).

Your supervisor and business sponsor can only assess your project report. A poorly presented report on even the most brilliant research will underwhelm your examiners. On the other hand, a well-presented report may not totally make up for an imperfect project, but it may tip the scales between passing and failing. How well you define, design and do your project report is a critical aspect of your research. Moreover, anything worth doing is worth doing well: a good project report is something you can be proud of, and writing well is a valuable skill.

To prepare a good report, you need to visualise your finished product – is it a written research report, an oral presentation, a viva, or a combination of these? Your report's structure and content should reflect the characteristics of a good project report, but they will also depend on your project requirements and assessment criteria.

Section 14.1 presents the structure and content of a generic project report, which you can vary to reflect your research approach or customise for a business report. An academic audience will be interested mainly in your findings and theoretical contribution, but a business audience will be interested in your recommendations and practical contribution. If you must present your research to both academic and business audiences, you may need to consider how they differ and what they have in common.

Section 14.2 describes how to manage the writing process better. This is especially important if you are writing a long or technically complex report, or if you are writing with other people. If you have been writing all along, then well done you. You should have enough time to write, edit and polish up your report into a brilliant piece of work without staying up all night consuming massive amounts of caffeine and chocolate or panicking. If you haven't, you should find some practical tips and strategies for rescuing your project or keeping it on track.

Section 14.3 focuses on the technical skills you need to write for either an academic or a business audience. You can use ideas about rhetoric, voice and style to create a high-quality project report, rather than one that just gets the job done.

After you have read this chapter, you should be able to visualise your finished report and work towards achieving it. You should be able to develop a writing plan, develop a detailed outline of your presentation and identify the most appropriate content, structure and style for your audience.

14.1 DELIVERING YOUR PROJECT REPORT

Writing is essential to each stage of the research process (O'Leary 2004: 206), not just the end stage. This is critical to 'beginning with the end in mind'– this is the end you should have been keeping in mind. Earlier we recommended that you visualise your finished project report early on in your project and work backwards to see what you must do to get there. Now you should treat your final write-up as a mini-research project. There are three issues you should think about now:

- *Defining your report* – How are you going to present your research? Why are you writing your report? Who will read it? What should go in and what should you leave out?
- *Designing your report* – What are the major themes of your report? How should you structure your report? What is the main evidence you need to include in your report? What other evidence do you need to support this?
- *Doing your report* – How can you put together a rough draft? How can you turn this rough draft into a first draft? How can you edit this into a finished report?

Most students find the first hurdle not how to write (style), but what to write (content and structure). Although you may need to learn new technical skills to write your project report, you can use a reference book such as *The Oxford Style Manual* (Ritter 2002) to find the answers to specific questions about formal writing such as referencing, page numbering, tables of contents and so on. You are unlikely to find a technical manual that tells you specifically how to write a report for your own unique project. There may be more than one way to do things, depending on what you are writing about and who you are writing it for.

We begin by identifying generic contents and structure for a typical project report. We then explain how you can vary this generic report for an academic or business audience, or to report quantitative or qualitative research.

14.1.1 Visualising your finished product

In our experience, visualising your finished project report *before* you start writing it – ideally even before you start researching it – makes it much easier to manage your writing process and produce a high-quality report. As you learnt in the defining stage of the overall research project – if you do a good job defining your project report, it will be easier to write it; if you drift into it without a plan, you will end up wasting your time and effort.

Beginning with the end in mind is especially important if you are preparing a formal or lengthy written report or presentation. Your project report may be the longest and/or most complex piece of writing you have done, or indeed may ever do if you are writing up a final-year project or dissertation. It is usually impossible to keep everything in your head at once when you are writing a long or complex project report.

The more you can apply a structured process for visualising, outlining and writing your project report or presentation, the easier it will be to see whether you have accomplished it. Similarly, if you are writing with other people, it is easier to work to a clear vision, and you can only achieve this if you can articulate it. If you are a type 2 student (see **Chapter 2**), you may have been able to muddle along in writing essays, coursework or short project reports where you can keep everything in your head and complete the process in one or two writing sessions. However, you may have to abandon your type 2 ways to do a good job on your project report, to avoid the usual 'beginning, muddle, end'.

The key questions to ask yourself here are:

- How will you present your research?
- Who will read this report?
- Why are they reading it?
- What do they expect to get out of it?

How will you present your research?

The first step in visualising your research project is to think about how you will present it. What form will it take – a written project report, an oral presentation, a viva, or more than one of these? Some of the most common formats for research reports are:

- Short project report – 20 pages
- Long project report – 100 pages
- Brief oral presentation – 15 minutes
- Long oral presentation – 1 hour
- Viva.

This will affect not only how you physically present your research, but also how much depth you can go into and what you need to include. Your project requirements should tell you how you will present your research and how it will be assessed. You should also have agreed with your business sponsor, if you have one, what they expect as far as any additional reports or presentations in your project brief.

Who will read your project report?

Besides the physical format, O'Leary (2004: 206) suggests that you should visualise your research as a conversation with your audience. It is important to identify this audience before you start writing or preparing your project report. Who is your ideal or actual **reader**? You need to target not only the contents and structure of your report, but also its style to your audience.

Most project reports are written for an examiner and/or business sponsor, as we discuss in **Chapter 15**. However, your project report may be read by your project supervisor, your academic advisors, your business sponsors, the people who have supported or participated in your research and the wider community of business and management researchers and managers. These different readers may not all bring the same knowledge, assumptions or expectations to your report.

Why are they reading it?

Your academic readers will be more interested in the conceptual, rather than the practical, side of your research problem. They may be less intrigued by the specific details of your answers than the theoretical aspects; the empirical context of your research may be no more than 'local colour'. In presenting your research to an academic audience, therefore, you should focus on showing how you have translated your research topic into research questions, and designed your research to answer those questions. Your report will focus on developing and evaluating your knowledge claim and presenting evidence to support or disprove it.

On the other hand, your business readers will be more interested in the practical, rather than the conceptual, side of your research. Your empirical analysis and recommendations will be more intriguing to them than the most elegant theory or model. Therefore, in presenting your research to business readers, you should focus especially on the practical problem: your analysis, potential solutions and recommendations.

What do you want your reader to get out of it?

Academic readers and business readers will actually read a project report or listen to a project presentation very differently. Your academic readers will expect you to be comprehensive and thorough – within the project guidelines of course. They may even turn to your references first, before they read anything else. On the other hand, the more senior the manager you are presenting your research to, the less time he or she will actually spend reading it. Most senior managers, in fact, will probably only read your report's executive summary or sit through a brief presentation, rather than go into the details.

Given these differences, you may wonder if you can get by with writing just one report if you are presenting your research to both academic and business audiences. Although you may be able to identify common themes and elements across both audiences, it is probably best to think at this stage of your target being two different reports, with some differences but as much in common as possible. We will talk about differences in content, structure and style between academic and business reports in **Section 14.1.3**.

14.1.2 A generic report structure

Once you have visualised your project report and your audience, you can define the basic parameters of your project report – the structure and content. This will help you to answer the following questions:

- How should you structure your report?
- What are the major themes of your report?
- What is the main evidence you need to include in your report?
- What other evidence do you need to support this?

Students often find getting started difficult because they do not know what the project report should contain or how it should be structured. A short informal report and a long formal report will differ substantially in details, but the structure and content will be similar. Your reader expects to read a project report in a familiar structure that presents information in a logical order (Denscombe 2003: 291). We describe this below as a generic project report, which we will show you how to vary depending on how you did your research and your audience.

We start off with the model that would be most appropriate for research that takes the scientific approach, since scientists have developed a standard report. The model that an ethnographer would take is an improvisation on this standard report to reflect the unique characteristics of the research.

Based on these elements, which we will describe below, you should try to develop an outline for your project report before you start writing. Even if you need to revise it later, the process of outlining will help you to clarify your thinking and visualise the finished project report. As you prepare your outline, think not only about what you want to say, but what evidence you want to include, in the form of charts, tables and figures, and how you will include these in your project report. This is also a good time to think about what material you need to include in the body of your report, and what should be put in appendices, especially if you have a limit on the number of words and/or pages in your report.

If you are writing up a report that takes the scientific approach, all you have left to do is write and edit it; if you are writing up a report from the ethnographic perspective, you need to think about how to make these elements part of your story or narrative. Many of the elements will be exactly the same for both kinds of reports, for example the prelims and endmatter should be identical – the main variation will be in the core chapters of the report.

Main text

The **main text** of your report includes everything between the first word of your introduction and the last word of your conclusions. Your main text should be divided into sections (short report) or chapters (long report) that are signalled by headings. You may want to check whether your project requirements for word or page length refer to just this main text or the entire project report.

In a generic project report, your main text would include these sections or chapters in this order:

- *Abstract* – A brief overview of the research problem, argument, themes
- *Introduction* – The problem this research addresses and why it was worth doing
- *Literature review* – What other people found out about this problem
- *Research methods* – How I/we investigated this problem
- *Findings* – What I/we found out about the problem and what it means
- *Discussion* – What our findings say about the more general research problem that I/we investigated
- *Conclusions* – What I/we now know about this problem as a result of this research project.

Introduction

Your **introduction** is an overview of your entire project report. It tells your reader what you did in your project, why it was important, and what you found out. The introduction should, at a minimum, tell the reader the background, aims, definitions and overview of your report:

- What your research is about
- Why your research is important and interesting
- What your research questions are
- How you answered those questions
- What your main findings were
- A preview of the rest of the paper.

It is usually easier to write your introduction last, even though it comes first in the main text. Word for word, your readers will probably pay more attention to your intro-duction than any other part of your project, and it pays to put in a lot of effort here to get things just right. Imagine that you have just this chapter to tell someone what your research is about.

Some students believe that if you tell your readers what you found out in your intro-duction, the reader will not want to read any farther. A research report is not a detective novel: you need to report your findings early on, rather than leaving them to the last chapters.

Literature review

In the introduction, or immediately following it, you should include a **literature review** that provides a critical analysis of the business and management research on your research topic. We discussed doing a literature search and writing a literature review in depth in **Chapter 4**, and mentioned Chris Hart's two excellent books, *Doing a Literature Review* (1998) and *Doing a Literature Search* (2001).

Your literature review should show a critical perspective on business and management research on your research topic, establish any conceptual framework you plan to use (theories, models, concepts, relationships between concepts) and provide the basis for your research questions. If your readers are unfamiliar with your research topic, after they have read your literature review they should know (O'Leary 2004:78–9):

1. The developments in the field
2. If the researcher is credible
3. If the topic is worth studying.

The structure of your literature review may follow a deductive logic, which Dunleavy (2003) describes as a **focus-down strategy**. This structure starts with a broad overview of the topic and progressively narrows it down. This is in line with the hierarchy of concepts model introduced in **Chapter 3** and is based on how scientists report their research, in keeping with the scientific ideal. However, you are not required to follow this model. Your literature review may be more convincing if you compare and contrast themes in the literature you are reviewing. The literature review is a concep-tual exploration of your research problem and research questions: once you have finished this chapter, your reader should be able to anticipate your findings, even though you have not yet described how you gathered and analysed your data or what your findings were.

If you wait to start your literature review until you are writing up, you may find that analysing and synthesising the relevant academic literature is just as difficult and time-consuming as analysing your data. You may find it difficult to do a good job on both at once. It is much easier if you have been constantly revisiting the literature as you gather data, analyse it and interpret your findings. Mistakes that students commonly make in writing literature reviews in their final report include:

● Being uncritical or hypercritical
● Lacking focus or having too many focuses
● Not linking the literature review to their research questions
● Not leaving enough time to search and review the literature
● Using the wrong sources.

Research methods

Once you have established your research questions in your literature, you are ready to describe how you will answer them in your **research methods** chapter. You should describe your research design (*how*) and your sources of data (*who* and *where*). You need to tell your reader how the research problem was investigated and why this was the best way to investigate it.

Your research methods chapter should explain how you investigated your research problem and why you used the particular methods and techniques that you did (Bell 1999). Say what you did, but don't feel compelled to report in detail everything you did. You may also be expected to address issues such as validity and reliability in this section. Key aspects of your research you should address include:

● Why you collected the data you did
● What data you collected, where you collected them, when they were collected and how they were collected
● How you analysed the data
● Why you choose these methods
● Strengths and weaknesses of your choices, perhaps with reference to alternative approaches that you might have taken, but didn't.

You may also need to include references for your specific research techniques, for example if you are using a case study, Stake (1995) or Yin (2003), or for action research, Stringer (1996). If you have chosen a well-established set of techniques and procedures for investigating your particular research topic, this may be a fairly short chapter. If there is controversy over the best method, or you have used a nontraditional method, you may need to delve deeper into your research approach.

Some students use their research methods chapter for an extended discussion of research philosophy (**Chapter 5**). The scientific versus ethnographic approach discussion in **Chapter 5** may be relevant here, if you are taking a nonstandard approach and need to justify it. Otherwise, unless you have been instructed by your project guidelines or academic supervisor to discuss research philosophy as part of this chapter (or you are a postgraduate research student), it is usually a good idea to leave it out. It is extremely difficult to get the discussion right, and even experts haven't managed to agree on the core issues.

You may want to use your research methods chapter to describe the research setting and sample, although you may have done this in the introduction for a project that started with a practical problem or qualitative research. This may include a description of the company or industry you studied, how you identified and selected your sample, details of your sample, including population, sampling frame, sample, sample size, and related issues such as response rates and nonrespondent bias.

Findings

Your **findings** chapter will introduce your reader to your data (Denscombe 2003: 294). This chapter tells what you found out in your research and what it means. You need to make sense of the data you have collected in your study, and relate them to both the theoretical literature and the overall research question or problem. Dunleavy (2003) suggests that if you think of this chapter as the answer to 'what does the reader need to know?', then you will focus on reducing the data and communicating them clearly. If your project is data-driven, you may need to summarise your analysis in the main text, in the form of charts and tables, and provide the full analysis and data in an appendix. As we covered this in **Chapter 13**, you should look at this chapter again if you get stuck. Here, to understand what you need to include in your findings, you might spend some time thinking about:

● What is the main evidence you need to include in your report?
● What other evidence do you need to support this?
● What are the major themes of your report?

Discussion

You should also provide a **discussion** of your findings, whether in your findings chapter or as a separate chapter. You need to present your findings before you analyse them and interpret them in light of your research questions (Denscombe 2003). As well as presenting the details of what you found out, you will also need to discuss what they mean within the broader context of the research project, including the theoretical literature and/or the frameworks presented in the literature review. This chapter should describe whether your research answered your research questions, or how it addressed the research problem. Your discussion will focus on your findings with respect to the conceptual models and the literature. It will also look beyond the current research project:

● Your main/most important findings
● How your results relate to the literature
● Any weaknesses/limitations of your findings
● The contribution to knowledge.

The structure of your results section may follow a deductive structure, the structure of your research questions or hypotheses or the main themes of your analysis.

Conclusions and recommendations

In this final chapter you should draw some general **conclusions** and suggest a way forward. Some issues you might address in your conclusions are:

● The main lessons learnt from the study
● The problems you faced and how you overcome them
● What you would do differently if starting the work now
● Any future research that should be conducted
● The implications for stakeholders – academics, managers or policy makers.

You should make sure that you have written a really good conclusions chapter. As we have noted, examiners often read selectively – they skim the middle of your project report and start reading closely again when they reach the conclusions and recommendations. Grab their interest again and help them to make sense of your research.

Preliminary matter (prelims)

All but very informal project reports include some additional material before the main text. You will include more **prelims** for formal or long reports. The prelims help your reader to navigate through your project report, so it is essential for long or complex projects and optional for short and simple projects. Unless otherwise noted, you should number these pages with lower-case Roman numbers (i, ii, iii, ...), although the page number is not usually shown on the front pages. The table of contents lists those pages following the contents, with the page numbers visible. You will restart your page numbers with your introduction and use Arabic numerals.

The first page of any report is the **title page**. Your project requirements will usually specify the content and format of this page, which may include the title of your project, the name of the author(s) (unless you are being marked anonymously), the date and the unit or degree for which you are submitting this report.

Make sure that your title expresses your research topic clearly and concisely. Your main research questions may be the best source of your title. Avoid obscure or clever titles – you are supposed to communicate your research to your reader, not show off.

In an academic report, an **abstract** usually follows the title page. Your abstract summarises your research topic, the main themes of your research and your main findings. An abstract may be as brief as 75 words or as detailed as 250 words. Students often make the mistake of writing their abstract as though it is the first part of the introduction – it is separate. Think of the abstract as a mini-report that may be circulated separately from your report, like a commercial for your research.

In a business report, an **executive summary** usually follows the title page instead of an abstract. The executive summary is a brief summary of the practical problem (normally about one page), your analysis of the practical problem, the alternative solutions, your recommendations and any implementation issues. You should write your executive summary so that a busy executive who only reads the executive summary (and not the rest of your report) can make a decision. As with the abstract, you should never write your executive summary as though it is the first part of your introduction – it is separate. In fact, it may well be circulated separately.

What other prelims you include depend on your project requirements and the complexity of your report. A long project (20 pages or more) may include: a **table of contents**, which lists the major elements of the report and their page numbers; a **list of figures**; a **list of tables**; a **list of illustrations**; and a **glossary** and/or a **list of abbreviations** that define unfamiliar terms in one location.

You may want to thank anyone who has helped you with your research. You should put these **acknowledgements** on a separate page in your project report. Only thank people who have contributed to your research. It's not really appropriate to thank your current girlfriend/boyfriend/best mate unless they have provided you with project resources or data. (Plus, be careful who you thank, as we have noted before in another context, you will have to live with it for a long time!) You may want to thank your academic supervisor or project sponsor, although try not to be too smarmy, especially if he or she will be marking your work.

Endmatter

While the prelims help your reader to navigate through your report, you may also need to include **endmatter** to help your reader to understand what you have presented and amplify their understanding.

The most important endmatter is your **list of sources** or references. This may list either all the resources you consulted for the research project, or only those sources you have actually cited in the main text. You should consult your project guidelines and/or project supervisor to see which one is appropriate.

Make sure that your references are complete, you have included every source you have cited in your main text and have not included irrelevant sources just to pad out your list. This will be much easier if you have been keeping good records of your sources during your project. Many examiners will turn first to your references, as we noted in **Chapter 4**, and interpret the quality of your citations and references as an overall guide to the quality of your research. If your project requirements do not specify a format, you should use the Harvard author–date system.

You should put anything that might be useful to understanding the report, but is not important enough to go in the main text, in an **appendix**. If you have included any appendices, these will follow your list of sources. This might include:

- Copies of your research instruments, such as a blank questionnaire or an interview schedule
- Full details of your research setting and sample, which you have summarised in the main text
- Full details of your analysis, which you have summarised in the main body.

Don't include all completed questionnaires or interview transcripts unless you have been instructed to do so by your supervisor or project requirements. One example of a questionnaire or transcript will usually do. You should make sure not to hide any of your key points in your appendices (many examiners do not bother to read them), but you should make sure that you don't waste space in your main text with material that doesn't belong there.

Table 14.1 Prelims and endmatter

	Academic report		Business report	
	Short/informal	Long/formal	Short/informal	Long/formal
Title page	✓	✓	✓	✓
Abstract	✓	✓		
Executive summary			✓	✓
Table of contents		✓		✓
Acknowledgements		(✓)		
References	✓	✓	(✓)	(✓)
Appendices	(✓)	✓	✓	✓

14.1.3 Variations on the generic structure

This generic report is commonly used for quantitative research, where researchers fill in the blanks of the generic structure with details of the particular research project. This generic project report structure is based on the scientific reporting style central to quantitative research, but ethnographers also need to report their work. While the generic report suits the deductive approach of quantitative research well, it may not be the best way to report qualitative research. Although you could use the generic structure and the chapter contents described above for any sort of project report, the structure of your report should reflect your research approach.

From this book you will know that qualitative research follows a different research process, and is analysed and interpreted differently. Researchers often report qualitative research using structures (and sometimes content) that reflect the difference between these two approaches. Instead of following the prescribed, highly structured format of quantitative research, qualitative research reports are usually written in a more fluid way, reflecting their emergent nature.

Qualitative research

If you have taken a qualitative approach to your research design, your project report or presentation may reflect this approach in its structure, which is usually more flexible than a quantitative report. Although you still need an introduction and conclusions, you may want to describe your research methods immediately following the introduction.

In **Chapter 13**, we described how to interpret qualitative research. Since in qualitative research you will often identify several themes rather than converge on a single theme through deduction, as in quantitative research, you will probably want to structure the core of your report around these themes. This means that you will probably integrate your literature review and your findings around your theme or themes. You may want to follow the advice given by Miles and Huberman (1984), who suggested structuring qualitative research reports around themes, rather than a focus-down structure. You might want to integrate your literature review with the findings and discussion, especially if you are following a grounded theory approach.

The main body of a typical qualitative research report or presentation might look like this:

- *Introduction* – The problem this research addresses and why it was worth doing
- *Research methods* – How I/we investigated this problem
- *Theme 1* – The first thing I/we found out about this problem and what it means
- *Theme 2* – and so on
- *Theme 3* – and so on
- *Conclusions* – What I/we now know about this problem as a result of this research.

Business report structure

You may want to write a separate report for a business sponsor if you are required to hand in both an academic report for marking and a business report to your business sponsor. In some circumstances, your business sponsor may be satisfied with a copy of your project report, but expect you to make an oral presentation.

Easterby-Smith et al. (2002: 154) argue that the distance between academic and business audiences is decreasing as more managers study business and management. However, we argue that you should consider them as two different audiences because managers and academics will want to know different things and the constraints on their time and attention differ so much.

A business audience will mainly be interested in your recommendations on the particular practical problem they face, and only in anything else such as what you did and how you did it insofar as it supports these recommendations. A top manager has only a few minutes to spend on your project report and will typically only read through a few pages of your report, and at best skim read the rest. Even a manager who reads your report closely, however, may not have any interest in the theoretical aspects of your research project. This means that the sections that are most interesting to your academic reader, including the literature review, research methods, findings and discussion, are completely wasted on the manager.

You should focus on the things that will most interest your project sponsor in the main body of your report or presentation:

1. Your analysis of the practical problem
2. Potential solutions to this practical problem
3. Your recommendation of a particular solution
4. Your implementation, including time, cost, feasibility.

Therefore, we recommend a structure that looks like this:

- *Introduction* – The problem this research addresses
- *Analysis* – Why this problem exists
- *Potential solutions* – How we could solve this problem
- *Recommendation* – How we should solve this problem
- *Implementation* – How we can put this recommendation into practice.

If you are not writing a separate report but do need to provide your business sponsor with a report, you might condense or append your literature review, methods and discussion chapters. However, you should still include the academic literature where it relates to your analysis, options and recommendations, and where you need to give credit to other people's words and ideas. Keep details of any important theory or models and your sample in the main body of the text. You still need to demonstrate to your sponsor or manager that your analysis and recommendations are credible and valid, and backing them up with the weight of the literature will help you do this.

 ### Oral presentations and vivas

Many research projects involve a formal or informal presentation, such as an oral presentation or a viva. Oral presentations include informal presentations to fellow students, and formal presentations to examiners and sponsors, which may be assessed individually or collectively.

Oral presentation

You should prepare an **oral presentation** as carefully as a written report. If you plan to do otherwise, you will not succeed. Planning and rehearsal are essential to successful oral presentations.

Issues you should think about during the planning stage include:

- What should the presentation include?
- Who should present it?
- How sophisticated does it need to be?

If the people attending your presentation haven't read your report in advance, your emphasis should be on summarising the key points and conveying the research story. A typical structure will be:

1. Title slide – project title, researcher name(s), sponsor (if any)
2. Aims and objectives
3. Background and context of the research
4. How you did the research
5. Your key findings
6. Your analysis and discussion
7. Your conclusions and recommendations.

If your audience has thoroughly read your written report in advance, you should try to avoid simply repeating the main points in your report, and instead try to add value through your presentation. Don't forget that your main goal should be communicating your research to your audience, but try to bring something new to the material you are presenting or present some aspects of your research that perhaps you could not include in the written report.

Most students nowadays can use presentation software such as Microsoft PowerPoint to create a professional-looking set of slides. The danger, of course, is that the content is often not as carefully thought out as the presentation. Before you get too wrapped up in selecting colours, music, special effects and so on, you need to plan the content of your presentation. Many of the tips for structuring a written report apply to formal presentations.

Try to avoid slides that are too busy or too dense. These will distract your audience from your content. Try not to overload slides with text – on the other hand, don't put up an overhead with just a few words. A good rule of thumb is to prepare one slide for every five minutes if your presentation is over an hour; one slide for every three minutes if under an hour.

You should rehearse your presentation enough times so that you can deliver your presentation smoothly and in the right amount of time. Rehearsing with technical aids is essential. If you haven't used an overhead projector, slide projector, whiteboard, flip chart, video/DVD, visualiser or other aid before, you should practise with it until you are comfortable. You should also work carefully on timing – presentations that are much longer or shorter come across as ill-prepared.

You might want to consider whether all group members will take turns presenting, or only the strongest and most confident. If you are presenting to examiners, you should probably make every effort to include every team member in the presentation, unless there is a genuine reason why someone cannot actively participate. It is usually better for everyone to play at least some role, even if only to introduce the people who will do the substantive speaking. If you are presenting to a business audience, you may want to let the more confident members dominate, but everyone should still participate.

If you are being assessed on your oral presentation, you should review your project requirements to see if any criteria apply specifically to your presentation or if they differ from the written project criteria. The main things examiners look for are:

- How confidently you present your report
- How well you bring your material to life
- How well you have prepared your materials and visual aids
- How well you can answer questions and, if necessary, depart from the script.

Although many students feel nervous or self-conscious about oral presentations, these help you to build career skills and self-confidence. They can also enhance your written project report by building enthusiasm and support for the project, allowing you to explore project angles you missed in the written report and expand the discussion of interesting areas of the project.

You will sound much better and feel less nervous if you take a deep breath before you speak your first word. If you are not normally a confident speaker, you should practise alone or with friends until you feel comfortable speaking. Practise in front of a mirror to see whether you are using your body language and gestures effectively. Get a friend to give you feedback if possible. If you are really nervous, you might try some sort of humour as an icebreaker – Dilbert cartoons are currently popular – but remember that humour can fall flat. You should also think about any questions that are likely to come up and how you might answer them. Once you get started, your audience will focus on what you are presenting, unless you distract them. As long as you don't fall down, giggle uncontrollably, pass out or run off stage – all things we have seen presenters do – the audience will stick with you.

Even experienced speakers expect to have some butterflies before they start speaking – in fact, many believe that if you don't, your delivery will be flat. Tony Blair, the UK prime minister and an experienced public speaker, has been known to finish presentations with a wringing wet shirt, but he still gets his message across.

Vivas

You may also be expected to answer questions about your research in an oral examination known as a **viva**. This may be relatively informal, such as a question-and-answer session, or a formal examination by one or more examiners.

Murray (2003: 17) suggests that the main concerns of the examiner will be:

- Did you do the work yourself?
- Do you understand the business and management research?
- Do you have a good knowledge of the research project?
- Are you a competent researcher?
- Did you learn anything?

You can look up past projects to see what they are like, but you cannot usually observe a viva to see what one is like, which makes some students nervous. On the brighter side, rarely will you get one or more intelligent examiners to listen so intently to you talking about your research project! If you are facing a viva, you might talk to students who have undergone the same examination to see what it is like – but beware horror stories. Everyone likes to tell stories about awful examinations, as they do about driving tests. You might also look at Rowena Murray's book *How to Survive Your Viva* (2003), although it is primarily aimed at doctoral students.

14.2 MANAGING THE WRITING PROCESS

Once you have identified the structure and content of your project report, writing it should be straightforward, shouldn't it? Well no, in fact the report-writing phase of your research will be cyclical, like the rest of your project. As noted earlier, your project report may often be the biggest written project you have done to date. Word lengths of 10,000–40,000 words (80–150 pages) are not uncommon. They are written differently from short projects of 20 pages or so. Because the project is so much longer and more complex, you will need to help your readers by explicitly guiding them through the main body of the text, for example by linking sections together and signposting what is coming up.

If you are working on a large piece of research such as a dissertation, you might be able to complete much of your written report early on in the research process. About half of a quantitative research project will have been completed before you begin your field research. You will have identified your research problem, research questions and any propositions or hypotheses you are putting forward in your research proposal; defined your methodology, including methods for gathering and analysing data, early on as well; and selected your analysis. This means that you should be able to write your first few sections or chapters whilst you are collecting and analysing your data.

In qualitative research, you will typically be collecting and analysing data and reviewing the literature at the same time, so you won't be able to do as much finished writing early in the project. However, you should be taking field and reflective notes during the process, and therefore you should have much of the text to hand by the time you finish your field work. The challenge is then to work out the structure for presenting your research.

Writing will be much easier if you set yourself a schedule and stick to it. A good description of productive writing habits can be found in Bell (1999: 199), who suggests that writing effectively will be much easier if you create a rhythm of work and get support from others.

If you have been working in a group, this may be the first time you have written anything substantial with other people. The skills that have got you this far in your studies may no longer be adequate. The main challenge will be to manage the group process, as discussed in **Chapter 2**. You will need to manage yourself and/or your group so that you not only finish on time, but also leave yourself plenty of time to get your project report right in the process. This is so important that we discuss this in detail.

14.2.1 Drafting and editing your project report

As soon possible, you should start writing your project report. The main milestones of your project will be a rough draft, a first draft and a finished report. However, some parts of your project may be finished before you start collecting your data, while others may only come together at the last minute.

Your rough draft

We suggest you start by putting together a **rough draft** of your core chapters only – the literature review, methods, findings and discussion – and hold back on the introduction, conclusions, prelims and endmatter until later. Otherwise, you will waste time editing them to reflect a constantly changing report. Your rough draft of these core chapters is critical, because this is the first time you will write down your complete argument in a more or less coherent form. You should aim for a rough draft that is about 60 per cent of your total word length, since you have quite a bit to add to this.

Writing your rough draft will be considerably easier if you have been writing all along, for example early drafts of quantitative research or theoretical memos for grounded research. You shouldn't worry about getting the detailed writing exactly right, but instead try to cover all the points and get the argument right. You can turn this rough draft into a first draft, and then polish up this first draft into your final project report.

Once you have written this rough draft, you can:

1. Add to it – new material, ideas, or thinking
2. Subtract from it
3. Change the structure around
4. Make it communicate better to your readers.

You should try to complete a chapter at a time, rather than lots of unconnected bits. Keep going back to your outline if you need to. You may want to write deductively – 'sculpting in marble' – write an initial draft of complete or longer length, then edit and revise it until it fits the requirements; or inductively – 'sculpting in clay' – start with an outline and fill in each of the points in greater detail until the report is written.

Your first draft

You can revise and edit this rough draft into your **first draft**, your first complete version of your report. The quality of your final report is determined by the quality of this first draft – at least for projects with deadlines – so make sure that you start and finish your first draft on time. Many project reports are marked down because they are essentially edited rough drafts, rather than polished first drafts. After you have written a first draft, you should read through your text and see if you have achieved the following:

● Presented the information in a logical sequence
● Made sure each section has a central message
● Made sure each item leads to the next
● Identified any unnecessary material that could go into an appendix.

You should go back to the outline and see how well the overall structure of your report is working, especially if you have taken a qualitative approach and there is more than one way to present your research.

At this point, don't worry too much about polishing your written text. Booth et al.

(2003: 201) suggest that: 'Since readers read each sentence in light of how they see it contributing to the whole, it makes sense to diagnose first the largest elements, then focus on the clarity of your sentences, and only last on matters of correctness, spelling and punctuation.' You may end up editing out or rewriting large sections of your rough draft, so it doesn't really matter how well written those sections were.

The major change between the rough draft and the first draft is in the perspective. Whereas you can write your rough draft from your own perspective, make sure that you write your first draft from your reader's perspective. Constantly remind your reader of the structure of your report and where they are in the report. Write what your reader wants to know, rather than what you want to say.

Most of your editing should focus on making your work communicate to your readers. In particular, you will need to include quite a lot of text that is not about the content of your research but helps your reader to navigate through the document and highlights the important or interesting things you have done. Murray (2003: 195–200) suggests four key things you should do for your reader:

1. *Repetition* – repeating concepts, arguments and other key points for linking and emphasis
2. *Forecasting* – letting readers know in advance what you will and will not be doing in your project report
3. *Signalling* – highlighting links and other key aspects of the text
4. *Signposting* – constantly reminding your readers where they are in the thesis, using headings, topic sentences and other devices.

Students sometimes say to us that they don't need to use repetition, forecasting, signalling and signposting because what they have written is so obvious and straight-forward – at least when they read it! However, these writing devices can be key to communicating with your reader.

Editing

Make sure that you have allowed enough time to edit your project report. No matter how bad your rough draft, your skill in editing it into a first draft and a final draft can 'turn a pig's ear into a silk purse'. This kind of editing is not spell-checking and other proofreading but revising how you have organised your paper to make sure that your argument is clear, and revising how you have written it so that it is understandable to your readers.

The length of your first draft is a good guide to whether your report is within the word limit specified in your project requirements. If you haven't formatted your report, a good estimate is 250 words per page (in double-spaced, standard margin, 12-point Times Roman font).

Although some people write concisely and economically even in their first draft, most of us can reduce the number of words by 25–50 per cent without losing any content. Look for wordy phrases you can replace such as 'in the way that' with 'how' or 'in order to' with 'to'. Use charts, figures and tables wherever they make sense. A picture can often replace 1000 words, as tables, diagrams, charts and other forms of illustration are often much clearer than written descriptions. However, make sure that you link these back to the text and interpret them – or highlight their implications – in the text rather than just inserting them anywhere and expecting them to be self-explanatory.

When you are satisfied with your first draft, then, and only then, you should include any additional elements required of your project as a piece of formal writing. These elements may include the title page, table of contents, table of figures, acknowledgements, abstract, executive summary, glossary, index, reference list or bibliography, index and/or appendices. You should check that your page numbering, headers, footers and so on are right and in the correct format. If you start including these too early in the writing process, you will waste a lot of time playing with them. We will describe special issues associated with final editing in **Section 14.3**.

As you edit your project report, you may need to consult a number of specialised sources. You can find dozens of good reference books in your library or book shop on the technical aspects of formal and academic writing. Every writer needs a basic set of reference books, including a dictionary, usage manual and thesaurus.

You may also want to consult a professional style and usage guide such as *The Oxford Style Manual* (Ritter 2002) or *The Chicago Manual of Style*, which are good for answering practical questions such as preparing a table of contents, page numbering, referencing and so on. They are especially useful when you start the final editing, since this will bring up many specific questions. Some standard academic reference books are listed at the end of the chapter.

If you are working on a long report and it contains many tables or figures or several different people are working together and combining electronic documents, you may find it worthwhile investing in a specialist guide to whatever word-processing program you are using. In preparing complicated documents (such as the various drafts of this book), being able to automatically update various fiddly bits of your document such as cross-references or figure numbers and page numbers can save you time and frustration.

If you have time to learn them, you may want to take advantage of the advanced technical capabilities built into modern word-processing software programs such as Microsoft Word. These programs now have many of the same features as professional page-setting programs. You can use these features if you are writing a long document. It can be useful to keep your text broken up into smaller units such as chapters, especially if different people are writing different bits of the text, and then use your word-processing software to edit and print them as a single virtual text.

14.2.2 Managing yourself

Students often turn in poor quality project reports, even if they have done a good job on designing and doing their research project, if they have allowed too little time to write and edit. You will have to manage yourself (and your project group if you have one) as well as your writing process.

Creating a good working environment

One key to writing up is to work consistently and without wasting your writing time. Make sure that you aren't trying to work somewhere that actively destroys your concentration. You don't need to go into monastic solitude – many people write better with some background noise such as the radio, television or music, but choose it carefully so that it isn't distracting.

For many of us, writing is bound up with elaborate rituals and habits. You should be aware of **comfort habits**, those habits and rituals that many of us engage in when getting down to a major piece of writing, for example clearing the desk, cleaning the oven, using a particular kind of writing pad/writing instrument. One PhD student, for example, could not start writing until he had made a cup of tea and allowed it to cool down completely. As Becker (1986) points out, we are often aware of our own habits but ashamed to admit to them, because we assume we are the only ones to have such rituals. Nearly everyone has a different comfort habit, but all are equally embarrassing. You should be mindful of your own habits if they are keeping you from writing well or even writing at all, or take advantage of them if they can help you to start or keep going. A trick that works for Kate when she is desperate is to line up the contents of a bag of Skittles and reward herself with a Skittle each time she completes a set amount of writing. One bag of Skittles later, the entire job is done. Healthier-minded students may promise themselves a run or a session in the gym after they've done a set quota of writing.

Even if you are working alone, finding someone to be a moral support can be an effective way to overcome procrastination. For example, you can talk about your writing with someone else or ask someone else to be your conscience.

Avoiding or overcoming procrastination

Many good research projects are not translated into good project reports because of **procrastination** (Blaxter et al. 1996: 209), the art of putting off until tomorrow what we should be doing today. We are all experts at avoiding things we don't really want to do. Although many students use deadlines to motivate themselves, waiting until the last possible minute does not result in significantly better project reports, but does increase the possibility that something will go wrong.

Procrastination stimulates students (and academics) to new heights of creativity in **displacement activities**, substituting an activity that is indeed worthwhile but not essential to your writing, for example cleaning the cooker, tidying your room/desk or walking the dog. These displacement activities are really just excuses for not sitting down to writing.

From a long list of ways to overcome procrastination provided by Blaxter et al. (1996: 210), four of the most useful are:

1. Make notes on your reading, the results of your research or your discussion with your supervisor or manager.
2. Write one of the easier sections of your report, such as the table of contents, references or bibliography.
3. Prepare the outline of one of the sections or chapters and start adding quotations, points and so on.
4. Set yourself a target for writing a set number of words or a set amount of time; don't do anything else until you have done it and give yourself a treat once you have finished it.

Recognising when you have done enough

Some type 1 students finish early and then keep working because they don't know when to stop. This is unlikely for most of us because we have procrastinated. Most students stop writing only when they absolutely have to stop in order to turn their project report in on time. However, if you have finished early and have met your objectives for the report, hand it in. No project report is ever completely finished, just abandoned.

14.2.3 Strategies for group writing

Many students may find writing the project report challenging, because they must write it as part of a team. Writing collaboratively involves not only technical challenges but also significant interpersonal challenges.

If you are working on a group project, you should discuss as a group how you will organise writing up the research report. Some groups prefer to assign roles, with a single person – or a pair – responsible for editing, and others writing the text. Other groups divide up responsibility equally for writing and editing.

You may find that you will have to solve interpersonal challenges as well as technical challenges in writing as a group. Some may be due to different writing habits, so it might be useful for your team to go through the issues mentioned above before you start writing the full project report draft.

As a project team, you may want to stick with the same strategy you have used in defining, designing and doing your research project, or you may want to try a new pattern. The two basic strategies for dividing up the writing responsibilities are writing individually and writing collaboratively.

If you have taken a quantitative approach, you may find that it is easy to split up the project report chapters or even sections so that individual team members can write independently. One person could take responsibility for the research methods chapter, one the literature review and so on. This may be difficult if you have taken a qualitative approach, since it is much more difficult to split up the different elements.

Although you may find that splitting up the writing task between individuals (or small teams) reduces interpersonal conflicts, if you cut and paste the resulting text together, as in **Figure 14.1a**, you can create a number of problems for your team. First, not everyone on the team may be equally good at writing, so that your overall report will be only as good as your weakest writer. Second, individual writers may go 'off message', so that your report contradicts itself, confusing your readers. Third, since team members will have different styles, it may be difficult to keep a consistent voice and style across the chapters. Thus, you will need to put a lot more effort into editing your report.

Your project report may be more consistent if you switch writing and editing responsibilities, as shown in **Figure 14.1b**. Since different people are responsible for writing and editing, the differences can be homogenised across the different individuals or teams. In addition, if different people are writing and editing, you have more chances to catch any mistakes or misstatements that may creep in. Achieving consistency is more of a challenge than you would think in a group working to deadlines. Some student project reports we have read fail even to agree on a consistent research topic – each section starting with a slightly different interpretation of the main topic! Needless to say, this didn't really impress the examiner, who would have preferred some consensus on whether the topic was corporate social responsibility, corporate ethics or corporate governance.

Your report may also be more consistent if you appoint a **master editor**, as shown in **Figure 14.1c**, to be responsible for editing all the chapters and making sure they are consistent. If you have a group member who is particularly talented at editing, this is a

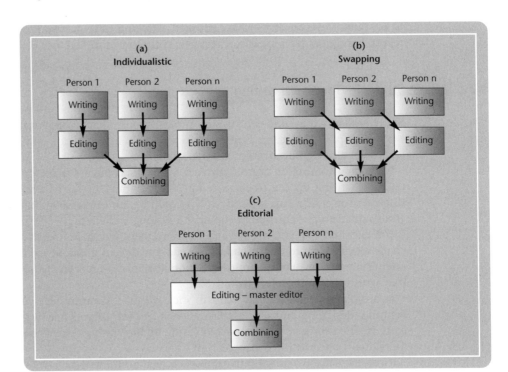

Figure 14.1 Strategies for writing and editing

good way of using his or her talent, but it can also be easy to burn that person out if the editing task is too big and there is too little time left to do it well.

If you are writing up quantitative research, shared responsibility for writing and editing may work well, since there are generally accepted conventions for structure and style that most people understand and can imitate. If you are writing up qualitative research, on the other hand, it may work better to have a single editor, especially if different people are writing different sections. It is often difficult to maintain a consistent style across writers, but the use of a master editor can help you attain a seamless style. However, it can be more difficult to identify discrete sections which you can assign to different writers, since you are weaving together your data, conceptual framework and findings as you present them, rather than having them in separate sections.

14.3 GETTING IT RIGHT

Thus far in the research project, you have had to learn and use various sets of skills. Writing the project report is no different. Every project report will be unique, but the process of writing any project report will call on the same set of generic technical skills, which are writing persuasively, correctly and stylishly.

A quick checklist for the technical details is to see whether your report or presentation does each of the following:

● Achieves a good standard of spelling and grammar
● Develops logical links from one section to another

- Uses headings and subheadings to divide the text into clear sections
- Is consistent in the use of the referencing style
- Uses care with the page layout
- Presents tables and figures properly.

14.3.1 Writing correctly

To write correctly, you need to master the basic mechanics of writing: spelling, grammar and punctuation. Some students may believe that writing correctly is old-fashioned: we think that you should do it anyway. You may not know who is marking your project report, it might be someone who cares deeply about language. Even if your reader isn't so punctilious, if you make more than a few errors, a reader will mentally downgrade his/her opinion of the quality of your research report and, by extension, your research. At the very least, errors cause the reader's attention to slip, and he/she may notice problems with your logic or other core aspects of your research that might otherwise have gone unnoticed. Finally, if you have put time and effort into your research, why not try to do a good job on the writing? Would you patronise a five-star restaurant where the chef is famous, the ingredients are top-notch, the cooking is superb, but the ingredients are slopped onto a paper plate and slapped down in front of you?

Many students have problems producing error-free prose. You may have dyslexia or another learning impairment. You may not have been taught how to write correctly, but your readers will consciously or unconsciously judge your research as being of poor quality if you make spelling, grammar and punctuation errors in your project report, presentation handouts and overheads, covering letters and any other documents you produce.

Although many students whose native language is not English write English tolerably or even exceptionally well, others find it a challenge. Many universities offer assistance to international students, including pre-sessional English courses, continuing English training and even personal coaching. You should investigate which of these are available to you. You may want to ask your supervisor or project coordinator whether you are allowed to use a proofreader (it is not ethical to hire someone to actually write the report for you).

Spell check

Most readers will assume that, if you misspell more than a few words in your project report, you have spent too little time to do a good job or you are satisfied with shoddy work. Most word-processing programs nowadays include spell-checking routines that highlight misspelt words. Some even query correctly spelt words that are commonly misused – 'it's' for 'its' or 'they're', 'their', 'there'. However, if you substitute a correctly spelt word for the word you meant to write, for example if you mean to write 'from' and type 'form' instead, even the most sophisticated computer spellchecker will not catch your mistake.

You will catch more misspellings if you:

- Use a dictionary when you write

- Leave time between your final editing and printing out your report, so that you can read through with a fresh eye
- Get someone else to read through your report
- Read through your report backwards – from back to front, bottom to top and left to right.

Don't forget to check you have correctly spelt the names of any people or organisations you mention in your report. Misspelling the name of a major researcher in your literature review – which happens more frequently than you would think – makes your command of the literature look shaky. Similarly, if you get the name of a major organisation wrong (Wal-Mart, not Walmart or WalMart), how likely is it that your reader will assume that your data and analysis are right?

You should also refer to your dictionary to make sure that you use words correctly. Students often misuse words when they want to appear more sophisticated than they actually are. This is not usually a good idea and you will come across like Mrs Malaprop, a character in one of Sheridan's plays who constantly misused words to try to impress her listeners.

A good dictionary will also help you avoid clichés and other hackneyed expressions in your writing. Some of the 'usual suspects' listed by O'Connor (1996) are acid test, bite the bullet, bottom line, can of worms, foregone conclusion, foreseeable future, tip of the iceberg and viable alternative.

Grammar check

As well as checking your spelling in your final draft, you should also check to make sure that you are grammatically correct. Grammar refers to the technical rules governing the parts of speech (nouns, verbs, adjectives, adverbs and pronouns), and how we employ them (agreement, phrases and clauses). A report that is filled with grammatical mistakes gives your reader the impression that you don't really care enough about your research to do a good job in presenting it.

Grammar poses a number of fiendish traps for writers of all types. 'Grammar is a sine qua non of language, placing its demons in the light of sense, sentencing them to the plight of prose' (Gordon 1993a: xv). Cook (1985: viii) suggests that the errors that most commonly cause readers problems in reading and understanding are:

- *Needless words* – A good editor can spot needless words and eliminate them. This is essential for editing your writing to the word limit, if your first draft is lengthy. It will also help with the clarity of what you are writing.
- *Words in the wrong order* – Words are in the wrong order for one of two reasons. First, word-processing makes it easy to shift sentence elements around and leave orphans or dangling bits. It is the editor's responsibility to hunt down and eradicate these. A more subtle problem occurs when words are not in the wrong logical order, but are not in the order that a native English speaker would put them. This takes a more practised ear to find, because it is usually difficult to articulate why 'the red big house', for example, sounds awkward, whereas the 'big red house' doesn't.
- *Equivalent but unbalanced sentence elements* – Writing your entire report in simple sentences would start to sound monotonous after a while. (It worked for Hemingway though!) Whenever we combine simple sentences into complex ones, we run the risk of creating inconsistencies between the joined-up phrases. A simple

example would be 'Harvey designed the survey chapters, the data were analysed by Kate, and writing all the report was the job of Helen.' Three different kinds of sentences are joined up here. It would be more consistent to write 'Harvey designed the survey, Kate analysed the data and Helen wrote the report.' Any time you use 'and' or 'or' to join up sentences (or sentence elements, which are incomplete sentences), you should check to make sure they are parallel, that is, written the same way. This may perhaps seem a subtle point but it can definitely distract your reader if you get it wrong.

- *Imprecise relations between subjects and verbs and between pronouns and antecedents –* This is perhaps a fancy way of saying that this is a tricky area of grammar. Make sure that your subjects agree with their verbs. This sounds easy, but it gets difficult when you have a compound subject (Bob and John … are … is?), when your subject and verb are separated by other elements of your sentence (the experiment that was carried out by the students under controlled conditions in a laboratory setting … are … is?), or when you have a tricky subject such as 'per cent' or 'none'. The same goes for pronoun agreement. Most of us wouldn't say 'John … she' but things can get tricky (the company … its or their?), especially when you are trying to avoid sexist terms (the examiner awarded his … her … their? mark).
- *Inappropriate punctuation –* the subject of our discussion below.

If you know you have problems with grammar, consult a good usage guide and/or a friend or professional with a good ear for language and a good understanding of the rules. There are many good guides to grammar for beginners and advanced students – see **Additional resources** at the end of this chapter.

Punctuation

Checking punctuation is the final task of the editor. Punctuation is essential to style and communicating with your reader. Punctuation clarifies the structure of a sentence and prevents you from misreading it (Cook 1985: 108).

If you know that you have trouble with punctuation, you can find a wide range of reference manuals in your library or book shop. We can enthusiastically recommend the following two books (full details in the **References**):

- Patricia T. O'Connor's *Woe is I: The Grammarphobe's Guide to Better English in Plain English* (1996: x), which the author describes as a 'survival guide for intelligent people', which provides 'commonsense tips on how to avoid stumbling into … the worst pitfalls of everyday language'
- Karen Elizabeth Gordon's *The New Well-tempered Sentence: A Punctuation Handbook for the Innocent, the Eager, and the Doomed* (1993b: vii), in which 'the punctuation marks themselves [are] stirring up trouble and inviting raffish comrades in for drinks', not to mention 'taking off their clothes, throwing masked balls, [and] sending insinuating letters to cellists, divas, and Eurobankers'.

Punctuation is also one of the key aspects of style. 'Prose writers are interested mostly in life and commas', argues Ursula Le Guin (1998: 35), a bestselling science fiction writer and expert on creative writing. You can use punctuation to decorate your writing, says Cook (1985). Lynne Truss's book on punctuation, *Eats, Shoots & Leaves* (2003), was a recent bestseller on both sides of the Atlantic.

Punctuating badly is like weaving all over the road when you are driving – you are likely to be pulled over and given a stern warning. It would be nice to think that people only have problems with sophisticated punctuation marks such as the colon, but even the poor full stop is abused in student writing. If you're not confident with your punctuation, stick to simple, short sentences. Your report may sound a bit choppy, or you may come across as the next Ernest Hemingway, but this may help you to write correctly, if not beautifully.

14.3.2 Writing with style

As we have noted above, your examiners will mark your project report based not only on the quality of your research, but also how well you report it. This includes not only the structure of your report, but also how well you describe what you have done – its style. Style also includes the sound of the language you use, punctuation, syntax, sentences and paragraphs.

Style distinguishes a good report from a great report, if they both have the same content. A great chef not only knows how to prepare a good meal, she/he also knows how to arrange it on the plate for maximum impact.

Your audience will not read your project report for its writing style only, unlike readers of poetry or fiction, but how you write does affect their ability to make sense of what you have written and interpret your meaning. Your readers may expect you to write a project report on quantitative research in a scientific style, using the third person, past tense and many passive sentences (Denscombe 2003: 289). On the other hand, for a project report on qualitative research, they may expect an ethnographic style, using the first person, present tense and many active sentences.

Beyond choosing an appropriate style for your research approach, remember that your readers will focus not so much on the aesthetics of your writing, as on your ability to construct sentences and paragraphs, and generate and order ideas (Williams 1990: xiv). O'Leary (2004: 209) suggests that you approach writing as a craft, which includes selecting the style and finding a voice. Another craft element is constructing your report: finding a story and making convincing arguments.

Many books deal with the finer points of style. Strunk and White's short (less than 100 pages) book *The Elements of Style* (1999) has withstood the test of time for generations of American students. Two invaluable handbooks for more advanced skills are Joseph M. Williams' *Style: Toward Clarity and Grace* (1990) and Jacques Barzun's *Simple and Direct* (1985). Both books focus on improving not only the style but also the structure of professional writing. Instead of prescribing rules such as 'avoid passive sentences', these books will help you to understand how to communicate complicated ideas in a simple manner.

Activity

If you are having problems writing clearly, here are some things that you should focus on:

1. *Narrative* – Remember that a research report is a type of story, and try

to put yourself in the shoes of the person who is hearing the story for the first time and trying to make sense of it.

2. *Agency* – Name the subjects of your sentences. This is why you are told to 'avoid passive sentences' – passive sentences evade responsibility – 'the staff were laid off' versus 'the division managers laid off the staff'. These subjects can be people, organisations, collectivities or figurative ('studies').

3. *Action* – Use active verbs wherever possible. Avoid weak verbs – is, are, were – if you can replace them with stronger verbs that describe physical movements, mental processes, feelings or relationships. If you combine active verbs with agency, you can't help but improve your writing.

4. *Cohesion* – Link your sentences.

Take a representative page from somewhere in your first draft and do one or more of the following activities:

● Circle the subjects of your sentences and underline the verbs. How many sentences have explicit subjects? How many have active verbs? Passive, indirect sentences are like a long stretch of the motorway – they can lull you to sleep.

● Count the number of words in the sentences on the page. Most people average about 20 words per sentence. Make some sentences shorter, and some longer, to vary the pace of your writing.

● If you are using word-processing software such as Microsoft Word, then check out the readability statistics for your work. If you are writing at too high a level (pseudo-academic), look at ways of simplifying your writing. If you are writing at too low a level (elementary), bring up the level.

● Circle the last sentence of each paragraph and first sentence of the next paragraph on the page and see how they relate to each other. If you are having continuity problems, this is a good way to see why this happens.

As well as the technical points we have covered, you will also need to edit for style, so that you end up with a well-written, as well as accurate, account of your research. This is especially important for qualitative research, where your style will help you to paint a picture of the real-life context where you have observed people and organisations. It is also important for quantitative research, because it helps you to establish and maintain the credibility of what you have done, by writing authoritatively.

Style is probably one of the hardest things for beginners to get right. New writers often try to imitate academic writing, and end up with an impenetrable mess. Joseph Williams (1990) suggests three reasons why good writing is difficult:

1. We don't actually intend to write well: we try to impress other people with pretentious writing or academic writing when we think our ideas won't be good enough, like trying to cover up a bad steak with a fancy sauce.

2. We never learnt how to write well: we think that technically correct writing (no spelling or grammatical errors) is enough, without writing clearly as well.

3. We can't write this particular report well: we don't have enough experience in doing this kind of writing or we don't really know for whom we're writing.

The following are some hints for editing by ear from Howard S. Becker (1986: 127), who probably writes better than any other sociologist (or even any social scientist) around:

1. Substitute active verbs for passive verbs when you can. Put crucial actions into verbs and make some important character in the story you are telling the subject of the verb.
2. Use fewer words. Avoid 'throat-clearing' phrases. 'An unnecessary word does no work.'
3. Avoid repeating phrases.
4. How you structure your writing (syntax) should reflect its content. Put important ideas first in the sentence.
5. Use concrete rather than abstract words wherever possible. Use concrete details to give body to abstractions.
6. Avoid overworked metaphors and clichés.

Writing clearly

A logical and clear report is likely to receive higher marks than a report that is muddled and hard to follow, even if both report the same research and same content. For your project report to document and communicate your research, an important part of your job is to write clearly: 'Whatever else a well-educated person can do, that person should be able to write clearly and to understand what it means to do that' (Williams 1990: 2).

As in the old joke about modern art, we may not be able to define clear writing, but we do know it when we see it. Williams (1990) suggests that writing clearly begins with writing clear sentences. These sentences then need to be joined up into coherent paragraphs, which maintain the flow of meaning between sentences. Paragraphs are joined up into sections. Sections are combined in a chapter. Each chapter needs to flow into the next.

Writing concisely

Good writing is not only clear but also concise. You should use as few words as possible. We can often cut 20 per cent or more words out of our writing without losing any meaning. Most first drafts are full of excess words – the equivalent of verbal throat-clearings such as 'erm' and 'you know' when we speak. The *Journal of Consumer Research*, in fact, suggests that authors cut 20 per cent of the length of their final draft before sending in a paper to the journal.

For example, the sentence 'Williams (1990) suggests that writing clearly begins with writing clear sentences' above started as 'Williams (1990) suggests that the process of writing clearly begins with the ability to write clear sentences.' The new sentence is 50 per cent shorter.

Voice

Good writing also has a distinct voice as well as style. *Voice* refers to the tone that is taken in the relationship between reader and writer, how you express yourself (Blaxter et al. 1996: 221), whilst *style* describes how you write up your research. In choosing a voice, it is important to think about your audience. In quantitative research, you are addressing an academic audience, usually your academic supervisor and/or examiner(s). Choosing a voice in qualitative research can be tricky. Who is your audience? Is it the same audience as for a quantitative report, or is it different? Miles and Huberman (1994) suggest that you should consider your reader as a co-analyst, looking at and interpreting the evidence in your qualitative report. If you are part of a group project, is the paper being written by the group, or by a collective 'we' persona?

Another way of thinking about voice is that it represents the *point of view*. Is the person writing the report omniscient, a perspective typically taken in quantitative research, or is the author's viewpoint limited to what he/she observed, as in much qualitative research?

A final word

Many students do their research project a great disservice by not taking care with how they present it. We would never argue that how you present your research is more important than what you present. However, in our experience, how you present can either detract from or enhance what you have done significantly. If you get the presentation right, your reader should not actually pay any attention to the voice, style or grammar in your report, and your research will be free to speak for itself. If you get the presentation wrong, your reader will be distracted from the content and focus on the presentation and quibble with the research.

SUMMARY

In **Section 14.1**, we describe the process for planning your project report, writing your rough draft, revising your rough draft into a first draft, and editing your project report into a finished draft. **Section 14.2** briefly discusses some of the technical aspects of project report writing: developing an argument, writing correctly and writing with style. **Section 14.3** concludes with some tips for writing alone or as part of a project group.

ANSWERS TO KEY QUESTIONS

How should I report my research?

- This depends on the requirements of your project – it may be a report and/or a presentation
- The formats for each of these are well defined
- You should follow one of the recommended formats

What are the differences between a report on quantitative research and one on qualitative research?

- The formats for quantitative reports are based on a generic format with little variation
- The formats for qualitative research may vary depending on the narrative or story being told

What are the differences between an academic and a business report?

- Length, audience, purpose and format are all different between these two forms

How can I manage the writing process effectively?

- Plan before you start
- Start early and write often
- Get regular feedback on the process
- Manage your group and yourself

How do I write and edit the project report?

- You should pay attention to style, voice and the technical content of your work

How do I prepare for an oral presentation or viva?

- Prepare your formal presentation
- Check the audience – their interest and purpose for attending
- Practise what you will say
- Anticipate questions

REFERENCES

Barzun, Jacques. 1985. *Simple and Direct: A Rhetoric for Writers*, rev. edn. Chicago: University of Chicago Press.

Becker, Howard S. 1986. *Writing for Social Scientists*. Chicago: University of Chicago Press.

Bell, Judith. 1999. *Doing Your Research Project: A Guide for First-Time Researchers in Education and Social Science*, 3rd edn. Maidenhead: Open University Press.

Blaxter, Lorraine, Hughes, Christine and Tight, Malcolm. 1996. *How to Research*. Buckingham: Open University.

Cook, Claire Kehrwald. 1985. *Line by Line: How to Edit Your Own Writing*. Boston, MA: Houghton Mifflin.

Denscombe, Martyn. 2003. *The Good Research Guide for Small-Scale Social Research Projects*, 2nd edn. Maidenhead: Open University Press.

Dunleavy, Patrick. 2003. *Authoring a PhD: How to Plan, Draft, Write and Finish a Doctoral Thesis or Dissertation*. Basingstoke: Palgrave Macmillan.

Gordon, Karen E. 1993a. *The Deluxe Transitive Vampire: The Ultimate Handbook for the Innocent, the Eager, and the Doomed*. New York: Pantheon Books.

Gordon, Karen E. 1993b. *The New Well-Tempered Sentence: A Punctuation Handbook for the Innocent, the Eager, and the Doomed*, Boston, MA: Houghton Mifflin.

Hart, Chris. 1998. *Doing a Literature Review: Releasing the Social Science Research Imagination*. London: Sage.

Hart, Chris. 2001. *Doing a Literature Search: A Comprehensive Guide for the Social Sciences*. London: Sage.

Le Guin, Ursula K. 1998. *Steering the Craft: Exercises and Discussions on Story Writing for the Lone Navigator or the Mutinous Crew*. Portland, OR: Eighth Mountain Press.

Miles, Matthew B. and Huberman, A. Michael. 1994. *Qualitative Data Analysis*, 2nd edn. Beverly Hills, CA: Sage.

Murray, Rowena. 2003. *How To Survive Your Viva: Defending a Thesis in an Oral Examination*. Maidenhead: Open University Press.

O'Connor, Patricia T. 1996. *Woe Is I: The Grammarphone's Guide to Better English in Plain English*. New York: Riverhead Books.

O'Leary, Zina. 2004. *The Essential Guide to Doing Research*. London: Sage.

Ritter, Robert M. 2002. *The Oxford Style Manual*. Oxford University Press.

Stake, Robert E. 1995. *The Art of Case Study Research.* London: Sage.

Stringer, Ernest T. 1996. *Action Research: A Handbook for Practitioners.* London: Sage.

Strunk, William I. and White, E.B. 1999. *The Elements of Style.* New York: Allyn & Bacon.

The Chicago Manual of Style: For Authors, Editors and Copywriters, 2003 15th edn. Chicago: University of Chicago Press.

Truss, Lynne. 2003. *Eats, Shoots & Leaves: The Zero Tolerance Approach to Punctuation.* London: Profile Books.

Williams, Joseph M. 1990. Style: *Toward Clarity and Grace.* Chicago: University of Chicago Press.

Yin, Robert K. 2003. *Case Study Research: Design and Methods,* 3rd edn. London: Sage.

ADDITIONAL RESOURCES

Booth, Wayne C., Columb, Gregory G. and William, Joseph M. 2003. *The Craft of Research,* 2nd edn. Chicago: University of Chicago Press.

Easterby-Smith, Mark, Thorpe, Richard and Lowe, Andy. 2002. *Management Research: An Introduction,* 2nd edn. London: Sage.

Locke, Lawrence F., Silverman, S.J. and Spirduso, W.W. 2004. *Reading and Understanding Research,* 2nd edn. London: Sage.

Van Maanen, J. 1982. 'Fieldwork on the beat'. In Von Maanen, J., Dabbs, J.M. Jr and Faulkner, R.R., (eds). *Varieties of Qualitative Research.* Thousand Oaks, CA: Sage.

Key terms

abstract, 404
acknowledgements, 404
appendix, 405
comfort habits, 413
conclusions, 403
discussion, 403
displacement activities, 414
endmatter, 405
executive summary, 404
findings, 402
first draft, 411

focus-down strategy, 401
glossary, 404
introduction, 400
list of abbreviations, 404
list of figures, 404
list of illustrations, 404
list of sources, 405
list of tables, 404
literature review, 401
main text, 400
master editor, 415

oral presentation, 408
prelims, 404
procrastination, 414
reader, 398
research methods, 402
rough draft, 411
table of contents, 404
title page, 404
viva, 409

FREQUENTLY ASKED QUESTIONS

How long will writing the report take?

Experience suggests that any piece of written work will take 110 per cent of the time you have available to do it in. However, you can plan for preparing, writing and editing early on.

If you know the length of your project, either total number of words or pages, you can estimate how long it will take based on how quickly you normally work. An average page formatted with double-spacing, 12-point Times Roman font will be about 250 words. The most you can reasonably expect to write in a single day is 6000 words, working at a frenetic pace. A more reasonable target is 2000 words working at a steady pace, or 1000 words if you are a slow writer.

This would require you to work the following amounts of time, just on writing (not researching or reading):

● 1–5 days for a coursework project of 1500–5000 words (6–20 pages)
● 5–20 days for a dissertation of 20,000 words.

You will also need to include time for collecting your materials and planning your report structure, and editing your first draft. Thus, you should allow about three times as long for the entire writing process as for the writing itself. Obviously, if you write as you go along, you will be able to streamline this stage of the research process; if you leave it all to the last minute, forget about it and just go into panic mode, work all night and drink lots of caffeinated beverages.

What should the report look like?

If you have been given specifications for the format of the written report, you should follow these – exactly. In this case, you can use this section to help understand what to do and how to get there. You will probably find it useful to consult student reports from previous years, if you have access to them, so that you can see how other students have presented their research.

If you are not working to a specified format, Section 14.2 will help you visualise your format and decide how to get there.

Who will read this report?

Unlike most things that you have read during your course and research, research reports are typically written for a minute audience. Your main 'customers' will be your supervisor, your examiners (if different), your sponsor (if you have one) and perhaps the participants in your study. Sometimes research reports from student projects will reach a wider audience, but this isn't usual or even desirable.

Discussion questions

1. Why is it important to approach your project report as a special kind of writing rather than just 'business as usual'?

2. Is there a special format that all project reports must follow?

3. Why is it important to understand who will be reading your report before you start writing?

4. Should you write your report in the same order as the chapters?

5. Where can you go to get help with writing if English is not your first language?

6. What challenges occur when you are writing as part of a group that are not relevant when you are writing alone?

7. Why is procrastination an enemy of good reports rather than just a different way of working?

8. Do you have any habits or rituals that you associate with writing? Are these productive or counterproductive?

9. How can good writing help your reader to understand your research project? How can it help you?

10. Why might quantitative and qualitative research reports differ? Academic and business reports? Individual and group reports?

Workshop

Go back to three of the core readings in your literature review (if a quantitative study) or theory (if a qualitative study such as a grounded theory project).

1. Analyse the overall structure of each piece.
2. Is this structure 'standard' or 'customised'?
3. Identify the major uses of literature.
4. How does the contributions and conclusions section build on the findings?

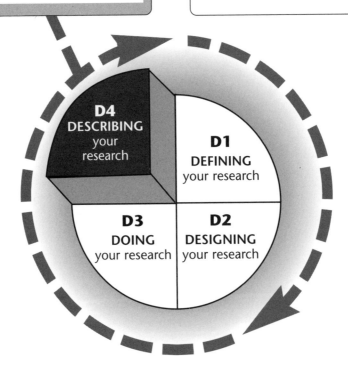

Closing the loop
Reflecting on and learning from your research

 Key questions

- What do examiners look for when they assess a project report?
- What can I do that will make my project fail or achieve a distinction?
- What can I learn from this project that will help me in the future?
- What should I do when I finish the project?

 Learning outcomes

At the end of this chapter, you should be able to:
- Explain the criteria that lead to a failed project, pass or distinction
- Identify the process for the assessment of your work
- Reflect on the lessons from your project for your personal objectives and career

Contents

INTRODUCTION

In **Chapter 1** we suggested that you should 'begin any research project with the end in mind'. We strongly suggest that you take time between completing your research and submitting your project report to reflect on what you have learnt about your topic and your research, and incorporate these insights into your report. In **Section 15.1**, we describe the criteria you will need to meet to pass your piece of coursework. For instance, your project is almost guaranteed to fail if you don't turn it in on time or violate other project guidelines, or get caught plagiarising or violating other ethical guidelines. You must absolutely avoid these.

Working on a research project can be stressful, even if everything goes well. Towards the end of a research project, many students console themselves with the knowledge that they are nearly finished. If the project, for example a dissertation, meets your final degree requirements, then you do not ever have to do this again. In **Section 15.2**, we describe how projects are marked and what examiners look for when they mark a project. In particular, we show the characteristics that distinguish *really* good projects from good projects.

Once you have completed your project or course, we suggest that you should not stop just yet. Many people feel that it would be great if they could go through the process again and do it all better the second time around. Not only would you know more about your research topic, you would also be far more familiar with the research process. As D. H. Lawrence commented:

> If only one could have two lives, the first in which to make one's mistakes ... the second in which to profit by them.

In **Section 15.3**, we will suggest how you can reflect and learn from your project. You should 'close the loop' – reflect on what you have learnt in your project about business and management, about the research process and yourself. Think of this as a brief history lesson – remind yourself of your original personal and research objectives and your intended outcomes. We will conclude with some reflections about research and the research process.

Our suggestions include debriefing yourself (and your project team) at the end of the project, using your project experience to get a 'leg-up' in the job market and launch an exciting career as a researcher (despite the conclusion drawn by some that the term 'academic career' is an oxymoron).

You can also apply what you have learnt to your studies, career and personal development. The business and management world will value research skills, the ability to take a critical perspective and draw together knowledge, and the discipline of writing that you have acquired. Just as important is your ability to be reflective about what you have done. These are tough skills to learn, but can become habits of thought – if you practise them.

15.1 FINALISING YOUR PROJECT REPORT – AVOIDING FAILURE

Few students begin their research project intending to fail, but inevitably some research projects do fail. Some fail to achieve one or more objectives; others fail resoundingly on every aspect. These disasters make everyone associated with them look and feel bad. Most projects, mercifully, don't fail.

In retrospect, the seeds of failure are usually visible from the first day of the project and sometimes even before. Many projects fail when students ignore what they ought to do in favour of what they'd like to do. Others fail when students ignore good advice. We identify two mistakes that will *nearly always* make your project fail: committing plagiarism or other ethical violations, or disobeying project guidelines.

15.1.1 Plagiarising or other unethical behaviour

As mentioned in **Chapters 4, 9** and **14**, you must absolutely avoid unethical behaviour if you want to have any credibility as a researcher. The penalty for unethical behaviour can be quite severe.

In academia, plagiarism is one of the most serious of these behaviours. Being caught plagiarising is a guaranteed way to fail. If your university has a policy on plagiarism, and you have had a reasonable chance to read it (for example if it is in the student handbook you were given on the first day of your first year), you are expected to obey it. When you write the final draft of your project report, double-check that you have credited the source of any ideas or words you have taken directly or indirectly from someone else and listed all the relevant sources in your reference list or bibliography.

In many universities, there is no right of appeal if you are caught plagiarising. The penalties may range from failing the work being assessed (your research project) to being expelled from your degree course. You can be punished for plagiarising whether your plagiarism is inadvertent – accidentally leaving out the source – or advertent – deliberately plagiarising, for example using material you have downloaded from the web. Your examiners will not take into account the effect that this might have on your glittering career prospects.

These points are illustrated by three recent cases in **Student research in action 15.1**.

Student research in action 15.1
GO AHEAD PUNK ...

1. I like what you've written, but it only got a 2.2 when I wrote it ...

Students on a course recently must have thought that they had 'got away with it' when they submitted assignment work to their marking institution. The work was moderated, given good marks and sent to the external examiner. The external examiner recognised much of the work, as it came directly copied from his own book. The students were failed for plagiarism and required to leave the institution. This is so common it has even become an 'urban myth'.

2. I found this neat dissertation on 'weapons of mass stupidity' on the internet, so ...

A student went to the library of a neighbouring institution, copied a dissertation report and submitted it with his name on it. This was easily picked up as the literature review was at least 10 years out of date and contained references to many sources that the student would not have

> had access to. It didn't take long for the assessor to track down the original.
>
> **3. The way to really impress your friends and family …**
>
> Our final cautionary tale is about a student who plagiarised on a resit examination. His tutors spotted the (poorly executed) cut-and-paste job and easily found the references that he had copied from. He was expelled from the master's programme, one week before graduation, and his offer of a postgraduate research place was immediately rescinded. He was also barred from campus, so that he couldn't even see his friends graduate. For the sake of an hour's extra work, he put his whole future in jeopardy.

It may appear that we are overstating plagiarism as a problem in research projects, but in our experience, the occurrence of unfair practice is not diminishing. Preventing the problem in the first place is better than having to deal with it once it has occurred. As we noted in **Chapter 4**, it is increasingly easy for students to plagiarise, as the mechanics of internet sources ('cut and paste') make plagiarism even more tempting.

It is also increasingly easy for examiners to search for the same sources and demonstrate plagiarism has occurred using software. Internet sources are easily traceable through search engines or specialised software programs for detecting unauthorised copying. Even if your examiner does not use computer software and does not recognise the material you have plagiarised, material you have not written yourself will usually stand out stylistically from the material you have written, particularly when you are not a fluent writer or a native English speaker.

If you get away with plagiarism in your written report, you can still be detected during an oral presentation or viva. Your examiners can ask you detailed questions about any source you cite, any facts or opinions you have not cited a source for, or any material they suspect you have cut and pasted.

Here are a few links that you may find helpful if you are still confused:

- The Writing Tutorial Services at the University of Indiana.
- The student judiciary at the University of California at Davis.
- The Faculty of Arts at the University of British Columbia.

Be equally scrupulous when preparing your report for your business sponsor or placement manager in checking for plagiarism. They may not care that much about academic integrity but they will expect full value for the money they have paid you and the access they have given you to their organisation. Plagiarising in your business report is just as bad as misrepresenting your data or not honestly interpreting your findings.

 ### Missing the project deadline and other project guideline no-nos

A second way to make sure that your project fails is to ignore the project guidelines, such as the deadline for handing in your project and the format and other guidelines about its presentation.

Handing in your project on time is critical, and unlikely to have any flexibility. Unless you have a genuine medical or personal emergency, and you have asked your course director (or the person named in your course handbook) in advance of your project deadline, do not hand in an incomplete project or fail to hand one in at all. Your examiners may have no choice but to fail you.

Make sure not to disobey other important project guidelines such as your word limit. Most project guidelines state a minimum and maximum word length for your project report. You should always obey the project word limit if you have been given one. Some students treat word limits as a recommendation, not an absolute, much in the same way many motorists regard speed limits. However, examiners are more likely to treat word limits as though they are speed cameras, so keeping between the minimum and maximum is essential.

Do not, as some students do, try to creatively adjust font sizes or page margins to squeeze in more words or disguise too few words. Experienced examiners are difficult to fool. Even though most examiners will not bother to count the words in your report, an experienced examiner can easily tell the difference between a 20,000-word and a 30,000-word report. If you are caught cheating on the guidelines, as well as the word limit, your examiner is well within his rights to fail you.

Most students worry about the minimum word limit – 'Will I be able to write 40,000 words?' or whatever it is – before they start writing. However, few students have trouble reaching the minimum number of words in their first complete draft. Few students will have written less than the minimum number of words, whilst many will have written substantially more. If your report is too long, edit it down (leaving out every fourth word, however, is not the most effective strategy). Your examiner awards a mark based on reading your report, not weighing it.

A concisely written report will communicate your work and your command of the topic more than a rambling, overlong report. Your examiner will thank you. The rain forest will thank you. And you will have learnt more about your project than when you started editing. If you are writing for a business sponsor, it is likely that he or she will only read a few pages of your report, anyway.

Similarly, you should stick to the upper and lower time limit when you are making an oral presentation of your project report. If your examiners have given you 15 minutes to present, then going over looks bad and gives the impression that you haven't bothered to plan your presentation properly. If you go on substantially longer than the project guidelines allow, your examiners may stop the presentation and you may not get to make the key points that pull your research project together. At the very least, your audience will stop listening to your presentation and start thinking about marking exams, what's for dinner or the summer holidays. Again, while you may not think that your examiners have anything better to do with their time, your business sponsors definitely do. Time is money. Don't waste their time or yours.

Finally, please don't try to be clever-clever. If something is in the project regulations, it has usually been found to be essential over generations of research projects. We recently heard a story about a doctoral student who handed in his thesis printed entirely on bright turquoise paper! Even though the thesis regulations did not specifically prohibit coloured paper, they did require that the thesis be legible, which unfortunately this was not. He had to have his thesis reprinted and rebound, which cost him time and money. His supervisor and examiners were not too impressed, either. If you do have a problem interpreting the guidelines, or if you think they are wrong, you might take the matter up with your supervisor or the project coordinator, but don't turn in a project that deliberately ignores the guidelines. You will just annoy everyone.

15.2 FROM FAIL TO PASS TO DISTINCTION

Most students are concerned not just with not failing their research project, they want to do well on it. Even if you have done all of the above, your project may still receive a pass, rather than the distinction you may feel is deserved. In this section, we build on the basic requirement – to receive a pass – and look at what makes an excellent project and how it will be assessed. Understanding both the standards your project will be marked against and the process by which your examiners will mark your project will help you to put those finishing touches to your work.

15.2.1 The characteristics of a distinction

To be awarded a distinction, it is not enough just to do everything to the letter – you must also produce a project that is distinguished, in concept, execution and contribution to knowledge. Probably the best guideline to whether a project gains a distinction or not is if the examiner comes away thinking 'I'd like to have done that project'.

Table 15.1 lists several factors that often weigh on whether a report receives a pass or a distinction. You should of course consider these factors in conjunction with any that are produced by the organisation or individuals who will be assessing your work.

15.2.2 The marking process

If you are a 'strategic learner', you will spend some time even before you choose your research topic understanding how your research project will be assessed, as suggested in **Chapter 3**. You should think about *who* will assess your project as well as *how* your project will be assessed.

Project marking, as we shall see, is more of a craft than an exact science. However, we can draw some lessons from our experience that may both help you to put the finishing touches to your current work, and help you 'close the loop' for your next project, understanding the result when you do receive your project mark.

Who will assess your project

Your project guidelines will tell you who has input into your project mark. Any of the following may provide input to your project mark:

- Your project supervisor
- An internal examiner who is not your project supervisor
- An external examiner who does not work at your university
- Your business sponsor.

Many students get so wrapped up in their research that they forget they are not the main client of the research. Your findings only count when you have delivered them to your project examiner; similarly, your recommendations only count when you have delivered them to your business sponsor. Your project examiner and/or your business

Table 15.1 Characteristics of a distinction

Issue	Characteristic
The fundamentals	Like the foundations of a great building, the work is nothing unless it has a good basis. The report presented must at least be acceptable on all the criteria outlined in **Section 15.1**. This is a *qualifier*, without which you will not get a distinction, no matter how well any of the other criteria are rated.
Interest	The work has answered the 'so what?' question, not only in the context of the particular research setting, but also says something to a wider audience.
Critique	The report has assimilated a wide literature and had something interesting to say about the wider issues in the literature, including identification of inconsistencies, contradictions and gaps.
The story	It is a defining characteristic of distinction-level projects that the quality starts at the first page. Here the story is outlined and the rest of the document picks it up and guides the reader through the work and, like a good story, it leaves you wanting more, for example explicitly stating identified areas for further research.
Sense-making	The scenario may be complex and the literature certainly will be. An excellent piece of work will take all of this in, and find ways to turn the complexity into something accessible, without oversimplifying it.
Initiative	As a marker, a piece of work distinguishes itself when it has done something that sets it aside from the rest of the pile of your marking – possibly in the level of effort that has gone into the method, or the unusual twist that someone has added to an established research method or the 'extra mile' that has been travelled in preparing the literature review (for example inclusion of hard-to-find journal articles).
Learning is evident	One of the great disappointments in reading a project report is when you check it against the question – 'could the person have produced this work without taking the course of study?' If the answer is yes, one is left wondering what value the course has added. On the other hand, a distinction-level project leaves the reader in no doubt that the writer has come through a tremendous personal journey and this report is the culmination of the thinking processes and perspectives gleaned, not necessarily from the whole course, but at least from substantial chunks of it.

sponsor are your most important 'customers', not the rest of your research group or anyone else.

If you can identify your examiners (but see the caveats below), you may want to target your project report to their interests and expertise. In some cases, you might be able to discuss briefly what they look for in a project and project report. A discussion of how the project might be marked (rather than what mark you might get) is usually acceptable when your project supervisor is marking your project. In other cases, this will be considered unethical, for example phoning up your external examiner is never a good idea.

We are not suggesting that you 'pander' totally to the main marker, but examiners are human and the marking process is subjective. We do suggest that if you can discuss with them what they consider absolutely essential or absolutely unacceptable, you can use this information to focus your report appropriately. You may want to know what he or she is expert in, because this will probably be what he or she focuses on most critically in your report. For instance, if your examiner:

● Specialises in the area you are researching, make sure that everything related to that area is as perfect as you can make it. For example, if she or he specialises in corporate finance, you should double-check any financial data you present.
● Has done research in this area, you should mention it in your literature review, even if critically. This said, don't mention irrelevant research just to 'soft-soap' him or her. Your examiner will have seen his or her name in print before.
● Has written a book on your particular research method, you should make sure that you have described and executed it perfectly. If your examiner has written 'the book' or 'the article' on case study research, for example, and you have used a case study approach, make sure that you have taken his or her advice on board.

Pay special attention to any **cues** your supervisor gives you about likes and dislikes, especially if he or she will be marking it. Some supervisors can't stand reports written in the first person; others prefer it. If your supervisor tells you to use the author–date system for referencing, using footnotes in a project report may really annoy him/her, not only because he/she prefers a certain system, but also because the student has not listened to him/her. A supervisor is rarely pleased when a student wastes his or her time by asking for advice or feedback and then ignoring it. Even if your supervisor will not be marking your report, your supervisor will certainly be reading it through the eyes of a prospective examiner, and is the closest you can get.

Most work is marked initially by someone from your institution, known as an **internal examiner**. You may or may not know who this is. Beware of overtargeting your work to a particular internal examiner, because most universities have a dual-marking system where more than one person assesses each major piece of work (that is, each one that contributes to your final classification). Although currently many reports are marked by a project supervisor, best practice is moving towards 100 per cent **double marking** of anonymous scripts, so the days of being marked by your supervisor may be numbered.

Marking may be done independently by each examiner without knowledge of the other person's mark (**blind marking**), or with one examiner checking and verifying the first examiner's mark (**moderating**). Your project mark may also be checked by an **external examiner**, who may review all marks or just borderline and extreme (distinctions and fails) cases.

In some cases, such as sponsored or placement project, your examiner may have feedback from your project sponsor. They will usually take this feedback seriously, because it will describe the value of your research to the company, and also whether you behaved ethically. Very seldom, however, can a business sponsor actually assign a mark that counts towards your final degree classification.

How will your project be marked?

Students often assume that examiners assign marks arbitrarily, one popular theory being that examiners use the stairs method for marking! Here, the marker stands at the top of a flight of stairs with a pile of reports and drops them. The landing position of the reports determines the mark: any paper that lands on the top step receives 80 per cent, decreasing 5 per cent per step below this. Other popular theories include the use of a random number generator, or weighing rather than reading your work. Although these techniques would save examiners much time in marking, in reality your examiners must follow the **assessment guidelines** when they mark your project.

The mark must be traceable and reproducible. Examiners are typically given a detailed list of criteria they must use in marking your project. These are (hopefully) exactly the same criteria you were given at the beginning of your project in your project guidelines. This is both good and bad. Good, because examiners cannot impose additional requirements on your project that have not been stated earlier. Bad, because they must assess you on those guidelines, even if what you have done as an alternative is excellent. There is rarely much leeway for them to reinterpret the rules as to how you will be assessed.

You should therefore check your project report so that it explicitly shows that you have addressed each of these criteria. If one of these is not addressed in the report, then it is likely to be marked down. For instance, if you are asked to relate your project findings to business and management research, make sure that you do it. You may even want to explicitly mention this in the chapter or section title or the introduction. Likewise, if you are asked to reflect on what you have learnt from the project, include a discussion of this.

As stated in **Chapter 14**, you should direct the attention of the readers to specific features of your report that are good or innovative. One of the easiest ways to do this is in the summaries at the start and end of each section. These provide explicit cues as to the quality of your work. Such cues will highlight these features (and take attention away from other features). The table of conclusions presented in **Table 13.3** is an example of such a focusing device. As a further example, in **Student research in action 12.3**, the students' written report failed to signal that the students had carried out covert observation of supermarket shoppers, even though this was innovative. They also failed to highlight their more interesting research findings, such as the rituals people go through in choosing fresh product. Thus, their research project came across as pedestrian, even though their research wasn't. This was a shame, as their research was original and definitely different.

A sample marking scheme is shown below:

- A careful selection of a management problem/issue that is relevant to the field of management.
- A clear definition of the problems/issues to be investigated.
- A well-justified and appropriate research design to investigate the specified issue.
- A demonstration that literature and secondary data sources have been thoroughly investigated. The literature review has to be comprehensive and presented in an analytical and critical manner. There should be a clear demonstration of the limitations of existing literature and the author's opinions should be presented with detailed reasons.
- A consistent and careful implementation of the adopted research plan.
- A systematic, objective and efficient analysis of the collected data.
- The drawing of relevant conclusions from the analysis. Conclusions should be supported by the data, compared and contrasted with the findings of previous studies and put into the context of existing literature.
- A demonstration of a good grasp and understanding of relevant theory that has been well integrated into the project report.

● Demonstration of originality and initiative in pursuing the objectives of the study, allied to thoughtful reflections on what has (or has not) been achieved in the project.

15.2.3 Is it a well-written report and does it reflect what you have done?

There is no substitute for a well-written report. Whilst your project supervisor will have discussed many aspects of your research with you along the way, other examiners may not have met you personally – and may not even recognise your name (or increasingly, number) – and only have your report to go on in assessing the quality of your work. Your examiners only know your research through your project report, whether that is a written project report, an oral presentation, a viva, or a combination of these. Your report is the only link between your research and the examiner, as shown in **Figure 15.1**.

Also make sure to highlight your report's contributions realistically. Your examiner will expect you to make some original contribution to business and management research, which may be any of the following:

● To review and synthesise existing knowledge
● To investigate some existing situation or problem
● To provide solutions to a problem
● To explore and analyse more general issues
● To construct or create a new procedure or system
● To explain a new phenomenon
● To generate new knowledge.

You do not need to show a major theoretical breakthrough in a project for an undergraduate or taught master's degree, as you would for a doctorate, but you do need to make a contribution in one or more of the areas listed above.

To understand why you need to 'market' your research findings, imagine yourself in your examiner's shoes, facing a towering stack of project reports. State what you did in concise terms, yes, but don't forget to draw attention to what you did differently, that adds real value or points of interest to your work. Highlight where you have used your imagination and creatively tackled the problem. This shows that you put yourself out to do the work.

Whilst your project will not pass or fail on presentation alone, as stated in **Chapter 14**, a neat and attractive presentation does contribute substantially to an examiner's favourable impression. A point worth repeating here is that many examiners do consciously mark down for flaws that could be eliminated with modern spelling and grammar checkers. Such avoidable errors are especially dangerous since they attract the examiner's attention to the lower quality aspects of your report. Put simply, if they find

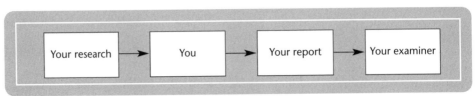

Figure 15.1 Your examiner only sees your research project indirectly

such a poor level of attention to what they may consider 'basics', the more likely they are to look for other errors or problems in your work. As we said earlier, assessment is a subjective process – don't give them a chance to nit-pick.

Always keep in mind that a report is no stronger than its weakest section (or link between sections). You must create a thesis or story that links your whole report together. You must also make sure that no section is over- or underemphasised relative to its importance. This is illustrated in **Figure 15.2**.

Excellent reports identify the themes of the research at the very beginning and carry them through each of the major sections. These themes are explicitly developed through the literature review, and the implications of the literature for those themes noted at the end of the literature review. These are passed to the methodology chapter as research questions that are specifically addressed through an appropriate methodology. The methodology is carried out (demonstrate this) and the results (your data) presented, structured around your key themes. Your discussion takes the themes and provides comparison with the relevant theory (and hence expectations) that were generated in your literature review. These provide the points of similarity and difference in those themes as the basis for the discussion. The conclusions include the outcomes and recommendations, relative to the themes.

These linkages are shown in **Figure 15.2**. If you can do all this, and see where it is going (a diagram really helps), you only need to be able to answer one further question – and that is 'so what?' Many studies focus on an interesting area but don't make the connection back to reality. In other words, they don't say anything useful based on the work carried out. This process of connecting back to reality and making something useful from your work is called *synthesis*. **Student research in action 15.2** is an example of where the 'so-what?' question appeared to be forgotten.

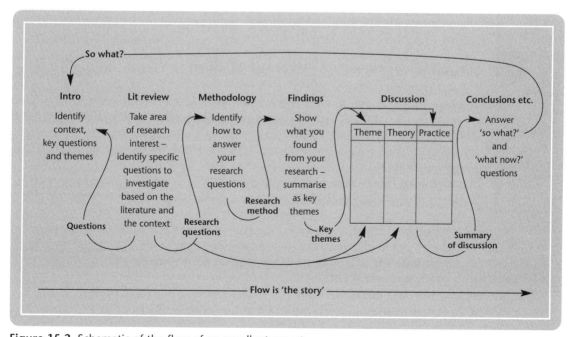

Figure 15.2 Schematic of the flow of an excellent report

> ### *Student research in action 15.2*
> **I'M FREE!**
>
> A student group looked at the scheduling routines for small businesses to see how owner-managers decided which order to work on first. They found many different algorithms in the scheduling literature. They collected data from three firms, to use in the algorithms, and this was where the project ended – with the outcomes from the algorithms showing how they could have scheduled their systems.
>
> The 'so what?' question revealed that this made no contribution at all to any of the firms (about how they should schedule their work, for instance to improve their cash flow). Neither did it increase knowledge about the area (about the algorithms and their applicability, for instance they may only work well where there is considerable accurate historic data about how long a job will take, and they don't handle the uncertainty inherent in a small business). All in all, there was no link back to reality.

Make sure that you can answer the 'so what?' question about your research. If you could have answered your research questions without having done your project, you are in big trouble. If you are in any doubt, imagine you have met one of your colleagues from your course in the street who doesn't know what you have been doing in your project. In 15 seconds (no more, otherwise they will get bored) you need to give them the 'punch lines' – what you have *done* and *found*. The student group in the above example might have reported:

> I worked with three SMEs to look at how they scheduled work. They were not optimally scheduling their resources and, by the use of a simple algorithm, could have improved their turnovers by 23 per cent in one year.

15.3 WHAT TO DO WHEN YOU HAVE FINISHED YOUR PROJECT

You have turned in your project report and presented your recommendations to your company sponsor. What next? Among the suggestions made by Rugg and Petre (2004: 208) are to relax by reading a good book or taking a long bath, or to get organised by tidying and filing your research materials, sorting out your wardrobe or otherwise getting rid of junk.

These are all constructive activities. But before you completely abandon researcher mode, we suggest that you **PARTY**:

- P – **persist** until the project is truly finished, not 95, or 99, but 100 per cent complete, printed, bound and 'pushed over the edge'
- A – **arrange** a holiday, a trip or discussion on a new project
- R – **reflect** on your learning
- T – **take time out** to allow the real lessons from the project to come to you
- Y – **yield manage** – make sure that you maximise any benefits to yourself and others from the project.

If you abandon your **learning process** when you submit your project report, though, you will lose an opportunity to reflect on and learn from your research. Research projects are a special type of project from a learning perspective, not least because they are so personal and all-involving. In his book *Project Management* (2003), Maylor suggests that the final phase of any project is to develop the process by which you carried out your project so that you can do it better next time. Why? Well, we find that at the end of most projects, people are so focused on moving on to the next thing (always pressing, generally more 'sexy' than what has just been finished) that they miss many opportunities for learning. As a result, in future projects they repeat the same mistakes, and run into the same problems caused by project novelty or uncertainty. Also, they overlook key findings and learning points about what did work, or simply do not give them the brain-space they deserve.

One thing you can do is to capture what you have learnt about yourself. In **Chapter 2**, we suggested that you should identify personal as well as research objectives for your project. Doing a research project is a good way to learn about your own strengths and weaknesses, in academic, personal and interpersonal skills. Make a list of what you have learnt about yourself from doing your research. Include both good and bad things, for example you might have learnt that you are good at planning things, but not so good at carrying them out. Some people find out that they are bad at writing, but good at editing. You might find out that you are good at teamwork, or that you never want to work on a team project again (at least with certain people or types of people).

Also remind yourself of any unexpected benefits, such as any friends you have made or contacts you have added to your personal network. One student found that the other students in the project group pulled together and covered the work she missed when a family member died. On the other hand, another student found out that her best friend was not very reliable, going clubbing on days she had claimed to be too ill or too busy to attend group project meetings! As we discuss below, many students use the contacts they make during their placements or projects to find a job after graduation.

Persist – closing down the project

The list above suggested that you should make sure the project is totally complete, then tidy and file your research materials when you finish your project. You might also:

- Send a thank you letter to everyone who provided support to the project. Enclose a copy of your findings to anyone who participated in the project. If you did an in-company project, this might be better as a one or two page summary of the project and its findings, rather than the entire report. Make sure that you don't violate any confidentiality agreements.
- Thank your project supervisor and coordinator and give him or her any feedback about the project process that might help them next time. Your supervisor might like a copy of the report, if he or she doesn't already receive one.
- Return any books you have borrowed to the library or their owners. You can lose your sponsor's or supervisor's goodwill if you don't, which may cost you dearly when it comes to getting recommendation letters.

Arrange – don't just sit there, do something!

We recommend booking something for a few days after the deadline for a project – you may well have earned a holiday if you have just completed a major project such as a dissertation that marks the end of a course of study. Taking a break has a number of benefits, not least:

- Avoiding the last mood phase of the project (deflation), identified in **Chapter 2**.
- Ensuring that you have really finished everything – there's nothing like a holiday deadline to make sure that you have cleared your desk and completed your work.
- People who have a holiday booked have never, in our experience of student projects, missed their submission deadline.
- Going on a break forces you to take time out and perhaps to use the time to reflect.

Reflect – project review

Probably the last thing you want to do when you have just handed in a project is talk about your project again. However, according to Maylor (2003: 348), you should carry out an immediate **project review** at the end of a project. If you have been working on a group project, then a brief meeting, perhaps over coffee or in the pub, would be a good way to do this. If you have been working on a project solo, then you could do this in front of *Casualty*, or while waiting for the bus, anywhere you have a few minutes to think. You will find that if you don't capture this information within a week or so of completing your project, you will forget about it until the next time you face the same situation. You will certainly wish you had.

In your project review (or post mortem), you should review how the project went, identify any long- or short-term changes you should make to improve your performance on the next project and identify any challenges or obstacles you faced and how you overcame them. If you have done well on your project, your review should focus on what you think you did well, so you can repeat it, and what you could improve next time. If you did more poorly than you wanted to, you should think about what you could do better next time, but also about anything that went right with your project so you can build on it. Some supervisors ask that this step is included explicitly in the final chapter of your project report.

Take time out

If you review your project immediately after you have completed it, you will capture many insights that might otherwise be lost. Other insights from the work you have done, however, are only revealed as time elapses. Your subconscious works on issues over time. This can give you a 'eureka' moment – often when you least expect it. On the other hand, it is difficult to capture this insight in your project report so that your examiner can give you credit for it!

These insights *will* be useful when you are working on projects or having to manage yourself or others in the future. For instance, one student studied enterprise and entrepreneurship in his project. The student found the project interesting at the time, but the long-term benefit was that it greatly helped him later on to understand the processes that a small company, one of his suppliers, was going through during the development of a new product.

Taking time out, though, is not just for intellectual purpose. Most people find creating a report and submitting it emotionally draining, and you need time for both your mind and body (and sometimes your soul) to recuperate.

Yield manage – use your research experience in the job market

If you are finishing a degree course and looking for a job, you can draw on your project experience as a key selling point in job interviews. Potential employers may not be interested in the particular content of your research project, but they do want to know about your strengths and weaknesses, and you can mine your project experience for examples. You can also use a successful group project as evidence that you can work well in groups, a skill highly sought after by employers.

Perhaps more relevantly, you can use many of your research skills in your job search. After all, it is also a research process. You can use your *generic* project skills for:

- Searching for information
- Recording and keeping track of information
- Managing the process using project management
- Writing skills (applications and thank you letters)
- Time management

and *specific* skills for:

- Interviewing (think about what it's like to be on the other side of the desk)
- Working or visiting organisational settings (what to wear, how to act)
- Observation (useful when you are starting a new job).

15.3.1 Using your research experience to begin a research career

If you have enjoyed your research project, you might want to consider a **research career** by enrolling in a postgraduate research programme to study for a master's in research or a doctoral degree. If you get on well with your supervisor, you might want to talk to him or her about opportunities to do further research. Although being good at research isn't a guarantee that you will complete an MPhil or a PhD, it's a prerequisite.

You might get a studentship to continue your research. The two main funding bodies that support postgraduate research in business and management in the UK are the Engineering and Physical Science Research Council (EPSRC), which supports mainly numbers-oriented areas of business and management such as operations management, finance, or accounting, and the Economic and Social Research Council (ESRC), which supports mainly meaning-oriented areas of business and management, such as organisational behaviour.

If you don't want to commit to a research career, you might still be interested in a summer job doing research or a short stint as a research officer. This requires a much shorter commitment that the three years (minimum) for a doctorate. You will typically not have any input into the design of the research project, but it can be a good way to hang around your institution (or another) for a while.

If you are interested in a research career, you should keep an eye on the following sources:

- *The Times Higher Education Supplement* – www.thes.ac.uk
- The www.jobs.ac.uk website and email newsletters
- The *Guardian* weekly Education supplement and website
- *The Chronicle of Higher Education*, for opportunities in North America.

And finally, despite all that has been written already about business and management, there is still much that we know very little about. A research project is a wonderful opportunity for researchers to contribute not just to their own knowledge base, but in some way, however small, to make new findings that will improve what we know overall. The experience we have had as supervisors of student projects over the past 15 years reinforces this – many projects have questioned, critiqued, confirmed or denied what has been accepted as 'knowledge', and in so doing contributed to the knowledge base.

As we always suggest at the end of a piece of work, you should ask yourself two questions. The first is 'so what?' The 'so what?' is that you should now have a good knowledge of the content and process of research – if you have read this book, studied the questions, identified relevant areas of further reading, you have all that you need for now. The second question is 'what now?' Your 'what now?' depends on whether you have been using this book as part of a course on research methods or to support you in doing your research project (or both). Whatever, we wish you every success and hope that you profit from the challenges, grow through the frustrations and, in the end, enjoy the great satisfaction that researching business and management can bring.

 ## SUMMARY

In this chapter, we suggest that you should take a little time between completing your work and submitting it, to make sure that it has the best chance of achieving your objectives. Also, instead of abandoning your project when you have finally delivered your report(s), you should spend some time reflecting on your project and seeing what you can learn from it.

We start by discussing some issues that cause projects to fail in **Section 15.1** – avoid them at all costs. Some mistakes will only cost you marks, but you should try to avoid them as well.

In **Section 15.2**, we discussed some of the characteristics of excellent work which we hope will provide you with something to aim for – gaining a distinction is not a science, but we hope we have enlightened the art just a little. Also, we opened the lid on the art and process of assessment. Later on, as well as the general reflection and learning discussed in the first section, we suggest that you reflect on and learn from your project mark. This section is intended to help make sense of that.

We concluded in **Section 15.3** by suggesting that you take some time to review your project, as well as relaxing and celebrating. You can use a project review to capture any insights into your research and personal objectives, and identify any feedback you need to provide to others. You can also note what went well and badly, and what you should work on next time. We also suggest that you reflect on how you can use what you have learnt in the process in planning for the next stage of your career. Research skills will be helpful in searching for a job, and perhaps even provide the first step on the career ladder.

ANSWERS TO KEY QUESTIONS

What do examiners look for when they assess a project report?

- They look at the quality of your research report
- They look at the quality of your research project (the process you have described in your report)
- They must mark you by the assessment criteria

What can I do that will make my project fail or achieve a distinction?

- You will nearly certainly fail if you behave unethically or disobey the project guidelines
- You will almost certainly lose marks if you do not achieve one or more of the project objectives

What can I learn from this project that will help me in the future?

- You can use your research skills and your research findings in the research and application for a job
- You can use your research skills as the basis for postgraduate work or study

What should I do when I finish the project?

- Relax and celebrate
- Conduct an immediate project review

REFERENCES

Maylor, Harvey. 2003. *Project Management,* 3rd edn. London: Financial Times Management.

Rugg, Gordon and Petre, Marian. 2004. *The Unwritten Rules of PhD Research.* Maidenhead: Open University Press.

ADDITIONAL RESOURCES

Bell, Judith. 1999. *Doing Your Research Project: A Guide for First-time Researchers in Education and Social Science,* 3rd edn. Maidenhead: Open University Press.

Bryman, Alan and Bell, Emma. 2003. *Business Research Methods.* Oxford: Oxford University Press.

Campbell, John P., Daft, Richard L. and Hulin, Charles L. 1982. *What to Study: Generating and Developing Research Questions.* Beverly Hills, CA: Sage.

Collis, Jill and Hussey, Roger. 2003. *Business Research,* 2nd edn. Basingstoke: Palgrave Macmillan.

Easterby-Smith, Mark, Thorpe, Richard and Lowe, Andy. 2002. *Management Research: An Introduction,* 2nd edn. London: Sage.

Sagan, Carl. 1997. *The Demon-Haunted World: Science as a Candle in the Dark.* New York: Ballantine Books.

Saunders, Mark, Lewis, Phillip and Thornhill, Adrian. 2003. *Research Methods for Business Students,* 3rd edn. Harlow: Financial Times/Prentice Hall.

Stringer, Ernest T. 1996. *Action Research: A Handbook for Practitioners.* London: Sage.

University of Bath. 1999. *MSc in Management, Dissertations and Projects,* University of Bath, School of Management.

Wilkinson, Barry. 1998. *Project Guidance Notes 1998/99,* Executive MBA Programme. School of Management, University of Bath, November.

Yin, Robert K. 2003. *Case Study Research: Design and Methods,* 3rd edn. London: Sage.

Zikmund, William G. 2000. *Business Research Methods,* 6th edn. Orlando, FL: Dryden Press/Harcourt College Publishers.

Key terms

arrange, 440
assessment guidelines, 437
blind marking, 436
cues, 436
double marking, 436
external examiner, 436
internal examiner, 436

learning process, 441
moderating, 436
PARTY, 440
persist, 440
project marking, 434
project review, 442
reflect, 440

research career, 443
take time out, 440
yield manage, 440

Workshop

Carry out a personal learning review of previous projects you have been involved with. You should consider:

1. What was the outcome of each of the projects – were you pleased with the outcome? If not, why not?

2. Your structuring of the technical (or subject-specific) issues around the project – how did you handle the complexity of the subject in particular?

3. How did you manage the process – did you set up a plan, use it to control your process, did you finish on time, was there an adequate buffer if problems arose?

4. Based on the above, what will you try to do differently next time?

Appendix
Readings in research

Aldridge, Alan and Levine, Ken. 2001. *Surveying the Social World: Principles and Practice in Survey Research*. Buckingham: Open University Press.

Baker, Michael J. 2000. Writing a literature review, *Marketing Review*, 1(2): 219–47.

Barzun, Jacques. 1985. *Simple and Direct: A Rhetoric for Writers,* rev. edn. Chicago: University of Chicago Press.

Becker, Howard S. 1986. *Writing for Social Scientists*. Chicago: University of Chicago Press.

Belbin, R.M. 1993. *Team Roles at Work*. Oxford: Butterworth Heinemann.

Bell, Judith and Opie, Clive. 2002. *Learning from Research: Getting More From Your Data*. Buckingham: Open University Press.

Bell, Judith. 1999. *Doing Your Research Project: A Guide for First-time Researchers in Education and Social Science,* 3rd edn. Buckingham: Open University Press.

Bell, Robert. 1992. *Impure Science: Fraud, Compromise, and Political Influence in Scientific Research*. New York: John Wiley & Sons.

Black, Thomas R. 1999. *Quantitative Research Design for the Social Sciences*. London: Sage.

Blaikie, Norman. 1993. *Approaches to Social Enquiry*. Cambridge: Polity Press.

Blaikie, Norman. 2000. *Designing Social Research*. Cambridge: Polity Press.

Blaxter, Lorraine, Hughes, Christine and Tight, Malcolm. 2001. *How to Research,* 2nd edn. Buckingham: Open University.

Block, P. 1981. *Flawless Consulting*, Austin, TX: Learning Concepts.

Bogdan, Robert and Taylor, Stephen J. 1984. *Introduction to Qualitative Research Methods: The Search for Meanings*. New York: John Wiley & Sons.

Booth, Wayne C., Columb, Gregory G. and William, Joseph M. 2003. *The Craft of Research,* 2nd edn. Chicago: University of Chicago Press.

Bryman, Alan. 1988. *Quantity and Quality in Social Research*. London: Routledge.

Bryman, Alan and Bell, Emma. 2003. *Business Research Methods*. Oxford: Oxford University Press.

Bryman, Alan and Burgess, R.G. (eds). 1994. *Analysing Qualitative Data*. London: Routledge.

Bryman, Alan and Cramer, D. 2000. *Quantitative Data Analysis with SPSS Release 10 for Windows*. London: Routledge.

Buchanan, D., Boddy, D. and McCalman, J. 1988. 'Getting in, getting on, getting out and getting back'. In Bryman, A. (ed). *Doing Research in Organisations*. London: Routledge.

Buzan, A. 2000. *The Mind Map Book*. London: BBC Books.

Cameron, S. 2001. *The MBA Handbook*. Harlow: Financial Times/Prentice Hall.

Campbell, John P., Daft, Richard L. and Hulin, Charles L. 1982. *What to Study: Generating and Developing Research Questions*. Beverly Hills, CA: Sage.

Collis, Jill and Hussey, Roger. 2003. *Business Research,* 2nd edn. Basingstoke: Palgrave Macmillan.

Cook T. D. and Campbell D. 1979. *Quasi-Experimentation: Design and Analysis Issues for Field Settings*. London: Houghton Mifflin.

Cook, Claire Kehrwald. 1985. *Line by Line: How to Edit Your Own Writing*. Boston: Houghton Mifflin.

Covey, Stephen. 1986. *The Seven Habits of Highly Effective People*. London: Simon & Schuster.

Creswell, John W. 1994. *Research Design: Qualitative and Quantitative Approaches*. Thousand Oaks, CA: Sage.

Crotty, Michael. 1998. *The Foundations of Social Research: Meaning and Perspective in the Research Process*. London: Sage.

Daft, Richard L. 1984. 'Antecedents of significant and not-so-significant organizational research'. In T.S. Bateman and G.R. Ferris (eds). *Method and Analysis in Organizational Research*. Reston, VA: Reston Publishing.

Davis, Gordon B. and Parker, Clyde A. 1997. *Writing the Doctoral Dissertation: A Systematic Approach*. Hauppage, NY: Barron's Educational Series.

Davis, Murray S. 1971. That's interesting! Towards a phenomenology of sociology and a sociology of phenomenology, *Philosophy of Social Science*, 1: 309–44.

Delamont, Sara, Atkinson, Paul and Parry, Odette. 1997. *Supervising the PhD: A Guide to Success*. Buckingham: Open University Press.

Delamont, Sara, Atkinson, Paul and Parry, Odette. 2004. *Supervising the Doctorate*. Maidenhead: Open University Press.

Denscombe, Martyn. 2003. *The Good Research Guide for Small-Scale Social Research Projects,* 2nd edn. Maidenhead: Open University Press.

Denzin, Norman. 1970. *The Research Act: A Theoretical Introduction to Sociological Methods*. Chicago: Aldine.

Denzin, Norman and Lincoln, Y. 1994. *Handbook of Qualitative Research*. Thousand Oaks, CA: Sage.

Dillon, William R. and Goldstein, Matthew. 1984. *Multivariate Analysis: Methods and Application*. New York: John Wiley & Sons.

Dubin, Robert. 1978. *Theory Building: A Practical Guide to the Construction and Testing of Theoretical Models,* 2nd edn. New York: Free Press.

Dunleavy, Patrick. 2003. *Authoring a PhD: How to Plan, Draft, Write and Finish a Doctoral Thesis or Dissertation*. Basingstoke: Palgrave Macmillan.

Easterby-Smith, Mark, Thorpe, Richard and Lowe, Andy. 2002. *Management Research: An Introduction,* 2nd edn. London: Sage.

Eisenhardt, Kathleen M. 1989. Building theories from case study research, *Academy of Management Review*, **14**(4): 532–50.

Eisenhardt, Kathleen M. 1991. Better stories and better constructs: The case for rigor and comparative logic, *Academy of Management Review*, **16**(3): 620–7.

Foddy, William. 1994. *Constructing Questions for Interviews and Questionnaires: Theory and Practice in Social Research*. Cambridge: Cambridge University Press.

Forsythe, Diana E. 2001. *Studying Those Who Study Us: An Anthropologist in the World of Artificial Intelligence*. Palo Alto, CA: Stanford University Press.

Gahan, Celia and Hannibal, Mike. 1998. *Doing Qualitative Research Using QSR Nud*IST*. London: Sage.

Geertz, Clifford. 1973. *Interpretation of Cultures*. New York: Basic Books.

Gill, John and Johnson, Phil. 2002. *Research Methods for Managers,* 3rd edn. London: Sage.

Girden, Ellen R. 2001. *Evaluating Research Articles from Start to Finish,* 2nd edn. Thousand Oaks, CA: Sage.

Glaser, Barney G. and Strauss, Anselm L. 1967. *The Discovery of Grounded Theory: Strategies of Qualitative Research*. London: Wiedenfeld & Nicholson.

Gomm, Roger, Hammersley, Martyn and Foster, Peter (eds). 2000. *Case Study Method: Key Issues, Key Texts*. London: Sage.

Gordon, Karen E. 1993a. *The Deluxe Transitive Vampire: The Ultimate Handbook for the Innocent, the Eager, and the Doomed*. New York: Pantheon Books.

Gordon, Karen E. 1993b. *The New Well-Tempered Sentence: A Punctuation Handbook for the Innocent, the Eager, and the Doomed*. Boston, MA: Houghton Mifflin.

Gray, David E. 2004. *Doing Research in the Real World*. London: Sage.

Guba, E. 1985. 'The context of emergent paradigm research'. In Lincoln, Y. (ed.). *Organizational Theory and Inquiry: The Paradigm Revolution*. Thousand Oaks, CA: Sage.

Gummesson, Evert. 2000. *Qualitative Methods in Management Research,* 2nd edn. Thousand Oaks, CA: Sage.

Hart, Chris. 1998. *Doing a Literature Review: Releasing the Social Science Research Imagination*. London: Sage.

Hart, Chris. 2001. *Doing a Literature Search: A Comprehensive Guide for the Social Sciences*. London: Sage.

Hollis, M. 1994. *The Philosophy of Social Science: An Introduction*. Cambridge: Cambridge University Press.

Hughes, John A. and Sharrock, Wesley W. 1997. *The Philosophy of Social Research*. Harlow: Longman.

Jankowicz, A.D. 2000. *Business Research Projects,* 3rd edn. London: Business Press/Thomson Learning.

Jick, Todd. Mixing qualitative and quantitative methods: Triangulation in action, *Administrative Science Quarterly*, **24**: 602–11.

Johnson, Phil and Duberley, Joanne. 2000. *Understanding Management Research: An Introduction to Epistemology*. London: Sage.

Kaplan, Abraham. 1964. *The Conduct of Inquiry*. San Francisco: Chandler Press.

Kolb, David A. 1985. *Experiential Learning*. Englewood Cliffs, NJ: Pearson.

Kolb, D.A., Rubin, I.M. and MacIntyre, J.M. 1984. *Organisational Psychology*. Englewood Cliffs, NJ: Prentice Hall.

Kuhn, Thomas S. 1996. *The Structure of Scientific Revolutions,* 2nd edn. Chicago: University of Chicago Press.

Latour, Bruno and Woolgar, Steve. 1986. *Laboratory Life: The Construction of Scientific Facts*. Princeton: Princeton University Press.

Lawrence, Paul R. 1992. The challenge of problem-oriented research, *Journal of Management Inquiry*, **1**(2): 139–42.

Lee, R.M. 2000. *Unobtrusive Methods in Social Research*. Buckingham: Open University Press.

Le Guin, Ursula K. 1998. *Steering the Craft: Exercises and Discussions on Story Writing for the Lone Navigator or the Mutinous Crew*. Portland, OR: Eighth Mountain Press.

Locke, Karen D. 2000. *Grounded Theory in Management Research*. London: Sage.

Locke, Lawrence F., Silverman, Stephen J. and Spirduso, Waneen W. 2004. *Reading and Understanding Research,* 2nd edn. Thousand Oaks, CA: Sage.

Lundberg, Craig C. 1976. Hypothesis generation in organizational behavior research, *Academy of Management Review*, **3**(1/2): 5–12.

Lundberg, Craig C. 1999. Finding research agendas: Getting started Weick-like, *The Society for Industrial and Organizational Psychology*, (TIP) Newsletter, American Psychological Society.

Lynch, P. 2001. 'Professionalism and ethics'. In Sadler, S. (ed.). *Management Consultancy,* 2nd edn. London: Kogan Page.

May, Tim. 2001. *Social Research: Issues, Methods and Process*. Buckingham: Open University Press.

Maylor, Harvey. 2003. *Project Management,* 3rd edn. London: Financial Times Management.

McClintock, C., Brannon, D. and Maynard-Moody, S. 1979. Applying the logic of sample surveys to qualitative case studies: The case cluster method, *Administrative Science Quarterly*, **24**(4): 612–29.

Miles, Matthew B. and Huberman, A. Michael. 1994. *Qualitative Data Analysis,* 2nd edn. Beverly Hills, CA: Sage.

Mintzberg, Henry. 1979. An emerging strategy of 'direct' research, *Administrative Science Quarterly*, **24**: 582–9.

Morgan, Gareth. 1997. *Images of Organization.* Thousand Oaks, CA: Sage.

Murray, Rowena. 2002. *How to Write a Thesis.* Maidenhead: Open University Press.

Murray, Rowena. 2003. *How To Survive Your Viva: Defending a Thesis in an Oral Examination.* Maidenhead: Open University Press.

O'Connor, Patricia T. 1996. *Woe Is I: The Grammarphone's Guide to Better English in Plain English.* New York: Riverhead Books.

O'Leary, Zina. 2004. *The Essential Guide to Doing Research.* London: Sage.

Oakshott, Lee. 2001. *Essential Quantitative Methods for Business, Management, and Finance,* 2nd edn. Basingstoke: Palgrave – now Palgrave Macmillan.

Oppenheimer, A.N. 1992. *Questionnaire Design, Interviewing, and Attitude Measurement,* new edn. London: Continuum.

Partington, David. 2002. *Essential Skills for Management Research.* London: Sage.

Peterson, Robert A. 2000. *Constructing Effective Questionnaires.* London: Sage.

Potter, Gary. 2000. *The Philosophy of Social Science: New Perspectives.* Harlow: Prentice Hall.

Ragin, Charles and Becker, Howard S. (eds). 1992. *What is a Case?* Cambridge: Cambridge University Press.

Remenyi, Dan, Williams, Brian, Money, Arthur and Swartz, Ethne. 1998. *Doing Research in Business and Management: An Introduction to Process and Method.* London: Sage.

Reason, Peter and Bradbury, Hilary (eds). 2000. *Handbook of Action Research.* London: Sage.

Richardson, S.A., Dohrenwend, B.S. and Klein, D. 1965. *Interviewing: Its Forms and Functions.* New York: Basic Books.

Ritter, Robert M. 2002. *The Oxford Style Manual.* Oxford: Oxford University Press.

Robson, Colin. 2002. *Real World Research: A Resource for Social Scientists and Practitioner-Researchers,* 2nd edn. Oxford: Blackwell.

Root-Bernstein, Robert S. 1989. *Discovering.* Cambridge, MA: Harvard University Press.

Rosen, M. 1991. Coming to terms with the field: Understanding and doing organisational ethnography, *Journal of Management Studies*, **28**(1): 1–24.

Rosenthal, R. and Fode, K.L. 1963. The effect of experimenter bias on the performance of the albino rat, *Behavioural Science*, **8**: 183–9.

Rosnow, R.L. and Rosenthal, R. 1997. *People Studying People: Artifacts and Ethics in Behavioural Research.* New York: W. H. Freeman.

Rugg, Gordon and Petre, Marian. 2004. *The Unwritten Rules of PhD Research.* Maidenhead: Open University Press.

Sagan, Carl. 1997. *The Demon-Haunted World: Science as a Candle in the Dark.* New York: Ballantine Books.

Salant, Priscilla and Dillman, Don A. 1995. *Conducting Surveys: A Step-by-step Guide to Getting the Information You Need.* New York: John Wiley & Sons.

Saunders, Mark, Lewis, Phillip and Thornhill, Adrian. 2003. *Research Methods for Business Students,* 3rd edn. Harlow: Financial Times/Prentice Hall.

Schragenheim, E. 1998. *Management Dilemmas.* London: St. Lucie Press.

Schutt, R.K. *Social World: The Process and Practice of Research.* Thousand Oaks, CA: Pine Forge Press.

Searle, C. *The Quality of Qualitative Research.* London: Sage.

Sekaran, Udo. 2000. *Research Methods for Business,* 3rd edn. Chichester: Wiley.

Shermer, M. 1997. *Why People Believe Weird Things: Pseudoscience, Superstition, and Other Confusions of Our Time.* New York: W.H. Freeman.

Shipman, M.D. 1982. *The Limitations of Social Research,* London: Longman.

Silverman, David. 2001. *Interpreting Qualitative Data: Methods for Analyzing Talk, Text and Interaction.* New York: Sage.

Stake, Robert E. 1995. *The Art of Case Study Research.* London: Sage.

Strauss, Anselm L. and Corbin, Juliet. 1999. *Basics of Qualitative Research: Grounded Theory Procedures & Techniques,* 2nd edn. Thousand Oaks, CA: Sage.

Stringer, Ernest T. 1996. *Action Research: A Handbook for Practitioners.* London: Sage.

Strunk, William I. and White, E.B. 1999. *The Elements of Style.* New York: Allyn & Bacon.

Sutton, Robert I. and Staw, Barry M. 1995. What theory is not, *Administrative Science Quarterly,* **40**(3): 371–84.

Swift, Louise. 2001. *Quantitative Methods for Business, Management and Finance.* Basingstoke: Palgrave – now Palgrave Macmillan.

Symon, G. and Cassell, C. (eds) 1998. *Qualitative Methods and Analysis in Organisational Research: A Practical Guide.* Thousand Oaks, CA: Sage.

The Chicago Manual of Style: For Authors, Editors and Copywriters, 15th edn. Chicago: University of Chicago Press.

Travers, Max. 2001. *Qualitative Research Through Case Studies.* London: Sage.

Truss, Lynne. 2003. *Eats, Shoots & Leaves: The Zero Tolerance Approach to Punctuation.* London: Profile Books.

Tsoukas, Harimas. 1994. What is management? An outline of a metatheory, *British Journal of Management,* **5**: 289–301.

Turabian, Kate L. 1996. *A Manual for Writers of Term Papers, Theses and Dissertations,* 6th edn. Chicago: University of Chicago Press.

Van Bruggen, Gerrit H., Lilien, Gary L. and Kacker, Manish. 2002. Informants in organizational marketing research: Why use multiple informants and how to aggregate responses, *Journal of Marketing Research,* **39**(4): 469–78.

Van Maanen, John. 1982. 'Fieldwork on the beat'. In Von Maanen, J., Dabbs, J.M. Jr and Faulkner, R.R. (eds). *Varieties of Qualitative Research.* Thousand Oaks, CA: Sage.

Wakeley, Tim. 1999. *DBA Project Guidelines 1999–2000,* School of Management, University of Bath, September.

Webb, E. and Weick, K.E. 1979. Unobtrusive measures in organisational theory: A reminder. *Administrative Science Quarterly,* **24**(4): 650–9.

Webb, E.J., Campbell, D.T., Schwartz, R.D. and Sechrest, L. 1966. *Unobtrusive Measures: Nonreactive Research in the Social Sciences.* Chicago: Rand McNally.

Weick, Karl E. 1979. *The Social Psychology of Organising,* 2nd edn. Reading, MA: Addison-Wesley.

Weick, Karl E. 1983. 'Management thought in the context of action'. In S. Srivastva (ed.). *The Executive Mind.* San Francisco: Jossey-Bass.

Weick, Karl E. 1989. Theory construction as disciplined imagination, *Academy of Management Review,* **14**(4): 516–31.

Weick, Karl E. 1992. Agenda setting in organizational behavior: A theory-focused approach. *Journal of Management Inquiry,* **1**(3): 171–82.

Whyte, William F. 1955. *Street Corner Society.* Chicago: University of Chicago Press.

Whyte, William F. 1978. 'Interviewing in field research'. In Burgess, R.G. (ed.). *Field Research: A Source-book and Field Manual,* pp. 300–18. New York: Allen & Unwin.

Williams, Joseph M. 1990. *Style: Toward Clarity and Grace*. Chicago: University of Chicago Press.

Williams, Malcolm and May, Tim. 1996. *An Introduction to the Philosophy of Social Research*. London: Routledge.

Yin, Robert K. 2002. *Applications of Case Study Research,* 2nd edn. London: Sage.

Yin, Robert K. 2003. *Case Study Research: Design and Methods,* 3rd edn. London: Sage.

Zikmund, William G. 2000. *Business Research Methods,* 6th edn. Orlando, FL: Dryden Press/Harcourt College.

Index